Exploring Contemporary English Language Education Practices

Truong Cong Bang
*University of Economics and Law, Ho Chi Minh City, Vietnam
& Vietnam National University, Ho Chi Minh City, Vietnam*

Cuong Huy Nguyen
International University, USA

Hung Phu Bui
University of Economics, Ho Chi Minh City, Vietnam

A volume in the Advances in Educational Technologies and Instructional Design (AETID) Book Series

Published in the United States of America by
IGI Global
Information Science Reference (an imprint of IGI Global)
701 E. Chocolate Avenue
Hershey PA, USA 17033
Tel: 717-533-8845
Fax: 717-533-8661
E-mail: cust@igi-global.com
Web site: http://www.igi-global.com

Copyright © 2024 by IGI Global. All rights reserved. No part of this publication may be reproduced, stored or distributed in any form or by any means, electronic or mechanical, including photocopying, without written permission from the publisher.
Product or company names used in this set are for identification purposes only. Inclusion of the names of the products or companies does not indicate a claim of ownership by IGI Global of the trademark or registered trademark.

                      Library of Congress Cataloging-in-Publication Data

Names: Bui, Hung Phu, editor. | Bang, Truong Cong, 1978- editor. | Nguyen,
   Cuong Huy, 1982- editor.
Title: Exploring contemporary English language education practices / edited
   by Hung Bui, Truong Bang, Cuong Nguyen.
Description: Hershey, PA : Information Science Reference, [2024] | Includes
   bibliographical references. | Summary: "This book reflects on
   contemporary perspectives and recent research in teaching and learning
   English as a second/ foreign language (L2)"-- Provided by publisher.
Identifiers: LCCN 2024009386 (print) | LCCN 2024009387 (ebook) | ISBN
   9798369332948 (hardcover) | ISBN 9798369332955 (ebook)
Subjects: LCSH: English language--Study and teaching--Vietnamese speakers.
   | English language--Study and teaching--Foreign speakers.
Classification: LCC PE1128.A2 E947 2024 (print) | LCC PE1128.A2 (ebook) |
   DDC 428.0071/05--dc23/eng/20240318
LC record available at https://lccn.loc.gov/2024009386
LC ebook record available at https://lccn.loc.gov/2024009387

This book is published in the IGI Global book series Advances in Educational Technologies and Instructional Design (AETID) (ISSN: 2326-8905; eISSN: 2326-8913)

British Cataloguing in Publication Data
A Cataloguing in Publication record for this book is available from the British Library.

All work contributed to this book is new, previously-unpublished material.
The views expressed in this book are those of the authors, but not necessarily of the publisher.

For electronic access to this publication, please contact: eresources@igi-global.com.

Advances in Educational Technologies and Instructional Design (AETID) Book Series

ISSN:2326-8905
EISSN:2326-8913

Editor-in-Chief: Lawrence A. Tomei, Robert Morris University, USA

MISSION

Education has undergone, and continues to undergo, immense changes in the way it is enacted and distributed to both child and adult learners. In modern education, the traditional classroom learning experience has evolved to include technological resources and to provide online classroom opportunities to students of all ages regardless of their geographical locations. From distance education, Massive-Open-Online-Courses (MOOCs), and electronic tablets in the classroom, technology is now an integral part of learning and is also affecting the way educators communicate information to students.

The **Advances in Educational Technologies & Instructional Design (AETID) Book Series** explores new research and theories for facilitating learning and improving educational performance utilizing technological processes and resources. The series examines technologies that can be integrated into K-12 classrooms to improve skills and learning abilities in all subjects including STEM education and language learning. Additionally, it studies the emergence of fully online classrooms for young and adult learners alike, and the communication and accountability challenges that can arise. Trending topics that are covered include adaptive learning, game-based learning, virtual school environments, and social media effects. School administrators, educators, academicians, researchers, and students will find this series to be an excellent resource for the effective design and implementation of learning technologies in their classes.

COVERAGE

- Virtual School Environments
- Higher Education Technologies
- K-12 Educational Technologies
- Bring-Your-Own-Device
- Instructional Design
- Educational Telecommunications
- Hybrid Learning
- Digital Divide in Education
- Classroom Response Systems
- Social Media Effects on Education

IGI Global is currently accepting manuscripts for publication within this series. To submit a proposal for a volume in this series, please contact our Acquisition Editors at Acquisitions@igi-global.com or visit: http://www.igi-global.com/publish/.

The Advances in Educational Technologies and Instructional Design (AETID) Book Series (ISSN 2326-8905) is published by IGI Global, 701 E. Chocolate Avenue, Hershey, PA 17033-1240, USA, www.igi-global.com. This series is composed of titles available for purchase individually; each title is edited to be contextually exclusive from any other title within the series. For pricing and ordering information please visit http://www.igi-global.com/book-series/advances-educational-technologies-instructional-design/73678. Postmaster: Send all address changes to above address. Copyright © 2024 IGI Global. All rights, including translation in other languages reserved by the publisher. No part of this series may be reproduced or used in any form or by any means – graphics, electronic, or mechanical, including photocopying, recording, taping, or information and retrieval systems – without written permission from the publisher, except for non commercial, educational use, including classroom teaching purposes. The views expressed in this series are those of the authors, but not necessarily of IGI Global.

Titles in this Series

For a list of additional titles in this series, please visit:
http://www.igi-global.com/book-series/advances-educational-technologies-instructional-design/73678

Effective and Meaningful Student Engagement Through Service Learning
Sharon Valarmathi (Christ University, India) Jacqueline Kareem (Christ University, India) Veerta Tantia (Christ University, India) Kishore Selva Babu (Christ University, India) and Patrick Jude Lucas (Christ University, India)
Information Science Reference • copyright 2024 • 293pp • H/C (ISBN: 9798369322567)
• US $275.00 (our price)

Integrating Cutting-Edge Technology Into the Classroom
Ken Nee Chee (Universiti Pendidikan Sultan Idris, Malaysia) and Mageswaran Sanmugam (Universiti Sains Malaysia, Malaysia)
Information Science Reference • copyright 2024 • 425pp • H/C (ISBN: 9798369331248)
• US $300.00 (our price)

Embracing Technological Advancements for Lifelong Learning
Mahmoud M. Kh. Hawamdeh (Al-Quds Open University, Palestine) and Faiz Abdelhafid (Al-Istiqlal University, Palestine)
Information Science Reference • copyright 2024 • 365pp • H/C (ISBN: 9798369314104)
• US $230.00 (our price)

Unlocking Learning Potential With Universal Design in Online Learning Environments
Michelle Bartlett (Old Dominion University, USA) and Suzanne M. Ehrlich (University of North Florida, USA)
Information Science Reference • copyright 2024 • 286pp • H/C (ISBN: 9798369312698)
• US $240.00 (our price)

Navigating Innovative Technologies and Intelligent Systems in Modern Education
Madhulika Bhatia (Amity University, India) and Muhammad Tahir Mushtaq (Cardiff Metropolitan Univesity, UK)

For an entire list of titles in this series, please visit:
http://www.igi-global.com/book-series/advances-educational-technologies-instructional-design/73678

701 East Chocolate Avenue, Hershey, PA 17033, USA
Tel: 717-533-8845 x100 • Fax: 717-533-8661
E-Mail: cust@igi-global.com • www.igi-global.com

Table of Contents

Preface xii

Chapter 1
Applying Process-Based Writing Instruction to Teach IELTS Writing Task 2:
An Action Research Project in Vietnam 1
    Mai Thi Thanh Vo, Tra Vinh University, Vietnam
    Chau Thi Hoang Hoa, Tra Vinh University, Vietnam

Chapter 2
Difficulties in L2 English Essay Writing: A Case in Vietnam 23
    An Nguyen Thi Thu, University of Social Sciences and Humanities,
       Vietnam National University, Ho Chi Minh, Vietnam

Chapter 3
Learning Strategies, Emotional Intelligence, and Academic Performance: A
Case in Spain 40
    Isabel María García Conesa, Centro Universitario de la Defensa de San
       Javier, Spain

Chapter 4
Relationships Between Emotional Intelligence, Willingness to Communicate,
and Classroom Participation: Results From Secondary Education in Spain 70
    Antonio Daniel Juan Rubio, Universidad de Granada, Spain

Chapter 5
Revisiting Oral Corrective Feedback in Second Language Acquisition:
Existing Debates and Directions for Further Studies 97
    Hung Phu Bui, University of Economics Ho Chi Minh City, Vietnam
    Thanh Huynh Vo, Ho Chi Minh City Open University, Vietnam

Chapter 6
Teaching English Literature in the Vietnamese EFL Context: Towards a
Language and Literature-Integrated Model 116
    Lien-Huong Vo, HUFLIS, Hue University, Vietnam
    Thanh-Hai L. Cao, HUFLIS, Hue University, Vietnam

Chapter 7
Technology Integration in English Language Education: An Evolving
Paradigm 131
    Truong Cong Bang, University of Economics and Law, Ho Chi Minh
        City, Vietnam & Vietnam National University, Ho Chi Minh City,
        Vietnam

Chapter 8
The Impact of Visual Corrective Feedback on Pronunciation Accuracy in L2
Sound Production: Empirical Evidence 158
    Rizgar Qasim Mahmood, The University of Wollongong, Australia

Chapter 9
The Role of Research in Applied Linguistics 190
    Jacqueline Żammit, University of Malta, Malta

Chapter 10
Vietnamese EFL Teachers' and Students' Perceptions of Using
Translanguaging in Language-Integrated Literature Courses: A Qualitative
Study 220
    Tuyet-Nhung Thi Nguyen, Tra Vinh University, Vietnam
    Phuong-Nam Thi Nguyen, Tra Vinh University, Vietnam
    Ngoc-Tai Huynh, Tra Vinh University, Vietnam

Compilation of References 249

About the Contributors 290

Index 294

Detailed Table of Contents

Preface xii

Chapter 1
Applying Process-Based Writing Instruction to Teach IELTS Writing Task 2:
An Action Research Project in Vietnam 1
    Mai Thi Thanh Vo, Tra Vinh University, Vietnam
    Chau Thi Hoang Hoa, Tra Vinh University, Vietnam

This study aims to investigate the effects of process-based writing instruction on Vietnamese EFL students' writing in an IELTS preparation course. An action research design was used, and the participants included 12 EFL students attending an IELTS course at a foreign language center in Vietnam. Data was gathered from students' essays, as well as through observations made by the teacher during two cycles. The students' essays were assessed by using the IELTS Writing Task 2 descriptors. Results showed a significant improvement in students' Writing Task 2 performance, particularly argumentative essays when process-based writing instruction was applied. They were able to respond appropriately to the prompt, maintain relevance to their chosen position, and support their main ideas with strong explanations and examples. The student initially negatively responded to the application because they were unfamiliar with the several stages of the application, but they eventually showed their willingness to participate in the activities, especially in Cycle 2.

Chapter 2
Difficulties in L2 English Essay Writing: A Case in Vietnam 23
    An Nguyen Thi Thu, University of Social Sciences and Humanities,
      Vietnam National University, Ho Chi Minh, Vietnam

Writing has been recognized as the most difficult skill for EFL learners and essay writing is one of the fundamental abilities that Vietnamese tertiary students are required to attain. This chapter aimed to investigate Vietnamese EFL learners' difficulties in learning English essay writing (EEW). It employed qualitative design using semi-structured interviews with 12 EFL learners studying EEW at several universities in Ho Chi Minh City. The findings show that the students encountered several major difficulties, such as inadequate sources of grammar and vocabulary, ineffective ideation and writing style, insufficient motivation and interest, poor planning and structure, and other issues during their EEW. Among those problems, learners found a lack of grammar and vocabulary sources and poor idea generation and writing style the most challenging. The findings from this study contribute to the literature on EFL teaching and learning in Vietnamese tertiary education in general and EEW in particular.

Chapter 3
Learning Strategies, Emotional Intelligence, and Academic Performance: A Case in Spain..40
Isabel María García Conesa, Centro Universitario de la Defensa de San Javier, Spain

Learning strategies, emotional intelligence, and academic performance have been proposed as variables with great impacts on language learning processes, which can be reinforced in distance university education. In this educational modality, learning is completely autonomous and independent, which implies the need to develop particular skills that make it possible to take advantage of previously provided learning experiences and resources. This chapter reports a study on the relationships between learning strategies, emotional intelligence, and academic performance in a course of English 3. Data were collected from a sample of 132 students in distance education at a university in Spain. For the analysis of the variables, a non-experimental design was used, making use of descriptive and correlational statistics. The results showed a high average rating on the learning strategies scales, as well as adequate understanding and emotional regulation in the students, in contrast to emotional perception, a dimension that obtained a low average rating.

Chapter 4
Relationships Between Emotional Intelligence, Willingness to Communicate, and Classroom Participation: Results From Secondary Education in Spain 70
Antonio Daniel Juan Rubio, Universidad de Granada, Spain

There is a proliferating research interest in emotional intelligence (EI) as it plays a significant role in learning processes. The chapter reports a study on the relationship between EI and the willingness to communicate (WTC) in the foreign language studied in secondary school (English). A positive correlation between both factors would be very significant since the use of the language of study is essential in the learning process. To assess the existence of this relationship, the questionnaires of 119 CSE students were analysed, and it was concluded that there is a statistically significant correlation between EI and the WTC. The general objective is, on the one hand, to analyse the relationship between emotional intelligence and the willingness to communicate in the Foreign Language (English) class at the secondary education stage, and whether there is a relationship between emotional intelligence, the willingness to communicate, and class participation.

Chapter 5
Revisiting Oral Corrective Feedback in Second Language Acquisition:
Existing Debates and Directions for Further Studies..97
    Hung Phu Bui, University of Economics Ho Chi Minh City, Vietnam
    Thanh Huynh Vo, Ho Chi Minh City Open University, Vietnam

Corrective feedback is acknowledged with a growing research interest in the second language acquisition literature. In the classroom, the teacher's and peer's oral corrective feedback (OCF) can be used to modify students' language and facilitate language learning. From the existing debates in the literature, the authors argue that corrective feedback should be broadly defined as the use of language and artifacts not only to correct language inaccuracies but also to signal unacceptable instances and/or suggest alternatives. To provide effective OCF, the teacher might need to consider the appropriateness of OCF types of strategies for the context, learners' age and preferences, and probably the relationship between the feedback provider and receiver. Finally, directions for further studies are discussed. Driven by a desire to provide updated literature regarding OCF, this chapter can be a reference for students, teachers, and novice researchers.

Chapter 6
Teaching English Literature in the Vietnamese EFL Context: Towards a
Language and Literature-Integrated Model 116
    Lien-Huong Vo, HUFLIS, Hue University, Vietnam
    Thanh-Hai L. Cao, HUFLIS, Hue University, Vietnam

This chapter is intended as an academic paper that proposes an integrated model of teaching English literature in the EFL courses at higher education level in Vietnam. The chapter begins with an overview of the importance of literature in language teaching and the teaching of English literature in Vietnam. It then presents a discussion of Carter and Long's models of teaching literature in language classes. These models are accompanied with discussion of the challenges EFL teachers encounter while teaching English literature in EFL contexts. The chapter ends with a proposal of an integrated model of teaching English literature in EFL classrooms with ideas and examples of material modification for classroom procedure and activities. The integrated model is expected to help develop students' language skills and proficiency, promote their higher-order thinking skills, and raise their (inter)cultural awareness.

Chapter 7
Technology Integration in English Language Education: An Evolving
Paradigm 131
    Truong Cong Bang, University of Economics and Law, Ho Chi Minh
        City, Vietnam & Vietnam National University, Ho Chi Minh City,
        Vietnam

This chapter conducts a comprehensive exploration of technology integration in English language education, chronicling its historical evolution and scrutinizing contemporary pedagogical frameworks amalgamating technological tools. A panoramic examination encompasses digital resources spanning online platforms, mobile applications, virtual/augmented reality, gamification, and intelligent tutoring systems. Challenges deliberated include the digital divide, teacher training imperative, privacy ramifications, and equilibrating technology with traditional pedagogies. Illustrative case studies and practitioner insights elucidate effective practices. Emerging technologies' potential impact, including artificial intelligence and learning analytics, is probed. The chapter delineates implications for policy, curricula, and teacher education to optimize technology integration. By synthesizing scholarship and pedagogical paradigms, stakeholders are furnished a comprehensive perspective on cultivating engaging, equitable, and efficacious technology-enhanced language learning environments.

Chapter 8
The Impact of Visual Corrective Feedback on Pronunciation Accuracy in L2
Sound Production: Empirical Evidence 158
    Rizgar Qasim Mahmood, The University of Wollongong, Australia

This chapter investigates the influence of visual corrective feedback (henceforth VCF) techniques on enhancing pronunciation accuracy among ESL learners (N = 40) from various countries and L1 backgrounds. Utilizing a mixed-methods approach, the research examines the efficacy of various VCF modalities, such as interactive software: Praat and YouGlish, in improving learners' pronunciation skills. Quantitative analysis involves pre- and post-assessment of pronunciation accuracy using standardized metrics. At the same time, qualitative data is gathered through learner interviews to gauge perceptions and experiences with VCF methods. The findings suggest a significant correlation between the use of VCF and enhanced vowel production accuracy. Additionally, the qualitative insights reveal positive learner attitudes towards VCF tools, highlighting their motivational and corrective influences on pronunciation improvement. This study offers several theoretical and pedagogical implications.

Chapter 9
The Role of Research in Applied Linguistics 190
    Jacqueline Żammit, University of Malta, Malta

This chapter shows the importance of research in applied linguistics. The chapter defines applied linguistics and explains the crucial function of research in this field. This defines teaching methods, laws, and interpretations for acquiring a language through definition and description. It consists of a section that discusses research methodologies in the area and language acquisition including quantitative as well as qualitative methods. Moreover, the chapter explains how different approaches are used to assess language teaching and learning environments including education and other factors that influence human knowledge. Finally, the chapter underscores the role played by research in applied linguistics urging for more investigations to improve understanding of language in daily life contexts.

Chapter 10
Vietnamese EFL Teachers' and Students' Perceptions of Using Translanguaging in Language-Integrated Literature Courses: A Qualitative Study 220
    Tuyet-Nhung Thi Nguyen, Tra Vinh University, Vietnam
    Phuong-Nam Thi Nguyen, Tra Vinh University, Vietnam
    Ngoc-Tai Huynh, Tra Vinh University, Vietnam

This chapter reports a case study on Vietnamese EFL student and teacher perceptions of the benefits and difficulties of using translanguaging in literature courses. Using semi-structured interviews and thematic analysis, this study engaged seven students and five teachers to address the research questions. The results revealed that the students perceived benefits in using Vietnamese in teaching English literature courses, including improving understanding and analyses of literary works, cultural connections, and group interactions. Similarly, the teachers recognized benefits such as increasing comprehension, student engagement, cultural awareness, and confidence. However, students encountered difficulties related to the use of colloquial language, translation complexities, and cultural disparities. Likely, teachers observed diminishing student engagement, hindrances to students' English language proficiency, and comprehension difficulties. These results thereby contribute to the existing understanding of translanguaging in the classroom.

Compilation of References 249

About the Contributors 290

Index 294

Preface

The field of English language education has undergone a remarkable evolution in recent decades, propelled by globalization, advancements in educational technology, and a deepening understanding of second language acquisition processes. This edited volume, *Exploring Contemporary English Language Education Practices*, represents a comprehensive and timely exploration of the current trends, challenges, and innovative approaches that shape the landscape of teaching and learning English as a second or foreign language.

Expertly curated by Dr. Truong Cong Bang, Dr. Cuong Huy Nguyen, and Dr. Hung Phu Bui, this anthology brings together a diverse array of scholarly perspectives, drawing from a broad spectrum of research interests and pedagogical contexts. The contributing authors, hailing from various academic and professional backgrounds, offer a rich tapestry of insights, empirical findings, and reflective analyses that collectively address the multifaceted nature of contemporary English language education practices.

The chapters encompass a wide range of topics, including the integration of technology in English language classrooms, oral and visual corrective feedback strategies, literature-integrated language teaching models, challenges in L2 writing instruction, the role of emotional intelligence in language learning, and the importance of research in applied linguistics and language education. Through these explorations, readers will gain a nuanced understanding of the current debates, evidence-based practices, and emerging directions that are shaping the field.

Notably, this edited volume extends beyond theoretical discourse by offering practical implications and actionable strategies for language educators, researchers, and stakeholders alike. Whether you are a student, a scholar, a practitioner, or a policymaker in the realm of English language education, this book promises to be a valuable resource, fostering critical reflection, inspiring future research endeavors, and informing pedagogical decision-making processes.

The editors, with their collective expertise and unwavering commitment to advancing the field of English language education, have curated a remarkable compilation that captures the vibrancy and complexity of contemporary practices.

Preface

"Exploring Contemporary English Language Education Practices" serves as a testament to the editors' dedication to promoting excellence, innovation, and inclusivity in the pursuit of enhancing English language teaching and learning experiences worldwide.

Truong Cong Bang
University of Economics and Law, Ho Chi Minh City, Vietnam & Vietnam National University, Ho Chi Minh City, Vietnam

Cuong Huy Nguyen
International University, Vietnam National University, Ho Chi Minh City, Vietnam

Hung Phu Bui
University of Economics Ho Chi Minh City, Vietnam

Chapter 1
Applying Process-Based Writing Instruction to Teach IELTS Writing Task 2:
An Action Research Project in Vietnam

Mai Thi Thanh Vo
Tra Vinh University, Vietnam

Chau Thi Hoang Hoa
 https://orcid.org/0000-0002-5738-9147
Tra Vinh University, Vietnam

ABSTRACT

This study aims to investigate the effects of process-based writing instruction on Vietnamese EFL students' writing in an IELTS preparation course. An action research design was used, and the participants included 12 EFL students attending an IELTS course at a foreign language center in Vietnam. Data was gathered from students' essays, as well as through observations made by the teacher during two cycles. The students' essays were assessed by using the IELTS Writing Task 2 descriptors. Results showed a significant improvement in students' Writing Task 2 performance, particularly argumentative essays when process-based writing instruction was applied. They were able to respond appropriately to the prompt, maintain relevance to their chosen position, and support their main ideas with strong explanations and examples. The student initially negatively responded to the application because they were unfamiliar with the several stages of the application, but they eventually showed their willingness to participate in the activities, especially in Cycle 2.

DOI: 10.4018/979-8-3693-3294-8.ch001

1. INTRODUCTION

Writing in an academic style can be tough for students learning English as a foreign language (EFL) (Evans & Green, 2007; Lee & Tajino, 2008). EFL students often struggle with putting together their academic work and following instructions (Wang & Xie, 2022). Hence, it is suggested that English teachers should find good ways to teach EFL students how to do academic writing (Fareed et al., 2016; Tseng, 2019).

Among various types of academic writing, argumentative writing is often considered the most challenging (Crasnich & Lumbell, 2005; Gárate & Melero, 2005). This type of writing requires responding to a problem, expressing thoughts, and providing convincing reasons (Crowhurst, 1990). Particularly, clarity and relevance are immensely crucial when making arguments (Zhu, 2001).

Observations and final writing tests collected from IELTS (International English Language Testing System) classes at a language center in South Vietnam reveal that students often lack sufficient guidance on effective writing. In particular, many encounter difficulties with the task response in IELTS Writing Task 2 since their scores for this criterion are often recorded to be comparatively lower than the other criteria. Hence, figuring out an effective teaching application is crucial to help these learners enhance their writing performance. Among useful teaching methods used to increase students' writing performance, some researchers highly recommend that applying process-based writing which helps students acquire writing skills throughout various stages is more beneficial than simply providing model answers like in product-based writing (Akinwamide, 2012; Sarhady, 2015).

However, product-based writing instruction has been constantly applied in IELTS writing classes. Many learners observed from the IELTS writing classes at this center have not only struggled with their academic writing but also shown their negative participation in product-based writing instruction used by most teachers here. Particularly, in each writing lesson, students are given a model answer with some important topic-related words and asked to follow the structures or format to make their writing products. Thus, students do not actively participate in writing activities because they know that they are always given model answers which include essential ideas for their final writing product. Even though this problem of learning and teaching IELTS writing in Vietnam has continuously occurred, there have not been any studies discovering and analyzing how process-based writing instruction affects IELTS learners' writing Task 2 performance, especially on task response criterion which is regularly reported to be a big challenge for IELTS students. From the observation of IELTS classes at the language center in Vietnam and the discovery of some significant benefits of process-based instruction, the researchers conducted this action research to answer two questions:

(1) How can process-based writing instruction be applied to teaching IELTS writing Task 2 to EFL students, particularly task response criterion?
(2) How do the students respond to the application of process-based writing instruction in IELTS Writing Task 2?

2. LITERATURE REVIEW

2.1 Theoretical Background

2.1.1 Argumentative Essays and Challenges to Students

Various definitions of the argumentative essay have been offered by various researchers. An argumentative essay, according to White and Billings (2008), is a style of speech in which writers attempt to persuade their audience to accept their point of view by presenting a pattern of reasoning that is supported by specific evidence. An argumentative essay should contain facts or arguments that are clear and logical. Another similar definition of an argumentative essay is that it is a piece of writing in which writers drive to persuade their readers to embrace an opinion supported by logical, well-organized evidence (Hung & Van, 2018; Zhu, 2001).

Composing argumentative essays is widely recognized as one of the most challenging forms of academic writing due to complex requirements for students (Crasnich & Lumbell, 2005; Gárate & Melero, 2005). Particularly, in an argumentative essay, students are required to fully comprehend the nuances of the essay prompt to address specific aspects of the question (Zhu, 2001). Additionally, Maharani (2022) reveals that one of the most challenging requirements of argumentative essays is that EFL learners should expand and develop their ideas in a coherent and logical manner. Similarly, Crasnich and Lumbell (2005) show that EFL students may face difficulties in providing convincing and relevant examples to support their arguments. This can result in argumentative essays that lack depth and fail to persuade the reader.

2.1.2 IELTS Writing Task 2 and Task Response Criterion

In recent times, the (IELTS) has witnessed a substantial increase in the number of test takers, including a notable number of Vietnamese candidates. Among four skills evaluated in the test, IELTS Writing Task 2, which is completing an argumentative essay, is often reported to be the biggest challenge for EFL students because examinees are reported to misunderstand the task because of disregarding the background of the given information in the task, causing them to inappropriately respond to the question. Additionally, identifying topics too generally without adequate supporting ideas is another common problem that EFL learners often encounter (Alavi et al., 2020; Bagheri & Riasati, 2016; Cullen, 2017). These hardships, in general, are related to the task response criterion which is one of four main criteria in the writing band descriptor used to evaluate test takers' writing Task 2 performance.

The IELTS Writing Task 2 assessment criteria consist of task response, coherence and cohesion, lexical resource, and grammatical range and accuracy. The 0–9 scale is used to define each criterion and assess specific IELTS test takers' abilities. Because it is believed that getting a high score on the task response is more challenging for IELTS students than getting a high score on the other IELTS Writing Task 2 criteria (UCLES, 1996), the task response was, therefore, the only element focused on and examined in this research.

Task response is a term of assessment to determine whether students construct a convincing argument in response to the prompt provided in the task. One of the most fundamental aspects of argumentative writing is a consistent point of view. Their knowledge, individual experiences, solid proof, and convincing examples all strengthen the argument (Uysal, 2009). Task response criterion in IELTS Writing Task 2 carefully evaluates the ideas or content, which appears to be the most important component overall. The essays of the students in this study were assessed based on the IELTS writing Task 2 band descriptor, only focusing on the task response criterion listed above.

2.1.3 Process-Based Writing Instruction

Process-based writing instruction, as defined by Nordin (2017), is an approach that places a strong emphasis on teaching writing as a dynamic process. Its primary goal is to empower students to uncover their unique expressions, select their preferred writing methods, and motivate them to revise their compositions. Another description suggested by Rashtchi and colleagues (2019) is that process-based writing instruction places the prime focus on the process in which writers go from the beginning to the end of the written product with clear instructions for each stage from teachers.

In general, there are diverse process-based instruction cycles that have been introduced and suggested by researchers. For example, Flower and Hayes (1981) present a process-based writing instruction model that involves students in a continuous cycle of comprehensive processes. These processes encompass planning (such as generating ideas, organizing, and setting goals), transforming (including generating text), and reviewing (involving evaluation and revision). Another recognized process-based writing model is suggested by White and Arndt (1991) involving a cycle of focusing, structuring, drafting, reviewing, evaluating, and generating stages. Despite various models of process-based writing instruction, this research was conducted using the model suggested by Kraklow and Slimon (2016) who suggest that the writing process should be instructed within five main stages explained in detail below, namely prewriting, organizing, drafting, reviewing (revising), and rewriting.

Kraklow and Slimon's model of process-based writing instruction (2016)

Prewriting: Quick thinking that enables students to explore their thoughts on the topic without worrying about making mistakes should be encouraged throughout the prewriting phase. Grammar and mechanics can be taught in a later stage of the process, which helps students be equipped to write ideas without restriction. Through brainstorming exercises, group discussions, and presentations, students can improve their ability to come up with good ideas that are relevant to the topic.

Organizing: Students are provided instructions on how to select the most appropriate ideas and carefully arrange them to get ready for the first draft. While one-on-one help is possible at this point, it shouldn't take more than a minute or two per student. A short outline for a well-planned draft is provided with a brief overview from the organizing stage.

Drafting: Students attempt to compose the paragraphs as rapidly as possible to create the first draft during the writing stage by using the outline or plan created in the second step. It's critical that teachers advise their students to put expression of ideas first and grammar later. Since there is no time for revisions or adjustments until the ideas are actually on paper, students learn to write their ideas without hesitating to change them.

Reviewing: Students' drafts are then reviewed by their peers and their teacher who gives overall comments. By providing a clear, step-by-step self-assessment rubric that allows both reviewers and writers to see their progress during this stage, the teacher may assist students as they go through the reviewing process.

Rewriting: Following the reviewing stage, students create a final draft using the comments from their peers and teacher. Students now have everything needed to produce a well-developed essay.

All things considered; process-based instruction could bring many benefits to English learners. Firstly, they promote students' self-initiation in their writing by having them establish clear writing objectives and structuring and arranging their ideas. (Widodo, 2008). Furthermore, they help students learn how to transform their ideas into sentences and paragraphs (Rashtchi et al., 2019). Moreover, EFL learners can learn to assess and revise their written work to align it with their objectives and effectively convey their ideas (Chien, 2012). These positive aspects are related to challenges that EFL students often struggle in meeting the requirements of task response criterion in IELTS Writing Task 2, leading to the importance of applying Kraklow and Slimon's model of process-based writing instruction in this research to improve students' writing performance on task response criterion in IELTS Writing Task 2.

2.1.4 The Importance of Process-Based Writing Instruction to EFL Learners' IELTS Writing Task 2

The task response criterion in IELTS Writing Task 2, as mentioned above, is considered as a radical challenge to EFL learners due to its complex requirements including an efficient response to the statement or question(s), relevant content to stick to the position, and supporting ideas to support the argument. Thus, IELTS teachers should carefully examine an effective approach to assist EFL students in enhancing their performance on IELTS academic Writing Task 2, with a particular focus on the task response criterion. Based on the enormous benefits of process-based writing instruction to students' writing process mentioned earlier, more studies have been recently conducted to check how this approach impacts EFL learners' IELTS writing performance. This also encouraged this research to be carried out to explore more aspects of process-based writing instruction.

2.2 Related Studies

Alodwan and Ibnian (2014) conducted a study to examine how employing the process approach to writing impacted the development of essay writing skills among university students. The research employed a quasi-experimental design, involving two groups comprising 90 non-English major students selected from English 101 sections at the World Islamic Sciences and Education University in Amman. One group was the experimental group while the other functioned as the control group. To gauge the influence of the process approach to writing, which was administered as a treatment to the experimental group, the researchers conducted both pretests and posttests for both groups. During the implementation of the process approach with the experimental group, these students effectively utilized the various stages of writing to explore, connect, and generate new ideas. Interestingly, in this stage, the students were reported to discover surprisingly related examples to support their main ideas. Additionally, they were noticed to feel comfortable expressing themselves and generating new ideas when asked to draw special attention to the flow of ideas rather than grammatical structures during the application of the process approach, particularly in the pre-writing stage.

Auliyah and Arrasyid (2019) explored the significance of process-based academic writing in the context of argumentative essays. Their study employed a descriptive qualitative approach, and the data sources for this study included argumentative essays, questionnaires, interview transcripts, audio recordings, and documents. After the process-based writing application, there were some considerable strengths such as preparing adequately before essay writing, creating interesting content, narrowing down effectively the ideas to have the strongest ones to support their position, and gathering the most topic-related information. Nevertheless, some challenges for these participants were inevitable. One of the major obstacles was stated that learners who were only used to the product writing found it extremely difficult to compose the final product without knowing the sample answer at the beginning.

Firoozjahantigh and colleagues (2021) conducted a study to investigate the impact of process-based writing instruction on the performance of Iranian EFL learners in the IELTS Writing Task 2, with a particular focus on the use of hedging and boosting techniques. The research revealed that the application of process-based writing instruction, with an emphasis on hedging and boosting, had a significantly positive effect on the academic writing proficiency of the learners. The study involved 115 Iranian EFL learners who were enrolled in IELTS preparation courses at the Farazmon IELTS institute. These participants were divided into two groups: a control group and an experimental group. The instructional phase consisted of process-based writing instruction delivered through two weekly sessions, each lasting 90 minutes, for a total of 30 sessions. The lesson plans encompassed various aspects, including different forms of argumentative writing, a wide array of sample questions and texts, and the prescribed writing formats for each specific type of writing. The systematic process-based writing instruction introduced the stages of prewriting, writing, revising, and editing. The results of the study demonstrated that process-based writing instruction had a positive and beneficial impact on the IELTS writing achievements of the learners. To be more specific, one of the most considerable benefits of this application was to substantially help learners enhance their skills of responding to the questions properly, which used to be a considerable problem for them before the application. In addition, the prewriting step was useful for the learners to carefully choose and stick to the generated ideas. This helped them avoid thinking about new ideas, which was a waste of time and led to poor performance on the final writing.

Maharani (2022) a descriptive qualitative study involving 28 junior participants who were in an Essay Writing course at ELESP, Faculty of Teacher Training and Education, Universitas Mahasaraswati Denpasar. The study was carried out to determine the impact of the writing instruction-based process approach on the students' EFL argumentative writing skill. To get at the results, the learners' argumentative essays were gathered and assessed by three different data collection techniques which were group discussion, interviews, and observation. The results showed that the prewriting, drafting, revising, editing, and publishing elements of the writing instruction-based process method used in EFL writing classrooms assisted students in improving their competence in argumentative writing. The students carefully followed each activity's instructions, allowing them to take notes and develop their ideas into writing pieces. The most significant improvement gathered from the observation was that the students always checked whether their ideas were clear and related enough for the audience to know their chosen position. Most of the participants firmly supported using the approach to help them improve their argumentative writing. Their methods of expressing their ideas were noticeably more creative.

In conclusion, numerous studies have explored the efficacy of process-based writing instruction in enhancing the writing performance of EFL learners. Nevertheless, not many researchers have taken into consideration how to apply process-based writing instruction to improve EFL learners' performance on IELTS Writing Task 2 and what students' perceptions of the application were. In addition, most previous studies have only mentioned generally the advantages of process-based writing instruction to improve EFL students' writing elements instead of focusing on one specific writing criterion, for instance, task response or coherence and cohesion in writing (Bui, 2022). These gaps led to the motive of conducting this research which focused on seeing how process-based writing instruction was applied in teaching IELTS Writing Task 2 to EFL students to improve students' writing performance on task response criterion and how the students responded to the application of process-based writing instruction in IELTS Writing Task 2.

3. METHODOLOGY

This research was conducted at a language center in Vietnam, employing Classroom Action Research methodology that involved cyclic activities including planning, acting, observing, and reflecting on the data acquired from the teaching and learning process (Kemmis & McTaggart, 1988). The research ran into two cycles, each of which lasted three meetings. The targeted students of the research were 12 IELTS students whose ages ranged from 16 to 22 at a language center in Vietnam. They already finished the IELTS Foundation and at the end of April, and started to attend another IELTS course which was approximately assessed at Band 4.5. Their coursebook was Mindset for IELTS Level 1 by Cambridge English. Regarding carrying out the research, there was the participation of a researcher who acted as the teacher applying process-based writing instruction in her IELTS class, observing, and reporting the findings while her collaborator mainly assisted her in evaluating the students' essays, suggesting activities conducted in two cycles, and cooperatively scrutinizing the research's findings and spotting limitations and recommendations for the researcher.

The researcher utilized observation and students' essays from the Essay 1 and Essay 2 to see how process-based writing instruction was applied in teaching IELTS writing Task 2 to EFL students to improve students' writing performance on task response criterion and how the students responded to the application of process-based writing instruction in IELTS Writing Task 2. Initially, in the proposal, interviews were planned to gather information about how the students responded to the application. However, when asked about participating in interviews, all the students expressed their disapproval, leading to the decision to observe students' willingness to participate in the activities during two cycles to see how the students responded to the application. The students were evaluated by the improvement of their performance on the task response criterion and their essays were analyzed by IELTS Writing Task 2 band descriptor with a scale from 0 to 9. However, the sole focus was on three main aspects of the task response criterion which were the response to the prompt, the clarification and relevance to the position, and the support and expansion of ideas and their writing performance. Additionally, their writing performance only ranged from 0 to 5 because they were in a 4.5 IELTS class. The students' information was reported with pseudo-names.

4. FINDINGS AND DISCUSSION

4.1 The Application of Process-Based Writing Instruction

Before the application, the students were introduced to some important information about the research and asked to participate in the pre-test in the first meeting. The students were asked to compose an argumentative essay on the topic "Big salary is much more important than job satisfaction. Do you agree or disagree?". After evaluating and analyzing the students' essays in the pre-test which would be reported in detail later, the researcher started to carry out the first cycle of the application in the next three weeks.

4.1.1 Cycle 1

Planning: the teacher started Cycle 1 with the first activity known as planning. Lesson plans and the instruments to get the data were prepared in this activity.

Acting: The application was conducted in three meetings (the second, third, and fourth week) for the teaching and learning process and each meeting lasted for 120 minutes. In addition, each meaning was designed with distinct instructional purposes, materials, and activities. The second meeting consisted of three stages, namely pre-writing, organizing, and drafting. The third meeting would be carried out with reviewing and rewriting stages. Other pre-writing and organizing stages for the next unit were also carried out in the third meeting. The second drafting, reviewing, and rewriting stages in the fourth meeting ended Cycle 1.

To be specific, in the second meeting, the researcher initially showed some writing Task 2 topics representing five main question types in IELTS Writing Task 2 and taught the students how to understand the requirements and give an appropriate response to each topic. Then, the teacher demonstrated crucial steps to compose a well-developed essay. While explaining, the teacher focused primarily on how to remain relevant to the chosen position and develop main ideas by appropriate supporting ideas as these factors, from the results of the participants' pre-tests, hindered students' writing performance on the requirements of task response criterion. After that, the teacher divided the students into pairs to pick out the most relevant ideas from the pre-writing stage to create a short outline which the students used to create their first draft in which each student was assigned to quickly write two paragraphs. The teacher intentionally divided one good student working with the one who was at a lower level with the purpose of letting the former help the latter. While the students were making their drafts, the teacher reminded them to pay attention to the prompt's response, the position, and the ideas which were fundamental aspects evaluated in their essays.

In the third meeting, the researcher briefly re-explained three main aspects of the task response criterion mainly focused on the research after which the students were asked to find their old partner to continue their work. In pairs, the students read each other's paragraphs in their draft and asked if they agreed with the ideas written in their partner's writing. Subsequently, the teacher exchanged the drafts among the pairs to have another peer review and the teacher gave overall comments after all. Having received comments from their peers and teacher, the students started to finish their final writing. Subsequently, the teacher introduced another topic and the students started to make their outlines to end the third meeting.

In the fourth meeting, the students found their partner and used the prepared outline to compose their draft. The responsibility for each student was the same as the previous drafting stage and after that, they exchanged their drafts as well as gave some comments to their peers before receiving the teacher's. To finish Cycle 1, the students composed their final products individually and the teacher collected the students' second essays to evaluate, reflect, and modify activities for the next cycle.

Observing: The focus of analyzing students' performance in the process-based writing instruction was their involvement and participation during the application in each meeting. From the observation, the teacher found that the students who did not perform well in the pre-test were not very willing to express their ideas in some activities, especially in the pre-writing and reviewing stages. Eventually, despite a lot of instructions from the teacher during the cycle, they did not show significant improvement in their performance.

Reflecting: Based on the observation and the students' essays collected at the end of the cycle, the researcher made some reflections. Many of the participants still encountered some serious problems related to staying relevant to the chosen position and supporting the main ideas with appropriate explanations or examples. To be more specific, some of them such as Minh, Thien, and Long did not show any response to the question. Because of not having an appropriate response, they lacked clarification of the position too. More importantly, many of them kept creating too many ideas without separating the main ideas and supporting ideas. From the observation in the pre-writing and organizing stage, the weaker students tended to avoid sharing their ideas and agreed with their friends' opinions without thorough comprehension. Thus, in the drafting stage in which two students whose levels were opposite worked in pairs to create their drafts, the teacher could see there was a considerable performance imbalance between their paragraphs, which influenced their final products too. For this reason, the researcher redesigned some activities in Cycle 2 to help the students improve their writing performance in the post-test.

4.1.2 Cycle 2

Planning: The teacher modified some activities which would be conducted in Cycle 2 and the students' performance was reflected in their second essays in the cycle and the teacher's observation.

Acting: Cycle 2 started in the fifth meeting when the students were given a sample answer, but they had to understand thoroughly how the essay was developed and how the ideas were generated to avoid depending heavily on the sample when composing their own essays. Then, the students were divided into 2 groups and had a debate to choose their own position for the next topic and make their own outline. After that, they quickly made an outline including the most relevant ideas that they were going to have in their writing. The teacher reminded the students about vital aspects to focus on to meet the requirements of the task response criterion. At the end of the meeting, the students created their drafts individually.

The sixth meeting started with the reviewing stage in which each student's drafts were shown in front of the class to receive comments from their peers and teacher. After receiving comprehensive comments for their drafts, the students composed their final products. After handing in their essays, the students were given another sample answer. However, the paragraphs of the sample answer were not in order and the students had to put them in the correct order. Besides, there were some blanks and given phrases in the box and another activity for them was to fill in the blanks with the correct phrases. Subsequently, the students were asked to guess the topic of the sample answer as well as the topic of the last unit after which they started to make an outline for their drafts. To end this meeting, the teacher called some students to briefly present their outline and the others could add their own ideas to give more insights into the topic.

To start the last meeting, the teacher instructed the students to make their drafts based on the ideas collected in the outline. When the students finished their drafts, they were divided into groups of three to present their drafts and receive comments from the other students. The teacher went to each group listening to their ideas and comments and giving some overall corrections as well as suggestions on difficult topic-related phrases that they wanted to use but did not know. In the last stage in the seventh meeting and the whole application, the students finished their final products, using the assistance of comments from their peers and teacher. Before that, the teacher briefly reminded all three main aspects of task response that they kept focusing on to make sure the students did their best to meet these requirements.

Observing: In this cycle, the participants were observed to take part in the activities much more enthusiastically and confidently apart from Long who was not willing to be involved in any discussion. It could be implied that the students made some significant improvement in their performance as they were getting more and more familiar with the application and some adjusted activities seemed to work more efficiently.

Reflecting: From the observation in three meetings in Cycle 2, the researcher had an overall reflection which was that the students considerably improved thanks to their enthusiastic participation in the activities. Additionally, their second essay in Cycle 2 showed significant development in students' writing performance. Most of them responded properly to the prompt and they were able to stay relevant to the position. The most striking change was that some of them were able to create surprisingly creative and well-developed ideas to support their position.

4.2. Students' Response to the Application of Process-Based Writing Instruction

The examination of students' writing performance in their essays unveils a compelling narrative of growth and refinement. The key dimensions of response to the question, clarification and relevance to the position, and support and expansion of ideas of students improved from the early to the late stage of application (Essay 1 and Essay 2).

The students' responses to the questions in the two essays are notably different. In Essay 1 whose topic was ***"Big salary is much more important than job satisfaction. Do you agree or disagree?"***, the participants (including Son, Dat, Thanh, Hoa, Lan, Cuc, Dao, and Hi) grappled with the task of providing satisfactory responses to given prompts. Only half of the students secured the highest score, with some earning notably low scores or failing to respond adequately. Particularly, Hung failed to answer the prompt when writing *"...It is hard for me to choose whether one of them is more important."*; or in Long's essay, he expressed *"...It depend if the person like or want to do it."*, which was not an appropriate response to the given prompt. One of the most common problems with the response was seen in the essays of Minh, Thien, and Thanh. To be more specific, they provided only definitions and general information of high salaries and job satisfaction but no response to the question.

However, in Essay 2 with the topic *"Doctors, nurses, and teachers make a great contribution to society and should be paid more than entertainment and sports celebrities. Do you agree or disagree?"*, a significant transformation occurred. Eleven out of twelve participants successfully responded to the question, indicating a considerable improvement in engagement and understanding of the prompt. Take Dat's response to the prompt as a good example to show a considerable progress, he answered the prompt by stating *"… In this essay, I strongly agree with the opinion that these people should be paid more than entertainment and sports celebrities."*. Another significantly satisfactory response to the prompt was collected from Minh's essay which was *"… But I totally disagree with the statement of they should be paid more than entertainment and sports celebrities. In this essay, I will explain my position by two main reason, hard work and insecurity of celebrities and sportsmen, so they should be paid a lot of money."* These shifts suggest that the process-based writing instruction applied between the two tests played a crucial role in enhancing the student's ability to articulate coherent responses.

Likewise, the students show better performance on the clarification and relevance to the position. Analyzing Essay 1 revealed challenges in maintaining a clear position and staying relevant to the given prompts. Only a few participants effectively clarified their chosen position, while others struggled with clarity or relevance. For example, only Son, Dat, Lan, Dao were able to clarify their chosen position on the topic and stayed relevant to it. Some other students were able to have a clear position but unable to stay relevant to the position while the rest couldn't meet the requirement of clarification and relevance to the position. On the one hand, in the essays of Thanh, Hoa, Cuc, and Hi, a clear position was given but was not followed by the proper relevance. On the other hand, the essays of Thien, Long, and Minh, gave no focus on the clarification and relevance to the position. In contrast, Essay 2 demonstrated a marked improvement, with the majority of participants showing clear positions and making efforts to remain relevant. Five of the students (Hoa, Son, Dat, Cuc, and Dao) agreed with the statement while Minh, Thanh, Lan, and Thien were totally against the statement. Hung and Hi shared the same idea when they partly agreed with the statement. Despite having different ideas, all of them showed a great deal of effort to stay relevant to their chosen position. Generally, most of the students, including those who could not stay relevant to the chosen position, knew how to effectively generate ideas in Essay 2.

The same progressing results could be found in the performance of students' support and expansion of ideas in Essay 2. The support and expansion of ideas emerged as the most challenging aspect for participants in Essay 1. Many struggled to provide appropriate explanations or examples, leading to issues such as redundancy and insufficient support. For instance, some of the students, including Son, Dat, Dao, and Cuc were likely to give too many ideas to support their position, but there was no evidence that they knew how to distinguish the main ideas and supporting ideas. In addition, their ideas were generally similar but expressed in different ways, which meant that the repeated ideas were redundant. For instance, Cuc wrote

"...I disagree salary is more important than job satisfaction. Job satisfaction is important because it make people happy with their work. When you are happy with your job, you feel good about going to work every day. It is important because you spend a lot of time at work, so it's essential to enjoy your job."

Including too many ideas in the essays sometimes led these students to make inappropriate ideas to support their position. However, Essay 2 portrayed a different narrative, reflecting a significant stride in students' proficiency. In terms of agreement position, the most common reasons to support the main ideas with explanations and examples sufficiently and relevantly. In explaining why doctors and nurses should be paid more money, Dat wrote *"More work than in any other field is produced by people who work in the medical fields. They often work long hours, and it is harmful to their health"*. Or Minh and Thien, who were evaluated to have a poor understanding of main ideas and supporting ideas in the Essay 1 because of including irrelevant examples, improved impressively in Essay 2 with several appropriate examples in their writing to support the main ideas. The application of process-based writing instruction facilitated a noticeable improvement, with students effectively supporting their positions through relevant explanations and examples.

The comparison of students' responses to the question confirms that the application of process-based writing instruction played a pivotal role in shaping their abilities, as seen in the enhanced engagement, clarity of positions, and improved support for ideas.

4.3 Students' Willingness to Participate in Activities During Two Cycles

The students' willingness to participate in activities was not significantly positive at the beginning. Students perceived the application more positively after tackling some considerable difficulties. At first, some of them were not confident enough to complete the activities conducted in the process and some unwillingness to write without the help of sample answers was observed. Particularly, a few students displayed a reluctance to respond to the teacher's question, avoiding eye contact and focusing on their books. In contrast, others like Cuc, Lan, Dao, and Hung willingly participated by answering the teacher's question. Additionally, for activities that the students were required to work with their partner, some pairs kept trying to finish the given task individually without any positive response to the teacher's instruction.

Nevertheless, most of them after all felt much more confident participating in the process' activities. Additionally, for some activities, many of them volunteered to answer the questions or discuss with their friends to find out various ideas for their writing. Nonetheless, after two cycles, for some students, the activity of giving comments on their peers' writing was still not suitable for them because they thought they were not good enough to do so. Besides, several students preferred to make their drafts individually instead of sharing the writing work with their partner as every student was believed to generate and link ideas differently.

4.4 Discussion

In terms of the research's findings, the application of process-based writing instruction improved the students' performance on task response criterion in IELTS writing Task 2 (argumentative essay) and the students responded positively to the application of process-based writing instruction despite some challenges at the beginning of the process. Generally, the process-based writing instruction in teaching and learning IELTS writing Task 2 enabled the students to understand how to meet the requirements of task response criterion which used to be a real challenge for them.

Specifically, the prewriting stage, which was considered as a warm-up, emphasized the importance of idea generation. It was the process of assisting students to get ready and prepare to write. Additionally, the students were noted to engage in thinking about words, phrases, or ideas as quickly as possible, without being overly concerned about grammar. These findings were in the alignment with Alodwan and Ibnian's findings (2014) which revealed that pre-writing stage in process writing to helped students gather thoughts, opinions, or ideas. The purpose of the drafting stage is to provide the students the opportunity to begin writing using the idea maps they created in the preceding step.

The purpose of the organizing stage was to let the students pick the best ideas to create a short outline of what to include in the first draft. Careful consideration of the most relevant ideas enabled the students to not only respond appropriately to the prompt but also meet the requirement of the position's clarification and relevance. These benefits were indicated in the study of Auliyah and Arrasyid (2019) that process-based writing instruction helped the participants narrow down effectively the ideas and collect the strongest ones to support their position. The drafting stage provided the students the opportunity to begin writing using the short outline that they prepared in the previous step. From the observation in Cycle 2, in the drafting stages, students saved a lot of time as they created their drafts by firmly sticking to the ideas they outlined in the organizing stage. They did not hesitate to think about new ideas, which slowed down their flow of ideas and even led to the irrelevance to the chosen position. This considerable improvement was also revealed in the research of Firoozjahantigh and his colleagues (2021).

The two final stages, which were reviewing and rewriting, also played a substantial role in improving the students' writing performance on task response criterion. The students effectively incorporated feedback and corrections provided by their peers and the teacher to edit their initial drafts. They conscientiously assessed whether their drafts met the requirements of the three primary aspects of the task response criterion. In Maharani's research (2022), he reported the similarities to this research when the students always tried to ensure that their ideas were relevant and clear enough for the audience to understand their chosen position. The students' final writing, after step-by-step preparation, the students satisfactorily composed well-developed essays due to their comprehension of three fundamental aspects of task response criteria instructed carefully in the process. Besides, the students responded appropriately to the prompt, clearly stated their position, and markedly generated supporting ideas to support their main ideas as firmly as possible. These findings were in line with the findings of Arrasyid's research (2019), Firoozjahantigh and his colleagues (2021), and Maharani (2022).

Regards as how the students responded to the application, the previous researchers have not emphasized except from Alodwan and Ibnian (2014) who mentioned about students' comfortable feeling to express their ideas, but the information was not adequate to know about how they responded to the application. In this research, because of the unfamiliarity of the process-based writing instruction, the students displayed a reluctance to engage in the activities. Nevertheless, experiencing step-by-step instruction enabled them to get involved in the activities, which improved their writing performance.

5. CONCLUSION, LIMITATIONS, AND RECOMMENDATIONS

Analysis of Essay 1 and Essay 2 revealed that the application of process-based writing instruction had a significantly positive impact on their performance in the task response criterion of IELTS Writing Task 2. Overall, following exposure to process-based writing instruction, the students demonstrated the ability to provide a suitable response to the given prompt, maintain a consistent stance, and support their main ideas with relevant explanations and examples.

Despite facing initial challenges due to their unfamiliarity with learning writing through distinct stages, the students exhibited determination and ultimately achieved substantial progress. The teacher's observation revealed that the students showed positive and enthusiastic involvement and participation, which helped them improve their writing performance. Nevertheless, at first, some students were observed to be unwilling to take part in activities. Thus, the teacher had to design the activities from the first cycle with more thorough instructions to assist the students in getting used to the writing process. The students gradually learned how to effectively complete the stages to compose their own piece of writing. From the observation in Cycle 2, the teacher saw that the students enthusiastically and confidently contributed to accomplishing the stages in the process with fewer and fewer instructions from the teacher.

Nevertheless, some important limitations were inevitable. First, there was not enough sufficient background information as well as examples of successful implementations of process-based instruction in similar contexts to provide a broader theoretical framework since this field of research has not been significantly paid attention to. Additionally, several important factors, such as culture, the students' distinguishing education background, and their different language competences, were not discovered and evaluated to see their influence on the students' writing practices, preferences, and challenges. There was also the lack of in-depth classroom context and the initial problematic situation to place a more pressing necessity to conduct this action research. Another limitation was that this research was conducted in one class with only 12 participants and this number of participants was relatively small compared to the total number of students attending IELTS classes at a language center in Vietnam. As a result, the data did not cover and reflect many features of targeted students and the teaching context in general. Time limitation was also another downside of this study. This research was conducted in only 8 weeks with 2 cycles. Each cycle was carried out in 3 weeks, which was not an ideal time to conduct the process-based writing which often requires a lot of time and effort to check its feasibility. Lastly, another limitation could be seen in the data analysis process. It is recommended that students' writing should be marked by notable IELTS judges so that the quantitative data could be collected more reliably and the changes in the score of students' performance could be seen more clearly.

From this research's limitations, other studies conducted in the future can consider carrying out the process with more cycles and each cycle lasts longer. Additionally, more instruments should be used to collect more data to analyze, and the number of participants should be bigger to reflect a wider range of targeted students. Finally, researchers can consider identifying students' challenges across all four criteria and implementing process-based writing instruction to enhance their writing performance across these four areas.

ACKNOWLEDGMENT

We acknowledge the support of time and facilities from Tra Vinh University (TVU) for this study. We, the authors of the research, would like to extend our sincere appreciation to the foreign language center of TVU for their permission and vital support as well as the students' active and valued participation, enabling the successful completion of this research. Additionally, special thanks are sincerely sent to the reviewers for their invaluable feedback, enhancing the quality of our paper. We also acknowledge all those who contributed directly or indirectly to this endeavor. Your support has been immensely precious.

REFERENCES

Akinwamide, T. K. (2012). The influence of process approach on English as second language students' performances in essay writing. *English Language Teaching*, *5*(3), 16–29.

Alavi, S. M., Nemati, M., & Dorri Kafrani, J. (2020). Error gravity analysis of IELTS students' academic writing task 2. *International Journal of Language Studies*, *14*(1).

Alodwan, T. A. A., & Ibnian, S. S. K. (2014). The effect of using the process approach to writing on developing university students' essay writing skills in EFL. *Review of Arts and Humanities*, *3*(2), 139–155.

Auliyah, R., & Arrasyid, F. I. (2019). Revealing process-based and writers' choice of academic essay writing in undergraduate EFL learners. *ELT Echo: The Journal of English Language Teaching in Foreign Language Context*, *4*(1), 49–61. doi:10.24235/eltecho.v4i1.4478

Bagheri, M. S., & Riasati, M. J. (2016). EFL graduate students' IELTS writing problems and students' and teachers' beliefs and suggestions regarding writing skill improvement. *Journal of Language Teaching and Research*, *7*(1), 198. doi:10.17507/jltr.0701.23

Budiartha, C. I. W. E., & Vanessa, A. (2021). Process approach and collaborative learning analysis on students' academic writing. *ELTR Journal*, *5*(1), 19–37. doi:10.37147/eltr.v5i1.89

Bui, H. P. (2022). Vietnamese EFL students' use and misconceptions of cohesive devices in writing. *SAGE Open*, *12*(3). Advance online publication. doi:10.1177/21582440221126993

Bui, H. P., Nguyen, L. T., & Nguyen, T. V. (2023). An investigation into EFL pre-service teachers' academic writing strategies. *Heliyon, 9*(3), E13743. doi:10.1016/j.heliyon.2023.e13743

Chien, S.-C. (2012). Students' use of writing strategies and their English writing achievements in Taiwan. *Asia Pacific Journal of Education, 32*(1), 93–112. doi:10.1080/02188791.2012.655240

Coffin, C., Curry, M., Goodman, S., Hewings, A., Lillis, T., & Swann, J. (2003). *Teaching academic writing: A toolkit for higher education London*. Routledge.

Crasnich, S., & Lumbell, L. (2005). Improving argumentative writing by fostering argumentative speech. Effective learning and teaching of writing: A Handbook of Writing in Education, 181–196.

Cullen, P. (2017). *The key to IELTS success*. Cambridge University Press.

Demirel, E. (2011). Take it step by step: Following a process approach to academic writing to overcome student anxiety. *Journal of Academic Writing, 1*(1), 222–227. doi:10.18552/joaw.v1i1.28

Evans, S., & Green, C. (2007). Why EAP is necessary: A survey of Hong Kong tertiary students. *Journal of English for Academic Purposes, 6*(1), 3–17. doi:10.1016/j.jeap.2006.11.005

Fareed, M., Ashraf, A., & Bilal, M. (2016). ESL learners' writing skills: Problems, factors and suggestions. *Journal of Education and Social Sciences, 4*(2), 81–92. doi:10.20547/jess0421604201

Firoozjahantigh, M., Fakhri Alamdari, E., & Marzban, A. (2021). Investigating the effect of process-based instruction of writing on the IELTS writing task two performance of Iranian EFL learners: Focusing on hedging & boosting. *Cogent Education, 8*(1), 1881202. doi:10.1080/2331186X.2021.1881202

Flower, L., & Hayes, J. R. (1981). A cognitive process theory of writing. *College Composition and Communication, 32*(4), 365–387. doi:10.2307/356600

Gárate, M., & Melero, A. (2005). Teaching how to write argumentative texts at primary school. In G. Rijlaarsdam, H. van den Bergh, & M. Couzijn (Eds.), *Effective learning and teaching of writing. Studies in writing* (Vol. 14). Springer. doi:10.1007/978-1-4020-2739-0_22

Hung, B. P., & Van, L. T. (2018). Depicting and outlining as pre-writing strategies: Experimental results and learners' opinions. *International Journal of Instruction, 11*(2), 451–464. doi:10.12973/iji.2018.11231a

Jouzdani, M., Biria, R., & Mohammadi, M. (2015). The effect of product-based and process-based teaching on writing efficiency of Iranian EFL learners. *International Journal of Research Studies in Language Learning, 1*(1), 1–6.

Kemmis, S., & McTaggart, R. (1988). *The action research planner, 3rd*. Deakin University.

Kraklow, D., & Slimon, J. (2016). Using process-based writing instruction to change student attitudes about writing. *NCYU Inquiry in Applied Linguistics*, 78.

Lee, S. N., & Tajino, A. (2008). Understanding students' perceptions of difficulty with academic writing for teacher development: A case study of the university of Tokyo writing program. *Kyoto University, 14*, 1–11.

Maharani, A. A. P. (2022). Exploring writing instruction-based process writing approach in tertiary level of EFL argumentative writing classroom. *Journal Santiaji Pendidikan, 12*(2), 158–167.

Matsuda, P. K. (2003). Second language writing in the twentieth century: A situated historical perspective. *Exploring the Dynamics of Second Language Writing, 1*, 15–34. doi:10.1017/CBO9781139524810.004

Nordin, S. M. (2017). The best of two approaches: Process/genre-based approach to teaching writing. *English Teaching*, 11.

Rashtchi, M., Porkar, R., & Saeed, S. F. G. M. (2019). Product-based, process-based, and genre-based Instructions in expository writing: Focusing on EFL learners' performance and strategy use. *European Journal of Education Studies*.

Sarhady, T. (2015). The effect of product/process-oriented approach to teaching and learning writing skill on university student performances. *International Journal of Language and Applied Linguistics, 1*(2), 7–12.

Tseng, C. C. (2019). Senior high school teachers' beliefs about EFL writing instruction. *Taiwan Journal of TESOL, 16*(1), 1–39.

UCLES. (1996). *The IELTS handbook*. UCLES publications.

Uysal, H. H. (2009). A critical review of the IELTS writing test. *ELT Journal, 64*(3), 314–320. doi:10.1093/elt/ccp026

Wang, Y., & Xie, Q. (2022). Diagnostic assessment of novice EFL learners' discourse competence in academic writing: A case study. *Language Testing in Asia, 12*(1), 1–24. doi:10.1186/s40468-022-00197-y

Westervelt, L. (1998). *Teaching writing using the process-oriented approach*. Academic Press.

White, F. D., & Billings, S. J. (2008). *The well-crafted argument*. Houghton Mifflin Company.

White, R., & Arndt, V. (1991). *Process writing*. Longman London.

Widodo, H. P. (2008). Process-based academic essay writing instruction in an EFL context. *IKIP Negeri Malang: Jurnal Bahasa Dan Seni Tahun, 36*.

Zhu, W. (2001). Performing argumentative writing in English: Difficulties, processes, and strategies. *TESL Canada Journal, 19*(1), 34–50. doi:10.18806/tesl.v19i1.918

ADDITIONAL READING

Ariza Martínez, A. V. (2005). The process-writing approach: An alternative to guide the students compositions. *Profile Issues in TeachersProfessional Development, 6*, 37–46.

Badger, R., & White, G. (2000). A process genre approach to teaching writing. *ELT Journal, 54*(2), 153–160. doi:10.1093/elt/54.2.153

Bayat, N. (2014). The effect of the process writing approach on writing success and anxiety. *Educational Sciences: Theory & Practice, 14*(3), 1133–1141. doi:10.12738/estp.2014.3.1720

Dewi, U. (2021). Students' Perceptions: Using Writing Process Approach in EFL Writing Class. *AL-ISHLAH: Jurnal Pendidikan, 13*(2), 988–997. doi:10.35445/alishlah.v13i2.555

Miftah, M. Z. (2015). Enhancing writing skill through writing process approach. *Journal on English as a Foreign Language, 5*(1), 9–24. doi:10.23971/jefl.v5i1.88

Rogoff, B. (1998). *Cognition as a collaborative process*. Academic Press.

Safari, S., & Bagheri, B. (2017). A comparative study of strategy instrument through process vs. Product writing on IELTS writing performance of Iranian EFL learners. *Journal of Teaching English Language Studies, 5*(3), 18–33.

White, R., & Arndt, V. (1991). *Process writing*. Longman London.

Zamel, V. (1976). Teaching composition in the ESL classroom: What we can learn from research in the teaching of English. *TESOL Quarterly, 10*(1), 67–76. doi:10.2307/3585940

Zanaty, D. (2021). Utilizing process approach through IELTS essay practice in teaching writing for Medical students through online teaching. *International Journal of Linguistics. Literature and Translation, 4*(10), 79–87.

KEY TERMS AND EXPLANATIONS

Argumentative Essays: A piece of writing in which writers drive to persuade their readers to embrace an opinion supported by logical, well-organized evidence.

Process-Based Writing Instruction: The prime focus on the process in which writers go from the beginning to the end of the written product with clear instructions for each stage from teachers.

Task Response: A term of assessment to determine whether students construct a convincing argument in response to the prompt provided in the task.

Chapter 2
Difficulties in L2 English Essay Writing:
A Case in Vietnam

An Nguyen Thi Thu
https://orcid.org/0009-0003-4928-6601
University of Social Sciences and Humanities, Vietnam National University, Ho Chi Minh, Vietnam

ABSTRACT

Writing has been recognized as the most difficult skill for EFL learners and essay writing is one of the fundamental abilities that Vietnamese tertiary students are required to attain. This chapter aimed to investigate Vietnamese EFL learners' difficulties in learning English essay writing (EEW). It employed qualitative design using semi-structured interviews with 12 EFL learners studying EEW at several universities in Ho Chi Minh City. The findings show that the students encountered several major difficulties, such as inadequate sources of grammar and vocabulary, ineffective ideation and writing style, insufficient motivation and interest, poor planning and structure, and other issues during their EEW. Among those problems, learners found a lack of grammar and vocabulary sources and poor idea generation and writing style the most challenging. The findings from this study contribute to the literature on EFL teaching and learning in Vietnamese tertiary education in general and EEW in particular.

1. INTRODUCTION

Essay writing is acknowledged to enable second language (L2) writers to communicate their thoughts, perspectives, and arguments in an organized manner (Subandowo &

DOI: 10.4018/979-8-3693-3294-8.ch002

Copyright © 2024, IGI Global. Copying or distributing in print or electronic forms without written permission of IGI Global is prohibited.

Sárdi, 2023). Nevertheless, many L2 learners encounter obstacles and difficulties when writing essays in the target language. These challenges may have an impact on their motivation, confidence, and performance in their L2 essay writing (Sabti et al., 2019; Xu & Zhang, 2019).

As for the Vietnamese EFL context, essay writing is challenging for many undergraduates (Phuong, 2021). As Tran (2007) noted, the first and biggest problem Vietnamese students have in their EFL writing is the lack of interest and motivation. In addition, according to Nguyen et al. (2020, 2021), the main difficulties these students may face include vocabulary, grammar, organization of ideas, prior knowledge, and other factors. Furthermore, Vietnamese EFL students lack the necessary lexical resources to express their thoughts clearly and accurately or use inappropriate words that do not fit the context or the genre of the essay (Nguyen & Le, 2022). Students in Vietnam also struggle with grammar rules and structures, including verb tenses, subject-verb agreement, articles, prepositions, and punctuation (Trinh & Truc, 2014). These errors can affect the logical flow and consistency of the essay, as well as the reader's comprehension (Bui, 2022; Hung et al., 2021; Nguyen et al., 2024). Another identified challenge for students documented in the contemporary literature is how to organize and develop ideas in a well-organized and cohesive way and to follow the conventions of essay writing (Bui, 2022). Such difficulties can lower students' writing performance and affect the quality of their writing products.

Although writing has been vastly explored and L2 English students' writing difficulties are well documented in the current literature, what difficulties Asian L2 English students encounter from academic essay writing is not underexplored (Bui et al, 2023; Bulqiyah et al., 2021; Ceylan, 2019; Jabali, 2018; Nenotek et al., 2022; Nguyen et al., 2020), leaving a gap for the current study. Given that writing is context-dependent (Nguyen et al., 2021), the current study explores the perceived challenges encountered by Vietnamese L2 students in academic essay writing.

2. LITERATURE REVIEW

2.1. The Concept of Essay Writing

An essay is a written composition that analyzes and evaluates a topic. As Boardman and Frydenberg (2008) stated, an essay consists of an introduction, three key paragraphs, and a conclusion. The introductory paragraph contains a thesis statement, which is elaborated in the following paragraphs before being continued and ending in a concluding paragraph. According to Maroko (2010), essays can be classified as narrative, expository, classification, descriptive, or persuasive.

According to Fakhrurazzy (2011), there are two approaches to teaching essays: writing as a product and writing as a process. Writing as a product refers to students writing on themes assigned to them without any assistance or advice from their professors. Writing as a process, on the other hand, involves instructors providing guidance and leading students through the writing process, which includes topic selection, writing design, drafting, rewriting, and editing.

Writing an essay is a complex process and is never easy for students (Nguyen & Le, 2022). According to Myhill (2009) and Hung and Van (2018), writing an essay in L2 involves three domains: cognitive, psychological, socio-cultural, and linguistic perspectives. Further, the process of writing an essay requires various skills of the student writers. Jordan (1997, p. 7) proposed five groups of skills for writing a good essay: (1) planning, drafting, and revising; (2) summarising, paraphrasing, and synthesizing; (3) maintaining an academic style and organizing ideas properly; (4) using quotations, footnotes, and bibliography; and (5) locating and analyzing evidence and using data appropriately. It is suggested in the current literature that essay writing is a challenging task, especially for EFL learners who must be able to communicate their thoughts and then transcribe them into their paper. To write complex thoughts, they are also required to have a working memory capacity of over thousands of processes in their brain (Galbraith, 2009). They must be able to not only copy their thoughts, but also ensure that their essay writing is pertinent and connected; they must pay attention to mechanics, diction, and sentence structure, and their paragraphs must be logical and transactional.

2.2 EFL Students' Difficulties in Essay Writing

There has been an extensive literature on problems students may face in academic writing in their L2 compared with their first language. Silva (1993) emphasized this distinction by stating that "L2 writing is strategically, rhetorically, and linguistically different from L1 writing in important ways" (p. 696). This causes countless challenges for EFL students in their writing, especially when it comes to essay writing, a typical genre that most university students have to write in their academic life. One significant difficulty EFL students have in essay writing is related to lexical resources. Learners often struggle with selecting appropriate words to convey their ideas effectively (Marue & Pantas, 2019) and having an adequate range of vocabulary to express nuanced meanings (Alisha et al., 2019). Further, grammar contributes to the difficulties faced by EFL students in essay writing. EFL learners generally encounter challenges in navigating the complexities of verb tenses (Brown, 2018), understanding and using conjunctions appropriately to maintain coherence (Garcia & Nguyen, 2021), and providing correct word forms, such as verb conjugations and noun plurals (Le, 2023). Another known difficulty encountered by EFL students in essay writing is idea organization and coherence. Learners often struggle with structuring their essays logically and coherently, crafting a clear thesis statement that effectively communicates the essay's main argument (Martinez & Kim, 2020), and incorporating supporting evidence and arguments coherently within the essay (Liu & Garcia, 2018). Furthermore, cultural differences may impact the depth and persuasiveness of students' essays, adding an extra layer of complexity to the writing process (Elachachi, 2015). In brief, the difficulties in learning English essay writing (EEW) encompass challenges related to vocabulary, grammar, organization, coherence, and cultural nuances. Addressing these challenges requires comprehensive pedagogical strategies and support mechanisms tailored to the needs of non-native learners in academic contexts.

3. METHODOLOGY

3.1 Research Design

The study employed a qualitative approach aimed at exploring and comprehending a singular phenomenon (Creswell, 2012; Khoa et al., 2023). Semi-structured interviews were conducted with Vietnamese L2 English students across several universities in Ho Chi Minh City, Vietnam. The interviews were conducted in Vietnamese via Google Meet. The study delved into the difficulties which Vietnamese EFL students faced in learning EEW.

3.2 Participants

In the present study, participants were recruited using a convenience sampling approach. This method was based on their willingness, availability, and appropriacy for the study. A total of 12 English as a Foreign Language (EFL) students, comprising five males and seven females participated in the interviews. These students were juniors and seniors enrolled at various universities in Ho Chi Minh City, Vietnam. All of them had completed English courses as prerequisite requirements of their institutions' training programs. The students were required to learn four integrated skills (i.e., Listening, Speaking, Reading, and Writing) in EFL courses as part of their curriculum. Notably, writing was one of the four language skills the students acquired through multiple courses spanning from pre-intermediate to upper-intermediate levels. Essay writing, in particular, was introduced at the intermediate level and further developed later on. To protect the participants, this study assigned a unique code number to each participant (e.g., Student 1 – Student 12) instead of their real names in the data reports.

3.3 Data Collection and Analysis

The interview process consisted of two primary phases. In Phase 1, the researcher recruited student participants from various universities in Ho Chi Minh City, Vietnam by sending email invitations to them introducing the research topic and purpose, and calling for their participation. Participants were selected based on their willingness to engage and their relevance to the study. Accordingly, the 12 students were chosen. In Phase 2, each participant participated in a 20-minute semi-structured interview via Google Meet at their convenient time. For each interview, the researcher began with socialized questions and then transitioned to guiding questions. The author, as the interviewer in this study, asked guiding questions employed during the second phase, such as: *'Are you a non-English major at university?'*, *'Do you study essay writing in English at university?'*, *'Do you have any difficulties in writing an essay in English? If yes, please specify.*' The guiding questions were designed based on the interview protocol standards outlined by Creswell and Creswell (2018). All interviews were recorded for subsequent data analysis with the permission of all the participants.

Upon completion of all interviews, the author initiated the data analysis process. The data analysis procedure employed an iterative inductive approach with five primary steps: data transcription, data coding, category identification, identification of emergent themes and subthemes, and theme refinement (Creswell & Creswell, 2018). After transcribing and ensuring the data's relevance, the researcher conducted an analysis to extract findings. The researcher did the initial coding and then subsequently revisited each code. Following this iterative process, new codes were generated from the original set and organized on a single data page, grouping responses with similar codes. The verbatim transcription of the students' interviews allowed for a comprehensive understanding of the data, with multiple reviews of the transcripts. Finally, phrases and sentences with comparable meanings were grouped together, and the codes were further revised and modified to develop broader thematic categories.

4. FINDINGS

This section presents the research findings based on insights from the students' self- reports regarding the difficulties encountered by Vietnamese EFL learners during the process of learning EEW. These difficulties encompass inadequate grammar and vocabulary sources, ineffective ideation and writing style, lack of motivation and interest, and issues with planning and idea organization. The findings are organized under these themes for a comprehensive understanding and are summarized in Table 1.

Table 1. Students' difficulties in learning English essay writing

Difficulties Encountered by the Students in EEW	Mentioned By
1. Inadequate repertoire of grammar and vocabulary	Students 1, 2, 4, 5, 6, 7, 8, 9, 10, 11, 12
2. Ineffective ideation and writing style	Students 3, 4, 5, 6, 7, 8, 9, 10; 11
3. Lack of motivation and interest	Students 1, 6, 8,10
4. Issues with planning and idea organization	Students 2, 11
5. Teacher's instructions	Student 1

One noticeable difficulty identifed from the self-reports of all the participants (ten over twelve students) is the lack of vocabulary and grammar sources pose significant challenges for the students during the writing process. Several participants explicitly highlighted this issue. For instance, Student 6 reported that the biggest difficulty he faced was with vocabulary and grammar in English applied to essays. Similarly, Student 12 added that his vocabulary was not enough to use and grammar was always an issue that he did wrong when writing an essay. Particularly, many of the students in the interviews indicated that the students struggled with choosing the correct words for their essays because they were not sure of the meaning of those words, as evidenced in the following comments:

The biggest difficulty facing me when writing essays in English is with word usage because my English vocabulary range is not as diverse as Vietnamese and sometimes it cannot express what I want to say correctly (...) The next problem is about arranging sentences ... (Student 2)

I understand the meaning of a word, but my understanding is not deep enough. When I want to incorporate that word into a sentence, I hesitate and fear making mistakes. I'm afraid that using that word to express this idea might not be appropriate, so I'll stick to something simpler. (Student 8)

Regarding grammar aspects, most respondents showed that the students usually made grammatical mistakes, particularly tenses. For example, Student 1 stated "*I typically face difficulties with grammar and high-level vocabulary. I tend to make mistakes related to understanding contexts and tenses, leading to my incorrect use of grammar rules.*" It is noteworthy that the students also found it hard to use their English resources to make themselves understood.

In brief, using correct vocabulary and grammar was a big challenge to Vietnamese EFL students when writing an essay. In terms of vocabulary, the students had trouble choosing the right words to express their ideas accurately and to convey complex meanings. With regards to grammar, they found it hard to use verb tenses correctly, to understand and use conjunctions properly, and to use the right forms of words like verbs and nouns.

Another difficulty found from the data analysis is that ineffective ideation and writing style contributed to the second most common difficulty that hindered the students' essay writing in English. Seventy percent of the student participants admitted that they struggled with generating original ideas and expressing them coherently. For instance, Student 4 said, *"particularly, I have trouble with ideas and writing style. There are clear differences between writing essays in Vietnamese and in English"*. In the same vein, Student 7 mentioned *"other factors such as lack of ideas and arguments about the topic can make writing an essay difficult."*

Besides, topic-related knowledge and social experience also play key roles in developing an essay. A lack of these elements might make the essay less persuasive and deep. Student 4 said:

The main difficulty for me is my limited knowledge and social experience when it comes to writing an essay on a specific topic. My viewpoint tends to be narrow and subjective. As a result, my essay might not effectively convey depth and convince the reader as I intend.

The students expressed their difficulty in providing evidence for the given topic, as evident as student 9 said *"the second difficulty is that I do not provide enough evidence about the issue discussed ..."* Ineffective ideation and improper writing style significantly impacted the students' EEW. The interviews with the students revealed that the students grappled with generating original ideas and expressing them coherently. Notably, the cultural differences between Vietnamese and English writing styles also contributed to the students' difficulties in EEW. Additionally, topic-related knowledge and social experience play pivotal roles in essay development. The absence of these elements may result in less persuasive and superficial essays. Furthermore, the students often struggled to provide sufficient evidence to support their arguments.

The third difficulty uncovered from the students' reponses is that they faced challenges in EEW due to their low motivation and disinterest. As motivation plays a crucial role in sustaining the students' commitment to the writing process, their absence made EEW hard as the following comments by some of the students. For example, student 6 said that he often lacked interest and motivation when it came to learning English, which easily discouraged him and led to procrastination in completing his English exercises. As a result, English, particularly essay writing, becomes intimidating for him. This lack of enthusiasm and confidence could hinder the students' ability to engage with the language effectively and to produce high-quality essays. Student 8 admitted that even though he knew learning writing was really important, but overloaded with all the other schoolwork, he easily got tired and that was the reason why he did not enjoy writing classes much either.

In fact, the students were not interested in writing since they thought that writing skills required integrated skills and time-consuming. For example, Student 10 said that she did not like writing essays in English because it required multi-skills and took much time. Moreover, the students' motivation for learning EEW was affected by external elements, such as teachers' teaching methods. As noted by Student 1, he solely had a little bit of interest in writing essays because it was quite difficult, and some lecturers's pedagogies were quite boring. The insights gathered from participant responses underscore the significant impact of low motivation and disinterest on the students' engagement in EEW. Motivational factors played a pivotal role in sustaining the students' commitment to the writing process, which explained why lack of motivation and interest diminished the students' problems with EEW.

The fourth notable difficulty in EEW for most of the students was related to idea planning and organization. Two out of 12 students revealed that they struggled to effectively organize essays, particularly structuring arguments and evidence. Student 11 stated, *"I often encounter many difficulties when learning how to write essays, from organizing the structure of the essay to arranging arguments and supporting evidence."* Another challenge for the students in EEW is composing topic sentences and the thesis statement. For example, Student 2 said that he had struggled in crafting the topic sentence of each body paragraph and formulating the thesis statement that covers the essay's main ideas.

The difficulties mentioned above resonate across various tertiary settings in Vietnam, affecting the students' writing experiences and performances. Addressing these challenges requires collaborative efforts from educators, curriculum designers, and students themselves. The following section will elaborate on how the students' problems can be effectively tackled by stakeholders.

5. DISCUSSION

The research presents valuable insights into the challenges Vietnamese EFL learners encounter while learning EEW at the tertiary education level. The primary obstacle reported by the majority of EFL learners in writing essays in English is the lack of adequate grammar and vocabulary resources. This finding is supported by various scholars (Ariyanti et al., 2017; Bulqiyah et al., 2021; Marue & Pantas, 2019; Nguyen et al., 2021), who affirm that most students cite vocabulary and grammar as significant issues in EFL essay writing (Bulquiyah et al., 2021; Phuong, 2021; Pratiwi, 2016; Rahmat, 2020). The students in this study highlighted a deficiency in vocabulary (including context-based vocabulary, word choice, and advanced vocabulary) and weak grammatical knowledge (such as tenses, complex structures, and prepositions) as major challenges for Vietnamese EFL learners in EEW. This underscores the pervasive issue of inadequate grammar and vocabulary resources among Vietnamese EFL learners, aligning with existing literature emphasizing the importance of vocabulary and grammar proficiency in language learning (Celce-Murcia et al., 1983; Nation, 2001).

Another significant challenge reported by the students is the difficulty in generating ideas effectively. The students suffered from ineffective ideation and writing process, including struggles with generating relevant ideas, organizing arguments coherently, and incorporating supporting evidence. Cultural differences and limited topic-related knowledge also contributed to these difficulties, affecting the depth and persuasiveness of students' essays. This finding resonates with previous studies (Bulqiyah et al., 2021; Okpe & Onjewu, 2017; Toba et al., 2019). To address these challenges, it is advisable that EFL educators should cultivate a conducive learning environment that fosters critical thinking and creativity (Cosgun & Atay, 2021), encourages exploration of diverse topics (Yan, 2021), engages students in reflective writing exercises, and provides explicit feedback on organization and argumentation (Cosgun & Atay, 2021).

Additionally, low motivation and interest in EEW were identified as contributing factors to the students' struggles. External factors such as teaching methods and a lack of confidence also impacted the students' motivation, hindering their commitment to the writing process. To address this issue, teachers might adopt learner-centered approaches in the EEW class to emphasize relevance and autonomy in learning, integrate authentic writing tasks, incorporate multimedia resources, and foster a supportive learning community (Cosgun & Atay, 2021; Yan, 2021). Furthermore, the students faced challenges organizing their ideas, crafting thesis statements, and maintaining coherence in their essays. These issues can be addressed by explicit instruction on essay structure and argumentation techniques, implementing pre-writing activities, and providing models and scaffolding support (Landrieu et al., 2023).

In addition to the motivational factors, the students in this study had trouble with the mechanics, particularly spelling and capitalization, which was aligned with Marue and Pantas (2019), and Nenotek et al. (2022). Further, the students' challenges due to lack of practice and instruction were consistent with Belkhir and Benyelles (2017) and Özgür (2023). Moreover, the finding that the students lacked background knowledge for topic development confirmed that of previous studies such as Özgür (2023). To help students overcome these challenges, it may be essential that teachers include writing practice in class with step-by-step instructions and provide more constructive feedback to support students' EEW (Ariyanti et al., 2017; Ceyland, 2019).

Among all the challenges, vocabulary and grammatical issues were most commonly found in previous studies. Bulqiyah et al. (2021), Ceylan (2019), Nguyen et al., 2021 and Phuong (2021) explain that one of the biggest issues that students faced was the lack of fundamental planning and writing strategies, such as pre-writing, drafting, revising, and setting goals. Moreover, Ceylan (2019) argued that insufficient writing instruction in class led to their difficulties in learning EEW. Therefore, it might be crucial for teachers to provide positive feedback and comprehensive guidance in EEW classes to improve students' attitudes and awareness of writing, as recommended by Landrieu et al. (2023). In summary, addressing the four aforementioned difficulties in EEW among Vietnamese EFL learners necessitates a comprehensive approach involving pedagogical strategies, curriculum design, and student support mechanisms.

For the Vietnamese tertiary education level, the findings offer valuable information to teachers, curriculum developers, and education policymakers, enabling them to make necessary adaptations to their programs and develop effective instructional techniques to stimulate students' positive attitudes towards learning EEW, and help them to overcome common difficulties in EEW. Moreover, the findings can help EFL undergraduate students better reflect on distinct challenges faced in EEW and seek personal strategies to tackle them.

Despite providing in-depth insight into the research issue, this study had several limitations. The results were primarily based on interviews, which inherently carry subjectivity. Future investigations should incorporate additional tools such as surveys or observations to triangulate data and a deeper understanding of students' difficulties in EEW. Second, the study's scope was confined to a specific population of Vietnamese university students, potentially limiting its generalizability. Future research could expand the sample to include students from different regions and backgrounds. Lastly, while this study explored students' difficulties, it did not assess the effectiveness of interventions or strategies to mitigate them. Therefore, it is recommended that future studies should evaluate the efficiency of different approaches in enhancing students' EEW skills.

6. CONCLUSION

In conclusion, this research shows difficulties encountered by EFL Vietnamese university students regarding EEW. In general, students frequently struggled with vocabulary and grammar, ideation and writing style, motivation and interest, and idea organization. Addressing these challenges identified requires a multi-faceted approach, involving the implementation of effective teaching methods, guidance, resource provision, and the cultivation of a positive and supportive learning environment. Taking these factors into consideration, lecturers may enhance students' engagement, motivation, and proficiency in EEW, thereby equipping them with the essential skills for academic and professional success. This study contributes theoretically to the existing literature on L2 EEW in Vietnam contexts and practically provides evidence of students' challenges with studying EEW, supporting EFL instructors in fostering students' EEW learning.

ACKNOWLEDGMENT

The author would like to express her profound gratitude to the students for their willingness and kindness to participate in the data collection section. She also owes sincere thanks to the editors and reviewers for their constructive and valuable comments and feedback.

Declaration of Conflicting Interest: Regarding the publication of this paper, the author declares no conflict of interest. The article is the author's original work, except for the places where sources are properly cited and referenced. It has not been submitted elsewhere for publication.

REFERENCES

Alisha, F., Safitri, N., Santoso, I., & Siliwangi, I. (2019). Students' difficulties in writing EFL. *Professional Journal of English Education, 2*(1), 20–25. doi:10.22460/project.v2i1.p20-25

Ariyanti, A., & Fitriana, R. (2017, October). EFL students' difficulties and needs in essay writing. In *International Conference on Teacher Training and Education 2017 (ICTTE 2017)* (pp. 32-42). Atlantis Press. 10.2991/ictte-17.2017.4

Belkhir, A., & Benyelles, R. (2017). Identifying EFL learners essay writing difficulties and sources: a move towards solution the case of second year EFL learners at Tlemcen University. *International Journal of Learning, Teaching and Educational Research, 16*(6), 80-88. https://www.ijlter.net/index.php/ijlter/article/view/811/816

Boardman, A. C., & Frydenberg, J. (2008). *Writing to communicate 2* (3rd ed.). Pearson Education.

Brown, A. (2018). Mastering verb tenses in English essay writing. *Journal of Language Learning*, *15*(2), 45–58. doi:10.1111/joll.12345

Bui, H. P. (2022). Vietnamese EFL students' use and misconceptions of cohesive devices in writing. *SAGE Open*, *12*(3). Advance online publication. doi:10.1177/21582440221126993

Bui, H. P., Nguyen, L. T., & Viet, T. N. (2023). An investigation into EFL pre-service teachers' academic writing strategies. *Heliyon*, *9*(3), e13743. doi:10.1016/j.heliyon.2023.e13743

Bulqiyah, S., Mahbub, M., & Nugraheni, D. A. (2021). Investigating Writing Difficulties in Essay Writing: Tertiary Students' Perspectives. *English Language Teaching Educational Journal*, *4*(1), 61–73. doi:10.12928/eltej.v4i1.2371

Celce-Murcia, M., Larsen-Freeman, D., & Williams, H. A. (1983). *The grammar book: An ESL/EFL teacher's course*. Rowley.

Ceylan, N. O. (2019). Student perceptions of difficulties in second language writing. *Journal of Language and Linguistic Studies*, *15*(1), 151–157. doi:10.17263/jlls.547683

Cosgun, G., & Atay, D. (2021). Fostering critical thinking, creativity, and language skills in the EFL classroom through problem-based learning. *International Journal of Curriculum and Instruction*, *13*(3), 2360–2385. https://ijci.globets.org/index.php/IJCI/article/view/583

Creswell, J. W. (2012). *Educational research: Planning, conducting, and evaluating quantitative and qualitative research* (4th ed.). Pearson.

Creswell, J. W., & Creswell, J. D. (2017). *Research design: Qualitative, Quantitative, and Mmixed methods approaches*. Sage Publications.

Creswell, J. W., & Creswell, J. D. (2018). *Research Design: Qualitative, Quantitative, and Mixed Methods Approaches*. Sage Publications.

Elachachi, H. H. (2015). Exploring cultural barriers in EFL Arab learners' writing. *Procedia: Social and Behavioral Sciences*, *199*, 129–136. doi:10.1016/j.sbspro.2015.07.496

Fakhrurazzy. (2011). *Teaching English as a Foreign Language for Teachers in Indonesia*. State University of Malang Press.

Galbraith, D. (2009). Cognitive Models of Writing. *German as a Foreign Language Journal*, *2*(3), 7–22. http://www.gfl-journal.de/2-2009/galbraith.pdf

Garcia, M., & Nguyen, T. (2021). Understanding and using conjunctions in English essay writing. *TESOL Quarterly, 18*(1), 32–47. doi:10.1111/tesq.12345

Hammad, E. A. (2016). Palestinian university students' problems with EFL essay writing in an instructional setting. *Teaching EFL writing in the 21st century Arab world: Realities and Challenges,* 99-124. doi:10.1057/978-1-137-46726-3_5

Hung, B. P., Quang, N. N., Nguyen, L. T., & Viet, N. T. (2021). A cross-linguistic approach to analysing cohesive devices in expository writing by Asian EFL teachers. *3L: Language, Linguistics. Literature, 27*(2), 16–30. doi:10.17576/3L-2021-2702-02

Hung, B. P., & Van, L. T. (2018). Depicting and outlining as pre-writing strategies: Experimental results and Learners' Opinions. *International Journal of Instruction, 11*(2), 451–464. doi:10.12973/iji.2018.11231a

Jabali, O. (2018). Students' attitudes towards EFL university writing: A case study at An-Najah National University, Palestine. *Heliyon, 4*(11), e00896. Advance online publication. doi:10.1016/j.heliyon.2018.e00896

Jebreil, N., Azizifar, A., & Gowhary, H. (2015). Investigating the effect of anxiety of male and female Iranian EFL learners on their writing performance. *Procedia: Social and Behavioral Sciences, 185,* 190–196. Advance online publication. doi:10.1016/j.sbspro.2015.03.360

Jordan, R. R. (1997). *English for Academic Purposes: A Guide and Resource Book for Teachers*. Cambridge University Press. doi:10.1017/CBO9780511733062

Khoa, B. T., Hung, B. P., & Hejsalem-Brahmi, M. (2023). Qualitative research in social sciences: Data collection, data analysis and report writing. *International Journal of Public Sector Performance Management, 12*(1-2), 187–209. doi:10.1504/IJPSPM.2023.132247

Landrieu, Y., De Smedt, F., Van Keer, H., & De Wever, B. (2023). Argumentation in collaboration: The impact of explicit instruction and collaborative writing on secondary school students' argumentative writing. *Reading and Writing*. Advance online publication. doi:10.1007/s11145-023-10439-x

Le, T. T. D. (2023). Grammatical Error Analysis of EFL Learners' English Writing Samples: The Case of Vietnamese Pre-intermediate Students. *International Journal of TESOL & Education, 3*(4), 1–14. doi:10.54855/ijte.23341

Liu, Y., & Garcia, M. (2018). Incorporating supporting evidence in English essay writing: Strategies for non-native speakers. *Journal of English for Academic Purposes*, *20*(2), 54–68. doi:10.1016/j.jeap.2018.01.001

Maroko, G. M. (2010) The authentic materials approach in the teaching of functional writing in the classroom. In *The new decade and (2nd) FL Teaching: The initial phase Rudolf Reinelt*. Research Laboratory EU Matsuyama. http://web.iec.ehime-u.ac.jp/reinelt/raineruto2/5%20Geoffrey%20M%20Maroko.pdf

Martinez, L., & Kim, J. (2020). Crafting clear thesis statements in English essay writing. *TESOL Quarterly, 17*(4), 89–103. https://doi.org/ doi:10.1111/tesq.12345

Marue, M. G., & Pantas, M. B. (2019). Challenges in descriptive essay writing: A case of Indonesian EFL leaners. *International Journal of Innovation, Creativity and Change, 8*(12), 88-103. https://www.ijicc.net/images/vol8iss12/81205_Marue_2019_E1_R.pdf

Myhill, D. (2009). Becoming a designer: Trajectories of linguistic development. In The Sage Handbook of Writing Development (pp. 402-13). Sage Publications.

Nation, I. S. P. (2001). *Learning vocabulary in another language*. Cambridge University Press. doi:10.1017/CBO9781139524759

Nenotek, S. A., Tlonaen, Z. A., & Manubulu, H. A. (2022). Exploring university students' difficulties in writing English academic essay. *Al-Ishlah: Jurnal Pendidikan*, *14*(1), 909–920. doi:10.35445/alishlah.v14i1.1352

Nguyen, L. Q., & Le, H. V. (2022). Improving L2 learners' IELTS task 2 writing: The role of model essays and noticing hypothesis. *Language Testing in Asia*, *12*(1), 58. doi:10.1186/s40468-022-00206-0

Nguyen, L. T., Bui, H. P., & Ha, X. V. (2024). Scaffolding in genre-based L2 writing classes: Vietnamese EFL teachers' beliefs and practices. *IRAL. International Review of Applied Linguistics in Language Teaching*, *62*(1), 1–19. doi:10.1515/iral-2023-0125

Nguyen, N. H. T., Nguyen, N. T. M., & Nguyen, T. T. T. (2021). Difficulties in writing an essay of English-majored sophomores at Tay Do University, in Vietnam. *European Journal of English Language Teaching*, *6*(5), 1–15. doi:10.46827/ejel.v6i5.3851

Nguyen, N. H. T., Pham, T. U., & Phan, T. M. U. (2020). Difficulties in writing essays of English majored sophomores at Tay Do University, Vietnam. *European Journal of English Language Teaching*, *6*(2), 1–14. https://oapub.org/edu/index.php/ejel/article/view/3518

Okpe, A. A., & Onjewu, M. A. (2017). Difficulties of Learning Essay Writing: The Perspective of Some Adult EFL Learners in Nigeria. *International Journal of Curriculum and Instruction*, *9*(2), 198–205. https://ijci.globets.org/index.php/IJCI/article/view/82

Özgür Küfi, E. (2023). Activation of Content-Schemata for Scaffolding L2 Writing: Voices from a Turkish Context. *Journal of Psycholinguistic Research*, *52*(6), 2405–2427. doi:10.1007/s10936-023-10002-3

Phuong, W. T. N. (2021). Difficulties in studying writing of English-majored sophomores at a university in Vietnam. *European Journal of Education Studies*, *8*(10). Advance online publication. doi:10.46827/ejes.v8i10.3962

Pratiwi, K. D. (2016). Students Difficulties in Writing English. A Study at the Third Semester Students of English Education Program of UNIB in Academic Year 2011-2012). *Journal of Linguistics and Language Teaching*, *3*(1). Advance online publication. doi:10.29300/ling.v3i1.106

Rahmat, N. H. (2020). Knowledge Transforming in Writing: An Analysis of Read-to-Write Process. *European Journal of English Language Teaching*, *594*(4), 1–17. doi:10.46827/ejel.v5i4.3103

Sabti, A. A., Md Rashid, S., Nimehchisalem, V., & Darmi, R. (2019). The Impact of writing anxiety, writing achievement motivation, and writing self-efficacy on writing performance: A correlational study of Iraqi tertiary EFL Learners. *SAGE Open*, *9*(4). doi:10.1177/2158244019894289

Silva, T. (1993). Toward an Understanding of the Distinct Nature of L2 Writing: The ESL Research and Its Implications. *TESOL Quarterly*, *27*(4), 657. Advance online publication. doi:10.2307/3587400

Subandowo, D., & Sárdi, C. (2023). Academic essay writing in an English medium instruction environment: Indonesian graduate students' experiences at Hungarian universities. *Ampersand (Oxford, UK)*, *11*, 100158. doi:10.1016/j.amper.2023.100158

Toba, R., Noor, W. N., & Sanu, L. O. (2019). The current issues of Indonesian EFL students' writing skills: Ability, problem, and reason in writing comparison and contrast essay. *Dinamika Ilmu*, *19*(1), 57–73. doi:10.21093/di.v19i1.1506

Tran, L. T. (2007). Learners' motivation and identity in the Vietnamese EFL writing classroom. *English Teaching*, *6*(1), 151–163. https://files.eric.ed.gov/fulltext/EJ832183.pdf

Trinh, Q. L., & Truc, N. T. (2014). Enhancing Vietnamese learners' ability in writing argumentative essays. *Journal of Asia TEFL*, *11*(2). http://journal.asiatefl.org/main/main.php?inx_journals=40&inx_contents=50&main=1&sub=2&submode=3&PageMode=JournalView&s_title=Enhancing_Vietnamese_Learners_Ability_in_Writing_Argumentative_Essays

Xu, L., & Zhang, L. J. (2019). L2 doctoral students' experiences in thesis writing in an English-medium university in New Zealand. *Journal of English for Academic Purposes, 41*, 100779. doi:10.1016/j.jeap.2019.100779

Yan, Z. (2021). English as a foreign language teachers' critical thinking ability and L2 students' classroom engagement. *Frontiers in Psychology*, *12*, 773138. Advance online publication. doi:10.3389/fpsyg.2021.773138

ADDITIONAL READING

Biggs, J. (1988). Approaches to Learning and to Essay Writing. In R. R. Schmeck (Ed.), *Learning Strategies and Learning Styles. Perspectives on Individual Differences*. Springer. doi:10.1007/978-1-4899-2118-5_8

Chen, Y. M. (2002). The problems of university EFL writing in Taiwan. *The Korea TESOL Journal, 5*(1), 59-79. https://mail.koreatesol.org/sites/default/files/pdf_publications/KTJ5-2002web.pdf#page=67

Cook, V. J. (2014). *The English writing system*. Routledge. doi:10.4324/9780203774236

Norton, L. S. (1990). Essay-writing: What really counts? *Higher Education*, *20*(4), 411–442. doi:10.1007/BF00136221

Sasaki, M. (2000). Toward an empirical model of EFL writing processes: An exploratory study. *Journal of Second Language Writing*, *9*(3), 259–291. doi:10.1016/S1060-3743(00)00028-X

KEY TERMS AND DEFINITIONS

Difficulty: A problem someone has in doing something. In the current study, difficulties refer to specific problems encountered by students in essay writing.

Essay: A short piece of writing on a specific topic or subject, structured with an introduction, body, and conclusion to provide information surrounding the topic and show the author's opinions. In the context of L2 English education, essay writing is used to examine students' writing proficiency.

Chapter 3

Learning Strategies, Emotional Intelligence, and Academic Performance:
A Case in Spain

Isabel María García Conesa
https://orcid.org/0000-0001-7005-2509
Centro Universitario de la Defensa de San Javier, Spain

ABSTRACT

Learning strategies, emotional intelligence, and academic performance have been proposed as variables with great impacts on language learning processes, which can be reinforced in distance university education. In this educational modality, learning is completely autonomous and independent, which implies the need to develop particular skills that make it possible to take advantage of previously provided learning experiences and resources. This chapter reports a study on the relationships between learning strategies, emotional intelligence, and academic performance in a course of English 3. Data were collected from a sample of 132 students in distance education at a university in Spain. For the analysis of the variables, a non-experimental design was used, making use of descriptive and correlational statistics. The results showed a high average rating on the learning strategies scales, as well as adequate understanding and emotional regulation in the students, in contrast to emotional perception, a dimension that obtained a low average rating.

1. INTRODUCTION

Students who opt for distance education are acknowledged to employ self-regulation to succeed on the learning journey, suggesting the need for learners'

DOI: 10.4018/979-8-3693-3294-8.ch003

Copyright © 2024, IGI Global. Copying or distributing in print or electronic forms without written permission of IGI Global is prohibited.

greater responsibility, dedication, and effort. Their learning does not depend primarily on the teacher but results from their interaction with learning resources, technologies, and other people, which differs from face-to-face traditional education. Learning becomes autonomous and independent, requiring maximum development of students' cognitive, affective, and procedural potential (Moore & Fodrey, 2021).

Learning strategies, an individual learner variable, have aroused great interest from the academic community. Learning strategies enable the development of skills, autonomous processes, and strategies that allow learners to accomplish their studies. Strategies can be conceived as promoters of independent and autonomous learning (Hajar, 2019). Also, the literature on language learning strategies suggests behavioral, cognitive, social, and affective dimensions (Bui et al., 2023). According to Mandasari and Oktaviani (2018), explorations into second language (L2) learning strategies usually have implications for language education.

Although the existing literature suggests the relationships between learning strategies, emotional intelligence, and academic performance (Guillén et al., 2021; Halimi et al. (2021)), there is scant literature on these learner variables in L2 English contexts and how these variables are related. Considering the implications and challenges of distance education, it is interesting to analyse the university students' learning strategies and emotional intelligence in this modality. The dynamics, means, and mediations of their learning processes differ from those of students whose training is face-to-face. Most of the research on these variables has been conducted on university students in face-to-face education.

To this end, this study aims to identify and analyse the relationship between learning strategies, emotional intelligence, and academic performance in a sample of university students taking the subject of English 3 in the open and distance modality. The intention is to provide a descriptive basis on which to generate intervention strategies that respond to students' educational and emotional needs, in accordance with the demands and conditions of distance education. To this end, a number of specific objectives have been determined: to conduct a theoretical review on learning strategies and emotional intelligence in university education; to identify and analyse the dimensions of students' emotional intelligence and the use of learning strategies; and to study the relationship between learning strategies, emotional intelligence, and students' academic performance.

2. LITERATURE REVIEW

2.1 Distance Education

Distance education was born as an alternative to academic and professional training, mainly because of the four factors that Rumble (2019) defined as socio-political advances, the need for lifelong learning, the lack of conventional systems, advances in the field of educational sciences, and technological transformations.

Rumble (2019) described the first factor in terms of the social demand that led to the massification of conventional education classrooms because of the demographic explosion and social pressure for all classes to have access to education. At this social juncture, neglected groups of the population, who, despite their motivation and ability to learn, had not been able to access education, became visible. This population included residents of remote geographical areas, working adults, housewives, and people with some physical disability that limited or prevented them from going to the classroom (Chau & Bui, 2023; Saykili, 2018).

The need for lifelong learning constitutes the second factor, which Rumble (2019) describes as "lifelong learning". This learning has been imposed in recent decades as a response to social, cultural, and technological changes that have led to education accompanying individuals during different stages of their lives.

The third factor relates to the limitations and shortcomings of conventional institutions that face the challenge of educational massification. On the one hand, the costs, physical resources, and human capital required to meet this demand are very high. On the other hand, the distances in countries with large territorial extensions did not allow them to bring classrooms to the entire population seeking access to education. Ultimately, the costs were very high; therefore, it was necessary to consider more viable and profitable alternatives that would increase access without affecting the quality of education (Baum & McPherson, 2019).

Advances in the educational sciences, the fourth factor, led not only to the reaffirmation of the need for lifelong learning but also to the renewal of the system to respond to the needs of societies. This is a challenge that conventional education faces, leading to the development of new ways of learning outside the classroom. Advances in psychology have also contributed to the development of pedagogical models that promote independent student work and the personalization of education (Pregowska et al., 2021).

Technological transformation, as the fifth and last factor, has also generated numerous transformations in our society (Bui, 2023). These transformations have made it possible to overcome the limitations of conventional education by reducing distance through the use of means of communication and resources. This has allowed the population to access quality training and content, enabling them to learn with the same efficiency as students in face-to-face centers (Sadeghi, 2019).

Unlike face-to-face education, the distance education modality has its own characteristics, among which five stand out, according to Sewart et al. (2020). First, this modality is characterized by physical separation between the teacher and students. Second, this separation is compensated by using communication media and technical resources. Third, the learning process is developed individually. Fourth, an organization provides resources, guides, and accompanies the students' processes. Finally, communication is bidirectional among the students, teachers, and institutions.

The students' role in this modality is particularly active, continuously developing autonomous and independent learning. It is independent of the extent to which students plan and schedule study sessions according to their pace and time availability. It is also autonomous because it is the student who develops the activities and exercises of the subjects on a permanent basis (Simonson et al., 2019).

On the other hand, the teacher's main role is not to give lectures but to guide students in developing knowledge, skills, and abilities through self-management strategies and control of their learning processes. Teachers become facilitators in creating learning resources and materials that lead students to interact in the process of acquiring knowledge. They are also tutors, as they orient, guide, and accompany each student's process. Finally, they are mediators, as they drive and motivate students to use the resources offered by new technologies as tools that promote independent learning (Traxler, 2018).

2.2 Learning Strategies

Learning strategies are circumscribed within different fields of education as a fundamental axis for understanding learning processes and their procedural characteristics (Lestari & Wahyudin, 2020). Different definitions can be found in different approaches and typologies from which researchers have approached or coined the concept of learning strategies.

According to Ramírez and Hernández (2022), learning strategies refer to thoughts, behaviours, beliefs, actions, and emotions that enable the acquisition of new information and its integration with previous knowledge. Through this process, new knowledge and skills were produced. Budiarti (2022) considered learning strategies to have an intentional character and implied a plan of action. Learning strategies are operations performed by thinking when confronted with learning, and as such, promote autonomous and independent learning.

Seng et al. (2023) stated that learning strategies are conscious and intentional processes in which the necessary knowledge is selected and retrieved to achieve a goal or accomplish a task. Although they respond to different typologies and approaches, they assume that learning strategies are dynamic processes in which different types of factors intervene. This last aspect has been enriching the concept precisely thanks to the inclusion of affective-motivational and supportive elements.

Finally, Teng considers learning strategies as "an organised, conscious, and intentional set of what the learner does to effectively achieve a learning objective in a given social context" (2023, p. 152). These strategies also integrate other aspects such as affective-motivational and supportive elements, such as metacognitive and cognitive elements.

Cohen and Wang's (2018) classification of learning strategies comprises four strategies: repetition, elaboration, organization, and regulation. Repetition refers to learning content through oral or written repetition. Elaboration strategies refer to the process of linking new information with previous knowledge by preparing summaries or outlines. Organizational strategies include content categorization processes. Finally, metacognitive learning strategies mainly refer to the strategies used by learners to regulate their learning.

Zormanová (2021) classified learning strategies into support, processing, knowledge personalization, and metacognitive strategies. Support strategies include motivation, attitudes, and affection. Processing strategies refer to the selection, organization, and processing of information. Knowledge personalization strategies include creative, critical, reflective, rational, and autonomous thinking. Finally, metacognitive strategies refer to the processes of planning, controlling, and evaluating actions.

Finally, Lin et al. (2021) classified strategies into five categories: rehearsal, elaboration, organization, comprehension control, and supportive or affective. The first refers to strategies of repetition of content. The second is the link between new information and previous knowledge. The third includes strategies of schematization and grouping of contents in which the processes of information relationships intervene. The fourth is related to metacognitive strategies, which allow students to be aware of the strategies used. Finally, support and affective strategies refer to the processes of motivation.

2.3 Emotional Intelligence

The concept of emotional intelligence has a multiplicity of definitions and approaches. Initially, the notion of the existence of emotional intelligence emerged as a tentative proposal that considered that some individuals possessed the ability to reason about their emotions. Therefore, they can be used to improve thinking more effectively (Guslyakova & Guslyakova, 2020).

Resnik and Deawaele's (2020) original definition conceptualized emotional intelligence as a series of interrelated abilities. However, this initial conception was amplified by other researchers into an eclectic mix of characteristics, many of which referred to dispositions such as happiness, self-esteem, optimism, and self-management. The initial conception of Vesely and Saklofske (2020) defined emotional intelligence as the ability to monitor one's own feelings and emotions using this information to guide one's own actions. Below, we describe three of the most representative models of emotional intelligence based on the classification made by Dewaele and Dewaele (2020).

The first model was developed by Goleman (1995). This model defines emotional intelligence as the skills of self-control, enthusiasm, persistence, and the ability to motivate oneself. The skills included the following: knowledge of one's own emotions; recognition of an emotion when it is generated; monitoring feelings from time to time; managing emotions; ability to calm down and get rid of anxiety; putting emotions in order at the service of a goal; delaying gratification and suppressing impulsivity; having the ability to enter a state of fluency; recognizing emotions in others; and ability to manage emotions in others.

The second model was introduced by Mayer and Salovey (1997). This model defines emotional intelligence as a series of skills that explain how accuracy varies in people's emotional perception and understanding. It is also defined as the ability to perceive and express emotions, assimilate them into thought and reason with emotion, and regulate one's own emotions and those of others. The specific skills covered by this model are perception and expression of emotions; identification and expression of emotions, thoughts, and physical states; identification and expression of emotions in language; assimilation of emotions into thought; understanding and analyzing emotions; ability to label emotions, including complex emotions and simultaneous feelings; ability to understand relationships associated with emotional changes; ability to stay open to emotions; and ability to monitor and regulate emotions reflexively and promote intellectual and emotional growth.

The third model was developed by Baron (1997). This model defines emotional intelligence as a variety of non-cognitive abilities, competencies, and abilities that influence one's ability to succeed in managing environmental pressures and demands. The skills included in this model are as follows: intrapersonal skills; self-awareness; assertiveness; self-esteem; self-realization; interpersonal skills and relations; social responsibility; empathy; problem solving; stress tolerance; impulse control; and optimism.

2.4 Academic Performance

The concept of academic performance or achievement is mostly understood from a quantitative perspective (Yan, 2022). Mahmud et al. (2020) described this construct as the flow of students moving from one level to another by comparing the number of new students entering a year with the number of graduates in the time provided. As a dichotomous variable, the term refers to the average grade, weighting the relationship between the credits passed and the credits taken. Finally, they narrowed the term to refer to the relationship between the number of subjects passed and taken within the period required to complete the program.

According to Fernández (2018), academic performance should not be placed exclusively at the operational level. He distinguished between objective, subjective, and dialectical conceptions of the term. He argued that, at the objective level, performance is understood as a set of properties that are observable, measurable, and translated into numerical grades to indicate a student's success or failure. From a subjective perspective, this construct is assumed to be the result or expression of the values and intentions of the agents involved in a particular educational situation. Finally, referring to the dialectical approach, academic performance is understood as the result of specific educational situations and practices that make its production possible within a specific context.

According to Liu (2022), academic performance refers to the relationship between what students should learn and what they have actually learned. This is circumscribed within an operational vision of the term, facilitating its measurement through the average grades obtained throughout the semester.

Referring to academic achievement, Alani and Hawas (2021) stated that this achievement has been understood as a product of the school process, whose evaluation reference is given by the achievement of the learning objectives set by an academic institution. They also added that academic achievement is determined through evaluations of how a student has learned through numerical or nominal indicators. Unlike these evaluations, pedagogical tests refer to the evaluation instruments created by teachers to account for students' academic achievement based on the results obtained, whether quantitative or qualitative, which is determined by the teacher himself (Rahman et al., 2022).

Based on this theoretical review of the terms performance and academic achievement, for the purposes of this study, this construct is based on the concept of academic achievement proposed by Hamoud et al. (2018) as a dependent variable. It is assumed to be the product of the school process, measured numerically through the average of grades obtained by each student in the evaluation processes conducted throughout the semester in the subject of English 3.

2.5 Relationship Between Learning Strategies, Emotional Intelligence, and Academic Performance

Different studies have analysed the variables of learning strategies and emotional intelligence have been analysed. Guillén et al. (2021) evaluated 278 undergraduate students' most commonly employed learning strategies, and how these strategies were related to their academic performance. The results indicate that academically successful students use more and better learning strategies than students who are not successful. Halimi et al. (2021) also analysed the relationship between learning strategies and academic achievement in a sample of 30 university students. Their findings suggest that the use of learning strategies in the language, arts, and mathematics positively influences academic performance.

Partido and Stafford (2018) studied the relationship among learning styles, learning strategies, and academic achievement in a sample of 312 students. Their results indicated that 42.6% of students used coding strategies but did not find a significant relationship between the variables analysed. MacCann et al. (2020) also analysed the possible relationship between learning strategies and academic performance in a sample of 54 students. The results suggest that there is no correlation between strategies and academic performance in the sample studied.

Duong et al. (2020) found a positive correlation between emotional intelligence and students' academic performance. They analyzed the contribution of emotional intelligence to the prediction of academic performance in 250 university students in technical and humanistic studies. The results revealed significant correlations between emotional intelligence measures and some academic performance indicators.

Romano et al. (2020) investigated the possible relationship between emotional intelligence and achievement obtained by a group of English as a foreign language students in reading comprehension. Their findings indicated that the scores obtained by the students in the experimental group on both emotional intelligence and reading comprehension tests were better than those obtained by the control group. Zhoc et al. (2018) also investigated the relationship between emotional intelligence and academic performance in a sample of 44 intermediate learners of English as a foreign language. They found that the experimental group had a significant improvement in their writing performance after implementing emotional intelligence.

Sánchez et al. (2020) analyzed the relationship between emotional intelligence and language proficiency in a sample of 123 undergraduate students teaching English as a foreign language. The results indicate a positive and high correlation between the results obtained in the emotional intelligence test and language proficiency tests. In their study, they found that although students appeared to be motivated and self-aware, a lack of self-regulation, empathy, and social skills was positively correlated with their academic performance.

Finally, Suleman et al. (2019) studied the relationship between learning strategies, emotional intelligence, and academic performance, and found positive relationships between the variables analyzed. Their results showed significant correlations between student performance and learning strategies and between performance and intrapersonal intelligence. Similarly, significant differences were found in the use of learning strategies according to components of emotional intelligence. They found that students with higher levels of emotional intelligence made greater use of metacognitive strategies.

3. METHODOLOGY

The general methodological objective of this study was to determine the relationship among learning strategies, emotional intelligence, and academic performance in the subject of English 3. We took a sample of university students studying their undergraduate programs in the open and distance modality. The research question is as follows: "Is there any relationship between academic performance in English, learning strategies, and emotional intelligence?".

Based on the objective of this research, the following general hypothesis was derived: we expect to find a positive relationship between academic performance in English, the learning strategies employed, and emotional intelligence. On the one hand, we expect to find differences in the learning strategies and emotional intelligence employed by students. On the other hand, we expected to find a positive relationship between learning strategies, academic performance, and emotional intelligence in English.

3.1 Research Design

Methodological design is a strategy implemented to achieve research objectives. This was a cross-sectional study, in which a non-experimental, descriptive, and correlational design was applied to test the proposed hypothesis. It is cross-sectional because data were obtained with a sample at a specific time cut-off, as opposed to longitudinal studies. The design was non-experimental because there was no manipulation of variables, and no treatment, intervention, or experiment was conducted. This method is descriptive because it seeks to narrate the observations obtained from the application of different instruments according to the analysis categories in a sample of university students. Finally, it is correlational because it analyses the relationships among the three variables.

We must also bear in mind that ethical considerations are fundamental in this type of research. Therefore, some key ethical considerations when conducting this research are privacy, confidentiality, data protection, transparency, and honesty.

3.2 Population and Sample

Population is defined as the set of all units of study (Hernández et al., 2014). Determining the population and sampling are essential to ensure the representativeness and validity of the results obtained. Population refers to identifying the group of elements that are the object of the study, and the sample involves the selection of an adequate sampling that represents the study population. A total of 132 students from open and distant faculties voluntarily participated in this study. This university currently offers 30 undergraduate programs across the country through its university service centres. The majority of the students enrolled in this university were working adults over 20 years of age who had finished their secondary education more than ten years ago, without having managed to enter higher education in the face-to-face modality.

The 132 students in the sample are part of a group of 358 students enrolled in level 3 of English for the first academic semester. The study sample comprised 88 women and 44 men. 86% of the participating students belonged to the Faculty of Humanities and the remaining 24% belonged to the Faculty of Education.

3.3 Variables, Measures, and Instruments

The correct research instruments helped us obtain the necessary information to achieve the objectives established at the beginning. Consequently, the variables analysed in this study are as follows:

- Learning strategies: a Questionnaire for the Evaluation of Learning Strategies for University Students (CEVEAUPEU) was used. The questionnaire consisted of 88 items divided into two scales: (1) Affective, supportive, and control strategies; and (2) Strategies related to information processing. For this study, some changes were made to the language of some of the items, and item 56 was eliminated. Language adaptations were reviewed and submitted to the English classroom teaching team to verify that each statement was as clear as possible to students.
- Emotional intelligence: The TMMS-24 questionnaire was used to assess this variable, based on the Trait Meta-Mood Scale (TMMS). The instrument consists of 24 items, through which three dimensions of emotional intelligence are evaluated: emotional perception, understanding feelings, and emotional regulation. Each dimension was evaluated using eight items. Students rated each item on a Likert scale ranging from 1 (not at all agree) to 5 (strongly agree). To obtain the students' scores in each of the three dimensions of emotional intelligence covered by the TMMS-24, the scores of items 1 to 8

were added for perception; items 9 to 16 for comprehension; and items 17 to 24 for regulation.
- Academic performance in English: For this variable, the final grade that each student obtained in the subject of English 3 was taken. This resulted from the average of the different online and face-to-face evaluation activities conducted throughout the semester. The average final grade obtained by students in the sample was 34.5 out of 50, which is acceptable. Of the total sample, 29.32% obtained a final grade between 30 and 35, they had an acceptable academic performance; followed by 25.56% whose final grades ranged between 35 and 40, thus achieving good academic performance in the subject. With the same number of students (21.05%), two groups of students were identified. On the one hand, those who obtained a final grade between 41 and 45 obtained an outstanding performance. On the other hand, those who failed the subject with a grade below 30 obtained poor or insufficient performance. Only three students in the sample achieved excellent performance in the subject with final grades ranging between 46 and 47.

3.4 Data Collection Procedure

First, a meeting was held with the centre's director to familiarize her with the research work and to request authorization to conduct the study with English 3 students. Once the endorsement was obtained, the learning strategies and emotional intelligence questionnaires were transferred to a digital format through the Google Forms tool for virtual distribution to all students, considering that this was the main learning mediation. This form allowed students to participate, giving them the option to fill it out when they considered the most appropriate.

The final version of the questionnaire was sent to English 3 students through the virtual classroom of the subject and through an e-mail message. Within the body of the message, the purpose of the questionnaire was explained to the students and instructions were given to answer it appropriately, also clarifying that participation was voluntary. The questionnaire was available for one month. Of the 358 students enrolled in the course, 132 (34%) responded to the questionnaire.

3.5 Data Analysis

An Excel database was created based on data collected through the virtual questionnaire and the results of the students' academic performance collected at the end of the semester. Data were analysed using the JASP statistical program. Descriptive statistics were applied to analyse the results of each of the variables studied, and correlation statistics were applied to evaluate the relationships among the three variables.

We used the Shapiro-Wilk normality test, which allowed us to measure the degree of agreement between the distribution data and the specific theoretical distribution. Considering this, the calculated value indicated that data had a normal distribution. The p-value obtained was also greater than the accepted degree of significance (0.05).

4. RESULTS

The first objective was to analyse the learning strategies used by the students in the sample based on their responses to the CEVEAPEU questionnaire. The first scale "affective, support, and control strategies" included motivational strategies, affective components, metacognitive strategies, and strategies for context control, social interaction, and resource management. Each of these strategy subscales is addressed with a descriptive analysis, indicating the mean, standard deviation (SD), minimum (Min), and maximum (Max).

From the analysis of the motivational strategies subscale, a high average score of 3.61 points was observed for all strategies. The task with the highest weighting was the value of the task with an average value of 4.55 points, followed by intrinsic motivation with 4.52 points. Also noteworthy are the averages obtained for external attributions and extrinsic motivation strategies, in which the scores were low at 2.08 and 2.46 points, respectively. The concept of intelligence as modifiable is at an intermediate level with 3.61 points, and it is also the strategy with the greatest dispersion (SD of 1.01).

From this analysis, it can be concluded that the students in the sample manifested a highly positive evaluation of strategies linked to internal issues. In contrast, the evaluation is low for strategies linked to external issues, such as the motivation and demands of the context. This indicates that students attributed greater importance to their academic performance and abilities than to external factors.

Regarding the affective components subscale, table 2 shows a high average score for physical and mental states, as well as anxiety levels. For the latter, the scores were closer to the average level, which, according to the answer options of the questionnaire scale, corresponded to a state of indecision. We can conclude that control of students' anxiety is at a medium level.

On the metacognitive strategies subscale, a high average rating was observed for knowledge of the objectives and evaluation criteria, self-evaluation and control, and self-regulation, with averages between 3.86 and 3.94. In contrast, planning obtained the lowest score of 3.39 points. This strategy corresponded to the items that inquired about the planning of time to work on different subjects or the schedule of an independent study. The results of this study are summarised in table 3.

Table 1. Descriptive data of motivational strategies

Item	Mean	SD	MIN	MAX
Intrinsic motivation	4.52	0.40	3.67	5.00
Extrinsic motivation	2.46	1.01	1.00	5.00
Task value	4.55	0.41	3.75	5.00
External attributions		2.08	0.70	1.00
Internal attributions		4.29	0.56	1.00
Self-efficacy and expectations	4.27	0.49	3.00	5.00
Conception of intelligence as modifiable	3.14	0.54	1.00	5.00
Motivational strategies	**3.61**	**0.27**	**3.06**	**4.43**

Table 2. Descriptive data of affective components

Item	Mean	SD	MIN	MAX
Physical and mental state	3.75	0.65	1.50	5.00
Anxiety	3.28	0.59	2.00	4.50
Affective components	**3.52**	**0.41**	**1.88**	**4.38**

Table 3. Descriptive data of metacognitive strategies

Item	Mean	SD	MIN	MAX
Knowledge of objectives and evaluation criteria	3.86	0.75	1.00	5.00
Planning	3.39	0.55	1.00	4.75
Self-assessment	3.94	0.49	2.67	5.00
Control and self-regulation	3.93	0.50	2.50	5.00
Metacognitive strategies	**3.78**	**0.40**	**2.25**	**4.67**

In the last subscale (context control, social interaction, and resource management strategies), the average ratings were different for each strategy. As shown in table 4, the average score obtained for the context control items was high at 4.01 points, while the score obtained for social interaction and learning skills with peers was medium at 3.40 points, also having a moderately high dispersion.

With respect to the scale of affective support and control strategies, we can conclude that students showed a high positive assessment of strategies related to internal components such as intrinsic motivation, internal attributions, self-efficacy, expectations, and the value of the task. In contrast, their assessment was medium-

Table 4. Descriptive data of context control, social interaction, and resource management strategies

Item	Mean	SD	MIN	MAX
Context control	4.01	0.65	1.00	5.00
Social interaction	3.40	0.91	1.00	5.00
Resource management strategies	**3.71**	**0.59**	**2.00**	**5.00**

low for external components such as extrinsic motivation and external attributions. Of the four subscales, metacognitive strategies had the highest overall rating, with control, self-regulation, and self-assessment strategies being the most highly valued.

The second scale, "Strategies related to information processing", includes strategies for searching for and selecting information, and strategies for processing and using information. These two subscales were addressed by conducting a descriptive analysis, again indicating the mean, standard deviation (SD), minimum (Min), and maximum (Max).

Table 5 shows a high score for the two types of strategies, with an overall average score of 3.77 points and scores of 3.71 and 3.83 points, respectively.

Regarding the strategies for processing and using information, the average score obtained for the global strategy was the same as that obtained for the first subscale with 3.77 points. However, when analysing the specific strategies, we observe that the highest scores are attributed to the strategies of acquisition, elaboration, and transfer of information with scores between 4.16 and 4.25 points. This was followed by storage strategies using mnemonic resources, organization, and resource management to use the information acquired, personalization, creativity, and critical thinking, with scores between 3.43 and 3.93 points. Finally, there is a simple repetition storage strategy with 2.47 points, obtaining the lowest rating and its dispersion being moderate and the most accentuated.

In general, it is observed that information processing strategies are positively valued by students, especially those related to how they acquire, integrate, expand, and understand information, and how they make use of what they have learned in

Table 5. Descriptive data of searching and selecting information strategies

Item	Mean	SD	MIN	MAX
Knowledge of sources and information search	3.71	0.70	1.67	5.00
Selection of information	3.83	0.46	2.50	5.00
Search and selection strategies and selection of information	**3.77**	**0.48**	**2.42**	**5.00**

Table 6. Descriptive data of processing and using information strategies

Item	Mean	SD	MIN	MAX
Elaboration	4.23	0.48	2.00	5.00
Acquisition of information	4.16	0.49	2.33	5.00
Organisation	3.77	0.72	1.80	5.00
Personalisation, creativity, and critical thinking	3.93	0.50	2.00	5.00
Storage (simple repetition)	2.47	0.93	1.00	5.00
Storage (use of mnemonic resources)	3.43	0.75	1.00	5.00
Resource management	3.92	0.57	2.00	5.00
Transfer	4.25	0.45	3.00	5.00
Strategies for processing and use of information	**3.77**	**0.33**	**3.10**	**4.56**

other subjects, situations, and contexts. The assessment is negative and has greater dispersion only for the simple repetition strategy, which is used as a means of learning or memorizing content.

The second objective was to assess the emotional intelligence of the sample of students based on their responses to the TMMS-24 questionnaire. The results obtained and their descriptive analysis are presented below, indicating the mean, standard deviation (SD), minimum (Min), and maximum (Max), as well as the distribution of frequencies for each of the three components of emotional intelligence that the test evaluates.

The results obtained for the dimensions of emotion comprehension and emotional regulation shown in table 7 suggest that they were adequate at 27.49 and 27.39 points, respectively.

Emotional perception obtained average negative rating of 22.89 points; 22.74 points for women and 23.18, men. This suggests that this is a dimension of emotional intelligence that the students in the sample need to improve.

When analysing the factor of emotional perception, it was found that 55% of the sample (73 students) should improve on this dimension because the results suggest that they pay little attention to their own feelings and the way they express them.

Table 7. Descriptive data of factors of emotional intelligence

Item	Mean	SD	MIN	MAX
Perception	22.89	6.43	10.00	39.00
Understanding	27.49	6.17	13.00	40.00
Regulation	27.39	6.41	12.00	40.00

Table 8. Descriptive data of factors of emotional perception by gender

Item	Mean	SD	MIN	MAX
Women	22.74	6.13	10.00	38.00
Men	23.18	7.07	12.00	39.00

Table 9. Distribution of frequencies of emotional perception

Item	Frequency	Percentage
Pay little attention	73	55
Adequate perception	54	41
Pay too much attention	5	4

54 students, representing 41% of the sample, had an adequate perception, and 4% (five students) needed to improve their perception, although they paid too much attention to their feelings and the way they expressed them.

Regarding the factor of comprehension of emotions, the results indicate that 62% (82 students) had an adequate understanding of emotions, 12% (16 students) had excellent comprehension, and 26% (34 students) had to improve this dimension of emotional intelligence.

For the emotional regulation factor, the results showed that 58% of the sample with 76 students had good regulation of their emotional states. Nineteen students (14%) stood out for their excellent emotional regulation, and the remaining 28% had to improve this dimension of emotional intelligence.

Table 10. Distribution of frequencies of feeling comprehension

Item	Frequency	Percentage
Comprehension needs to be improved	34	26
Adequate comprehension	82	62
Excellent comprehension	16	12

Table 11. Distribution of frequencies of emotional regulation

Item	Frequency	Percentage
Regulation needs to be improved	37	28
Adequate regulation	76	58
Excellent regulation	19	14

In summary, it was observed that the evaluations obtained by the students in the sample showed an adequate level of comprehension of emotions and their regulation, while the perception and expression of their own emotions were below the acceptable level, indicating that this is a factor of emotional intelligence in which students must improve.

The third objective was to study the relationship between learning strategies and academic performance in English 3 using a sample of students. Pearson's correlation was applied to analyse the learning strategies separately, which was also used in the descriptive analysis. Thus, we began with the affective, support, and control strategies scale, to which four subscales of strategies corresponded: motivational strategies, affective components, metacognitive strategies and strategies for context control, social interaction, and resource management. As shown in table 12, no statistically significant relationship was found between the academic performance of the sample of students and their scores for motivational strategies.

Regarding affective components, no significant relationship was found between academic performance, physical and mental states, and level of anxiety. The results of this study are presented in table 13.

As shown in table 14, as happened with the previous two subscales, no significant relationships were found between metacognitive strategies and students' academic performance on the English subject.

Table 12. Correlation between motivational strategies and academic performance

Variable	R	p
Intrinsic motivation	,162	,06
Adequate regulation	-,0.48	,58
Task value	,135	,12
External attributions	,040	,65
Internal attributions	,113	,20
Self-efficacy and expectations	,099	,26
Conception of intelligence as modifiable	-,095	,28

Table 13. Correlation between affective components and academic performance

Variable	R	p
Physical and mental state	,100	,26
Anxiety	-,144	,10

Table 14. Correlation between metacognitive strategies and academic performance

Variable	R	p
Knowledge, objectives, and evaluation criteria	-,002	,99
Planning	,042	,63
Self-assessment	,044	,61
Monitoring and self-regulation	-,013	,88

For the last subscale, no relationships were found between context control strategies, social interaction, learning with peers, and the academic performance of the students in the sample in the English subject.

Regarding the scale of strategies related to information processing, the analysis of its relationship with the academic performance of students in English 3 did not find any statistically significant relationship with the strategies of searching for and selecting information. The results are presented in table 16.

However, when analysing the relationship between English 3 performance, information processing, and the use of strategies, a significant relationship was found between English 3 performance and information acquisition. Therefore, there was a low positive correlation between academic performance in English and the sub-strategy of information acquisition, as shown in table 17.

In general, it can be stated that there is no statistically significant relationship between the learning strategies assessed through the CEVEAPEU questionnaire and the academic performance in English of the students in the sample.

Table 15. Correlation between strategies of contextual control, social interaction, and resource management, and academic performance

Variable	R	p
Contextual control	,071	,42
Social interaction skills and peer learning	,010	,91

Table 16. Correlation between information search and selection strategies and academic performance

Variable	R	p
Knowledge of sources and search for information	-,035	,69
Selection of information	,001	,99

Table 17. Correlation between information processing and use strategies and academic performance

Variable	R	p
Elaboration	,092	,30
Acquisition of information	,189	,03
Organisation	,060	,50

The fourth objective was to study the relationship between emotional intelligence and academic performance in English 3 using a sample of university students. Pearson's correlations were used to analyse the relationships between emotional perception, understanding of feelings and emotional regulation, and academic performance in English. The results indicate that there is no statistically significant relationship between any of the three dimensions of emotional intelligence and the academic performance of students in the English sample. Table 18 presents the results of this study.

The fifth objective was to analyse the relationship between emotional intelligence and learning strategies in a sample of students. Pearson's correlations were used to study how the three dimensions or factors of emotional intelligence, namely emotional perception, understanding of emotions, and emotional regulation, are related to the subscales of learning strategies.

Starting with the study of the relationship between emotional intelligence and affective support and control strategies, the results in table 19 show that there is a significant relationship between motivational strategies and understanding of emotions. This correlation is positive, which means that the greater the understanding of emotions, the greater is the value of motivational strategies. Similarly, a low positive correlation was found between the strategies of context control, social interaction, resource management, and emotional perception. In other words, the greater the emotional perception, the greater is the value of these strategies.

Table 18. Correlation between dimension of emotional intelligence and academic performance

Variable	R	p
Emotional perception	-,046	,60
Understanding feelings	-,079	,37
Emotional regulation	-,018	,84

Table 19. Correlation between dimensions of emotional intelligence and affective strategies of support and control

Variable	Emotional perception		Understanding emotions		Emotional regulation	
	R	p	R	p	R	p
Motivational strategies	-,001	,99	,209	,02	,164	,06
Affective components	,117	,18	,062	,48	,082	,35
Metacognitive strategies	,081	,35	,019	,83	,057	,52
Contextual control strategies	,189	,03	-,045	,61	,038	,66

The relationship between emotional intelligence and information-processing strategies was then examined. Table 20 presents the results of this study.

The results showed a significant relationship between information search, selection strategies and emotional regulation. There is also evidence of a significant relationship between information-processing strategies and the understanding of emotions and emotional regulation. Therefore, there is a low positive correlation between information-seeking and selection strategies and emotional regulation. The greater the emotional regulation, the greater is the assessment of search and selection strategies. Similarly, there is a low positive correlation between information processing and use strategies and an understanding of emotions and emotional regulation. The greater the understanding and emotional regulation, the greater is the value of processing strategies.

5. DISCUSSION

The aim of this research was to analyse the relationship between learning strategies, emotional intelligence, and academic performance in English 3, in a sample of university students who study their academic programs in the open and distance

Table 20. Correlation between dimensions of emotional intelligence and strategies related to information processing

Variable	Emotional perception		Understanding emotions		Emotional regulation	
	R	p	R	p	R	p
Information search and selection strategies	-,102	,25	,146	,09	,180	,04
Strategies related to information processing	,005	,95	,200	,02	,182	,04

modality. To achieve this, specific objectives and hypotheses are established, as discussed below.

The first objective was to analyse the learning strategies of a sample of university students. This hypothesis states that there are differences in learning strategies employed by students. The responses to the CEVEPEAU questionnaire, analysed by scales following the classification of groups of strategies, showed that students attributed a similar and high value to the different subscales of strategies, with average scores ranging between 3.52 and 3.78 points. In descending order, starting with the group of best-rated strategies, metacognitive strategies were followed by the two subscales of strategies related to information processing, which obtained the same average score of 3.77. Third, there are strategies for context control, social interaction, and resource management, followed by motivational strategies. And in the last place, with an average rating of 3.52, are the affective components. In this last subscale, the average score of 3.28 points given to anxiety management stands out, which accounts for a predominant state of indecision in the face of anxiety management.

The lowest scores obtained within the six subscales were for simple repetition storage strategies (2.47 points), external attributions (2.08 points), and anxiety (3.28 points). However, within the groups of best-rated strategies, the value of the task was 4.55 points, followed by intrinsic motivation with 4.52 points. Third, with 4.29 points being internal attributions and fourth, self-efficacy and expectations scored 4.27 points. All of these belong to the motivational strategies subscale. These results show that student populations attribute greater importance in their learning process to factors such as intrinsic motivation, objectives, and the value that subjects represent in the individual training process, rather than external factors such as external demands and expectations, as suggested by Teng (2023). Students express a high valuation of internal factors and a low valuation of factors, such as extrinsic motivation, and they show an average assessment of anxiety management according to the study conducted by Seng et al. (2023).

The second objective was to assess the emotional intelligence of a sample of students. This hypothesis posits the existence of differences in scores obtained for the three dimensions of emotional intelligence assessed in the test, as suggested by Resnik and Deawaele (2020). The descriptive analysis of the results confirms the hypothesis, finding that the average score obtained in the emotional perception dimension is negative at 22.89 points, suggesting that this is a dimension in which students must improve. The majority, represented by 73 students (55% of the sample), paid little attention to their feelings or how they expressed them. In addition, 4% of the students in the sample improved their perception by paying too much attention to their emotions, as Vesely and Saklofske (2020) mentioned in their study. For the comprehension and emotion regulation dimensions, the average scores were positive, accounting for adequate levels.

The third objective was to study the relationship between learning strategies and academic performance in English 3 using a sample of students. The hypothesis was expected to find a significant and positive relationship between the assessment of learning strategies and the academic performance of students, the latter represented by the final grade obtained in the subject of English 3, as stated by Guillén et al. (2021). No statistically significant relationship was found between students' academic performance and their scores on the different subscales of the CEVEAPEU learning strategies questionnaire, thus rejecting this hypothesis. However, a low positive correlation was found between academic performance in English and information acquisition sub-strategies, as defended by Halimi et al. (2021).

The fourth objective was to study the relationship between emotional intelligence and academic performance in English, using a sample of students. Duong et al. (2020) proposed the existence of a positive relationship between the two variables. The results rejected this hypothesis as no correlation was found between any of the three dimensions of emotional intelligence and students' academic performance in English 3.

The fifth objective was to examine the relationship between emotional intelligence and learning strategies. We hypothesized a positive relationship between learning strategies and emotional intelligence as suggested by Suleman et al. (2019). The results corroborate this hypothesis by reporting a series of positive correlations, although all of them are low, between some subscales of strategies and some dimensions of emotional intelligence. Within the group of affective support and control strategies, a positive correlation was found between motivational strategies and understanding of emotions, as well as between strategies of context control, social interaction, resource management, and emotional perception. Within the group of strategies related to information processing, a positive correlation was also found between information search, selection strategies, and emotional regulation. A positive relationship was also found between information-processing strategies and comprehension of emotions and emotional regulation.

6. CONCLUSION

From the analysis of the results obtained in this study and the discussion of each of the objectives and hypotheses raised at the beginning of the research, we can conclude that students showed a positive and high rating for the different subscales of learning strategies, with very close weightings between them. However, it is possible to relate the high value attributed to metacognitive strategies with the demands of the distance education modality, as the contact and supervision of teachers is limited and distant. In this order of ideas, the skills to search, select and process information are also decisive because the virtual classrooms constitute a repository of abundant information in this modality of education. Throughout this process, the teachers of each subject sought to cover a significant amount of information that it was not possible to address in the few face-to-face meetings. Although the scores attributed to physical and mental states were predominantly high, the assessment of anxiety management had a clear intermediate trend, which denotes the prevalence of significant levels of anxiety when presenting examinations, or interventions in public.

No correlation was found between the assessment of learning strategies and the academic performance of students in English 3, although there was evidence of a positive relationship between academic performance and information acquisition strategies. This finding can be related to the difference in academic performance achieved by students who reported constant access to and exploration of the classroom. This can be compared to the performance of students whose access to the classroom and resources is limited, the latter being those who fail the subject. In addition, there was no correlation between emotional intelligence and students' academic performance in English 3. However, there was a positive correlation between some learning strategies and dimensions of emotional intelligence.

By way of synthesis, it can be stated that the students in the sample highly valued most of the learning strategies, which shows the importance they attribute to them within the learning processes developed in their distance professional training. Likewise, their emotional intelligence was adequate for two of the three dimensions evaluated, with emotional perception being the dimension in which the students in the sample must improve. However, academic performance in English 3 was not related to learning strategies or emotional intelligence. However, there was a positive correlation between the learning strategies and students' emotional intelligence.

The present study has some limitations, mainly based on the type of instrument used and its application. The instruments consisted of self-reports with the aim of accounting for students' appraisals of their use of learning strategies and the three dimensions of their emotional intelligence. These conditions may have influenced the validity of the answers, as the students may have chosen the options that they perceived as correct or most appropriate, and not those that were closer to their reality. Although this is a difficult factor to control due to the nature of the instrument, it is possible to minimize these biases when the questionnaires are completed in person with the accompaniment and guidance of a counsellor.

This study could be replicated by expanding the sample to cover the six levels of English, thus providing a global overview of the assessment of learning strategies and emotional intelligence within the English program. This study could either be limited to addressing the study of strategies related to the learning of a foreign language or expanded by maintaining the focus on general strategies, more considering the academic performance of students in other subjects of their undergraduate programs.

REFERENCES

Alani, F. S., & Hawas, A. T. (2021). Factors Affecting Students Academic Performance: A Case Study of Sohar University. *Psychology and Education*, *58*(5), 4624–4635.

Baum, S., & McPherson, M. (2019). The Human Factor: The Promise & Limits of Online Education. *Daedalus*, *148*(4), 235–254. doi:10.1162/daed_a_01769

Budiarti, Y. (2022). Language Learning Strategies, Gender, and Motivation in Foreign Language Context. *Journal of English as A Foreign. Language Teaching Research*, *2*(1), 19–33. doi:10.31098/jefltr.vil.780

Bui, H. P. (2023). L2 teachers' strategies and students' engagement in virtual classrooms: A multidimensional perspective. In *Lecture Notes in Networks and System* (Vol. 617, pp. 205–213). Springer. doi:10.1007/978-981-19-9512-5_18

Bui, H. P., Nguyen, L. T., & Viet, N. T. (2023). An investigation into EFL pre-service teachers' academic writing strategies. *Heliyon*, *19*(3), e13743. doi:10.1016/j.heliyon.2023.e13743

Chau, M. K., & Bui, H. P. (2023). Technology-assisted teaching during the COVID-19 pandemic: L2 teachers' strategies and encountered challenges. In *Lecture Notes in Networks and Systems* (Vol. 617, pp. 243–250). Springer.

Cohen, A. D., & Wang, I. K. H. (2018). Fluctuation in the functions of language learner strategies. *System*, *74*, 169–182. doi:10.1016/j.system.2018.03.011

Dewaele, J. M., & Dewaele, L. (2020). Are Foreign Language Learners' Enjoyment and Anxiety Specific to the Teacher? An Investigation Into the Dynamics of Learners' Classroom Emotions. *Studies in Second Language Learning and Teaching*, *10*(1), 45–65. doi:10.14746/ssllt.2020.10.1.3

Duong, T. M., Tran, N. Y., Ha, A. T., & Phung, Y. (2020). The impact of emotional intelligence on performance: A closer look at individual and environmental factors. *Journal of Asian Finance Economics and Business*, *7*(1), 183–193. doi:10.13106/jafeb.2020.vol7.no1.183

Fernández, S. G. (2018). Rendimiento Académico en Educación Superior: Desafíos para el Docente y Compromiso del Estudiante [Academic Performance in Higher Education: Challenges for the Teacher and Student Commitment]. *Revista Científica de la UCSA, 5*(3), 55–63. doi:10.18004/ucsa/2409-8752/2018.005(03)055-063

Fojtík, R. (2018). Problems of distance education. *ICTE Journal, 7*(1), 14–23. doi:10.2478/ijicte-2018-0002

Guillén, M., Monferrer, D., Rodríguez, A., & Moliner, M. (2021). Does emotional intelligence influence academic performance? The role of compassion and engagement in education for sustainable development. *Sustainability (Basel), 13*(4), 1–18. doi:10.3390/su13041721

Guslyakova, N. I., & Guslyakova, A. V. (2020). Emotional Intelligence as a Driving Force in the Study of Foreign Languages in Higher Education. *Proceedings IFTE*, 781-792. DOI: 10.3897/ap.2.e0781

Hajar, A. (2019). A Critical Review of Research on Language Learning Strategies Used by Arab Learners of English. *Studies in Self-Access Learning Journal, 10*(3), 239–257. doi:10.37237/100303

Halimi, F., Al Shammari, I., & Navarro, C. (2021). Emotional intelligence and academic achievement in higher education. *Journal of Applied Research in Higher Education, 13*(2), 485–503. doi:10.1108/JARHE-11-2019-0286

Hamoud, K., Hashim, A. S., & Awadh, W. A. (2018). Predicting student performance in higher education institutions. *International Journal of Interactive Multimedia and Artificial Intelligence, 5*(2), 26–31. doi:10.9781/ijimai.2018.02.004

Hernández Sampiero, R., Fernández Collado, C., & Baptista Lucio, P. (2014). *Metodología de la investigación* [Research methodology]. McGraw-Hill.

Lestari, M., & Wahyudin, A. Y. (2020). Language Learning Strategies of Undergraduate EFL Students. *Journal of English Language Teaching and Learning, 1*(1), 25–30. doi:10.33365/jeltl.v1i1.242

Lin, L., Lam, W. I., & Tse, S. K. (2021). Motivational strategies, language learning strategies, and literal and inferential comprehension in second language Chinese reading: A structural equation modeling study. *Frontiers in Psychology, 12*, 1–13. doi:10.3389/fpsyg.2021.707538

Liu, M. (2022). The Relationship between Students' Study Time and Academic Performance and its Practical Significance. *BCP Education & Psychology, 7*, 1–4. doi:10.54691/bcpep.v7i.2696

MacCann, C., Jiang, Y., Brown, L. E. R., Double, K. S., Bucich, M., & Minbashian, A. (2020). Emotional intelligence predicts academic performance: A meta-analysis. *Psychological Bulletin*, *146*(2), 150–186. doi:10.1037/bul0000219

Mahmud, A., Chanda Antor, S., & Al Zabir, A. (2020). Factor Affecting the Academic Performance of University Students. *Social Work Education*, *7*(3), 373–382. doi:10.25128/2520-6230.20.3.11.

Mandasari, B., & Oktaviani, L. (2018). English Language Learning Strategies: An Exploratory Study of Management and Engineering Students. *Premise: Journal of English Education and Applied Linguistics*, *7*(2), 61–78. doi:10.24127/pj.v7i2.1581

Moore, R., & Fodrey, B. (2021). *Distance Education and Technology Infrastructure: Strategies and Opportunities*. Springer.

Partido, B. B., & Stafford, R. (2018). Association between emotional intelligence and academic performance among dental hygiene students. *Journal of Dental Education*, *82*(9), 974–979. doi:10.21815/JDE.018.094

Pregowska, A., Masztalerz, K., Garlińska, M., & Osial, M. (2021). A worldwide journey through distance education. *Education Sciences*, *11*(3), 1–26. doi:10.3390/educsci11030118

Rahman, M. W., Farid, K. S., & Tanny, N. Z. (2022). Determinants of Students' Academic Performance at the University Level. *International Journal of Agricultural Science, Research and Technology in Extension and Education Systems*, *11*(4), 213–222. 20.1001.1.22517588.2021.11.3.1

Ramírez Espinosa, A., & Hernández Gaviria, F. (2022). Learning strategies in action. *Revista Boletín Redipe*, *11*(4), 67–83. doi:10.36260/rbr.v11i04.1802

Resnik, P., & Dewaele, J. M. (2020). Trait Emotional Intelligence, Positive and Negative Emotions in First and Foreign Language Classes: A Mixed-methods Approach. *System*, *94*, 1–20. doi:10.1016/j.system.2020.102324

Romano, L., Tang, X., Hietajärvi, L., Salmela-Aro, K., & Fiorilli, C. (2020). Students' trait emotional intelligence and perceived teacher emotional support in preventing burnout: The moderating role of academic anxiety. *International Journal of Environmental Research and Public Health*, *17*(13), 4771–4786. doi:10.3390/ijerph17134771

Rumble, G. (2019). *The planning and management of distance education*. Routledge. doi:10.4324/9780429288661

Sadeghi, M. (2019). A shift from classroom to distance learning: Advantages and limitations. International. *Journal of Research in English Education*, *4*(1), 80–88. doi:10.29252/ijree.4.1.80

Sánchez Álvarez, N., Berrios Martos, M. P., & Extremera, N. (2020). A meta-analysis of the relationship between emotional intelligence and academic performance: A multi-stream comparison. *Frontiers in Psychology*, *11*, 1517. doi:10.3389/fpsyg.2020.01517

Saykili, A. (2018). Distance education: Definitions, generations, key concepts, and future directions. *International Journal of Contemporary Educational Research*, *5*(1), 2–17.

Seng, H. Z., Mustafa, N. C., Halim, H. A., Rahmat, N. H., & Amali, N. A. K. (2023). An Investigation of Direct and Indirect Learning Strategies in Learning Foreign Languages. *International Journal of Academic Research in Business & Social Sciences*, *13*(3), 322–338. doi:10.6007/IJARBSS/v13-i3/16492

Sewart, D., Keegan, D., & Holmberg, B. (2020). *Distance education: International perspectives*. Routledge.

Simonson, M., Zvacek, S. M., & Smaldino, S. (2019). *Teaching and Learning at a Distance: Foundations of Distance Education*. IAP.

Suleman, Q., Hussain, I., Syed, M. A., Parveen, R., Lodhi, I. S., & Mahmood, Z. (2019). Association between emotional intelligence and academic success among undergraduates: A cross-sectional study in KUST. *PLoS One*, *14*(7), 1–22. doi:10.1371/journal.pone.0219468

Teng, F. (2023). Language learning strategies. In Z. Wen, R. Sparks, A. Biedroń., & F. Teng (Eds.), Cognitive individual differences in second language acquisition: Theories, assessment, and pedagogy (pp. 147-173). De Gruyter. doi:10.1515/9781614514749-008

Traxler, J. (2018). Distance learning: Predictions and possibilities. *Education Sciences*, *8*(1), 1–13. doi:10.3390/educsci8010035

Vesely-Maillefer, A. K., & Saklofske, D. H. (2020). *Emotional Intelligence and the Next Generation of Teachers*. Springer.

Yan, C. (2022). Research on Student Academic Performance Prediction Methods. *Highlights in Science. Engineering and Technology*, *24*, 1–7.

Zhoc, K. C. H., Chung, T. S. H., & King, R. B. (2018). Emotional intelligence (EI) and self-directed learning: Examining their relation and contribution to better student learning outcomes in higher education. *British Educational Research Journal*, *44*(6), 982–1004. doi:10.1002/berj.3472

Zormanová, L. (2021). Learning strategies applied by university students in distance learning. *International Journal of Research in E-learning*, *7*(1), 1–20. doi:10.31261/IJREL.2021.7.1.04

ADDITIONAL READING

Adebola, O. O., Tsotetsi, C. T., & Omodan, B. I. (2020). Enhancing Students' Academic Performance in University System: The Perspective of Supplemental Instruction. *International Journal of Learning. Teaching and Educational Research*, *19*(5), 217–230. doi:10.26803/ijlter.19.5.13

Al Lily, A. E., Ismail, A. F., Abunasser, F. M., & Alhajhoj Alqahtani, R. H. (2020). Distance education as a response to pandemics: Coronavirus and Arab culture. *Technology in Society*, *63*, 1–11. doi:10.1016/j.techsoc.2020.101317

Ali Shoukat, Z. H., Khan, H., & Ahmed, A. (2023). Factors Contributing to the Students' Academic Performance: A Case Study of Islamia University Sub-Campus. *American Journal of Educational Research*, *8*(1), 283–289. doi:10.12691/education-1-8-3

Bergdahl, N., & Nouri, J. (2020). Covid-19 and Crisis-Prompted Distance Education in Sweden. *Technology, Knowledge, and Learning*, *26*(3), 443–459. doi:10.1007/s10758-020-09470-6

Brew, E. A., Nketiah, B., & Koranteng, R. (2021). A Literature Review of Academic Performance, an Insight into Factors, and their Influences on Academic Outcomes of Students at Senior High Schools. *OAlib*, *8*(6), 1–14. doi:10.4236/oalib.1107423

Chanderan, V., & Hashim, H. (2022). Language learning strategies used by ESL undergraduate students. *Creative Education*, *13*(3), 768–779. doi:10.4236/ce.2022.133049

Chang, C. H., & Liu, H. J. (2023). Language Learning Strategy Use and Language Learning Motivation of Taiwanese EFL University Students. *Electronic Journal of Foreign Language Teaching, 10*(2), 196-209. DOI: doi:10.56040/e-flt /e-FLT.sg

Endres, T., Leber, J., Bottger, C., Rovers, S., & Renkl, A. (2021). Improving lifelong learning by fostering students' learning strategies at university. *Psychology Learning & Teaching*, *20*(1), 144–160. doi:10.1177/1475725720952025

Fu Wong, J. C., & Yin Yip, T. C. (2020). Measuring Students' Academic Performance through Educational Data. *International Journal of Information and Education Technology (IJIET)*, *10*(11), 797–804. doi:10.18178/ijiet.2020.10.11.1461

Jamaluddin, N. S., Kadir, S. A., Alias, S. N., & Abdullah, A. (2021). A Review of Learning Strategies towards Learning Outcome. *International Journal of Social Science and Human Research*, *4*(12), 3647–3651. doi:10.47191/ijsshr/v4-i12-26

Khansir, A. A., Dehkordi, F. G., & Mirzaei, M. (2021). Learning Strategies and English Language Teaching. *Theory and Practice in Language Studies*, *11*(6), 734–741. doi:10.17507/tpls.1106.19

Khansir, A. A., Dehkordi, F. G., & Mirzaei, M. (2023). A Study on the Effectiveness of Learning Strategies in English. *Indian Journal of Language and Linguistics*, *4*(2), 18–31. doi:10.54392/ijll2323

Khumalo M. Utete R. (2023). Factors that influence academic performance of students: an empirical study. *The Seybold Report*, 1710-1722. DOI: doi:10.17605/OSF.IO/JCMKU

Kumar, S., Agarwal, M., & Agarwal, N. (2021). Defining and Measuring Academic Performance of Hei Students: A Critical Review. *Turkish Journal of Computer and Mathematics Education*, *12*(6), 3091–3105.

Macatuno-Nocom, N. (2022). Motivation and learning strategies on foreign language acquisition. *South Florida Journal of Development*, *3*(2), 2885–2896. doi:10.46932/sfjdv3n2-102

Makhambeova, A., Zhiyenbayeva, N., & Ergesheva, E. (2021). Personalized Learning Strategy as a Tool to Improve Academic Performance and Motivation of Students. *International Journal of Web-Based Learning and Teaching Technologies*, *16*(6), 1–17. doi:10.4018/IJWLTT.286743

Prasad Paudel, K. (2021). Dimensions of Academic Performance in the Context of Nepali Higher Education Institutions. *The Journal of Educational Research*, *11*(1), 29–48. doi:10.51474/jer.v11i1.497

Said Al Husaini, Y. N., & Ahmad Shukor, N. S. (2022). Factors Affecting Students' Academic Performance: A review. *Res Militares. The Social Science Journal*, *12*(6), 1–12.

Sivakumar, R. (2020). Effects of social media on academic performance of the students. *The Online Journal of Distance Education and e-Learning : TOJDEL, 8*(2), 90–97.

Syafryadin, S. (2020). Students' Strategies in Learning Speaking: Experience of Two Indonesian Schools. *Vision: Journal for Language and Foreign Language Learning, 9*(1), 34–47. doi:10.21580/vjv9i14791

Thomas, N., Bowen, N. E. J. A., & Rose, H. (2021). A diachronic analysis of explicit definitions and implicit conceptualizations of language learning strategies. *System, 103*, 1–19. doi:10.1016/j.system.2021.102619

Thomas, N., Rose, H., Cohen, A. D., Gao, X., Sasaki, A., & Hernández González, T. (2022). The third wind of language learning strategies research. *Language Teaching, 55*(3), 1–5. doi:10.1017/S0261444822000015

Wildschut, A., Megbowon, E., & Miselo, A. (2020). Impact of funding on academic performance: An exploration of two South African universities. *Journal of Education, 81*(81), 29–49. doi:10.17159/2520-9868/i81a02

KEY TERMS AND DEFINITIONS

Academic Performance: Academic performance is the measurement of student achievement across various academic subjects. Teachers typically measure achievement using classroom performance, graduation rates, and results from standardized tests

Distance Education: Distance education is the education of students who may not always be physically present at school, or where the learner and teacher are separated in both time and distance.

Emotional Intelligence: Emotional intelligence is defined as the ability to understand and manage one's emotions, as well as recognize and influence the emotions of those around. The term was first coined in 1990 by researchers John Mayer and Peter Salovey but was later popularized by psychologist Daniel Goleman.

Learning Strategies: A learning strategy is an individual's way of organizing and using a particular set of skills to learn content or accomplish other tasks more effectively and efficiently.

University Students: Undergraduates are students at universities and colleges who have graduated from high school and have been accepted to college, but they have not graduated yet.

Chapter 4
Relationships Between Emotional Intelligence, Willingness to Communicate, and Classroom Participation:
Results From Secondary Education in Spain

Antonio Daniel Juan Rubio
 https://orcid.org/0000-0003-3416-0021
Universidad de Granada, Spain

ABSTRACT

There is a proliferating research interest in emotional intelligence (EI) as it plays a significant role in learning processes. The chapter reports a study on the relationship between EI and the willingness to communicate (WTC) in the foreign language studied in secondary school (English). A positive correlation between both factors would be very significant since the use of the language of study is essential in the learning process. To assess the existence of this relationship, the questionnaires of 119 CSE students were analysed, and it was concluded that there is a statistically significant correlation between EI and the WTC. The general objective is, on the one hand, to analyse the relationship between emotional intelligence and the willingness to communicate in the Foreign Language (English) class at the secondary education stage, and whether there is a relationship between emotional intelligence, the willingness to communicate, and class participation.

DOI: 10.4018/979-8-3693-3294-8.ch004

1. INTRODUCTION

Willingness to communicate (hereinafter WTC) in a second or foreign language (L2) is construed as learners' readiness to get involved in the target language (Bui et al., 2022). The current literature shows that a high level of L2 WTC can enhance learners' communicative competence, language development, and speaking skills, resulting in knowledge development. Accordingly, L2 WTC can be divided into two main types: L2 WTC inside and outside the classroom. As L2 WTC side the classroom has implications for language teaching and learning, it is important for teachers to understand factors that affect learners' L2 WTC inside the classroom (Yashima, 2019; Fernández et al., 2020; MacIntyre, 2020; Dewaele & Pavelescu, 2021; Lee, 2022).

Previous studies indicate that L2 WTC is influenced by both situated (relationship with interlocutors and classroom setting) and individual factors (e.g. confidence and motivation) (Hoang & Bui, 2023; Vongsila & Reinders, 2016; Wang 2021), suggesting the potential relationship between L2 WTC inside the classroom and emotional intelligence. Although L2 WTC is vastly explored in the world, most previous studies (e.g. Aydin, 2017; Basöz & Erten, 2018; Derakhsan et al., 2021); Kant, 2019) focused on intermediate-level adult students, little is known about the relationship between learners' WTC inside L2 English classroom and emotional intelligence in a context of Spain.

This chapter reports a study on the relationship between L2 English learners' emotional intelligence, WTC, and participation level inside the classroom in a secondary school in Spain. This study can provide implications for language teaching and learning in the context of Spain and beyond.

2. LITERATURE REVIEW

2.1 WTC in English L2

WTC, together with many other factors such as motivation, personality, and the learner's active participation, is one of the elements that influence the learning of a foreign language (MacIntyre & Wang, 2021). Given the relevance of WTC in the foreign language learning process, it is particularly important for teachers to analyse the factors that might influence WTC, including emotional intelligence (hereinafter EI).

According to Katsaris (2019), the concept of WTC developed from three fundamental concepts: refusal to communicate, predisposition towards verbal behaviour, and shyness. Therefore, WTC is defined as a person's intention to start a communicative act when provided with the opportunity to do so. Furthermore, MacIntyre and Gregersen (2021) added that WTC represents a state of psychological readiness to use a foreign language when an opportunity arises.

According to several studies, WTC influences language learning, assuming that the greater the WTC, the more likely it is to achieve proficiency in the language that we are learning (Dewaele & Dewaele, 2018; Yashima et al., 2018; MacIntyre et al., 2020; Ghardirzade & Haniyeh, 2023). The significance of this relatively new concept is that leading experts, such as Zhou et al. (2023), consider WTC as the ultimate goal of instruction. The importance of WTC in language learning can be observed in MacIntyre et al.'s (1998) pyramid model. According to these authors, as learners move up the pyramid, they have greater control over the act of communicating in the target language.

As shown in figure 1, the pyramid is composed of six layers with 12 constructions. The layers are as follows: WTC behaviour; behavioural intention; situated antecedents; motivational tendencies; affective-cognitive context; and social and individual contexts. On the other hand, the 12 constructs are the following: foreign language use; WTC, WTC with a specific person; self-confidence; interpersonal motivation; intergroup motivation; self-confidence; intergroup attitudes; social status; competence; intergroup climate; and personality.

Therefore, WTC is located in the second layer, which means that it is a step prior to using a foreign language. According to this pyramid, there is a direct relationship between WTC and language use. In addition, the pyramid shows that there are a wide variety of factors that affect psychological readiness to speak. We can identify

Figure 1. Model of the variables that affect WTC in learning a foreign language

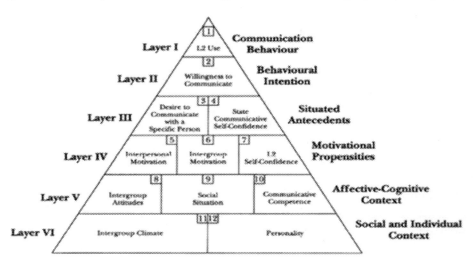

individual factors such as anxiety, motivation, attitudes, or personal attraction, as well as social factors such as ethno-linguistic vitality or language contact. These factors increase or decrease WTC when a person chooses to speak (Zarrinabidi et al., 2021).

Finally, it should be noted that although WTC has so far been regarded as a stable predisposition, Dewaele (2019) suggests that it can vary according to other variables that arise. Therefore, he proposes a new, more flexible definition of this concept of WTC: "it is a voluntary individual act to actively engage in communication in a specific situation, which may vary depending on the interlocutor, the topic, and the context of the conversation" (2019, p. 525).

Predisposition to speak can be a fundamental tool in the proper development of foreign language learning. For example, Lee and Hsieh (2019) argued that WTC is an essential component of foreign language learning. Similarly, Peng (2019) stated that learners with high WTC are more likely to use the foreign language they learn in authentic interactions. Similarly, Shirvan et al. (2019) stated that no matter how proficient a person is in using a foreign language. If they are not fully WTC, their attempts will not be fruitful. They also argued that these students would function better, as autonomous learners make efforts to learn the language and become more involved in learning activities.

Other studies have linked WTC and foreign language learning and have indicated that gender and age have an impact on WTC (Syed & Kuzborska, 2018; Weda et al., 2021). In fact, they argue that girls were of a higher level of WTC than boys. They also add that 14- and 15-year-olds have a better WTC than 13-year-olds, and that students who are more motivated also have better WTC.

Zarrinabadi et al. (2021) argued that there is a strong correlation between WTC and learner orientation in language learning. Broadly speaking, two types of orientation were identified: on the one hand, instrumental orientation occurs when a person pursues practical interests such as enhancing their academic curriculum or gaining professional qualifications; on the other, integrative orientation corresponds to the desire to learn a language.

According to Chen et al. (2022), any successful language learning programme should focus on encouraging WTC. They focus on key facets of language learning such as motivation, level of effort, confidence in language use, frequency, and duration of interventions in the learner's use of language. In fact, they argued that WTC should be the goal of second language instruction.

2.2 Emotional Intelligence (EI)

Historically, the concepts of intelligence and emotion have been considered areas with no apparent connections. However, from the 1970s onwards, the boundary between intelligence and emotion began to weaken, and studies began to establish how the two concepts interacted. In this context, the concept of emotional intelligence (hereinafter EI) can be defined as follows: "Emotional intelligence includes the ability to accurately perceive, appraise, and express emotion; the ability to access and/or generate feelings when they facilitate thoughts; the ability to understand emotion and emotional knowledge; and the ability to regulate emotions to promote emotional and intellectual growth" (Abatabaee & Pishghadam, 2021, p. 78).

This definition of EI can be understood as a set of skills that explains how people vary in their perceptions of feelings. Moreover, the better our knowledge of emotions, the better our ability to solve problems related to our emotional lives will be. In a slightly more formal way, Issah (2018) determined that EI is the ability to perceive and express feelings, assimilate these emotions, understand and reason with emotions, and control one's own emotions and those of others. According to O'Connor et al. (2019), this concept affirms that success depends on the different types of intelligence available and on the control of emotions. Based on these findings, Bujang et al. (2023) proposed that whether EI is so important in our lives, it should be taught in schools, as this would also mean future success for students. Regarding the skills that underlie EI, Singh et al. (2022) stated that an emotionally intelligent person is gifted in four areas: identifying, using, understanding, and regulating emotions. Similarly, Peixoto and Muñiz (2022) argued that EI consists of five parts: knowing one's own emotions, managing these emotions, self-motivation, recognising emotions in others, and managing interpersonal relationships.

Once the concept has been narrowed down, efforts have focused on determining how to measure EI. In this regard, it is worth highlighting the work of Robles et al. (2021), whose endeavour introduced a measure of EI with five scales and 15 sub-scales to define EI as follows. Accordingly, each scale consists of two to five sub-scales.

Scale 1: Intrapersonal Intelligence: the ability to know one's own emotions and management

- Awareness of one's own emotions (the ability to be aware of, recognise, and understand your own emotions)
- Assertiveness (the ability to express one's own feelings, beliefs, thoughts, and defend one's rights)
- Self-esteem (the ability to be aware of, understand, accept, and respect oneself)
- Self-realisation (the ability to realise and achieve your own potential)
- Independence (the ability to make decisions for oneself, and to be self-sufficient and free from emotional dependence).

Scale 2: Interpersonal Intelligence: the ability to manage relationships with other people.

- Empathy (the ability to understand other people's feelings)
- Interpersonal relationships (the ability to establish and maintain mutually satisfying relationships)
- Social responsibility (the ability to cooperate and be a constructive member of society).

Scale 3: Adaptability: ability to adjust to change

- Problem solving (the ability to solve problems effectively)
- Reality checking (the ability to recognise one's own feelings and thoughts by assessing the correspondence between what is subjectively experienced and what objectively exists)
- Flexibility (the ability to adapt to changes in one's feelings and thoughts).

Scale 4: Stress management: control of stress

- Stress tolerance (the ability to manage strong emotions, adverse events, and stressful conditions by coping with them in a positive way)
- Impulse control (the ability to control one's own feelings and resist temptation to act).

Scale 5: Mood: the ability to be optimistic and positive and to enjoy life

- Happiness (the ability to feel satisfied with one's life and have a good time)
- Optimism (the ability to look at the positive side of life and maintain a positive attitude when faced with problems).

Despite the enormous influence of EI in many fields, some studies have shown that it is of low importance in relation to certain points related to teaching. Adamakis and Dania (2021) found no empirical evidence to support previous theories. Both researchers concluded that there was no evidence that a higher level of EI was associated with more effective teacher job performance.

2.3 Emotional Intelligence and Foreign Language

Regarding the role of EI in foreign language learning, Bata and Castro (2021) found that academic success was strongly associated with several dimensions of EI (intrapersonal, stress management, and mood competencies). MacCann et al. (2020) found a positive relationship between EI and academic performance, particularly between EI and vocabulary knowledge. According to these researchers, EI is a good indicator of academic performance and vice versa. Similarly, Botes et al. (2020) found a significant relationship between foreign language learning anxiety and EI skills, whereas De Smet et al. (2018) found a correlation between stress management and EI.

In the work by Zhuo and Zhang, who analysed the role of EI in student behaviour and stress level, one of the conclusions reached was the following: "Evidence has been collected that emotionally intelligent students have better levels of psychological adjustment and emotional well-being; they have a higher quality and quantity of interpersonal and social support networks; they are less likely to engage in disruptive, aggressive or violent behaviour; they can achieve higher school performance by coping with stressful situations more easily, and they consume less addictive substances" (2020, p. 9).

Regarding the role of EI in foreign language learning, Alanoca (2019) advocated introducing EI into the classroom in a way that increases students' self-esteem in dealing with errors during language learning. According to Alanoca, "in the English classroom, the cognitive and communicative feature ends up materialising in linguistic expression" (p. 18). One of the key competencies to be developed in the area of English is linguistic competence; therefore, fostering EI facilitates achievement (Hung & Khoa, 2022).

Similarly, Kushkiev (2019) stated that interpersonal relationships are EI factors most clearly related to foreign language learning. According to Kushkiev, they provide a great opportunity to express one's language skills, but not only one of the variables involved. Learners who acquire a foreign language experience the initiation of more interpersonal encounters and greater academic opportunities.

Overall, the data seem to point to a key role of EI in academics and language learning, but there are still some fronts to explore. Consequently, some scholars have not been able to corroborate a direct relationship between EI and certain aspects of foreign language learning (Méndez, 2020). For example, Dewaele and Li (2020) found no statistically significant relationship between EI and foreign language vocabulary learning, contrary to the findings of previous studies.

2.4 The Relationship Between EI and WTC in a Foreign Language Class

Although several studies have pointed out the importance of both EI and WTC in successful language learning, few have analysed the interdependence between them (Aomr et al., 2020). Many studies have been conducted to determine the relationship between WTC and variables such as personality, self-confidence, attitudes, and motivation. However, few studies have been conducted to identify the relationship between EI and WTC. In one of the few studies examining both concepts, Iqbal et al. (2022) concluded that EI determined the degree of WTC. They found a significant correlation between the two terms, indicating that a high level of EI is related to a high level of WTC.

Rogulska et al. (2023) showed that EI is related to WTC and anxiety in a foreign language classroom. Regarding the relationship between EI and anxiety, the authors concluded that the higher the EI an individual possesses, the lower the level of anxiety that they have in class. For EI and WTC, the results showed a positive correlation. These results seem to indicate that foreign language learners are more willing to communicate when they are in a mood to do so and when they can overcome stress. Another study by Thao et al. (2023) found that multiple intelligences were responsible for the degree of WTC. The higher the scores for the different types of intelligence, the higher the chance of initiating interactions with others.

To confirm this WTC in a foreign language classroom, it is desirable to have other external data that could corroborate these figures. In this case, class participation can be related to WTC, as it can be assumed that the greater the WTC, the greater is the participation (Arias et al., 2022). The tangential aspect of this study was class participation. Data on students' participation in class were collected to observe whether there was any relationship between WTC, EI, and class participation. According to Li et al. (2019), participation is an active process that can be classified into five categories: preparation, contribution to discussions, group skills, WTC skills, and attendance. For example, Duong et al. (2020) assert that students are more motivated, whereas others, such as Dewaele et al. (2019), say that the older students are, the less they need to memorize and have better levels of interpretation, analysis, and synthesis.

Another study by Safranj and Zivlak (2019) found that EI was responsible for the degree of WTC. The higher the scores on the different types of intelligence, the greater the chance of initiating interactions with others (Jaime et al., 2021). It is desirable to have other external data because the greater the WTC students' level, the greater their participation in class is (Shirvan et al., 2019).

3. METHODOLOGY

Regarding research methodology, a field study was conducted to obtain data on secondary school students' EI, WTC, and classroom participation levels. This was a non-experimental correlational study of two variables: EI and WTC. Data were collected using two questionnaires measuring EI and WTC. Quantitative data on the degree of student participation in class were obtained using a rubric completed by the teacher. These questionnaires were developed for Compulsory Secondary Education (CSE) classes in a Spanish high school.

3.1 Methodological Design

This study aimed to establish the degree of relationship between secondary school pupils' EI and their WTC in a foreign language, and the influence that these two variables may have on class participation. Our research question was as follows: "Does emotional intelligence positively influence students' WTC in a foreign language?

Thus, the hypothesis is that the higher a student's EI score, the more willing he/she will be to communicate, and the more active his/her participation in class will be. To evaluate this relationship, a correlational study is conducted that allows us to measure the degree of the relationship and the way in which two or more variables interact with each other. Finally, the research presented here is classified as non-experimental because, when the researcher merely observes the events without intervening, non-experimental research is developed.

3.2 Sample

Population is defined as the set of all units of study. Therefore, the sample of the participants who took part in this study were students in the 1st, 2nd, 3rd, and 4th years of CSE at a public high school in Granada, Spain, because population determination and sampling are essential to ensure the representativeness and validity of the results. With regard to the age of the participants, the 119 pupils ranged from 12 to 17 years old. Regarding sex, 43.6% were female, and 67% were male. Table 1 shows the distribution of the samples according to age and sex.

3.3 Instruments

Selecting the correct research instruments helped us obtain the information necessary to achieve the initial objectives set at the beginning. I used three main instruments to collect data. The first instrument was the TMMS (Trait Meta-Mood Scale)-24 scale to measure the participants' degree of EI. This scale consists of 24 items that assess the degree of conformity of participants on a 5-point Likert scale. In this way, it is not a test in which there are right or wrong questions, neither good nor bad. Instead, answers must be provided according to individual preferences. This scale is divided into three parts to measure the key dimensions of EI. Each part is composed of eight items. These dimensions are: emotional perception (when an individual is able to feel and express feelings appropriately), understanding feelings (when an

Relationships Between Emotional Intelligence

Table 1. Sample distribution

Class	Age	Female	Male	Class Total	Percentage
1st CSE	12-13	12	19	31	26%
2nd CSE	13-14	6	19	25	21%
3rd CSE A	14-15	9	6	15	13%
3rd CSE B	14-15	8	10	18	15%
4th CSE	15-16	17	13	30	25%

individual has good knowledge of their emotional state), and emotional regulation (when a person is able to correctly regulate their emotional state).

To obtain the score for each subject for each dimension, the values assigned by the participants to each item were added. Thus, items 1 to 8 are calculated to obtain the perception factor; items 9 to 16 are the comprehension factors, and, consequently, items 17 to 24 are the regulation factors. In this test, the results always depend on each participant's answers' truthfulness, confidence, and sincerity.

The second instrument used was the WTC questionnaire, subdivided into two parts:

a. WTC in class: in this case, a total of 27 items were presented, all referring to WTC in-class tasks. The students were asked to rate their WTC on a scale of 1 to 5 (1 = I am almost never willing, 2 = I am sometimes willing, 3 = I am willing half the time, 4 = I am usually willing, and 5 = I am almost always willing). The items were grouped into four categories: speaking (eight items, α = .81), listening (five items, α = .83), reading (six items, α = .83), and writing (eight items, α = .88).

b) WTC outside class: A total of 27 items were presented, all referring to WTC outside class. As in the previous scale, students were asked to identify their WTC on a scale of 1 to 5 (1 = almost never willing, 2 = sometimes willing, 3 = half the time willing, 4 = usually willing, and 5 = almost always willing). The items were also grouped into four areas, although there was some difference in the total values: speaking (eight items, α = .89), understanding (five items, α = .89), listening (five items, α = .89), and communication (five items, α = .89).

The third and final instrument used to collect data was a rubric designed by the researcher to evaluate class participation. To prevent the possible bias of the questionnaire application, I used Cronbach's alpha coefficient to check the internal consistency of the questionnaire, which yielded a value of 0.83. This value indicates that the instrument was highly reliable; therefore, the questionnaire had a high internal reliability, and its measurements were stable and consistent.

3.4 Data Analysis

Data analysis was performed using Microsoft Excel, a statistical data processing software offered by Microsoft. The procedure followed was to prepare an Excel spreadsheet, and then data were statistically processed using the statistical programme JASP. Of all the questionnaires, two were eliminated because they forgot to complete part of the test. Our study used descriptive statistics to determine the means and standard deviations.

A normality test of the instrument was conducted to verify the validity of the hypothesis. For this purpose, we used the Kolmogorov-Smirnov normality test, which allowed us to measure the degree of agreement between the distribution of the data set and a specific theoretical distribution. After this test, the calculated Kolmogorov-Smirnov value (Ks c-value) was 0.1764, whereas the Kolmogorov-Smirnov table value (Ks t-value) which reflects the maximum permissible error, was 0.2534, with a p-value of 0.2738. Because the Ks c-value was lower than the Ks t-value and the p-value was greater than the accepted degree of significance (0.05), we had to take the null hypothesis because the data had a normal distribution.

4. FINDINGS

The analysis of data revealed that the mean EI of the participants was 77.9 which, according to the scale used to evaluate the participants' scores, was high. According to age range, students aged 12-13 years obtained an average of 81.9, which was the highest average among the four groups. The 13-14 age group obtained an average of 78.4, while the 14-15 and 15-16 age groups obtained an average of 75.4 and 76.1 respectively, which are several points below the average.

Regarding gender differences, data lead to the conclusion that men have a slightly higher EI than women. While males obtained an average of 77.9, females obtained 76.5.

Although the difference is very small, which may be due to factors such as sample size, it is interesting because there is evidence that women generally have a higher EI than men AS Bata and Castro suggested (2022) in their study. As shown in figure 5, data revealed that the average WTC coefficient of the participants was 156.2.

With respect to sex, females scored an average of 171.5, whereas males scored an average of 144.3 (figures 6 and 7). These data confirm previous studies that

Figure 2. Emotional intelligence in CSE students. Mean: 77.9

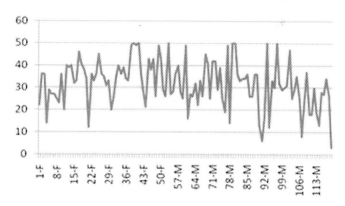

Figure 3. Males emotional intelligence in CSE. Mean: 79.0

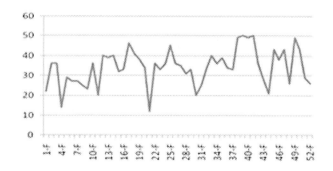

Figure 4. Females emotional intelligence in CSE. Mean: 76.5

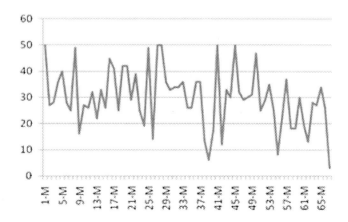

Figure 5. Mean total WTC

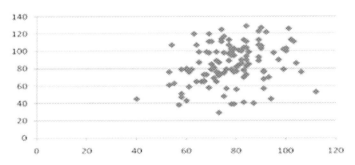

argue that girls are more willing to communicate than boys are, following De Smet et al. (2018).

By age range, the 15-16 age group scored best in terms of WTC with a mean of 166.9, followed by the 12-13 age group with 165.8. Groups 13-14 and 14-15 had significantly lower WTC in English than the first two groups, giving total scores of 154.8 and 138.4, respectively. Outside the class, WTC followed a similar trend, with the 15-16 group scoring the highest (77.6). The second highest average group was the 12-13 age group with 73.2, the third highest group was 13-14 with 70.9, and finally, the 14-15 age group had the lowest scores with an average of 63.2.

Because the main aim of this study was to determine the relationship between EI and WTC in secondary schools, in-class WTC was of utmost interest. The best results were obtained by students in the 12-13 age group, with an average of 92.6, while students in the 15-16 age group, who received the best results both outside the classroom and overall, obtained an average of 89.3. The lowest results were for the 13-14 age group, with 83.9, and the 14-15 age group, with an average of 75.2. In this case, although the best results were obtained by the older age group (15-16),

Figure 6. Total WTC in females. Mean 171.5

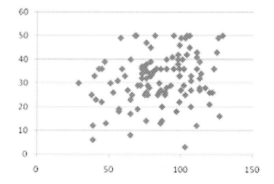

Figure 7. Total WTC in males. Mean 144

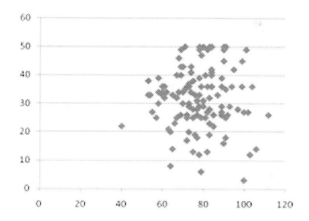

the younger age group (12-13) showed better results than the students in the 13-14 age group and significantly better results than the students in the 14-15 age group.

There was a clear difference in favour of in-class WTC (see Figures 8 and 9). While in-class WTC scored an average of 85.1, out-of-class WTC scored an average of 71, suggesting that students have much more WTC in English in class than out-of-class. This was one of the study's specific objectives, and the students were clearly more willing to speak a foreign language in class.

The best-performing items were in response to questions such as reading letters from a friend written in native English, talking to a stranger who entered the classroom, starting a conversation in English, and reading letters that used simple structures

Figure 8. In-class WTC with all learners. Mean 85.1

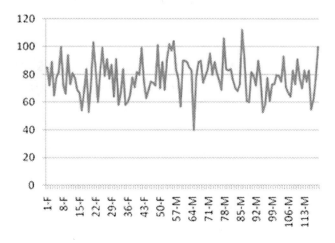

Figure 9. WTC outside class with all students. Mean 71

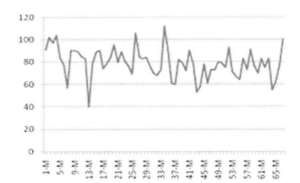

and words. In contrast, the items with the worst results responded to situations such as talking to a friend while waiting in line, playing a game in English, writing an article in a newspaper, or writing down a list of things to do the next day.

Regarding class participation, the average participation score of all secondary school students who participated in the study was 31.5 out of a total of 50 points, as shown in Figure 10.

Regarding gender, women obtained an average score of 34.1, almost five points higher than men (29.4), as shown in figures 11 and 12.

On the one hand, these data show that females participated significantly more than males in class (almost 5 points difference). On the other hand, they showed much similarity with the results obtained in WTC, where females obtained significantly better results than males. However, these results differ greatly from those obtained in

Figure 10. Class participation of all students. Mean: 31.5

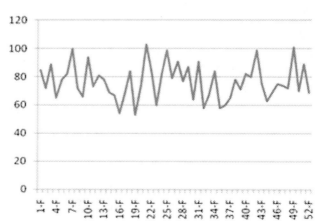

Figure 11. Female participation in class in CSE. Mean: 34.1

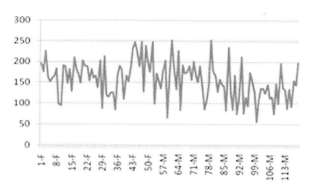

Figure 12. Class participation of males in CSE. Mean: 29.4

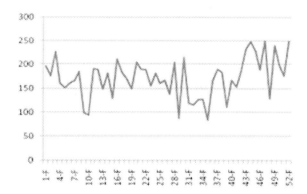

EI, where males scored 2.5 points better than females (the type of test and possible interactions between variables may have influenced the results).

Based on the age range, the four groups showed similar results. The 13-14 age group obtained the best results, with an average of 32.8. The 14-15 group, which obtained the worst results for both EI and WTC, obtained an average of 31.6, ahead of the 15-16 group (31) and the 12-13 group with an average of 30.7.

The relationship between EI and WTC (figure 13) was the focal point of this study. To explore whether there was a correlation between the two concepts, the Pearson correlation coefficient, which determines the linear mean between the two variables, was used. According to this test, the correlation between EI and WTC was positive (r= 0.27) and statistically significant (p= 0.01), although it was not as strong as predicted by the initial hypothesis and by Aomr et al. (2020).

Statistical analysis of the relationship between WTC and class participation showed a positive correlation coefficient of 0.23 (taking the combined data of all

Figure 13. WTC /EI correlation r= 0.27821523

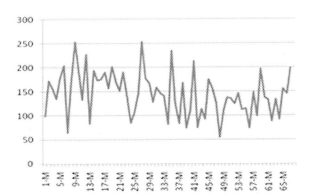

students), as Iqbal et al. (2022) already suggested. This means that the relationship was weak, although statistically significant (p= 0.009), as shown in figure 14.

The correlation coefficient between EI and class participation was -0.001, which means that the relationship between both concepts was very weak and negative. Moreover, the difference was not statistically significant (p= 0.98), despite the study by Anas et al. (2022).

There could be several possible reasons for this result. One reason could be that the sample size was too small. Another reason could be that this variable may interact with other variables, or that the questionnaires chosen to determine secondary school students' EI do not emphasise the factors that could most affect students'

Figure 14. Correlation WTC /Class participation r= 0.2378169

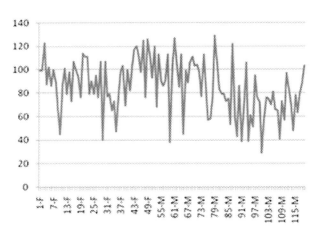

Figure 15. Correlation EI/Class participation r= -0.00154656

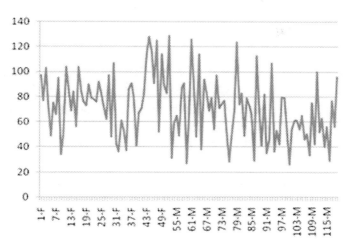

participation in class. More studies with larger sample sizes and different methods of quantifying EI and participation are needed to make a more realistic estimate.

Once the results were analysed, the extent to which class participation variable depended on the variables EI and WTC, because there was a correlation between both concepts as suggested by Li et al. (2019). For this purpose, a multiple regression test was conducted, the result of which proved that 6.24% of the variability shown by the marks depended on these factors. Individual analysis of the influence of the independent variables on participants' grades showed that their WTC influenced their grades (t-statistic = 2.60) in a statistically significant manner (p = 0.01). Although this percentage is not very high, it can be affirmed that it shows a certain tendency.

Regarding the EI variable, the results show that it is negatively related to class participation (t-statistic = -1.10) and that it is not statistically significant (p = 0.27), as stated by Rogulska et al. (2023). One possible explanation could be that the EI variable interacts with the WTC variable, because students with more WTC also had a high EI as anticipated by MacCann et al. (2020). Another explanation could be that the method chosen to measure EI did not emphasise interpersonal or intrapersonal factors, which were the most influential factors in the process. According to the results obtained, following Botes et al. (2020), an improvement in students' EI leads to better WTC in the foreign language classroom, which in turn leads to better results in terms of students' participation in class.

5. CONCLUSION AND DISCUSSION

The main objective of this research was to determine whether there was a relationship between emotional intelligence and willingness to communicate in a foreign language class during the CSE stage. The results showed a positive relationship between the two concepts, although less strong than expected based on previous studies, and statistically significant. The small sample size or the type of test used to quantify the different variables may have influenced the results.

The results indicate a positive correlation between WTC and class participation. The correlation was not as strong as expected but marked a positive trend. On the contrary, the relationship between emotional intelligence and class participation was negative and statistically non-significant, which is unexpected considering the previous literature. Several factors may have played a role, such as the limitations of the sample or the types of tests used to measure variables.

For these reasons, this study suggests that programs for developing emotional skills can be integrated into learning a foreign language in secondary school. It is possible to increase students' essential skills, such as self-confidence, or establish better relationships with classmates. With respect to future studies, it would be advisable to conduct more work to determine the influence of emotional intelligence programs in the secondary stage. It is also advisable to analyse the interactions between different variables and develop better mechanisms that reduce subjectivity.

One limitation of this study is that the questionnaires used to measure emotional intelligence and WTC were based on students' appraisals of themselves. In other words, students may perceive themselves as emotionally intelligent. Similarly, students may consider their WTC to be high, whereas reality may differ from this appreciation. Therefore, to reduce the subjectivity of the study, it would be convenient to focus on different tests to measure emotional intelligence and students' WTC. Another limitation was due to organizational reasons. Because of the logical limitations of the time available to organize the work, only one type of questionnaire was used to measure emotional intelligence and another to measure the WTC. The possibility of conducting other tests to measure both concepts would provide more certainty when assessing the resulting measurements. A third limitation refers to the number of participants. As this study had a limited number of participants, the conclusions drawn are exploratory and can only be extrapolated to the scope of the population under study. Therefore, it is necessary to expand the sample of secondary school students to determine the level of representation that allows for greater generalization. Finally, regarding applying strategies for developing emotional skills in students, we have to bear in mind that it is not only a school that intervenes in emotional development. The study evaluated the program's impact on emotional intelligence based on tests conducted before and after the program's implementation, but it could not determine the influence of other important factors such as family or friends.

As has been reiterated throughout this study, the influence of students' emotional intelligence in the educational field is very important. In addition to the impact of emotional intelligence on WTC, it would be interesting to analyse the benefits of developing emotional skills. Another aspect that should be explored is determining the real impact of emotional programs on the educational environment. The influence of several factors on students' emotional development, especially the family environment, makes it difficult to infer the significance of these educational programs. Related to the previous point is the influence of teachers on students' emotional improvement, and vice versa. Future studies should examine the relationships between teachers and students. In other words, they should explain how teachers' emotional intelligence affects students and how students' emotional intelligence affects teachers. It would also be interesting to analyse whether the students' gender has any influence on different variables. In this case, I did not present the data in depth for this variable because, if the sample of 119 students was very small, dividing it between men and women was less clear.

REFERENCES

Abatabaee Farani, S., & Pishghadam, R. (2021). Examining emotion in sense-based teaching: A cognitive task of sentence comprehension. *Language Related Research*, *12*(4), 73–104. doi:10.29252/LRR.12.4.3

Adamakis, M., & Dania, A. (2021). Validity of emotional intelligence scale in pre-service physical education teachers. *Journal of Physical Education and Sport*, *21*(1), 54–59. doi:10.7752/jpes.2021.01007

Alanoca, M. (2019). Emotional Intelligence Program to improve The Teaching-Learning Process of The English Language in Teaching and Translation of Language. *Educación Superior*, *6*(2), 14–23.

Aomr, J., Seng, G., & Kapol, N. (2020). Relationship between willingness to communicate in English and classroom environment among Libyan EFL learners. *Universal Journal of Educational Research*, *8*(2), 605–610. doi:10.13189/ujer.2020.080232

Arias, J., Soto-Carballo, J. G., & Pino-Juste, M. R. (2022). Emotional intelligence and academic motivation in primary school students. *Psicologia: Reflexão e Crítica*, *35*(1), 14–23. doi:10.1186/s41155-022-00216-0

Aydin, F. (2017). Willingness to communicate among intermediate-level adult Turkish EFL learners: Underlying factors. *Journal of Qualitative Research in Education*, *5*(3), 109–137. doi:10.14689/issn.2148-2624.1.5c3s5m

Başöz, T., & Erten, I. (2018). Investigating tertiary level EFL learners' willingness to communicate in English. *English Language Teaching*, *11*(3), 78–87. doi:10.5539/elt.v11n3p78

Bata, S., & Castro, C. (2021). English as a foreign language students' emotional intelligence management when taking speaking exams. *Profile: Issues in Teachers' Professional Development, 23*(2), 245–261. https://doi.org/.v23n2.8837 doi:10.15446/profile

Botes, E., Dewaele, J. M., & Greiff, S. (2020). The Foreign Language Classroom Anxiety Scale and Academic Achievement: An Overview of the Prevailing Literature and a Meta-Analysis. *Journal for the Psychology of Language Learning*, *2*(1), 26–56. doi:10.52598/jpll/2/1/3

Bui, H. P., Hoang, V. Q., & Nguyen, N. H. (2022). Encouraging Vietnamese students' willingness to communicate inside English L2 classrooms. *Language Related Research*, *13*(5), 1–23. doi:10.52547/LRR.13.5.17

Bujang, S., Heromi, N. A., & Hadil, H. (2023). Issues and gaps in emotional intelligence studies. *Science International (Lahore)*, *35*(1), 39–44.

Chen, X., Dewaele, J., & Zhang, T. (2022). Sustainable development of EFL/ESL learners' willingness to communicate: The effects of teachers and teaching styles. *Sustainability (Basel)*, *14*(1), 1–21. doi:10.3390/su14010396

De Smet, A., Mettewie, L., Galand, B., Hiligsmann, P., & Van Mensel, L. (2018). Classroom Anxiety and Enjoyment in CLIL and non-CLIL: Does the Target Language Matter? *Studies in Second Language Learning and Teaching*, *8*(1), 47–71. doi:10.14746/ssllt.2018.8.1.3

Derakhshan, A., Eslami, Z. R., & Ghandhari, N. (2021). Investigating the interplay of emotional intelligence and inter-language pragmatic competence in Iranian lower-intermediate EFL learners. *Journal of Issues in Language Teaching*, *10*(1), 37–66. doi:10.22054/ilt.2020.54334.527

Dewaele, J. M. (2019). The effect of classroom emotions, attitudes toward English, and teacher behavior on willingness to communicate among English Foreign Language Learners. *Journal of Language and Social Psychology*, *38*(4), 523–535. doi:10.1177/0261927X19864996

Dewaele, J. M., & Dewaele, L. (2018). Learner-internal and learner-external predictors of willingness to communicate in the FL classroom. *Journal of the European Second Language Association*, *2*(1), 24–37. doi:10.22599/jesla.37

Dewaele, J. M., Magdalena, A. F., & Saito, K. (2019). The Effect of Perception of Teacher Characteristics on Spanish EFL Learners' Anxiety and Enjoyment. *Modern Language Journal*, *103*(2), 412–427. doi:10.1111/modl.12555

Dewaele, J. M., & Pavelescu, L. (2021). The relationship between incommensurable emotions and willingness to communicate in English as a foreign language: A multiple case study. *Innovation in Language Learning and Teaching*, *15*(1), 66–80. doi:10.1080/17501229.2019.1675667

Duong, T. M., Tran, N. Y., Ha, A. T., & Phung, Y. (2020). The impact of emotional intelligence on performance: A closer look at individual and environmental factors. *Journal of Asian Finance Economics and Business*, *7*(1), 183–193. doi:10.13106/jafeb.2020.vol7.no1.183

Fernández Barrionuevo, E., Villoria Prieto, J., González Fernández, F. T., & Baena Extremera, A. (2020). Willingness to communicate in a foreign language in the four skills. Sex and age differences. *Espiral. Cuadernos del Profesorado*, *13*(27), 192–203. doi:10.25115/ecp.v13i27.3359

Ghadirzade Toosy, S., & Haniyeh Jajarmi, H. (2023). ESQ in L2 Willingness to Communicate and Communicative Ability. *Journal of Business. Tongxin Jishu*, 15–27. doi:10.56632/bct.2023.2202

Hoang, V. Q., & Bui, H. P. (2023). Encouraging EFL students' willingness to communicate inside Vietnamese high school classrooms: Teachers' strategies and students' beliefs. *Applied Research on English Language*, *12*(2), 19–44. doi:10.22108/ARE.2022.134674.1968

Hung, B. P., & Khoa, B. T. (2022). Communication strategies for interaction in social networks: a multilingual perspective. In I. Priyadarshini & R. Sharma (Eds.), *Artificial intelligence and cybersecurity* (pp. 2008–2020). CRC Press, Taylor & Francis.

Iqbal, J., Asghar, M. Z., Ashraf, M. A., & Yi, X. (2022). The impacts of emotional intelligence on students' study habits in blended learning environments: The mediating role of cognitive engagement during COVID-19. *Behavioral Sciences (Basel, Switzerland)*, *12*(1), 14–33. doi:10.3390/bs12010014

Issah, M. (2018). Change Leadership: The Role of Emotional Intelligence. *SAGE Open*, *8*(3), 1–6. doi:10.1177/2158244018800910

Jaime Romero, B., Castillejos López, W., & Reyes Toxqui, A. (2021). Intencionalidades y resistencias en el aprendizaje del inglés: Referentes para diseñar estrategias didácticas efectivas [Intentionalities and resistances in English language learning: references for designing effective teaching strategies]. *Revista de Investigación Educativa de la REDIECH, 12*, 1–19. doi:10.33010/ie_rie_rediech.v12i0.1013

Kant, R. (2019). Emotional intelligence: A study on university students. *Journal of Education and Learning, 13*(4), 441–446. https://doi.org/.13592 doi:10.11591/edulearn.v13i4

Katsaris, T. (2019). The Willingness to Communicate (WTC): Origins, significance, and propositions for the L2/FL classroom. *Journal of Applied Languages and Linguistics, 3*(2), 31–42.

Kushkiev, P. (2019). The role of positive emotions in second language acquisition: Some critical considerations. *Mextsol Journal, 43*(4), 1–10.

Lee, J. S. (2022). The role of grit and classroom enjoyment in EFL learners' willingness to communicate. *Journal of Multilingual and Multicultural Development, 43*(5), 452–468. doi:10.1080/01434632.2020.1746319

Lee, J. S., & Hsieh, J. C. (2019). Affective variables and willingness to communicate of EFL learners in in-class, out-of-class, and digital contexts. *System, 82*(1), 63–73. doi:10.1016/j.system.2019.03.002

Li, C., Dewaele, J. M., & Jiang, G. (2019). The Complex Relationship between Classroom Emotions and EFL Achievement in China. *Applied Linguistics Review, 11*(3), 1–26. doi:10.1515/applirev-2018-0043

MacCann, C., Jiang, Y., Brown, L. E. R., Double, K. S., Bucich, M., & Minbashian, A. (2020). Emotional intelligence predicts academic performance: A meta-analysis. *Psychological Bulletin, 146*(2), 150–186. doi:10.1037/bul0000219

MacIntyre, P. D. (2020). Expanding the Theoretical Base for the Dynamics of Willingness to Communicate. *Studies in Second Language Learning and Teaching, 10*(1), 111–131. doi:10.14746/ssllt.2020.10.1.6

MacIntyre, P. D., & Gregersen, T. (2021). The Idiodynamic Method: Willingness to Communicate and Anxiety Processes Interacting in Real Time. *International Review of Applied Linguistics in Language Teaching, 60*(1), 67–84. doi:10.1515/iral-2021-0024

MacIntyre, P. D., & Wang, L. (2021). Willingness to communicate in the L2 about meaningful photos: Application of the pyramid model of WTC. *Language Teaching Research, 25*(6), 878–898. doi:10.1177/13621688211004645

MacIntyre, P. D., Wang, L., & Khajavy, G. H. (2020). Thinking Fast and Slow About Willingness to Communicate: A Two-systems View. *Eurasian Journal of Applied Linguistics, 6*(3), 443–458. doi:10.32601/ejal.834681

Méndez López, M. G. (2020). Emotions attributions of ELT pre-service teachers and their effects on teaching practice. *Profile: Issues in Teachers'. Professional Development (Philadelphia, Pa.), 22*(1), 15–28. doi:10.15446/profile.v22n1.78613

Méndez López, M. G. (2022). Emotions experienced by secondary school students in English classes in México. *Colombian Applied Linguistics Journal, 24*(2), 219–233. doi:10.14483/22487085.18401

O'Connor, P. J., Hill, A., Kaya, M., & Martin, B. (2019). The Measurement of Emotional Intelligence: A Critical Review of the Literature and Recommendations for Researchers and Practitioners. *Frontiers in Psychology, 10*, 1–19. doi:10.3389/fpsyg.2019.01116

Peixoto, I., & Muniz, M. (2022). Emotional Intelligence, Intelligence and Social Skills in Different Areas of Work and Leadership. *Psico-USF, 27*(2), 237–250. doi:10.1590/1413-82712022270203

Peng, J. E. (2019). The roles of multimodal pedagogic effects and classroom environment in willingness to communicate in English. *System, 82*(1), 161–173. doi:10.1016/j.system.2019.04.006

Robles Bello, M. A., Sánchez Teruel, D., & Moreno, M. G. (2021). Psychometric properties of the Emotional Quotient Inventory: Youth Version-EQ-i:YV in Spanish adolescents with Down syndrome. *Journal of Applied Research in Intellectual Disabilities, 34*(1), 77–89. doi:10.1111/jar.12787

Rogulska, O., Rudnitska, K., Mahdiuk, O., Drozdova, V., Lysak, H., & Korol, S. (2023). The today's linguistic paradigm: the problem of investigating emotional intelligence in the learning of a foreign language. *Revista Românească pentru Educaţie Multidimensională, 15*(4), 458-473. https://doi.org/ doi:10.18662/rrem/15.4/804

Šafranj, J., & Zivlak, J. (2019). Effects of big five personality traits and fear of negative evaluation on foreign language anxiety. *Croatian Journal of Education, 21*(1), 275–306. doi:10.15516/cje.v21i1.2942

Shirvan, M. E., Khajavy, G. H., MacIntyre, P. D., & Taherian, T. (2019). A meta-analysis of L2 willingness to communicate and its three high-evidence correlates. *Journal of Psycholinguistic Research*, *48*(6), 1241–1267. doi:10.1007/s10936-019-09656-9

Syed, H. A., & Kuzborska, I. (2018). Dynamics of factors underlying willingness to communicate in a second language. *Language Learning Journal*, 1–49. doi:10.1080/09571736.2018.1435709

Thao, L. T., Thuy, P. T., Thi, N. H., Yen, P. H., Thu, H. A., & Tra, N. H. (2023). Impacts of Emotional Intelligence on Second Language Acquisition: English Major Students' Perspectives. *SAGE Open*, *13*(4), 1–15. doi:10.1177/21582440231212065

Weda, S., Atmowardoyo, H., Rahman, F., Said, M. M., & Sakti, A. E. F. (2021). Factors affecting learners' willingness to communicate in EFL classroom at higher institution in Indonesia. *International Journal of Instruction*, *14*(2), 719–734. doi:10.29333/iji.2021.14240a

Yashima, T., MacIntyre, P. D., & Ikeda, M. (2018). Situated Willingness to Communicate in an L2: Interplay of Individual Characteristics and Context. *Language Teaching Research*, *22*(1), 115–137. doi:10.1177/1362168816657851

Zarrinabadi, N., Lou, N. M., & Darvishnezhad, Z. (2021). To praise or not to praise? Examining the effects of ability vs. effort praise on speaking anxiety and willingness to communicate in EFL classrooms. *Innovation in Language Learning and Teaching*, *17*(1), 1–14. doi:10.1080/17501229.2021.1938079

Zhou, L., Xi, Y., & Lochtman, K. (2023). The relationship between second language competence and willingness to communicate: The moderating effect of foreign language anxiety. *Journal of Multilingual and Multicultural Development*, *44*(2), 129–143. doi:10.1080/01434632.2020.1801697

Zhuo C., Zhang, P. (2020). Trait Emotional Intelligence and Second Language Performance: A Case Study of Chinese EFL Learners. *Journal of Multilingual and Multicultural Development*, 1–15. https://doi.org/.2020.1767633 doi:10.1080/01434632

ADDITIONAL READINGS

Darasawang, P., & Reinders, H. (2021). Willingness to Communicate and Second Language Proficiency: A Correlational Study. *Education Sciences*, *11*(9), 1–12. doi:10.3390/educsci11090517

Ebadi, S., & Ebadijalal, M. (2022). The effect of Google Expeditions virtual reality on EFL learners' willingness to communicate and oral proficiency. *Computer Assisted Language Learning, 35*(8), 1975–2000. doi:10.1080/09588221.2020.1854311

Freiermuth, M., & Ito, M. (2020). Seeking the source: The effect of personality and previous experiences on university students' L2 willingness to communicate. *Learning and Motivation, 71*, 1–10. doi:10.1016/j.lmot.2020.101640

Henrya, A., Thorsen, C., & MacIntyre, P. D. (2021). Willingness to communicate in a multilingual context: A time-serial study of developmental dynamics. *Journal of Multilingual and Multicultural Development*, 1–20. doi:10.1080/01434632.2021.1931248

Jamalifar, G., & Salehi, H. (2020). The effects of rehearsal and strategic task planning on L2 willingness to communicate. *Language Learning Journal, 48*(2), 162–169. doi:10.1080/09571736.2017.1370605

Liu, F., Vadivel, B., Rezvani, E., & Namaziandost, E. (2021). Using games to promote English as a foreign language learners' willingness to communicate: Potential effects and teachers' attitude in focus. *Frontiers in Psychology, 12*, 1–10. doi:10.3389/fpsyg.2021.762447

Nguyen, C. H. (2024). Self-consciousness and unwillingness to communicate: An ethnographic case study. In H. P. Bui, T. C. Bang, & C. H. Nguyen (Eds.), *Teacher and student perspectives on bilingual and multilingual education* (pp. 51–67). IGI Global. doi:10.4018/979-8-3693-5365-3.ch004

Resnik, P., & Dewaele, J. M. (2020). Trait emotional intelligence, positive and negative emotions in first and foreign language classes: A mixed-methods approach. *System, 94*, 1–20. doi:10.1016/j.system.2020.102324

Sánchez Álvarez, N., Berrios Martos, M. P., & Extremera, N. (2020). A meta-analysis of the relationship between emotional intelligence and academic performance in secondary education. *Frontiers in Psychology, 11*, 1517. doi:10.3389/fpsyg.2020.01517

Tran, N. H., & Bui, H. P. (2024). Causes of boredom in language classrooms and students' coping strategies: A case in Vietnam. *Language Related Research, 15*(3), 1–24. doi:10.29252/LRR.15.3.1

Vo, T. H. (2024). Contextualizing Vietnamese students' willingness to communicate inside the classroom. In Teacher and student perspectives on bilingual and multilingual education (pp. 179-192). IGI Global.

KEY TERMS AND DEFINITIONS

Class Participation: The behaviours that students exhibit in class. This behaviour can take many formats, such as raising questions, responding to others' questions, participating in discussions, or providing feedback.

Emotional Intelligence: The ability to manage both one's own emotions and understand the emotions of people around them. There are five key elements of EI: self-awareness, self-regulation, motivation, empathy, and social skills.

Secondary Education: In Spain, secondary education includes grades 1-4 (called CSE, 12-16 years) and grades 5 and 6.

Willingness to Communicate: The intention to speak or to remain silent, given free choice. Initially developed in the L1 context of educational instruction, WTC was subsequently introduced to SLA.

Chapter 5
Revisiting Oral Corrective Feedback in Second Language Acquisition:
Existing Debates and Directions for Further Studies

Hung Phu Bui
 https://orcid.org/0000-0003-3468-4837
University of Economics Ho Chi Minh City, Vietnam

Thanh Huynh Vo
 https://orcid.org/0009-0001-2324-0352
Ho Chi Minh City Open University, Vietnam

ABSTRACT

Corrective feedback is acknowledged with a growing research interest in the second language acquisition literature. In the classroom, the teacher's and peer's oral corrective feedback (OCF) can be used to modify students' language and facilitate language learning. From the existing debates in the literature, the authors argue that corrective feedback should be broadly defined as the use of language and artifacts not only to correct language inaccuracies but also to signal unacceptable instances and/or suggest alternatives. To provide effective OCF, the teacher might need to consider the appropriateness of OCF types of strategies for the context, learners' age and preferences, and probably the relationship between the feedback provider and receiver. Finally, directions for further studies are discussed. Driven by a desire to provide updated literature regarding OCF, this chapter can be a reference for students, teachers, and novice researchers.

DOI: 10.4018/979-8-3693-3294-8.ch005

1. INTRODUCTION

Although corrective feedback (CF) has been gaining attention from researchers in applied linguistics and language education, books and journal articles mainly focus on specific aspects of CF. As CF is context-sensitive, it is essential to make CF adaptive to the local contexts where it is employed. Driven by a desire to provide a comprehensive view of CF, this chapter initially reviews the existing definitions of CF in the literature. Then, the types of CF and agenda of CF research are critically discussed. Finally, we outline the directions for further research in this area. We hope that this chapter will be added to public and school libraries and be of interest to researchers, practitioners, and students in the field.

2. REDEFINING CORRECTIVE FEEDBACK

CF began its childhood in the field of education as the teacher's attempt, parent, or caretaker to revise a child's inaccuracies (Hattie & Timperley (2007). Since it was first introduced in the field of language education, CF has gained attention from second language acquisition (SLA) researchers. The existing literature well documents different definitions of CF. Long (2015), Lyster (2015) and Schachter (1991) acknowledge *corrective feedback, negative evidence, and negative feedback* as three terms used interchangeably to correct an error. Regarding second or foreign language (L2) English contexts, CF evokes the concepts of intervention, inaccuracies, modification, and support (Long, 2007). As Lightbown and Spada (1999) noted, CF is conceptualized as the teacher' effort to revise when they identify a student's error. However, Gielen et al. (2010) argued that the teacher's feedback can be used for other purposes. In fact, feedback can be employed to correct unaccepted instances or affirm a behavior. Accordingly, the teacher may give corrective feedback to signal unaccepted instances to put forward students' performance or affirm students' behavior for further development, suggesting that feedback includes feed-forward and can be categorized into positive and negative types. The negative types are to correct inaccuracies but the positive types are to affirm students' performance or behavior (Long 2015; Lyster, 2015). Regarding L2 contexts, assessment of spoken and written language is not solely based on inaccuracies but L2 speakers' performance, for which rating criteria accurately indicate speakers' proficiency level (Baker 2012; Cumming et al., 2002). The proficiency level is broadly measured through language complexity metrics (Khabbazbashi, 2012). In the classroom, the teacher may enhance students' language development by using corrective feedback (Yan et al., 2021), suggesting that CF should not be simply conceptualized as a tool to correct errors or inaccuracies but signal instances, including language and strategies, which are considered unacceptable compared to the expected learning outcomes. Motivated by sociocultural theory, peers can also get involved in classroom assessment and provide feedback (Bui, 2023; Bui & Nguyen, 2022).

Considering the existing definitions of CF documented in the literature of second language acquisition, we argue for a broad definition of CF as a pedagogical intervention in which feedback on students' performance is used to modify students' concepts or behaviors for the purpose of improving learning and accomplishment. CF, focused or unfocused, can be delivered either formally or informally and directly or indrectly by an assessor. Thus, CF can delineate students' language problems or appraisals.

3. MISTAKES AND ERRORS: WHAT SHOULD BE CORRECTED?

What errors and mistakes are and how errors differ from mistakes have provoked many debates. Understanding the main distinction between errors and mistakes in the context of language learning is pivotal for understanding learners' linguistic competence and performance (Chomsky, 1965; Corder, 1975; Richard & Schmidt, 2002)). Those on the side of accuracy do not distinguish errors and mistakes. That is, all language instances that deviate from the standard language and demonstrate a lack of knowledge are called errors; errors, therefore, include mistakes (Simpson et al., 2020). However, those who believe that language problems are natural and process-related proposed a distinction between errors and mistakes. Accordingly, mistakes, unlike errors, are related to performance and may take place as a result of unconsciousness or carelessness (Nassaji, 2018). Corder (1975) further elaborated on this distinction that errors are reflections of a learner's partial grasp of a language system. Such errors are commonly observed in those who are yet to fully master an institutionalized language, including second language learners and dialect speakers, indicating gaps in their linguistic competence. Corder (1975) also points out that learners' language errors are systematically aligned with their current level of linguistic understanding within their interlanguage framework, implying that errors are not random but rather reflective of the learner's ongoing phase in acquiring a new language. They symbolize the developmental stages of linguistic competence as learners advance in their second language acquisition. Thus, these errors serve as crucial indicators of a learner's current standing within their transitional language system, marking their progress and areas for growth in language proficiency. In contrast, mistakes or lapses, are not seen as indicators of inadequate linguistic competence. Instead, as many scholars (e.g. Vanderheiden & Mayer, 2020; van der Westhuizen et al., 2020) describe, mistakes psychologically arise from the encoding and articulation of speech, suggesting that mistakes are natural, even among native speakers, who, despite having a comprehensive understanding of their native language, can make occasional slip-ups.

In language learning, as learners' interlanguage develops, the nature of errors and mistakes change dynamically. Initially, errors are more frequent due to the influence of the learner's first language (L1). Over time, as learners advance, their interlanguage evolves, leading to more sophisticated errors that reflect the complexities of the target language. Mistakes, however, may occur at any stage of language development, linked less to linguistic understanding and more to external or physiological factors. Notably, fossilization can occur in interlanguage, a complex process where certain language elements cease to evolve, highlighting the challenge of attaining native-like proficiency in a second language (Nguyen & Newton, 2021).

Ellis and Barkhuizen (2005) highlight the ongoing complexities and debates in language education by acknowledging that defining an 'error' in language learning is not straightforward or without issues. This reflects the nuanced nature of error identification and the various approaches to addressing it in educational contexts. Understanding the interplay of interlanguage with errors and mistakes is crucial for language educators. It allows teachers to tailor their instruction and feedback to the learner's current stage of language development. Acknowledging errors as a natural phenomenon of interlanguage development can lead to more effective and supportive teaching methods, focusing on guiding learners through their unique linguistic journey rather than merely correcting mistakes (Nassaji, 2018; van der Westhuize et al., 2020).

One key question may be whether educators should correct every single error made by learners or adopt a more selective approach. To answer this question, we may need to consider many aspects of language learning as the effectiveness of CF can rely on whether the CF strategy employed is appropriate for the error to be corrected and how it is applied. This perspective reminds us back to the questions around the nuanced differences between 'errors' and 'mistakes' in language learning. From an SLA perspective, while errors might indicate a lack of understanding, mistakes could be sporadic slips despite a general grasp of the correct language form. This distinction is vital for educators to provide feedback that is both appropriate and effective (Angelucci & Pozzo, 2020).

4. TYPES OF CORRECTIVE FEEDBACK

Corrective feedback (CF) emerges as a crucial pedagogical remedy in the growing agenda of SLA as it is believed to modify learners' language and defossilize systematic existing errors in students' language use. CF involves the identification and correction of learners' language inaccuracies and inappropriate cases. Highlighting the significance of feedback in education, Hattie and Timperley (2007) emphasized the potential of CF to positively and negatively influence student learning, with broad implications and meanings of feedback in educational settings. Supporting this view, Li & Vuono (2019) identified a surge in CF research agenda, underscoring its growing importance in the field of SLA. Accordingly, corrective feedback is broadly divided into two primary forms: oral and written feedback, each playing a distinct role in shaping the L2 learning journey.

In practice, CF can be delivered either in a written form, called written corrective feedback (WCT) or in an oral form, called oral corrective feedback (OCF) (Li & Vuono, 2019), or a mixed form, including both WCT and OCF. For instance, when rating students' L2 writing, the teacher may analyze and identify the errors that need to be orally further elaborated or treated in the classroom (Rassaei, 2013). The practice of WCT applied to students' works may assist students in avoiding making similar errors in their future assignments, and OCF delivered in the classroom personally or in front of the whole class, possibly on an anonymized basis, may explain further details of the addressed errors in a monologic or interactive manner.

OCF and WCF share some characteristics. First, from a theoretical view. Both OCF and WCF are used as artifacts to modify students' language. Researchers are concerned about the extent to which different types of CF can promote students' language development. Second, OCF and WCF may have either immediate or delayed effects on learning and development. What types of CF are used, how they are used, and if they are accepted by students are the main determinants of whether CF is effective in use (Li & Vouno, 2019).

Despite the aforesaid similarities, OCF differs from WCT in several main aspects (Table 1). According to Li and Vouno (2019) and Sheen (2011), OCF is so-called as it is delivered to students in the form of sound and in direct classroom communication in which the feedback receiver, usually students, is provided with feedback right in the session where their utterances are found unacceptable. However, WCF, addressed to students in the written form, is in general given later as the teacher usually needs time to read and rate students' written submissions. This difference suggests the interactive and timely nature of OCF provided to students in integrated classroom settings. Another difference is found in the focus of the feedback. As WTC is fundamentally applied to written assignments, feedback is not only about language but also about several aspects of writing, such as coherence, cohesion, unity, and completeness. It is explicitly provided in a direct or indirect manner. The teacher may decide to focus on one or several types of language and writing issues, depending on the expected learning outcomes, course objectives, and lesson focus. OCF, in contrast, may be given explicitly or implicitly, suggesting that OCF is sometimes not recognized by students as they might not be aware that they are implicitly corrected.

Table 1. A comparison of OCF and WCF

	OCF	WCF
Modality	Aural	Visual
Spontaneity	Synchronous/ immediate	Asynchronous/ delayed
Context	Integrated	Isolated
Focus	Language only	Language and content
Salience	Explicit and implicit	Explicit
Classification	Prompt and provide; Implicit and explicit	Direct and Indirect; Focused and unfocused

Every CF strategy is documented with distinct advantages, suggesting that how they should be employed depends on the learning context, type of error, and students' level of proficiency. To maximize the effectiveness of CF strategies, teachers may not only employ a diverse range of feedback techniques but also be keenly aware of both learner-internal and external factors. These factors significantly influence how learners notice and utilize the corrective feedback provided (Nassaji & Kartchava, 2021). For instance, explicit correction is clear and straightforward, making it suitable for more significant errors or beginner learners who generally need detailed and well-informed guidance (Varnosfadrani & Basturkmen, 2009).

5. ORAL CORRECTIVE FEEDBACK

5.1 Problematizing Oral Corrective Feedback

The timely and interactive nature of OCF in part makes it an integral part of pedagogy in L2 English classroom settings (Lyster et al., 2013), where direct communication is crucial, as interlocutors can address spoken instances deviating from standard language forms and unclear or inappropriate utterances (Oliver & Adams, 2021). The application and efficacy of OCF have sparked considerable debates and research, making it a focal point in the field of language learning over the past two decades (Ha et al., 2021).

Several studies have categorized OCF into different types. For example, Ranta and Lyster (2007) proposed six main CF types divided into two main groups: (1) reformulations (recasts and explicit correction) and (2) prompts (clarification request, metalinguistic feedback, elicitation, and repetition). This proposal of six CF types, widely accepted, has been used to frame several recent studies (e.g. Ha & Murray, 2020; Hartono et al., 2022).

Known as a type used to reconstruct students' language use, recasts (conversational and didactic) are generally known as reformulations of a student's spoken error. While a conversational recast is prone to implicitness, a didactic recast is inclined to explicitness. According to several studies (e.g. Choi & Li, 2012; Li & Vuono, 2019; Ha et al., 2021), recasts are frequently used in different settings. The effectiveness of recast relies mainly on the type of error, with these interventions being particularly salient for second language (L2) pronunciation errors (Saito, 2012, 2017). To modify students' language, the teacher may also deploy explicit correction, occurring when the teacher emphasizes students' problem and provides a acceptable language form (Ranta & Lyster, 2007).

Clarification requests, metalinguistic feedback, elicitation, and repetition are instrumental in promoting learner autonomy and activeness in language correction (Ranta & Lyster, 2007). According to Oliver & Adams (2021), these prompts are effective scaffolding tools in language production, especially when the necessary modifications fall within Zone of Proximal Development (ZPD). From a sociocultural perspective, prompts aid in enhancing self-regulated learning, underscoring the active role of learners.

The classification of OCF types remains a subject of ongoing debate among scholars. For example, recasts, widely used by teachers are typically classified as implicit (Ellis, 2021). However, Lyster & Mori (2006) argued that recasts are inclined to be explicit. This diversity in perspectives, as Oliver Adams (2021) emphasizes the nuanced and context-sensitive nature of OCF in the field of language learning and teaching. Furthermore, while numerous studies, including those mentioned by Ha et al. (2021), have demonstrated the overall effectiveness of various types of feedback in language learning, it is essential to note that several mediating factors influence their effectiveness. This suggests that the impact of OCF is not merely dependent on the type of feedback employed but also on how it interacts with other elements in the learning environment.

Despite the existing doubts about the effectiveness of OCF in the early development of SLA (e.g. Krashen, 1982), recent empirical evidence has demonstrated the positive and lasting impacts of OCF, particularly when it raises learners' awareness of the corrected items and is contextualized. Hattie and Timperley (2007) particularly emphasize the risks of not addressing errors through OCF, suggesting that it could lead to the reinforcement of the identified inaccuracies. Lyster et al. (2013) found that OCF can enhance learners' skills. The meta-analyses by Li (2010) and Lyster and Saito (2010) also support the usefulness of OCF for L2 development. Accordingly, the effectiveness of OCF is not discussed as an autonomous issue but in relation to what errors need correcting, when errors should be corrected, who corrects errors, and if the OCF strategies are appropriate for the context. This shift from initial skepticism to a recognition of its importance highlights OCF's integral position in effective language teaching and learning strategies.

Researchers recently raised a question about the effectiveness of different OCF types. According to Nassaji's (2009) study, recasts, particularly didactic recasts, were effective. Long (2007) argued for the use of recasts as they give examples of what learners' language is expected to be like while the communication is maintained by the feedback giver. Nevertheless, several researchers (e.g. Sheen, 2004) are skeptical about recast effectiveness as they do not function properly in some contexts and with some language items. Lyster (2004) argues that prompts, more explicit and salient than recasts, support students' L2 development further; some students, in fact, are not sensitive to error correction through repetition.

Lyster and Mori (2006) and Lyster and Saito (2010) support the use of peer corrective feedback (PCF). They argue that it facilitates L2 development through dynamic peer interactions in the classroom. These interactions enhance language learning and proficiency (Lyster et al., 2013). Sato (2017) further elaborates on the importance of PCF, noting its role in enabling learners to identify and amend errors and in fostering an environment conducive to collaborative learning. The study highlights that the effectiveness of PCF is contingent upon the social dynamics within the classroom and the learners' attitudes. It also stresses the mutual nature of PCF, where learners benefit from both providing and receiving feedback, thus contributing to the overall language development of the group (Bui, 2023; Bui & Nguyen, 2022). Selecting appropriate corrective techniques in classroom settings is crucial; however, inappropriate methods or excessive focus on correction can heighten learners' stress levels, potentially hindering the language acquisition process (Nguyen & Newton, 2021).

In summary, the selection of an appropriate feedback technique requires the careful consideration and experience of the teacher, who needs to consider the varied attributes and needs of students. Such aspects as the students' age, their motivation for learning the language, and the specific context of their learning are all vital factors (Nassaji, 2016). Oliver and Adams (2021) delineate the importance of learners' own preferences for CF types. However, the practice of OCF should not entirely be a rigid adherence to learners' preferred CF types. Instead, it is about modifying CF to maximize efficiency and foster better engagement among learners. It may be essential for teachers to understand that learners may not always express their preferences for feedback with clarity and that what learners think they prefer might not necessarily be the most effective for their linguistic development.

5.2 Addressing Errors and Mistakes

As in the aforesaid, errors typically arise from a lack of understanding or incomplete knowledge of language rules and structures, whereas mistakes usually are unaccepted performance-related issues that happen despite the learner having the necessary knowledge. In the process of language learning, addressing both errors and mistakes is essential (Lyster, 2004; Nassaji, 2017). When dealing with these issues, it is important to consider various factors, such as the learning objectives, the proficiency level of the learners, and the specific context in which the language is being used (Ammar & Spada, 2006).

In language teaching, deciding what errors should be corrected involves a complex process: a careful evaluation of errors, appropriateness of the technique, frequency of each error, and lesson focus (Ellis, 2017). This process, complicated by the potential negative effects of errors on learning (Sheen, 2010), demands prioritizing errors that affect intelligibility and are relevant to the lesson focus, such as target grammatical errors and word choice. Teachers must employ a diversity of correction strategies, including immediate or delayed and direct, peer-involved, or self-correction methods to accommodate the different preferences of students (Cohen, 1975). The approach to error correction should be flexible and learner-centered, suggesting that errors should be oriented to learning (Wong & Lim, 2018). This perspective aligns with the concept of handling errors through prevention, permission, and promotion, underscoring their educational value.

How feedback should be delivered, especially in contexts emphasizing fluency and confidence, is supported by a number of interdisciplinary studies. Krashen (1982) suggests that learners' emotions significantly influence language acquisition, advocating for a lower affective filter to facilitate learning, suggesting the practice of gentle correction or overlooking occasional mistakes to reduce anxiety and promote confidence. Swain (1985) highlights that making and correcting mistakes is a natural part of language development, proposing that learners benefit from the opportunity to take risks with language learning, probably causing mistakes. Selinker (1972) also recommends gradual refinement through subtle corrections for language development. Together, these perspectives advocate for a balanced approach to mistake correction.

In practice, striking a balance in CF is key. Overcorrection can hinder communication and affect learners' confidence while under-correction can lead to error fossilization (Truscott, 2007). The decision on when and how to correct errors should be guided by the educational context and the specific needs and goals of the learners (Nassaji, 2015, 2016). For instance, in a conversation-driven class, the focus might be more on fluency and less on correcting every error; thus, the use of recasts might fulfill the lesson focus and satisfy learners' preferences (Long, 2007).

In summary, both errors and mistakes present valuable learning opportunities for language learning. The approach to correction should be adapted to meet the specific needs of learners' and the context of learning (Ammar & Spada, 2006; Nassaji, 2016). Additionally, teachers need to recognize the importance of differentiating errors and mistakes, adopting a more positive perspective towards errors as opportunities for growth and understanding (Angelucci & Pozzo, 2020).

5.3 Timing

In language teaching, the timing of CF plays a crucial role, suggesting both the preparation and the time of its delivery. Immediate feedback, generally provided shortly after learners indicate emerging unacceptable utterances or commit errors, may facilitate instant correction and reinforcement. Conversely, delayed feedback, provided at a later time after students make errors, is acknowledged to support reflective learning (Li et al., 2018). The two main types of OCF may evoke a question about the most effective timing for feedback. The strategies regarding feedback timing are a subject of extensive research and debates, with differing opinions among teachers and students over the optimal delivery of OCF. The main reason for this discrepancy was ascribed to teachers' concern about students' emotional well-being and the possibility of disruption of OCF. This disparity makes the decision on timing a complex aspect of language education (Fu & Li, 2020). Many researchers, including Lyster and Saito (2010), have highlighted the effectiveness of immediate feedback, particularly in OCF. Immediate feedback, given as soon as an error occurs, is believed to be more effective in ensuring that learners can apply the correction in similar future contexts. Delayed feedback, on the other hand, might lose its effectiveness if provided after the relevant context has passed, making it harder for learners to apply the corrections in future communication (Canals et al., 2021).

According to Fu and Li's (2020) research, the timing of OCF timing should be viewed in relation to instruction. They argue that feedback is most impactful when closely linked to instruction. It is especially effective when given alongside instructions and relevant to the lesson focus. This proximity helps learners associate the feedback with the instruction, thereby reinforcing their understanding of the material, including both regular and irregular past-tense forms. Delayed feedback, for instance given three weeks after instruction, may become purely corrective rather than reinforcing, as learners may struggle to link it with the earlier instruction. These researchers argue that integrating instruction and feedback in close temporal proximity is preferred.

Research indicates a disparity in preferences for feedback timing between students and teachers. There is a consensus that students generally favor immediate feedback, wanting to be corrected soon after making errors, while teachers often prefer delaying feedback until the end of a speaking activity or lesson (Ha et al., 2021; Davis, 2003). The preference for OCF timing also depends on teachers' experience. Experienced teachers value both immediate and post-activity feedback, drawing from their teaching background, while novice teachers, influenced by their own learning experiences, tend to avoid explicit immediate feedback to reduce student anxiety. The discrepancy in the teachers' preference for OCF may derive from the teachers' adaptation. Rahimi and Karkami (2015) argue that, as OCF is context-dependent, it might be essential for teachers to consider individual learners' needs in order to optimize OCF delivery.

Based on the perspective that interlanguage naturally evolves, in which mistakes are a normal and developmental part of learning, Fu and Li (2020) suggest that errors should not be corrected immediately. This approach acknowledges that as learners advance, many errors may resolve themselves through increased exposure and practice, either controlled or uncontrolled. Therefore, teachers may not need to pay much attention to consistent mistakes but errors that occur systematically, focusing primarily on persistent errors that cannot be resolved in other ways. Mackey and Philp (1998) support this view, arguing that delayed feedback might be more effective in the long run because learners gain a deeper understanding of linguistic structures in the learning process, making them notice, process, and integrate feedback when it is given at a more advanced stage of their learning journey. Considering that language learning is a process, I would argue that error correction should not be deemed to provide "instant feed" but facilitate SLA and language development. Therefore, the teacher's error correction should be focused and relevant to the objectives of the lesson and the course. However, as earlier said, errors may root in many sources and be fossilized, requiring special and intensive rehabilitation (Guijarro Sanz, 2021). Teachers' expectation of absolute rehabilitation in a one-time feedback provision may be a driving force of learning anxiety, reducing classroom interaction (Krashen, 1982; Rahimi, 2015). A plan for using feedback to promote students' L2 development is essential (Yan et al., 2021).

To wrap up, the timing and nature of CF in language teaching is a multifaceted issue that requires careful consideration of various factors. While immediate feedback, occurring shortly after an error or during a task, can be effective for instant correction and reinforcement, delayed feedback, provided after a period of practice, offers opportunities for reflective learning and may be more suitable for errors that resolve themselves over time. The timing of CF in language teaching is a complex decision that hinges on balancing immediate and delayed feedback. Immediate feedback aids in quick correction and reinforcement, especially useful for straightforward errors, while delayed feedback facilitates reflective learning and can be more effective for complex or developmental errors. Preferences for feedback timing can vary between students and teachers, with students often favoring immediacy and teachers leaning towards a mix of both, based on their experience and the learners' needs. Ultimately, the effective use of CF requires a nuanced understanding of the learners' context, the nature of the errors, and the overall learning objectives, making it a tailored and dynamic aspect of language education.

5.4 Learner's Age

In SLA, young learners are known to acquire an additional language differently from adult learners (Ellis, 2015). Larsen-Freeman and Long (2014) further elaborate that the difference in the SLA process between the two groups is ascribed to exposure, language proficiency level, and psychological functioning, suggesting that they process feedback differently. According to Mackey et al. (2003), child dyads were more likely to respond to OCF than adult dyads. The researchers explained that the more willing a child is to accept feedback, the more comfortable they feel from error correction, resulting in their risk-taking inclination. Also, Oliver (2000) found that children exhibited more uptake than adults. The effects of the instructional setting, SLA process (Oliver & Azkarai, 2017), and interaction petterns (Azkarai & Imaz Agirre, 2016) are attributed to students' uptake of the provided feedback.

6. CONCLUSION

In conclusion, it is essential to note that CF is not always used to correct language forms that are supposed to deviate from the expected standards. In practice, teachers might use CF to construct learning and facilitate SLA. OCF, CF delivered orally, can be of two main types: reformulations and prompts. Although some arguments exist about the effectiveness of OCF in the early history of SLA, the contemporary literature shows positive impacts of OCF in recent studies. The effectiveness of OCF should be viewed in relation to what OCF strategies are used, how and by whom they are employed, and if the OCF strategies are appropriate for the context and target learners.

Although OCF is vastly explored and is shown to function differently in different social settings, little attention is so far paid to how to make OCF adaptive to specific cultures. Considering that different cultures may view and respond to OCF differently (Divaharan & Atputhasamy, 2002; Tang & Williams, 2000; Thanh & Gillies, 2010), it may be essential for future investigations to consider the adaptability of OCF in different contexts. In addition, as the advent of technology has provided language education with many innovative measures, researchers can examine the use of online OCF and bichronous online CF compared to offline CF delivered in the traditional face-to-face class.

REFERENCES

Angelucci, T. C., & María Isabel Pozzo, M. I. (2020). Errors and mistakes in foreign language learning: Drawing boundaries from the discourse of Argentine teachers. In E. Vanderheiden & C. Mayer (Eds.), *Mistakes, errors and failures across cultures: Navigating potentials* (pp. 383–398). Springer. doi:10.1007/978-3-030-35574-6_20

Baker, B. A. (2012). Individual differences in rater decision-making style: An exploratory mixed-methods study. *Language Assessment Quarterly*, 9(3), 225–248. doi:10.1080/15434303.2011.637262

Bui, H. P. (2023). Vietnamese university EFL teachers' and students' beliefs and teachers' practices regarding classroom assessment. *Language Testing in Asia*, 13(1), 10. doi:10.1186/s40468-023-00220-w

Bui, H. P., & Nguyen, T. T. T. (2022). Classroom assessment and learning motivation: Insights from secondary school EFL classrooms. *International Review of Applied Linguistics in Language Teaching*, 0(0). Advance online publication. doi:10.1515/iral-2022-0020

Canals, L., Granena, G., Yilmaz, Y., & Malicka, A. (2021). The relative effectiveness of immediate and delayed corrective feedback in video-based computer-mediated communication. *Language Teaching Research*. Advance online publication. doi:10.1177/13621688211052793

Choi, S.-Y., & Li, S. (2012). Corrective feedback and learner uptake in a child ESOL classroom. *RELC Journal*, 43(3), 331–351. doi:10.1177/0033688212463274

Chomsky, N. (1965). *Aspects of the theory of syntax*. MIT Press.

Corder, S. P. (1975). Error analysis, interlanguage and second language acquisition. *Language Teaching*, 8(04), 201–218. doi:10.1017/S0261444800002822

Cumming, A., Kantor, R., & Powers, D. E. (2002). Decision making while rating ESL/EFL writing tasks: A descriptive framework. *Modern Language Journal*, 86(1), 67–96. doi:10.1111/1540-4781.00137

Davis, A. (2003). Teachers' and students' beliefs regarding aspects of language learning. *Evaluation and Research in Education*, 17(4), 207–222. doi:10.1080/09500790308668303

Divaharan, S., & Atputhasamy, L. (2002). An attempt to enhance the quality of cooperative learning through peer assessment. *Journal of Educational Enquiry*, 3(2), 72–83.

Ellis, R. (2015). *The study of second language acquisition* (2nd ed.). Oxford University Press.

Ellis, R. (2017). Oral corrective feedback in L2 classroom: What we know so far. In H. Nassaji & E. Kartchava (Eds.), *Corrective feedback in second language teaching and learning: Research, theory, applications, implications* (pp. 3–18). Taylor & Francis. doi:10.4324/9781315621432-2

Ellis, R. (2021). Explicit and implicit oral corrective feedback. In H. Nassaji & E. Kartchava (Eds.), *The Cambridge handbook of corrective feedback in second language learning and teaching* (pp. 341–364). Cambridge University Press. doi:10.1017/9781108589789.017

Ellis, R., & Barkhuizen, G. (2005). *Analysing learner language*. Oxford University Press.

Fu, M., & Li, S. (2020). The effect of immediate and delayed correcitve feedback on L2 development. *Studies in Second Language Acquisition*, 1–33. doi:10.1017/S0272263120000388

Gielen, S., Peeters, E., Dochy, F., Onghena, P., & Struyven, K. (2010). Improving the effectiveness of peer feedback for learning. *Learning and Instruction*, 20(4), 304–315. doi:10.1016/j.learninstruc.2009.08.007

Guijarro Sanz, M. (2022). Fossilized mistakes in Spanish relative clauses learned by Chinese students. *International Review of Applied Linguistics in Language Teaching*, 60(4), 1227–1251. doi:10.1515/iral-2021-0062

Ha, X. V., & Murray, J. C. (2020). Corrective feedback: Beliefs and practices of Vietnamese primary EFL teachers. *Language Teaching Research*, 27(1), 137–167. doi:10.1177/1362168820931897

Ha, X. V., Nguyen, L. T., & Hung, B. P. (2021). Oral corrective feedback in English as a foreign language classrooms: A teaching and learning perspective. *Heliyon*, 7(7), e07550. doi:10.1016/j.heliyon.2021.e07550

Hartono, D., Basthomi, Y., Widiastuti, O., & Prastiyowati, S. (2022). The impacts of teacher's oral corrective feedback to students' psychological domain: A study on EFL speech production. *Cogent Education*, 9(1), 1–19. doi:10.1080/2331186X.2022.2152619

Hattie, J., & Timperley, H. (2007). The power of feedback. *Review of Educational Research*, 77(1), 81–112. doi:10.3102/003465430298487

Khabbazbashi, M. (2012). *On topic validity in speaking tests.* Cambridge University Press.

Krashen, S. D. (1982). *Principles and practice in second language acquisition.* Pergamon.

Larsen-Freeman, D., & Long, M. H. (2014). *An introduction to second language acquisition research.* Routledge. doi:10.4324/9781315835891

Li, S. (2010). The effectiveness of corrective feedback in SLA: A meta-analysis. *Language Learning, 60*(2), 309–365. doi:10.1111/j.1467-9922.2010.00561.x

Li, S., Ellis, R., & Kim, J. (2018). The influence of pre-task grammar instruction on L2 learning: An experimental study. *Studies in English Education, 23*(4), 831–857. doi:10.22275/SEE.23.4.03

Li, S., & Vuono, A. (2019). Twenty-five years of research on oral and written corrective feedback in System. *System, 84,* 93–109. doi:10.1016/j.system.2019.05.006

Lightbown, P. M., & Spada, N. (1999). *How languages are learned.* Oxford University Press.

Long, M. H. (2007). *Problems in SLA.* Lawrence Erlbaum.

Lyster, R. (2004). Differential effects of prompts and recasts in form-focused instruction. *Studies in Second Language Acquisition, 26*(3), 399–432. doi:10.1017/S0272263104263021

Lyster, R., & Mori, H. (2006). Interactional feedback and instructional counterbalance. *Studies in Second Language Acquisition, 28*(2), 269–300. doi:10.1017/S0272263106060128

Lyster, R., & Saito, K. (2010). Oral feedback in classroom SLA. *Studies in Second Language Acquisition, 32*(2), 265–302. doi:10.1017/S0272263109990520

Lyster, R., Saito, K., & Sato, M. (2013). Oral corrective feedback in second language classrooms. *Language Teaching, 46*(1), 1–40. doi:10.1017/S0261444812000365

Mackey, A., Oliver, R., & Leeman, J. (2003). Interactional input and the incorporation of feedback: An exploration of NS–NNS and NNS–NNS adult and child dyads. *Language Learning, 53*(1), 35–66. doi:10.1111/1467-9922.00210

MacKey, A., & Philp, J. (1998). Conversational interaction and second language development: Recasts, responses, and red herrings? *Modern Language Journal, 82*(3), 338–356. doi:10.1111/j.1540-4781.1998.tb01211.x

Nassaji, H. (2009). Effects of recasts and elicitations in dyadic interaction and the role of feedback explicitness. *Language Learning, 59*(2), 411–452. doi:10.1111/j.1467-9922.2009.00511.x

Nassaji, H. (2015). *The interactional feedback dimension in instructed second language learning: Linking theory, research, and practice.* Bloomsbury.

Nassaji, H. (2016). Anniversary article interactional feedback in second language teaching and learning: A synthesis and analysis of current research. *Language Teaching Research, 20*(4), 535–562. doi:10.1177/1362168816644940

Nassaji, H. (2018). *Errors versus mistakes. Teaching grammar.* doi:10.1002/9781118784235.eelt0059

Nassaji, H., & Kartchava, E. (Eds.). (2021). *The Cambridge handbook of corrective feedback in second language learning and teaching.* Cambridge University Press. doi:10.1017/9781108589789

Nguyen, L. T., & Newton, J. (2021). Enhancing EFL teachers' pronunciation pedagogy through professional learning: A Vietnamese case study. *RELC Journal, 52*(1), 77–93. doi:10.1177/0033688220952476

Oliver, R. (2000). Age differences in negotiation and feedback in classroom and pairwork. *Language Learning, 50*(1), 119–151. doi:10.1111/0023-8333.00113

Oliver, R., & Adams, R. (2021). Oral corrective feedback. In H. Nassaji & E. Kartchava (Eds.), *The Cambridge handbook of corrective feedback in second language learning and teaching* (pp. 187–206). Cambridge University Press. doi:10.1017/9781108589789.010

Oliver, R., & Azkarai, A. (2017). Review of child second language acquisition: Examining theories and research. *Annual Review of Applied Linguistics, 37*, 62–76. doi:10.1017/S0267190517000058

Rahimi, M., & Karkami, F. H. (2015). The role of teachers' classroom discipline in their teaching effectiveness and students' language learning motivation and achievement: A path method. *Iranian Journal of Language Teaching Research, 3*(1), 57–82. https://eric.ed.gov/?id=EJ1127336

Ranta, L., & Lyster, R. (2007). A cognitive approach to improving immersion students' oral language abilities: The awareness-practice-feedback sequence. In R. DeKeyser (Ed.), *Practice in a second language: Perspectives from applied linguistics and cognitive psychology* (pp. 141–160). Cambridge University Press. doi:10.1017/CBO9780511667275.009

Rassaei, E. (2013). Corrective feedback, learners' perceptions, and second language development. *System, 41*(1), 472–483. doi:10.1016/j.system.2013.05.002

Richards, J. C., & Schmidt, R. (2002). *Dictionary of language teaching and applied linguistics* (3rd ed.). Longman.

Roothooft, H., & Breeze, R. (2016). A comparison of EFL teachers' and students' attitudes to oral corrective feedback. *Language Awareness, 25*(4), 318–335. doi:10.1080/09658416.2016.1235580

Saito, K. (2012). Effects of instruction on L2 pronunciation development: A synthesis of 15 quasi-experimental intervention studies. *TESOL Quarterly, 46*(4), 842–854. doi:10.1002/tesq.67

Sato, M. (2017). Oral peer corrective feedback: Multiple theoretical perspectives. In H. Nassaji & E. Kartchava (Eds.), *Corrective feedback in second language teaching and learning: Research, theory, applications, implications* (pp. 19–34). Routledge. doi:10.4324/9781315621432-3

Schachter, J. (1991). Corrective feedback in historical perspective. *Second Language Research, 7*(2), 89–102. doi:10.1177/026765839100700202

Selinker, L. (1972). Interlanguage. *International Review of Applied Linguistics in Language Teaching, 10*(1-4), 209–232. doi:10.1515/iral.1972.10.1-4.209

Sheen, Y. (2004). Corrective feedback and learner uptake in communicative classrooms across instructional settings. *Language Teaching Research, 8*(3), 263–300. doi:10.1191/1362168804lr146oa

Sheen, Y. (2010). Introduction: The role of oral and written corrective feedback in SLA. *Studies in Second Language Acquisition, 32*(2), 169–179. doi:10.1017/S0272263109990489

Sheen, Y. (2011). Comparing oral and written corrective feedback. In Corrective feedback, individual differences and second language learning (pp. 113-127). Springer. doi:10.1007/978-94-007-0548-7_6

Simpson, A., Maltese, A. V., Anderson, A., & Sung, E. (2020). Failures, errors, and mistakes: A systematic review of the literature. In E. Vanderheiden & C. H. Mayer (Eds.), *Mistakes, errors and failures across cultures*. Springer. doi:10.1007/978-3-030-35574-6_18

Swain, M. (1985). Communicative competence: Some roles of comprehensible input and comprehensible output in its development. In S. Gass & C. Madden (Eds.), *Input in second language acquisition* (pp. 235–253). Newbury House.

Tang, T., & Williams, J. (2000). Who have better learning styles - East Asian or Western students? *Proceedings of the fifth European Learning Styles Information Network Conference.*

Thanh, P. T. H., & Gillies, R. (2010). Designing a culturally appropriate format of formative peer assessment for Asian students: The case of Vietnamese students. *International Journal of Educational Reform*, *19*(2), 72–85. doi:10.1177/105678791001900201

Truscott, J. (1999). The case for "The case against grammar correction in L2 writing classes": A response to Ferris. *Journal of Second Language Writing*, *8*(2), 111–122. doi:10.1016/S1060-3743(99)80124-6

Truscott, J. (2007). The effect of error correction on learners' ability to write accurately. *Journal of Second Language Writing*, *16*(4), 255–272. doi:10.1016/j.jslw.2007.06.003

van der Westhuizen, J., Tshabalala, M., & Stanz, K. (2020). Mistakes, errors and failures: Their hidden potential in cultural contexts – The power of a professional culture. In E. Vanderheiden & C. H. Mayer (Eds.), *Mistakes, errors and failures across cultures*. Springer. doi:10.1007/978-3-030-35574-6_30

Vanderheiden, E., & Mayer, C. H. (2020). "There is a crack in everything. That's how the light gets in": An introduction to mistakes, errors and failure as resources. In E. Vanderheiden & C. H. Mayer (Eds.), *Mistakes, errors and failures across cultures*. Springer. doi:10.1007/978-3-030-35574-6_1

Varnosfadrani, A. D., & Basturkmen, H. (2009). The effectiveness of implicit and explicit error correction on learners' performance. *System*, *37*(1), 82–98. doi:10.1016/j.system.2008.04.004

Wong, S. S. H., & Lim, S. W. H. (2018). Prevention–permission–promotion: A review of approaches to errors in learning. *Educational Psychologist*, *54*(1), 1–19. doi:10.1080/00461520.2018.1501693

Yan, Q., Zhang, L. J., & Cheng, X. (2021). Implementing classroom-based assessment for young EFL learners in the Chinese context: A case study. *The Asia-Pacific Education Researcher*, *30*(6), 541–552. doi:10.1007/s40299-021-00602-9

ADDITIONAL READING

Agudo, J., & de, D. M. (2012). An investigation into how EFL learners emotionally respond to teachers' oral corrective feedback. *Colombian Applied Linguistics Journal, 15*, 265–19. doi:10.14483/udistrial.jour.calj.2013.2.a08

Alsolami, R. (2021). Effect of oral corrective feedback on language skills. *Theory and Practice in Language Studies, 9*(6), 672–677. doi:10.17507/tpls.0906.09

Calsiyao, I. S. (2015). Corrective feedback in classroom oral errors among Kalinga-Apayao State College students. *International Journal of Social Science and Humanities Research, 3*(1), 394–400.

Pawlak, M. (2014). *Error correction in the foreign language classroom: Reconsidering the issues.* Springer. doi:10.1007/978-3-642-38436-3

Sakiroglu, H. U. (2020). Oral corrective feedback preferences of university students in English communication classes. *International Journal of Research in Education and Science, 6*(1), 172–178. doi:10.46328/ijres.v6i1.806

KEY TERMS AND DEFINITIONS

Corrective Feedback (CF): Teacher's or peer's feedback used to correct language errors and/or promote language learning.

Oral Corrective Feedback (OCF): Feedback provided orally, usually in the classroom.

Prompts: Hints or suggestions provided by the teacher to address error(s) and to facilitate self-correction.

Recast: A type of corrective feedback for which the teacher provides a form considered acceptable.

Chapter 6
Teaching English Literature in the Vietnamese EFL Context:
Towards a Language and Literature-Integrated Model

Lien-Huong Vo
https://orcid.org/0000-0001-7922-7416
HUFLIS, Hue University, Vietnam

Thanh-Hai L. Cao
HUFLIS, Hue University, Vietnam

ABSTRACT

This chapter is intended as an academic paper that proposes an integrated model of teaching English literature in the EFL courses at higher education level in Vietnam. The chapter begins with an overview of the importance of literature in language teaching and the teaching of English literature in Vietnam. It then presents a discussion of Carter and Long's models of teaching literature in language classes. These models are accompanied with discussion of the challenges EFL teachers encounter while teaching English literature in EFL contexts. The chapter ends with a proposal of an integrated model of teaching English literature in EFL classrooms with ideas and examples of material modification for classroom procedure and activities. The integrated model is expected to help develop students' language skills and proficiency, promote their higher-order thinking skills, and raise their (inter)cultural awareness.

DOI: 10.4018/979-8-3693-3294-8.ch006

1. INTRODUCTION

Language and literature have an undeniable mutually supportive relationship as literature has always been a vivid representation of the recurrent use of language. Literary works, therefore, have been useful sources of authentic material for language teaching (Hişmanoğlu, 2005). Brumfit and Carter (1986) described literature as "an ally of language" (p. 1) in language teaching and learning. Prior to the 1970s, when the grammar-translation approach to language teaching was in its heyday, literary works were used as a source of material typical of complex grammatical rules, which often caused a sense of unease among language learners. As the Communicative Language Teaching (CLT) took the forefront, literature has no longer been a preferred source of teaching material in English as a Foreign Language (EFL) context due to the linguistic and cultural complexity in the literary works. Findings from Truong's (2005) study carried out at a university in Hue, Vietnam showed that 65% of EFL students believed that they learned nothing about language through literature, but on the contrary, they had to be good at language to understand literature. Truong (2005) further explained that the reason behind this was the focus on analyzing the cultural and artistic values of literary works rather than creating opportunities for students to experience the language of literature. However, literature still constitutes a considerable proportion in the EFL curricula because the literary language, by its nature, "embodies a significant aspect of human experience" (Shrawan, 2019, p.2). Therefore, the literary works enable students to be "more familiar with patterns of social interaction in the country which uses the target language" (Collie & Slater, 1987, p.5). Arguably, literary works are still authentic in language classes to enrich learners' cultural and linguistic knowledge and motivate their personal experience and growth (Carter & Long, 1991).

Nonetheless, there arises a question as to how literature is used in language classes to optimize the role of literature in language development, especially in EFL classes where the target language is used almost exclusively within the class. This is the motivation for the current chapter. In this chapter, a big picture of literature in EFL classes and a description of the teaching of English literature in Vietnamese context is provided as a solid ground for the suggested model of teaching – the thrust of this chapter. A review of models of teaching literature (Carter & Long, 1991) is then presented with discussion about the benefits and challenges faced by teachers and learners. Accordingly, an integrated model of teaching literature to EFL classes is proposed, illustrated with ideas and examples of material modification to boost students' language proficiency, encourage students' higher-order thinking skills and raise their (inter)cultural awareness.

2. THE ROLES OF LITERARY WORKS IN EFL CLASSES

The term 'English literature' in this chapter refers to the literature written in the English language about the English-speaking world. In EFL classes, especially in Vietnam, the selected literary works for literature courses are still canonical texts of British and American literature. They come in different genres such as plays, novels, short stories and poems, and they vary in literary ages. For the important relationship between language and literature, literary works should be included in the language teaching, as Collie and Slater (1987) argued, to "develop a broader range of activities which are more involving for our students" (p. 5). In particular, literary works serve the following functions.

First, literary work functions as *authentic material* in language teaching. Although most literary works are not written for language teaching purposes, it exposes learners to actual speech events because its language depicts real-life contexts. Reading literary texts familiarizes learners with different linguistic forms and meanings, as well as communicative functions (Carter & Long, 1991), and so literature strongly supports language learning, accordingly.

Another role of literature is *cultural enrichment* (Isariyawat et al, 2020; Oktan & Kaymakamoğlu, 2017). Foreign language learners are unlikely to have first-hand experience in the target culture. Yet, they can develop their understanding about the society and history through literary works. The world in literary works, though an imagined one, depicts vivid contexts and social backgrounds of the characters in it. The development stages of literature also mirror the development of the country. Readers still understand their thoughts, emotions, and habits, as well as have a picture of what life was like during a certain period.

Literature is also useful for *language enrichment*. It increases the chance of learning a variety of languages. Collie and Slater (1987) argued that "literature provides a rich context in which individual lexical or syntactic items are made more memorable" (p. 7). Through literary works, learners familiarize themselves with linguistic features of the written language and cohesion devices, which improve their writing skills.

In addition, literature motivates learners' *personal involvement*. Literary works are not only universal in their subject matter, but they also allow readers to have an open interpretation. When learners study literary works, they must make inferences based on information in the work as well as connect ideas and events in the work with their own experiences. Therefore, learning English through literary works enables learners' critical reading and improves their emotional awareness (Lazar, 1993).

Although the roles of literature in foreign language classes were examined in Europe in the 1990s, the importance of literature seemed to be overlooked in Asia until the 2000s. Research by scholars in Asian contexts during the past two decades not only have proved the significance of literature in EFL teaching as posited in previous studies, but also have found several contributions of literature to EFL teaching, such as *developing learners' language skills* (Ainy, 2006; Setyowati et al., 2021) and *awareness of cultural differences* Isariyawat et al., 2020), as well as *increasing learners' critical thinking* (Khatib & Alizadeh, 2012) and *pragmatic competence* (Bataineh, 2014).

3. TEACHING ENGLISH LITERATURE IN VIETNAM

In Vietnam, English literature forms part of the compulsory courses in the curricula of programs leading to the bachelor degrees in English language studies. The classroom procedure does not follow a specific model, but it tends to have more characteristics of the cultural model, beginning with the exploration of information related to author, theme, and historical context. While exploring literary works, students read and answer comprehension questions related to the work. This is more like a language model, but it focuses on finding out the values of the literary work in the contemporary period.

Issues related to teaching literature in EFL programs have recently made a comeback and become an attention-getter to many EFL lecturers at higher education levels. Nguyen (2022) investigated the perceptions and practices of teachers in their teaching of English literature. The study, however, is based on the standpoint of English as a Lingua Franca, and thus the research produced similar findings to previous studies rather than explore locally specific findings. Seeing from the perspectives of university students in the Mekong Delta of Vietnam, N. Nguyen's (2023) study showed positive results that students recognized the assistance of literature in improving language knowledge and skills. In another study also conducted in the Mekong Delta, Do (2022) examined the materials used in a literature course as part of the evidence to support his argument about developing students' critical thinking. There has been, however, no proposal of a teaching model that can be applied in the Vietnamese context that satisfies the purpose of teaching language through literature. This makes the present chapter happen as it is of paramount importance to have a model of teaching and adapting material for English literature in EFL classes.

4. CARTER AND LONG'S MODELS OF TEACHING LITERATURE

For the importance of literature in language classes, researchers have made several attempts at teaching models highly effective for the sake of language education. Among these, Carter and Long (1991) proposed the cultural model, the language model and the personal growth model of teaching English literature. These models have been widely applied in language education. Depending on the goals of each teaching model, literature is viewed from different angles, which are summarized subsequently.

4.1 The Cultural Model

This teaching model emphasizes the relationship between culture and literature. Literary works in this model are seen as reflections of culture, and through studying literary works, learners will understand more about the culture and ideological system of the language they are learning. In a typical classroom procedure following this model, the literary work is regarded as a complete product and analyzed based on its cultural and social values, thereby not forgetting to focus on highlighting the author's personal creativity.

The strength of this model is that the aesthetic and artistic values of literary works are communicated to learners thoroughly and deeply. However, this teaching model places too much emphasis on promoting the role of the teacher, and is often carried out in the form of lecturing. Therefore, it does not motivate learners' initiative, which might create a hindrance to promoting a constructive learning environment. In addition, this model of teaching literature requires learners to have a good command of language, something that not all foreign language learners can easily achieve. Learners' insights into target language cultures are also crucial in this model since literary works, especially those belonging to earlier literary movements, are usually embedded with classic references representing cultural values, beliefs and even ideologies in such societies. This can pose challenges to both teachers and learners in decoding literary texts in this vein within the context of EFL in many countries in the expanding and outer circles in which teachers' and learners' intercultural competence still has room for improvement. A further issue that needs to be addressed should the application of this model be carried out is time allotment and resources for preparation on the teachers' part both inside and outside the classroom to ensure a successful teaching and learning experience. Given the time constraints and limited resources that EFL teachers can access, this may seem unfeasible.

4.2 The Language Model

The language model views literature as a source of material for learning a language. As mentioned, literature is the manifestation of language, so it provides the opportunity to come into contact with real-life language for learners, and therefore, it increases their chance to improve language proficiency (Lazar, 1993). In other words, literary works are used in this model for the purpose of expanding learners' knowledge of vocabulary or grammatical structures.

The advantage of this model is that it helps learners grasp common and natural ways of using language. However, this model requires a decent command of linguistic elements ranging from the sounds of English, syntax, morphology, semantics, pragmatics to different varieties of English. Too much emphasis on language itself leads to overlooking the fundamental role of literary works, which are composed primarily to convey the feelings, thoughts, and thoughts of people in real-life context. Moreover, it can be challenging for EFL learners whose language competence can be limited, resulting in more of the learner's efforts being placed on the linguistic features of the texts while overlooking the significance of the work itself. Thus, this teaching model detaches learners from appreciating life values through literary works, narrowing their opportunity of mental and ideological development.

4.3 The Personal Growth Model

This model encourages learners to have a connection between literary works and themselves. In this model, literature is used as a reference source to approach life, and learners are expected to become more mature in consciousness, thought and emotion through understanding and learning from characters in the literary works.

The strength of this model is to stimulate learners' ability to evaluate, and proactively share personal opinions about literary issues, thereby combining linguistic development and cultural appreciation. The teacher acts as a facilitator, helping learners discover the meaning of literary works and draw lessons for themselves. However, there is a lack of clear language focus in this teaching model, overlooking the opportunity to improve learners' language proficiency through literary works. In addition, the focus on learners' experiences and their ability to make connections with the literary texts invariably requires a certain level of language skills among learners to express themselves. EFL learners' relatively limited language skills may prove to be an obstacle. This is further exacerbated by cultural differences, and in many cases, learners' personalities whereby sharing ideas might not be fruitful.

5. AN INTEGRATED MODEL OF TEACHING ENGLISH LITERATURE

Several researchers in language education have tried to adopt an integrated approach to teaching literature in the EFL contexts (Duff & Maley, 1990; Divsar & Tahriri, 2009; Savvidou, 2004; Yimwilai, 2015). While Divsar and Tahriri (2009) and Yimwilai (2015) evaluated the effectiveness of using an integrated model in teaching literature, Duff and Maley (1990) emphasized the importance of using an integrated model in terms of linguistic, methodology and motivation. They aimed their attention at teaching techniques to develop language learners' skills, that is, using a literary text as a material source. Savvidou (2004), inspired by Duff and Maley's (1990) reasons for integrating those three elements into teaching literature in EFL context, proposed an integrated model of six stages. Stage 1 (Preparation and Anticipation) enables learners to experience the setting and theme of the literary work. Stage 2 (Focusing) exposes learners to the content of the literary work via listening or reading activities. Stage 3 (Preliminary Response) asks learners to respond to the content of the literary work via speaking or writing activities. Stages 4 and 5 (Working at it - I & II) let learners explore layers of meanings and the underlying messages, and the special uses of language within the literary work. Stage 6 (Interpretation and Personal Response) enhances learners' understanding and encourages them to develop their own interpretation.

Savvidou's (2004) model was a work of merit for its successful combination of three models suggested by Carter and Long (1991). The cultural model was present in stages 1, 4 and 5 having five out of six stages (stages 1 - 5) focusing on appreciation of literary content and values. Stages 2 and 3 pointed out particular language skills to practice and stage 6 was based on the personal growth model. Although the model combined all three models suggested by Carter and Long (1991), it opted for the cultural model, laying emphasis on literary knowledge.

Unlike Savvidou's (2004) model, the recommended model in this chapter is intended to be a merger of Carter and Long's (1991) three models, constituting a model of three stages, designated as *initiation, exploration,* and *reflection*. This integrated model aims to pinpoint what should be done in each stage in the classroom procedure, as well as what activities should be appropriate for each stage.

The classroom activities to illustrate the recommended teaching model are designed for a class of American literature in which Jerome Weidman's (1935) short story *My father sits in the dark* is taught. There are reasons for the story to be selected for the illustration. The story is not as culture-specific as others of the contemporary and the plot is simple and the image of the character was universal but symbolic (Gold, 2019). The story, therefore, is appropriate for EFL readers, and at the same time provoking universal themes for their discussion such as family relationship, the connection between past and present, and the impacts of the Holocaust.

My father sits in the dark is about a young boy waking up one night and finding his father sitting alone in the dark in the kitchen. The father replied to the boy that he was sitting there thinking about nothing. The young boy saw him sitting in the dark for many nights, and regardless of multiple queries in repeated conversations with his father and his very own speculations, he was unable to fathom the reasons why his father was there. The boy went through an array of emotions, changing from confusion to anger to worries and joy with ultimate relief when, in the end, he seemingly recognized what had been weighing on his father.

Stage 1: Initiation

This stage comprises the preliminary activities that teachers provide to ensure students' readiness for the lesson and stimulate their interest in exploring the literary work. These activities focus on the cultural model, emphasizing the explanation of literary terms, the influences of historical culture on the literary movement of the work, or the socio-cultural features of the literary age. While facilitating students with the readiness, teachers can apply techniques for teaching reading comprehension skills such as brainstorming and prediction to allow more interaction between teachers and learners.

Activity 1: Think Before You Read

1. *Have you ever wondered what people are thinking when you see them sitting alone?*
2. *How do you feel about sitting alone in the dark?*
3. *Do you have any memories that you would like to keep to yourself?*

This activity is similar to a warm-up for its introductory nature. It aims at creating context to familiarize learners with the situation in the literary work. Questions in this activity should be related to the theme of the literary work or, at least, related to the key words in the work.

Activity 2: What Do You Know About This Story?

1. *Who was the main character? Who was the narrator?*
2. *What is the relationship between the main character and the narrator?*
3. *What is the effect of having the narrator involved in the plot and having the narrator as an outsider?*
4. *How is the plot organized? (linear/ episodic/ parallel/ flashback)*

This activity prepares learners with the literary basics. In this activity, literary terms about narrative point of view and plot structure can be introduced to learners.

Stage 2: Exploration

In this stage, learning activities are based on the language model, emphasizing the expansion of the learner's knowledge of the target language. This stage takes up the majority of the time allotted to a literature lesson, with activities maximizing the value of the content and language of literary works. Arguably, both language knowledge and skills are acquired in this stage. Therefore, the activities should aim to develop students' language knowledge (vocabulary and sentence structures) and comprehension skills, so it is necessary to enrich the types of exercises such as multiple choice, matching, gap-filling, inference-making, and jig-saw reading.

Activity 1: Vocabulary

For each of the bold words in the following statements extracted from the story, choose the word or phrase with the closest meaning based on the context by circling A, B, C or D.

1. My father has a **peculiar** habit.
    A. familiar
    B. repeated
    C. special
    D. usual
2. Again I almost **stumble** across my father.
    A. step on
    B. trip over
    C. run
    D. knock
3. He is not **reticent** about that either.
    A. close-lipped
    B. ashamed
    C. worried
    D. anxious
4. And he would not **brood about** them like that.
    A. think happily
    B. care about
    C. remember
    D. grieve over
5. We are a bit **short on** money, but we are long on health.
    A. not have as much of it as one thinks one should
    B. have enough

C. almost not have
D. have plenty
6. I will be **puzzled**.
   A. tricked
   B. unable to understand
   C. surprised
   D. concerned
7. I climb the step softly, skipping the ones that **creak**.
   A. break
   B. make a harsh sound when pressure or weight is applied
   C. make no sounds
   D. open
8. He straightens up with a **jerk**, as though he has been struck.
   A. surprise
   B. smile
   C. sharp movement
   D. slow movement
9. I can see the deeper darkness of his **hunched** shape.
   A. straight
   B. slim
   C. curled up
   D. big
10. I see a small boy, crouched on a pile of twigs at one side of the huge fireplace, his starry **gaze** fixed on the dull remains of the dead flames.
    A. face
    B. head
    C. feature
    D. eyes

This activity helps learners to build up their vocabulary by guessing the meaning of the words in context, which ultimately contributes to enhancing their linguistic competence while simultaneously providing them with a leverage to understand the literary text.

Activity 2: Inference-Making

For each of the following items, please decide which portrays/can be inferred from which character. Put the corresponding letter into the appropriate group.

A. nostalgic about his childhood

B. deeply concerned about the father sitting in the kitchen in the dark
C. understanding and respectful to the father, acting normal
D. open about the family financial situation
E. seems thoughtful
F. determined to find out why the father keeps sitting in the dark
G. careful not to disturb everyone in the family

The father: ....
The son: ....
The mother and the sister: ....

This activity, making inference, helps learners to move beyond simple comprehension. This also lays the foundation for learners to grasp the themes and ultimately the writer's purpose when they engage in the activities in the final stage - reflection.

Stage 3: Reflection

The final stage involves activities developed based on the personal growth model, geared towards fostering learners' skill to reflect and contemplate as well as to make connections between their inner self with the outside world through the universal values inferred from the text. In this stage, teachers create opportunities for learners to express their own opinions and help them explore the social and humanistic values of the work. Activities include group discussion, reflective journals, and writing a new ending for the work. Some examples of these activities are as follows.

Activity 1: Sharing Ideas

In the story, we never meet the son's mother or his sister, but they were mentioned. Discuss what sort of relationship they had with the father?

Activity 2: Writing

Have you ever had a moment in your life when you suddenly understand something about your parents? Describe that moment.

These activities not only promote learners' critical thinking but also enhance learners' language skills for the sake of communicative language teaching. All in all, the model comprises 3 stages. It commences with the initiation stage - eliciting and stimulating learners' background knowledge and interest, which establishes their readiness and willingness to explore the text further while simultaneously enabling them to connect their prior knowledge to the forthcoming information in the lesson.

Subsequently, in the exploration stage, learners are conditioned to develop linguistic skills and knowledge in activities related to language development. Finally, in the reflection stage, learners can reflect on the themes and state or share their opinion in speaking or writing, which ultimately reinforces and builds up not only their outlook but also their communicative competence and language skills.

6. CONCLUSION

This chapter proposed an integrated model of teaching English literature in the Vietnamese context. In this chapter, the significance of literature in general and its role in the context of EFL in particular are highlighted. This is followed by the thorough review of Carter and Long's (1991) three models of teaching English literature in language classes, namely the cultural model, language model and personal growth model. A discussion of the practice of EFL teaching in Vietnam is also provided as a background for the suggested model of teaching literature in EFL classes in Vietnam. The critique of different approaches to combining a variety of teaching models is presented prior to the demonstration of the suggested model – the focus in this chapter – with specific activities designed for a lesson teaching Jerome Weidman's (1935) short story *My father sits in the dark* to EFL learners.

Underlying the suggested model are the principles of flexibility and adaptability merging the three models by Carter and Long. In particular, the model is consisted of three stages including initiation, exploration and reflection. The model can be applied across the board whether on the teaching of a poem, a short story, or an excerpt of a novel or a play. More specifically, this model helps unpack the common aspects found in literary works such as culture, linguistics and philosophy; which allows learners to develop different skills and bodies of knowledge in one lesson. In addition, the application of all the three models gives teachers a certain level of flexibility in designing and delivering lessons. As students may vary as individuals and cohorts, lessons can have a multitude of focuses appropriate for them according to their level of linguistic competence, experience and cultural background. In essence, the model gears towards developing EFL learners' linguistic competence, intercultural communication competence and ultimately critical thinking skills with a focus on the learners in every single stage. The perks of this suggested model is that it pays equal attention to the different components that should be enhanced in EFL learners, taking into consideration the context and challenges in EFL teaching and learning in order to maximize the potential of the original models.

REFERENCES

Ainy, S. (2006). *Use of literature in developing learner's speaking skills in Bangladeshi EFL contexts* [Doctoral dissertation]. University of Nottingham.

Bataineh, A. (2014). The effect of teaching literature on EFL students' pragmatic competence. *Journal of Education and Practice, 5*(3), 137–156.

Brumfit, C. J., & Carter, R. A. (Eds.). (1986). Literature and language teaching. Oxford University Press.

Carter, R. A., & Long, M. N. (1991). *Teaching Literature*. Longman.

Collie, J., & Slater, S. (1987). *Literature in the language classroom: a resource book of ideas and activities*. Cambridge University Press.

Divsar, H., & Tahriri, A. (2009). Investigating the effectiveness of an integrated approach to teaching literature in a EFK context. *Journal of Pan-Pacific Association of Applied Linguistics, 13*(2), 105–116.

Do, N. C. (2002). Vietnamese EFL students' critical thinking in an English literature course. *Journal of Ethnic and Cultural Studies, 9*(1), 77–94.

Duff, A., & Maley, A. (1990). *Literature*. Oxford University Press.

Gold, H. (2019). "My Father Sits in the Dark" by Jerome Weidman. In J. R. Bryer (Ed.), *Why I Like This Story* (pp. 162–167). Boydell & Brewer. doi:10.1017/9781787445352.024

Hişmanoğlu, M. (2005). Teaching English through literature. *Journal of Language and Linguistic Studies, 1*(1), 53–66.

Isariyawat, C., Yenphech, C., & Intanoo, K. (2020). The role of literature and literary texts in an EFL context: Cultural awareness and language skills. *Journal of Language and Linguistic Studies, 16*(3), 1320–1333. doi:10.17263/jlls.803748

Khatib, M., & Alizadeh, I. (2012). Critical thinking skills through literary and non-literary texts in English classes. *International Journal of Linguistics, 4*(4), 563–580. doi:10.5296/ijl.v4i4.2928

Lazar, G. (1993). *Literature and language teaching: a guide for teachers and trainers*. Cambridge University Press. doi:10.1017/CBO9780511733048

Nguyen, T. K. T. (2022). A study of Vietnamese teachers' perceptions and practice in teaching English literature in the context of English as a Lingua Franca. *HNUE Journal of Science, 67*(3), 3–13. doi:10.18173/2354-1075.2022-0039

Nguyen, T. T. N. (2023). Exploring Vietnamese EFL students' perceptions towards literature courses in English Studies program. *International Journal of Language Instruction, 2*(3), 80–96. doi:10.54855/ijli.23234

Oktan, D., & Kaymakamoğlu, S. E. (2017). Using literary texts in EFL classrooms: Cultural awareness and vocabulary enrichment. *International Journal of New Trends in Arts, Sports & Science Education, 6*(4).

Savvidou, C. (2004). An Integrated Approach to Teaching Literature in the EFL Classroom. *The Internet TESL Journal, 10*(12). Available at http://iteslj.org/Techniques/Savvidou-Literature.html

Setyowati, S., Sukmawan, S., & El-Sulukiyyah, A. A. (2021). The effect of literature as authentic materials for writing essays in a blended learning setting. *International Seminar on Language, Education, and Culture, KnE. Social Sciences, 2021*, 195–208.

Shrawan, A. (2019). *The language of literature and its meaning: A comparative study of Indian and western aesthetics.* Cambridge Scholars Publishing.

Truong, K. N. (2005). *Issues of Literature classrooms: An Investigation into the role of Literature in Language Classrooms at Hue College of Sciences* [BA thesis]. Hue University, Vietnam.

Weidman, J. (1935). *My father sits in the dark.* Available at https://msanaknudsen.weebly.com/uploads/9/3/6/8/9368722/my_father_sits_in_the_dark_by_jerome_weidma1.pdf

Yimwilai, S. (2015). An integrated approach to teaching literature in an EFL classroom. *English Language Teaching, 8*(2), 14–21. doi:10.5539/elt.v8n2p14

ADDITIONAL READING

Agathocleous, T., & Dean, A. C. (Eds.). (2003). *Teaching literature: A companion.* Palgrave MacMillan. doi:10.1057/9780230507906

Gonzales, W., & Flores, E. (2016). Stylistics in the Southeast Asian ESL or EFL classroom: A collection of potential teaching activities. *TESOL International Journal, 11*(1), 96–107.

McRea, J. (2002). *Literature with a small 'l': Developing thinking skills in language teaching and learning.* Wayzgoose Press.

Miri, M. A., & Hung, B. P. (2021). Contextualizing second language writing in literature courses: Locality of pedagogy for innovative practices. In *Futuristic and linguistic perspectives on teaching writing to second language students* (pp. 287–306). IGI Global. doi:10.4018/978-1-7998-6508-7.ch017

Sun, X. (2023). Literature in secondary EFL class: Case studies of four experienced teachers' reading programmes in China. *Language Learning Journal, 51*(2), 145–160. doi:10.1080/09571736.2021.1958905

Yopp, R. H., & Yopp, H. K. (2013). *Literature-based reading activities: Engaging students with literary and informational text*. Pearson Education.

KEY TERMS AND DEFINITIONS

Authentic Material: The language product of genuine source used for teaching purposes.

Cultural Awareness: A process of becoming conscious of values and beliefs of a culture.

Integrated Teaching Model: A guide that deliberately combines different teaching principles to achieve many different objectives.

Intercultural Awareness: A process of gaining an understanding about the similarities and differences between one's own culture and other cultures.

Intercultural Communicative Competence: The ability to communicate effectively and appropriately in different cultural context.

Chapter 7

Technology Integration in English Language Education:
An Evolving Paradigm

Truong Cong Bang
https://orcid.org/0000-0001-8840-252X
University of Economics and Law, Ho Chi Minh City, Vietnam & Vietnam National University, Ho Chi Minh City, Vietnam

ABSTRACT

This chapter conducts a comprehensive exploration of technology integration in English language education, chronicling its historical evolution and scrutinizing contemporary pedagogical frameworks amalgamating technological tools. A panoramic examination encompasses digital resources spanning online platforms, mobile applications, virtual/ augmented reality, gamification, and intelligent tutoring systems. Challenges deliberated include the digital divide, teacher training imperative, privacy ramifications, and equilibrating technology with traditional pedagogies. Illustrative case studies and practitioner insights elucidate effective practices. Emerging technologies' potential impact, including artificial intelligence and learning analytics, is probed. The chapter delineates implications for policy, curricula, and teacher education to optimize technology integration. By synthesizing scholarship and pedagogical paradigms, stakeholders are furnished a comprehensive perspective on cultivating engaging, equitable, and efficacious technology-enhanced language learning environments.

1. INTRODUCTION

The pervasive influence of technology has permeated various domains of education, including the field of English language teaching (ELT). The integration

DOI: 10.4018/979-8-3693-3294-8.ch007

of technology in language classrooms has garnered substantial attention due to its potential to enhance language learning and teaching processes (Pegrum, 2019). The rapid advancement of digital tools and resources has catalyzed a transformation in traditional instructional practices, offering novel opportunities for engaging learners and fostering communicative competence in English as a second or foreign language (Dash, 2022; Nehe et al., 2023).

In recent decades, the discipline of English language education has undergone a paradigmatic shift, as educators and researchers have recognized the value of incorporating technology into pedagogical practices. This shift is driven by the acknowledgment that technology can provide a multitude of benefits, such as increased learner motivation, authentic language use, personalized learning experiences, and access to a wealth of online (Negoescu & Mitrulescu, 2023; Nurmala et al., 2023). Furthermore, technology enables teachers to create interactive and collaborative learning environments that align with the principles of communicative language teaching (Kaur et al., 2023; Kim, 2015; Purnama, 2022).

The overarching purpose of this chapter is to provide a comprehensive examination of the role of technology in English language education. Drawing upon current research and pedagogical practices, the chapter aims to explore the evolution of technology integration in language teaching, examine pedagogical approaches and frameworks for incorporating technology, delve into the wide array of digital tools and resources available for English language learning, discuss the challenges and considerations in technology integration, present exemplary technology integration approaches and empirical illustrations, and outline future directions and implications for the field.

By critically analyzing the impact of technology on English language education, this chapter seeks to equip educators, researchers, and policymakers with a profound understanding of the potential benefits and challenges associated with technology integration. Moreover, it endeavors to provide practical insights and recommendations to guide effective technology integration practices in English language classrooms, ultimately contributing to the advancement of language teaching and learning in the digital age.

2. THE EVOLUTIONARY TRAJECTORY OF TECHNOLOGY INTEGRATION IN ENGLISH LANGUAGE EDUCATION

2.1 Historical Perspectives on Technology Adoption in Language Pedagogy

The integration of technology in language teaching has a long and multifaceted history, tracing its origins back to the mid-twentieth century when audio-visual aids were first adopted in educational settings (Chapelle, 2001; Softa, 2022). The introduction of language laboratories and the utilization of audio recordings marked the initial foray into using multimedia resources to enhance language learning experiences (Kumar & Prasad, 2022). As technology progressed, the advent of video and computer technology further expanded the possibilities for incorporating technological tools into language classrooms.

In the 1980s, the field witnessed the emergence of computer-assisted language learning (CALL), a pivotal milestone in the amalgamation of technology and language education (Chapelle, 2001). CALL encompassed a diverse array of computer-based activities and software specifically designed to support language acquisition, providing learners with interactive exercises, multimedia materials, and communication tools (Warschauer & Healey, 1998). This shift towards CALL reflected a growing recognition of the potential of technology to facilitate language learning processes and promote learner autonomy (Benyo, 2020; Lai, 2019).

2.2 Key Technological Advancements and Their Impact on Language Education

Over time, technological advancements have continued to shape and redefine the landscape of English language education. The proliferation of internet connectivity and the rise of mobile devices have revolutionized the way learners engage with language learning resources, creating new opportunities for ubiquitous and flexible learning experiences (Nehe et al., 2023).

Furthermore, the integration of adaptive learning systems and intelligent tutoring technologies has paved the way for personalized instruction, enabling learners to receive tailored feedback and individualized learning paths (Brudermann, 2015; Kupchyk & Litvinchuk, 2021; Zhao, 2020). These technological advancements have not only transformed the learning experiences of English language learners but have also influenced instructional practices, prompting educators to adopt learner-centered approaches and interactive pedagogies that leverage the affordances of technology (Kaur et al., 2023; Nagy, 2021; Nazli & Yahya, 2023).

2.3 Contemporary Landscape of Technology Integration in English Language Classrooms

The current state of technology integration in English language classrooms is characterized by a diverse range of practices and approaches, reflecting the varying degrees of adoption and implementation across different educational contexts. While some educators have fully embraced technology and seamlessly integrated it into their teaching routines, others continue to face challenges in effectively incorporating technology into their instructional contexts (Inyang, 2017; Lubis & Fithriani, 2023).

Research suggests that the integration of technology in English language classrooms is influenced by a multitude of factors, including teacher attitudes, institutional support, access to resources, and pedagogical beliefs (Bui, 2022; Gilakjani, 2012). While some classrooms have successfully adopted a blended learning model, combining face-to-face instruction with online activities (Albatti, 2023), others have implemented a flipped classroom approach, where learners engage with instructional materials online before attending class (Li, 2023; Mohammad & Khan, 2023; Ngo & Yunus, 2021).

Furthermore, the integration of technology has led to shifts in the roles of teachers and learners. Teachers have transitioned from being solely knowledge providers to facilitators, guiding learners in navigating digital resources and fostering critical thinking and digital literacy skills (Kung, 2005; Sinha, 2022). Learners, on the other hand, are encouraged to take ownership of their learning, actively engaging with online platforms and resources to enhance their language proficiency and develop self-regulated learning skills (Ginusti, 2023).

3. PEDAGOGICAL APPROACHES AND FRAMEWORKS FOR TECHNOLOGY INTEGRATION IN ENGLISH LANGUAGE EDUCATION

3.1 Communicative Language Teaching and Technology Integration

Communicative Language Teaching (CLT) has long been established as a prominent pedagogical approach in language education, emphasizing the development of communicative competence through meaningful interaction and authentic language use (Azizah et al., 2022; Bang, 2024). With the advent of digital technologies, CLT has evolved to incorporate a wide range of technological tools and resources, offering new opportunities for facilitating authentic communication and promoting meaningful language production (Teh, 2021).

The integration of technology within the CLT framework underscores the importance of interactive and communicative activities that simulate real-life language contexts (Haider & Chowdhury, 2012). Digital platforms, such as online discussion boards and video conferencing tools, enable learners to engage in collaborative tasks, negotiate meaning, and develop their communicative competence in English through meaningful interactions (Jeong, 2016; Vurdien, 2019).

3.2 Task-Based Language Teaching and Technology-Enhanced Tasks

Task-Based Language Teaching (TBLT) provides a framework for language instruction that centers on the completion of authentic, meaning-focused tasks (Guía et al., 2016; Huang, 2022). The integration of technology in TBLT has expanded the range of task possibilities and enriched the learning experience, offering new avenues for task design and implementation (Zhang, 2023).

Technology-enhanced tasks in TBLT leverage a wide array of digital resources, such as multimedia materials, online simulations, and virtual environments, to create engaging and interactive learning opportunities (Mısır, 2018). These tasks promote language production, negotiation of meaning, and the development of critical thinking skills, as learners engage with authentic, technology-mediated tasks that mirror real-world language use (Lee, 2002; Petek & Bedir, 2018).

3.3 Content and Language Integrated Learning (CLIL) and Technology Integration

Content and Language Integrated Learning (CLIL) represents an approach that integrates the teaching of language and subject matter, enabling learners to develop language proficiency while simultaneously acquiring subject-specific knowledge and skills (McDougald et al., 2023; Sujana et al., 2023). Technology integration in CLIL classrooms provides learners with access to authentic content materials, multimedia resources, and interactive platforms for language practice and content exploration (Begimbetova et al., 2022; Pellegrino et al., 2013).

The use of technology in CLIL enables learners to explore disciplinary content in English, develop subject-specific language proficiency, and engage in meaningful language use within a disciplinary context (Arnó-Macià & Mancho-Barés, 2015; Nikula, 2015). Digital tools, such as online databases, simulations, and content creation platforms, support the seamless integration of language and content learning in CLIL classrooms, facilitating the development of academic language proficiency and subject matter knowledge (Marenzi et al., 2010; Oddone, 2011; Yaguara et al., 2021).

3.4 Blended Learning Models: Integrating Face-to-Face and Online Instruction

Blended learning models combine face-to-face instruction with online learning activities, providing a flexible and interactive learning environment that leverages the strengths of both modalities (Batista-Toledo & Gavilan, 2022). In English language education, blended learning models have gained prominence due to their potential to effectively integrate technology and promote learner engagement and autonomy (Stanlee et al., 2022).

In English language classrooms, blended learning models combine in-person communication and interaction with a wide range of online resources, including multimedia materials, virtual classrooms, and online assessments (Albatti, 2023; Nassar et al., 2023). This approach allows for individualized learning experiences, increased learner autonomy, and access to a diverse range of digital resources, fostering language development and promoting learner-centered pedagogies (Menggo & Darong, 2022; Nassar et al., 2023).

3.5 Flipped Classroom Approaches: Leveraging Technology for Pre-Class Instruction

Flipped classroom approaches involve the reversal of traditional instructional practices, where learners engage with instructional materials online before class, and face-to-face class time is dedicated to interactive and collaborative activities (Ngo & Yunus, 2021). Technology integration plays a central role in facilitating the implementation of the flipped classroom model in English language education.

In a flipped classroom setting, technology enables learners to access instructional videos, online tutorials, and interactive exercises outside the classroom, promoting self-paced learning and personalized instruction. This approach allows for individualized learning experiences, tailored feedback, and efficient use of class time, which can be dedicated to communicative activities, language practice, and teacher-guided discussions (Ngo & Yunus, 2021). The flipped classroom model, facilitated by technology integration, supports learner autonomy, active engagement, and the development of communicative competence in English language classrooms.

4. EMERGING DIGITAL TOOLS AND RESOURCES FOR FACILITATING ENGLISH LANGUAGE ACQUISITION

4.1 Online Language Learning Platforms and Applications

The advent of online language learning platforms and applications has significantly transformed the landscape of English language education, providing a wealth of interactive resources and opportunities for learners to engage with the target language (Pichugin et al., 2022). These platforms leverage multimedia capabilities, virtual classrooms, and automated feedback mechanisms to create immersive and personalized learning experiences, thereby enhancing language acquisition and practice (Hampel & Stickler, 2012). Prominent examples include Duolingo, Rosetta Stone, and Babbel, which offer self-paced instruction tailored to individual learners' needs and schedules (Li & Bonk, 2023). The cross-platform accessibility of these resources via web browsers and mobile applications further amplifies their utility, allowing learners to seamlessly integrate language learning into their daily routines.

4.2 Mobile Applications for English Language Learning

In tandem with the ubiquity of smartphones and tablets, mobile applications have emerged as indispensable tools for English language learning, offering a multitude of resources and features (Kannan & Meenakshi, 2023). These applications encompass a wide range of language learning activities, including vocabulary builders, grammar exercises, pronunciation practice, and interactive language games, catering to diverse learning preferences and objectives (Fan et al., 2023; Rocque, 2022). Applications such as Memrise, Quizlet, and HelloTalk have gained significant traction due to their ability to facilitate on-the-go language learning, enabling learners to engage with English anytime and anywhere (Abarghoui & Taki, 2018; Al-Jarf, 2022; Wibowo & Raihani, 2019). The portability and convenience of mobile devices, coupled with these applications' personalized learning features, contribute to an enhanced and individualized language instruction experience (Kukulska-Hulme, 2016).

4.3 Virtual Reality (VR) and Augmented Reality (AR) in Language Education

Virtual Reality (VR) and Augmented Reality (AR) technologies have garnered considerable attention in language education due to their potential to create immersive and engaging learning environments. VR facilitates the transportation of learners into realistic and interactive virtual contexts, enabling them to practice language skills in simulated real-world scenarios (Dooly et al., 2023). AR, on the other hand, enhances the physical environment by overlaying digital information and language learning resources, providing learners with contextual support and enriched learning experiences (Weerasinghe et al., 2022). Applications such as Google Expeditions and AR-enabled language learning apps offer learners opportunities to explore cultural landmarks, interact with virtual objects, and engage in language-rich activities, thereby fostering a deeper understanding and application of the target language (Ebadi & Ebadijalal, 2022; Shadiev & Liang, 2024).

4.4 Gamification and Game-Based Language Learning

Gamification and game-based learning have emerged as effective strategies for enhancing learner engagement, motivation, and language acquisition in English language education. Gamified language learning platforms, such as Kahoot! and Quizlet Live, incorporate game elements such as leaderboards, badges, and rewards to create a competitive and enjoyable learning environment, thereby increasing learner participation and retention (Liu et al., 2022; Pham & Duong, 2022; Waluyo & Bucol, 2021).

Game-based learning, which involves the use of educational video games, simulations, and interactive storytelling, immerses learners in authentic language-rich contexts, promoting problem-solving, social interaction, and incidental language acquisition (Pereira, 2013). Games such as "The Sims" and "LingoBee" exemplify this approach, providing learners with engaging and enjoyable opportunities to practice language skills while fostering critical thinking and collaboration (Petersen et al., 2013; Wang, 2019).

4.5 Adaptive Learning Systems and Intelligent Tutoring for Personalized Instruction

Adaptive learning systems and intelligent tutoring systems leverage artificial intelligence (AI) algorithms to provide personalized instruction and support to English language learners, catering to their individual needs and learning styles (Troussas et al., 2019). These systems analyze learner performance data and dynamically adjust the content, difficulty level, and learning pathways, offering tailored feedback and scaffolding to address specific language proficiency gaps (Tafazoli et al., 2019). Prominent platforms such as Duolingo and Babbel employ adaptive algorithms to continuously assess learners' proficiency levels and adapt the exercises accordingly, ensuring an optimal balance between challenge and support (Kalsoom et al., 2024). By providing individualized instruction and targeted scaffolding, intelligent tutoring systems aim to enhance learner engagement, retention, and overall language acquisition outcomes.

5. CHALLENGES AND CONSIDERATIONS IN TECHNOLOGY INTEGRATION

5.1 Addressing the Digital Divide and Inequities in Technology Access

The digital divide, characterized by disparities in access to technology resources and internet connectivity, poses a formidable challenge to the integration of technology in English language learning (Chuang et al., 2010; Yaman, 2015). Learners from socioeconomically disadvantaged backgrounds or marginalized communities often lack access to essential devices, reliable internet connections, and digital literacy skills necessary for fully engaging with technology-enabled language learning opportunities. This uneven access to technology exacerbates existing educational inequalities, perpetuating disparities in language learning experiences and outcomes (Zhao, 2023). Bridging the digital divide requires concerted efforts from policymakers, educational institutions, and stakeholders. Comprehensive strategies encompassing infrastructure development, resource allocation, and targeted initiatives to provide equitable access to technology tools and training are imperative to ensure inclusive and equitable technology integration in English language education.

5.2 Enhancing Teacher Training and Professional Development for Effective Technology Integration

Effective integration of technology in English language learning hinges on the pedagogical expertise and technical proficiency of teachers (Nurmala et al., 2023). However, many educators face challenges in integrating digital tools due to inadequate training and limited opportunities for professional development (Soepriyanti et al., 2022). To address this gap, comprehensive professional development programs focused on cultivating teachers' technological pedagogical content knowledge (TPACK) are essential. Such programs should equip teachers with the skills to select appropriate digital tools, design technology-enhanced language learning activities, and provide meaningful feedback to learners (Adipat et al., 2023). Ongoing support, collaboration among teachers, teacher educators, and technology specialists, as well as opportunities for continuous learning and knowledge-sharing, are crucial for successful and sustained technology integration in language classrooms (Nurmala et al., 2023).

5.3 Prioritizing Privacy, Security, and Ethical Considerations in Technology Use

The integration of technology in language learning raises critical concerns related to privacy, security, and ethical considerations (Cassell, 2023). The collection and storage of learners' personal data, including sensitive information, by technology platforms and digital tools pose potential risks of privacy breaches. Furthermore, the prevalence of cyberbullying, online harassment, and exposure to inappropriate content can jeopardize learners' well-being and safety (Afifa et al., 2022). To mitigate these risks, policymakers, educators, and technology developers must prioritize data protection measures, informed consent processes, and the creation of secure digital environments. Establishing clear guidelines and ethical frameworks that safeguard learners' privacy and ensure responsible technology use in language education is paramount (Alier et al., 2021). Ongoing vigilance, stakeholder collaboration, and adherence to best practices are necessary to uphold ethical standards and protect learners in technology-enhanced language learning contexts.

5.4 Balancing Technology Integration with Traditional Pedagogical Approaches

Integrating technology in English language learning necessitates striking a judicious balance between digital tools and traditional teaching approaches (Kassem, 2018). While technology offers innovative and interactive learning opportunities, it should complement, rather than replace, face-to-face interactions, authentic language use, and meaningful teacher-student interactions that are essential for language acquisition (Guillén et al., 2020).

Educators must carefully consider the pedagogical goals, learning outcomes, and learner needs when selecting and integrating technology tools (Nurmala et al., 2023). A thoughtful blend of technology-enhanced activities and traditional classroom practices can create a synergistic learning environment that maximizes language learning outcomes and fosters a well-rounded educational experience (A, 2019).

5.5 Evaluating and Assessing Technology-Enhanced Language Learning

The evaluation and assessment of technology-enhanced language learning present unique challenges and considerations that necessitate innovative approaches (Akintunde & Angulu, 2020). Traditional assessment methods may not adequately capture learners' digital literacy skills, collaborative competencies, or creative use of technology tools in language learning contexts. To address this gap, alternative assessment strategies, such as portfolio assessment, self-assessment, and performance-based tasks, should be incorporated to holistically evaluate learners' technology-mediated language skills (Bahrani, 2011; Moqbel & Al-Kadi, 2023). Furthermore, the development of reliable and valid assessment instruments specifically designed for technology-enhanced language learning is crucial to ensure accurate measurement of learners' progress, proficiency, and achievement of learning outcomes in technology-integrated language learning environments.

6. TECHNOLOGY INTEGRATION IN ENGLISH LANGUAGE EDUCATION: PRACTICES AND EMPIRICAL EVIDENCE

6.1 Successful Implementations and Promising Pedagogical Approaches

A burgeoning body of literature has documented successful examples of technology integration in English language education, illustrating promising practices for enhancing language learning and teaching (Nurmala et al., 2023). One such practice is the implementation of the flipped classroom model, where instructional content is delivered online, and class time is dedicated to interactive activities and language practice. This approach has demonstrated positive outcomes for language learners, fostering active engagement and language skill development (Li, 2022).

Another promising practice involves the utilization of online discussion forums and collaborative writing platforms, such as Google Docs, which facilitate peer interaction, feedback, and revision in language learning (Purwaningtyas et al., 2023). These digital tools promote learner autonomy, foster a sense of community, and enhance language proficiency through collaborative processes.

Furthermore, the integration of authentic multimedia resources, including podcasts, videos, and online news articles, has been shown to enhance learners' listening and reading comprehension skills, as well as their cultural awareness (Kozhevnikova, 2014; Tan et al., 2010). Engaging with authentic materials exposes learners to real-world language use and promotes authentic language production (Mohammed, 2023).

6.2 Experiences and Insights from Practitioners and Researchers

Practitioners and researchers have contributed valuable experiences and insights regarding technology integration in English language education, providing guidance for effective implementation (Kumar et al., 2022). Case studies and action research projects have investigated various aspects of technology integration, such as the use of mobile applications, online learning platforms, and virtual reality, elucidating their benefits and challenges (Abarghoui & Taki, 2018; Dooly et al., 2023; Pichugin et al., 2022; Rocque, 2022).

Additionally, practitioner reflections and narratives have offered firsthand accounts of technology integration, highlighting the impact on learners, pedagogical approaches, and instructional design (Gönen, 2019; Lyddon, 2019). These qualitative insights provide a rich understanding of the practical considerations, successes, and limitations of technology integration in diverse educational contexts.

6.3 Lessons Learned and Recommendations for Effective Technology Integration

The cumulative lessons learned from successful technology integration initiatives in English language education have yielded valuable recommendations for effective implementation (Kumar et al., 2022). Paramount among these recommendations is the necessity for a pedagogical approach that aligns with language learning goals to guide technology integration efforts (Lyddon, 2019). Technology should be utilized purposefully and meaningfully to enhance language learning experiences, rather than being perceived as an end in itself.

Moreover, ongoing professional development and support for teachers are crucial to ensure effective technology integration (Nurmala et al., 2023). Teachers require opportunities to develop their technological and pedagogical skills, collaborate with colleagues, and share best practices. Furthermore, a learner-centered approach that promotes learner autonomy, collaboration, and critical thinking should underpin technology-enhanced language learning (Benyo, 2020; Lai, 2019).

Lastly, careful evaluation and assessment of technology integration initiatives are necessary to inform future practices and make evidence-based decisions (Bui, 2022). Evaluation frameworks and tools should be employed to assess the impact on language learning outcomes, learner engagement, and overall effectiveness (Nurmala et al., 2023). By collecting and analyzing data, educators and researchers can identify areas for improvement and make informed decisions regarding technology integration in English language education.

7. FUTURE DIRECTIONS AND IMPLICATIONS

7.1 Emerging Technologies and Their Potential Impact

The field of English language education stands to be profoundly transformed by rapid technological advancements. Emerging technologies such as artificial intelligence (AI), machine learning, virtual reality (VR), and augmented reality (AR) hold immense potential to revolutionize language learning and teaching practices.

AI and machine learning algorithms can facilitate personalized and adaptive instruction, intelligent tutoring systems, and interactive language assistants (Weng & Chiu, 2023). AI-powered chatbots and virtual assistants can simulate authentic conversations, providing learners with real-time feedback and opportunities for naturalistic language practice (Fryer et al., 2019). These technologies can enhance learner engagement, motivation, and ultimately, language proficiency.

Furthermore, VR and AR technologies offer immersive and interactive learning environments (Dooly et al., 2023). Learners can explore virtual contexts, engage in simulated communicative scenarios, and participate in interactive language tasks. These technologies have the potential to foster authentic language use, cultural understanding, and meaningful engagement with the target language (Ebadi & Ebadijalal, 2022).

7.2 Anticipated Trends and Developments in Technological Integration

Several emerging trends and developments are anticipated to shape the landscape of technology integration in English language education. Mobile learning is poised for continued growth, as learners increasingly turn to smartphones and tablets for language learning purposes (Alharbi, 2021). Mobile applications, gamified learning platforms, and social media tools are expected to play a pivotal role in promoting learner engagement, collaboration, and informal language learning opportunities (Thurairasu, 2022).

The Internet of Things (IoT) has the potential to transform language learning environments by connecting physical objects, wearables, smart classrooms, and language learning tools to the internet (Shinde & Bhangale, 2017). IoT-enabled language learning environments can provide real-time data, personalized learning experiences, and seamless integration of digital tools. Additionally, the advent of big data analytics and learning analytics is anticipated to inform instructional design, provide personalized feedback, and support data-driven decision-making (Ru, 2022; Volk et al., 2015).

7.3 Implications for Policy, Curriculum Design, and Teacher Education

The integration of technology in English language education necessitates a comprehensive approach addressing policy, curriculum design, and teacher education. Policymakers must recognize the significance of technology integration, allocate resources to bridge the digital divide, ensure equitable access, and establish guidelines for responsible and ethical technology use. Furthermore, policy initiatives should support professional development programs that equip teachers with the necessary technological and pedagogical skills (Adipat et al., 2023; Nurmala et al., 2023).

Curriculum designers should incorporate technology integration as an integral component of language learning goals, fostering digital literacies, multimodal communication, and intercultural competencies. The design of technology-enhanced language learning activities should align with communicative language teaching principles, facilitating authentic language use and meaningful interaction (Guillén et al., 2020).

Teacher education programs play a crucial role in preparing educators to effectively integrate technology into their pedagogical practices (Adipat et al., 2023; Nurmala et al., 2023). Pre-service and in-service training programs should equip teachers with technological and pedagogical knowledge and skills, provide hands-on experiences with emerging technologies, and cultivate a reflective and inquiry-based approach to technology integration. Ongoing professional development opportunities are essential to ensure teachers remain up-to-date with rapidly evolving technologies and best practices.

8. CONCLUSION

8.1 Synopsis of Salient Considerations

The present chapter has undertaken an examination of the integration of technology into English language education, accentuating its potential to augment the processes of language acquisition and instruction. Paramount topics elucidated encompass successful exemplars of technology integration within the realm of English language education, insights and experiential accounts from practitioners and researchers, lessons gleaned, and recommendations for effectual technology integration. Moreover, the chapter has scrutinized emerging technologies and anticipated trajectories in technology integration, together with their prospective impact on English language education. Ultimately, the implications for policy formulation, curriculum design, and teacher education have been deliberated upon in light of technology integration.

8.2 The Salience of Technology in English Language Education

The exploration of technology integration in English language education underscores its significance within contemporary contexts of language learning. Technology proffers opportunities to engage learners, foster interactive and authentic language use, promote learner autonomy, and furnish personalized feedback. It enables access to authentic materials, facilitates collaboration and communication, and enhances language proficiency. Furthermore, technology integration addresses the evolving needs and expectations of learners in the digital age, preparing them for communication and interaction in an increasingly interconnected world.

8.3 Exhortation for Further Research and Exploration in the Discipline

While significant strides have been accomplished in technology integration within English language education, a multitude of areas remain to be explored and researched. Further investigation is warranted to explore the optimal utilization of emerging technologies such as artificial intelligence, virtual reality, and the Internet of Things. Research should be focused on comprehending the impact of technology integration on various facets of language learning, including linguistic, cognitive, affective, and sociocultural dimensions. Additionally, research is necessitated to inform policy development, guide curriculum design, and enhance teacher education programs in relation to technology integration. By addressing these lacunae in research, the field can advance our understanding of effective technology integration in English language education and inform pedagogical practices for the benefit of learners and educators alike.

In conclusion, technology integration holds great promise for English language education, providing opportunities to enhance language learning experiences and outcomes. By embracing emerging technologies, considering the implications for policy and curriculum design, and fostering ongoing research and exploration, educators can harness the potential of technology to create engaging, effective, and inclusive language learning environments.

ACKNOWLEDGMENT

Funding for this project was provided by the University of Economics and Law, Ho Chi Minh City, Vietnam. I would like to express my sincere gratitude to the University for their support in making this research possible.

REFERENCES

A, A. M. (2019). The use of technology in English language teaching. *Frontiers in Education Technology, 2*(3), 168-180. doi:10.22158/fet.v2n3p168

Abarghoui, M. A., & Taki, S. (2018). Measuring the effectiveness of using "Memrise" on high school students' perceptions of learning EFL. *Theory and Practice in Language Studies, 8*(12), 1758–1765. doi:10.17507/tpls.0812.25

Adipat, S., Chotikapanich, R., Laksana, K., Busayanon, K., Piatanom, P., Ausawasowan, A., & Elbasouni, I. (2023). Technological pedagogical content knowledge for professional teacher development. *Academic Journal of Interdisciplinary Studies, 12*(1), 173–182. doi:10.36941/ajis-2023-0015

Afifa, S., Yelfiza, Y., & Merina, Y. (2022). Cyberbullying found in commentary on English educational Youtube channel for high school students. *Edumaspul: Jurnal Pendidikan, 6*(1), 717–722. doi:10.33487/edumaspul.v6i1.2039

Akintunde, A. F., & Angulu, Y. D. (2020). Technology in language learning: An effective innovation but not without Its challenges. *Sapientia Foundation Journal of Education Sciences and Gender Studies, 2*(4), 25–35.

Al-Jarf, R. (2022). Learning vocabulary in the app store by EFL college students. *International Journal of Social Science And Human Research, 5*(1), 216–225. doi:10.47191/ijsshr/v5-i1-30

Albatti, H. (2023). Blended learning in English language teaching and learning: A focused study on a reading and vocabulary building course. *World Journal of English Language, 13*(5), 121–130. doi:10.5430/wjel.v13n5p121

Alharbi, B. (2021). Mobile learning age: Implications for future language learning skills. *Psychology (Savannah, Ga.), 58*(2), 862–867. doi:10.17762/pae.v58i2.1960

Alier, M., Guerrero, M. J. C., Amo, D., Severance, C., & Fonseca, D. (2021). Privacy and e-learning: A pending task. *Sustainability (Basel), 13*(9206), 1–17. doi:10.3390/su13169206

Arnó-Macià, E., & Mancho-Barés, G. (2015). The role of content and language in content and language integrated learning (CLIL) at university: Challenges and implications for ESP. *English for Specific Purposes, 37*, 63–73. doi:10.1016/j.esp.2014.06.007

Azizah, S. N., Supriyono, Y., & Andriani, A. (2022). Projecting communicative language teaching (CLT) implementation in teaching spoken language at secondary school. *Journal of English Teaching Applied Linguistics and Literatures*, *5*(2), 179–197. doi:10.20527/jetall.v5i2.12873

Bahrani, T. (2011). Technology as an assessment tool in language learning. *International Journal of English Linguistics*, *1*(2), 295–298. doi:10.5539/ijel.v1n2p295

Bang, T. C. (2024). English in higher education: navigating Vietnam's academic landscape. In H. P. Bui, T. C. Bang, & C. H. Nguyen (Eds.), *Teacher and student perspectives on bilingual and multilingual education* (pp. 34–50). IGI Global. doi:10.4018/979-8-3693-5365-3.ch003

Batista-Toledo, S., & Gavilan, D. (2022). Implementation of blended learning during COVID-19. *Encyclopedia*, *2*(4), 1763–1772. doi:10.3390/encyclopedia2040121

Begimbetova, G., Abdigapbarova, U., Abdulkarimova, G., Pristupa, E., Issabayeva, D., & Kurmangaliyeva, N. (2022). *Use of ICT in CLIL-classes for the future teachers training*. 2022 the 4th International Conference on Modern Educational Technology (ICMET), New York.

Benyo, A. (2020). CALL in English language teaching. *International Journal of Advanced Science and Technology*, *29*(3), 1390–1395. http://sersc.org/journals/index.php/IJAST/article/view/6098

Brudermann, C. A. (2015). Computer-mediated online language learning programmes vs. tailor-made teaching practices at university level: A foul relationship or a perfect match? *Open Learning*, *30*(3), 267–281. doi:10.1080/02680513.2015.1100069

Bui, T. H. (2022). English teachers' integration of digital technologies in the classroom. *International Journal of Educational Research Open*, *3*, 1–15. doi:10.1016/j.ijedro.2022.100204

Cassell, M. (2023). Language technology applications: Current developments and future implications. *Journal of Linguistics and Communication Studies*, *2*(2), 83–89. doi:10.56397/JLCS.2023.06.11

Chapelle, C. A. (2001). *Computer applications in second language acquisition: foundations for teaching, testing and research*. Cambridge University Press. doi:10.1017/CBO9781139524681

Chuang, H.-H., Yang, Y.-F., & Liu, H.-C. (2010, December). *What digital divide factors matter in the motivation to use technology to learn English? A case of low SES young learners in Taiwan.* 2009 Joint Conferences on Pervasive Computing (JCPC), Tamsui, Taiwan.

Dash, B. B. (2022). Digital tools for teaching and learning English language in 21st century. *International Journal of English and Studies*, 4(2), 8–13. doi:10.47311/IJOES.2022.4202

Dooly, M., Thrasher, T., & Sadler, R. (2023). "Whoa! incredible!:" language learning experiences in virtual reality. *RELC Journal*, 54(2), 321–339. doi:10.1177/00336882231167610

Ebadi, S., & Ebadijalal, M. (2022). The effect of Google Expeditions virtual reality on EFL learners' willingness to communicate and oral proficiency. *Computer Assisted Language Learning*, 35(8), 1975–2000. doi:10.1080/09588221.2020.1854311

Fan, X., Liu, K., Wang, X., & Yu, J. (2023). Exploring mobile apps in English learning. *Journal of Education. Humanities and Social Sciences*, 8, 2367–2374. doi:10.54097/ehss.v8i.4996

Fryer, L. K., Nakao, K., & Thompson, A. (2019). Chatbot learning partners: Connecting learning experiences, interest and competence. *Computers in Human Behavior*, 93, 279–289. doi:10.1016/j.chb.2018.12.023

Gilakjani, A. P. (2012). An analysis of factors affecting the ue of computer technology in English language teaching and learning. *International Journal of Information and Education Technology*, 2(2), 135–142. doi:10.7763/IJIET.2012.V2.96

Ginusti, G. N. (2023). The implementation of digital technology in online project-based learning during pandemic: EFL students' perspectives. *J-SHMIC: Journal of English for Academic*, 10(1), 13–25. doi:10.25299/jshmic.2023.vol10(1).10220

Gönen, S. İ. K. (2019). A qualitative study on a situated experience of technology integration: Reflections from pre-service teachers and students. *Computer Assisted Language Learning*, 32(3), 163–189. doi:10.1080/09588221.2018.1552974

Guía, E., Camacho, V. L., Orozco-Barbosa, L., Luján, V. M. B., Penichet, V. M. R., & Pérez, M. L. (2016). Introducing IoT and wearable technologies into task-based language learning for young children. *IEEE Transactions on Learning Technologies*, 9(4), 366–378. doi:10.1109/TLT.2016.2557333

Guillén, G., Sawin, T., & Avineri, N. (2020). Zooming out of the crisis: Language and human collaboration. *Foreign Language Annals*, *53*(2), 320–328. doi:10.1111/flan.12459

Haider, M. Z., & Chowdhury, T. A. (2012). Promoting CLT within a computer assisted learning environment: A survey of the communicative English course of FLTC. *English Language Teaching*, *5*(8), 91–102. doi:10.5539/elt.v5n8p91

Hampel, R., & Stickler, U. (2012). The use of videoconferencing to support multimodal interaction in an online language classroom. *ReCALL*, *24*(2), 116–137. doi:10.1017/S095834401200002X

Huang, J. (2022). Task-based language teaching and rigorous instruction in beginning English as a second language classrooms. *New Directions for Adult and Continuing Education*, *2022*(175), 59–70. doi:10.1002/ace.20468

Inyang, J. B. (2017). The use of information and communication technologies (ICTS) in foreign language teaching in Nigeria: Prospects and challenges. *International Journal of Arts and Humanities*, *6*(1), 124–134. doi:10.4314/ijah.v6i1.11

Jeong, K.-O. (2016). Integrating a web-based platform to promote creativity and authenticity in language classrooms. *International Journal of Knowledge and Learning*, *11*(2), 127–136. doi:10.1504/IJKL.2016.079752

Kalsoom, T., Jabeen, S., Alshraah, S. M., Khasawneh, M. A. S., & Al-Awawdeh, N. (2024). Using technological-based models as digital tutors for enhancing reading and writing proficiency of foreign language undergraduates. *Kurdish Studies*, *12*(1), 1716–1733. doi:10.58262/ks.v12i1.118

Kannan, M., & Meenakshi, S. (2023). A critical overview of the implementation of language-immersion through the use of mobile apps. *Theory and Practice in Language Studies*, *13*(1), 186–191. doi:10.17507/tpls.1301.21

Kassem, M. A. M. (2018). Balancing technology with pedagogy in English language classroom: Teachers' perspective. *International Journal of English Language Teaching*, *6*(9), 1–19.

Kaur, D. J., Saraswat, N., & Alvi, I. (2023). Technology-enabled language leaning: Mediating role of collaborative learning. *Journal of Language and Education*, *9*(1), 89–101. doi:10.17323/jle.2023.12359

Kim, S. H. (2015). Communicative language learning and curriculum development in the digital environment. *Asian Social Science*, *11*(12), 337–352. doi:10.5539/ass.v11n12p337

Kozhevnikova, E. (2014). Exposing students to authentic materials as a way to increase students' language proficiency and cultural awareness. *Procedia: Social and Behavioral Sciences*, *116*, 4462–4466. doi:10.1016/j.sbspro.2014.01.967

Kukulska-Hulme, A. (2016). *Personalization of language learning through mobile technologies*. Cambridge University Press.

Kumar, M. N., & Prasad, B. B. N. (2022). Acquisition of English language through language laboratories- a paradigm shift in language learning. *International Journal of English Learning and Teaching Skills*, *4*(4), 1–9. doi:10.15864/ijelts.4409

Kumar, T., Shet, J. P., & Parwez, M. A. (2022). Technology-integration experiences in ELT classrooms as an effective tool: A theoretical study. *Journal for Educators. Teachers and Trainers*, *13*(1), 51–60. doi:10.47750/jett.2022.13.01.006

Kung, S.-C. (2005). Guiding EFL learners in the use of web resources. *GEMA: Online Journal of Language Studies*, *5*(2), 50–62.

Kupchyk, L., & Litvinchuk, A. (2021). Constructing personal learning environments through ICT mediated foreign language instruction. *Journal of Physics: Conference Series*, *1840*(1), 1–15. doi:10.1088/1742-6596/1840/1/012045

Lai, C. (2019). Technology and learner autonomy: An argument in favor of the nexus of formal and informal language learning. *Annual Review of Applied Linguistics*, *39*, 52–58. doi:10.1017/S0267190519000035

Lee, L. (2002). Enhancing learners' communication skills through synchronous electronic Iiteraction and task-based instruction. *Foreign Language Annals*, *35*(1), 16–24. doi:10.1111/j.1944-9720.2002.tb01829.x

Li, F. (2022). The impact of the flipped classroom teaching model on EFL learners' language learning: Positive changes in learning attitudes, perceptions and performance. *World Journal of English Language*, *12*(5), 136–147. doi:10.5430/wjel.v12n5p136

Li, G. (2023). On flipped classroom teaching of college English listening under the "Internet Plus" model. *Frontiers in Educational Research*, *6*(6), 101–104. doi:10.25236/FER.2023.060622

Li, Z., & Bonk, C. J. (2023). Self-directed language learning with Duolingo in an out-of-class context. *Computer Assisted Language Learning*, 1–23. Advance online publication. doi:10.1080/09588221.2023.2206874

Liu, Y.-J., Zhou, Y.-G., Li, Q.-L., & Ye, X.-D. (2022). Impact study of the learning effects and motivation of competitive modes in gamified learning. *Sustainability (Basel)*, *14*(11), 1–14. doi:10.3390/su14116626

Lubis, N. H., & Fithriani, R. (2023). Investigating vocational high school teachers' challenges in integrating computer assisted instruction (CAI) into EFL classes. *Jurnal Paedagogy, 10*(3), 809–819. doi:10.33394/jp.v10i3.7731

Lyddon, P. A. (2019). A reflective approach to digital technology implementation in language teaching: Expanding pedagogical capacity by rethinking substitution, augmentation, modification, and redefinition. *TESL Canada Journal, 36*(3), 186–200. doi:10.18806/tesl.v36i3.1327

Marenzi, I., Kupetz, R., Nejdl, W., & Zerr, S. (2010). *Supporting active learning in CLIL through collaborative search. International Conference on Web-Based Learning*, Shanghai, China. 10.1007/978-3-642-17407-0_21

McDougald, J. S., Gómez, D. P. D., Gutiérrez, L. S. Q., & Córdoba, F. G. S. (2023). Listening to CLIL practitioners: An overview of bilingual teachers' perceptions in Bogota. *Colombian Applied Linguistics Journal, 25*(1), 97–117. doi:10.14483/22487085.18992

Menggo, S., & Darong, H. C. (2022). Blended learning in ESL/EFL class. *LLT Journal: A Journal on Language and Language Teaching, 25*(1), 132-148. doi:10.24071/llt.v25i1.4159

Mısır, H. (2018). Digital literacies and interactive multimedia-enhanced tools for language teaching and learning. *International Online Journal of Education & Teaching, 5*(3), 514–523.

Mohammad, T., & Khan, S. I. (2023). Flipped classroom: An effective methodology to improve writing skills of EFL students. *World Journal of English Language, 13*(5), 468–474. doi:10.5430/wjel.v13n5p468

Mohammed, A. M. K. A. (2023). Authenticity in the language classroom and its effect on ELF learners' language proficiency. *Brock Journal of Education, 11*(1), 78–87. doi:10.37745/bje.2023/vol11n17889

Moqbel, M. S. S., & Al-Kadi, A. M. T. (2023). Foreign language learning assessment in the age of ChatGPT: A theoretical account. *Journal of English Studies in Arabia Felix, 2*(1), 71–84. doi:10.56540/jesaf.v2i1.62

Nagy, T. (2021). Using technology for foreign language learning: The teacher's role. *Central European Journal of Educational Research, 3*(2), 23–28. doi:10.37441/cejer/2021/3/2/9347

Nassar, Y. H., Al-Motrif, A., Abuzahra, S., Aburezeq, I. M., Dweikat, F. F., Helali, M. M., ... Gimeno, A. R. (2023). The impacts of blended learning on English education in higher education. *World Journal of English Language, 13*(6), 449–458. doi:10.5430/wjel.v13n6p449

Nazli, K., & Yahya, U. (2023). The role of computer-assisted language learning (CALL) in language teachers' professional development. *Pakistan Languages and Humanities Review, 7*(1), 1–11. doi:10.47205/plhr.2023(7-I)01

Negoescu, A. G., & Mitrulescu, C. M. (2023). Using technology to increase students' motivation for learning a foreign language. *International conference: Knowledge-based Organization, 29*(2), 210-214. 10.2478/kbo-2023-0059

Nehe, B. M., Mualimah, E. N., Bastaman, W. W., Arini, I., & Purwantiningsih, S. (2023). Exploring English learners' experiences of using mobile language learning applications. *Jurnal Teknologi Pendidikan, 25*(1), 76–90. doi:10.21009/jtp.v25i1.34883

Ngo, H. K., & Yunus, M. M. (2021). Flipped classroom in English language teaching and learning: A systematic literature review. *International Journal of Academic Research in Business & Social Sciences, 11*(3), 185–196. doi:10.6007/IJARBSS/v11-i3/8622

Nikula, T. (2015). Hands-on tasks in CLIL science classrooms as sites for subject-specific language use and learning. *System, 54*, 14–27. doi:10.1016/j.system.2015.04.003

Nurmala, I., Irianto, S., Franchisca, S., Amsa, H., & Susanti, R. (2023). Technology-enhanced language learning: A meta-analysis study on English language teaching tools. *Journal of Education, 6*(1), 2188–2195. doi:10.31004/joe.v6i1.3221

Oddone, C. (2011). Using videos from YouTube and websites in the CLIL classroom. *Studies about. Languages (Basel, Switzerland), 0*(18), 105–110. doi:10.5755/j01.sal.0.18.417

Pegrum, M. (2019). *Mobile lenses on learning languages and literacies on the move*. Springer., doi:10.1007/978-981-15-1240-7

Pellegrino, E., Santo, M. D., & Vitale, G. (2013). Integrating learning technologies and autonomy: a CLIL course in linguistics. *Procedia- Social and Behavioral Sciences, 106*(2023), 1514-1522. doi:10.1016/j.sbspro.2013.12.171

Pereira, J. (2013). Video game meets literature: language learning with interactive fiction. *E-TEALS: AN E-JOURNAL of Teacher Education and Applied Language Studies, 4*, 19-45.

Petek, E., & Bedir, H. (2018). An adaptable teacher education framework for critical thinking in language teaching. *Thinking Skills and Creativity, 28*, 56–72. doi:10.1016/j.tsc.2018.02.008

Petersen, S. A., Procter-Legg, E., & Cacchione, A. (2013). Creativity and mobile language learning using LingoBee. *International Journal of Mobile and Blended Learning, 5*(3), 34–51. doi:10.4018/jmbl.2013070103

Pham, T. N., & Duong, D. T. (2022). Using Kahoot! in vocabulary learning: Evidence from a Vietnamese higher education context. *VNU Journal of Foreign Studies, 38*(3), 138–152. doi:10.25073/2525-2445/vnufs.4849

Pichugin, V., Panfilov, A., & Volkova, E. (2022). The effectiveness of online learning platforms in foreign language teaching. *World Journal on Educational Technology: Current Issues, 14*(5), 1357–1372. doi:10.18844/wjet.v14i5.7861

Purnama, Y. (2022). The use of information and communication technology as learning sources in English language learning. *International Journal of Multidisciplinary Research and Analysis, 5*(9), 2302–2304. doi:10.47191/ijmra/v5-i9-02

Purwaningtyas, T., Nurkamto, J., & Kristina, D. (2023). EFL teacher intervention in mediating students' interaction in web-based collaborative writing environment using Google Docs. *Voice of English Language Education Society, 7*(1), 135–144. doi:10.29408/veles.v7i1.7912

Rocque, S. R. (2022). Evaluating the effectiveness of mobile applications in enhancing learning and development. *International Journal of Innovative Technologies in Social Science, 3*(35), 1–8. doi:10.31435/rsglobal_ijitss/30092022/7847

Ru, M. (2022). Research on the new model of data-driven teaching decision-making for university minority language majors. *Frontiers in Psychology, 13*, 1–8. doi:10.3389/fpsyg.2022.901256

Shadiev, R., & Liang, Q. (2024). A review of research on AR-supported language learning. *Innovation in Language Learning and Teaching, 18*(1), 78–100. doi:10.1080/17501229.2023.2229804

Shinde, K., & Bhangale, R. (2017). A model based on IoT for improving programming language skills among students. *International Journal of Students'. Research Technology Management, 5*(2), 38–40. doi:10.18510/ijsrtm.2017.521

Sinha, K. K. (2022). Role of modern technology in teaching and learning the English language in Indian educational institutions. *Indonesian Journal of English Language Studies, 8*(2), 71–82. doi:10.24071/ijels.v8i2.4713

Soepriyanti, H., Waluyo, U., Syahrial, E., & Hoesni, R. K. (2022). Pre-service English teachers' lived experiences in implementing technology for teaching practice. *Technium Education and Humanities, 3*(1), 16–26. doi:10.47577/teh.v3i1.7810

Softa, V. L. (2022). Technology as a method of teaching and learning foreign languages. *Intercultural Communication, 1*(7), 81–90. doi:10.13166/ic/712022.4948

Stanlee, T. J., Swanto, S., Din, W. A., & Edward, E. I. (2022). English language educators' approaches to integrate technology in the 21st century education practices. *International Journal of Education Psychology and Counseling, 7*(48), 301–307. doi:10.35631/IJEPC.748022

Sujana, I. M., Waluyo, U., Fitriana, E., & Sudiarta, I. W. (2023). The potentials and limitations of applying content and language integrated learning (CLIL) approach to English teaching for medical students. *World Journal of English Language, 13*(2), 331–335. doi:10.5430/wjel.v13n2p331

Tafazoli, D., María, E. G., & Abril, C. A. H. (2019). Intelligent language tutoring system: Integrating intelligent computer-assisted language learning into language education. *International Journal of Information and Communication Technology Education, 15*(3), 60–74. doi:10.4018/IJICTE.2019070105

Tan, H. Y.-J., Kwok, J. W.-J., Neo, M., & Neo, T.-K. (2010, December 5-8). *Enhancing student learning using multimedia and web technologies: students' perceptions of an authentic learning experience in a Malaysian classroom.* ASCILITE- Australian Society for Computers in Learning in Tertiary Education Annual Conference, Sydney, Australia.

Teh, W. (2021). Communicative language teaching (CLT) in the context of online learning: A literature review. *International Journal of TESOL & Education, 1*(2), 65–71. doi:10.11250/ijte.01.02.004

Thurairasu, V. (2022). Gamification-based learning as the future of language learning: An overview. *European Journal of Humanities and Social Sciences, 2*(6), 62–69. doi:10.24018/ejsocial.2022.2.6.353

Troussas, C., Chrysafiadi, K., & Virvou, M. (2019). An intelligent adaptive fuzzy-based inference system for computer-assisted language learning. *Expert Systems with Applications, 127*, 85–96. doi:10.1016/j.eswa.2019.03.003

Volk, H., Kellner, K., & Wohlhart, D. (2015). Learning analytics for English language teaching. *Journal of Universal Computer Science, 21*(1), 156–174.

Vurdien, R. (2019). Videoconferencing: Developing students' communicative competence. *Journal of Foreign Language Education and Technology, 4*(2), 269–298.

Waluyo, B., & Bucol, J. L. (2021). The impact of gamified vocabulary learning using Quizlet on low-proficiency students. *Computer-Assisted Language Learning Electronic Journal, 22*(1), 158-179.

Wang, J. Q. (2019). Classroom intervention for integrating simulation games into language classrooms: An exploratory study with the SIMs 4. *CALL-EJ, 20*(2), 101–127.

Warschauer, M., & Healey, D. (1998). Computers and language learning: An overview. *Language Teaching, 31*(2), 57–71. doi:10.1017/S0261444800012970

Weerasinghe, M., Biener, V., Grubert, J., Quigley, A. J., Toniolo, A., Pucihar, K. Č., & Kljun, M. (2022). Vocabulary: Learning vocabulary in AR supported by keyword visualisations. *IEEE Transactions on Visualization and Computer Graphics, 28*(11), 3748–3758. doi:10.1109/TVCG.2022.3203116

Weng, X., & Chiu, T. K. F. (2023). Instructional design and learning outcomes of intelligent computer assisted language learning: Systematic review in the field. *Computers and Education: Artificial Intelligence, 4*, 1–12. doi:10.1016/j.caeai.2022.100117

Wibowo, H., & Raihani, S. (2019). The effectiveness of Hellotalk app on English writing skills. *Lingua Jurnal Pendidikan Bahasa, 15*(2). Advance online publication. doi:10.34005/lingua.v15i2.581

Yaguara, J. A., Salinas, N. P. V., & Caviche, J. C. O. (2021). Exploring the implementation of CLIL in an EFL virtual learning environment. *Latin American Journal of Content and Language Integrated Learning, 14*(2), 187–214. doi:10.5294/laclil.2021.14.2.1

Yaman, İ. (2015). Digital divide within the context of language and foreign language teaching. *Procedia: Social and Behavioral Sciences, 176*, 766–771. doi:10.1016/j.sbspro.2015.01.538

Zhang, Y. (2023). Research on technology-mediated task-based teaching approach in oral English teaching based on the Chinese context. *Frontiers in Humanities and Social Sciences, 3*(6), 12–16. doi:10.54691/fhss.v3i6.5137

Zhao, B. X. (2023). Educational inequality: The role of digital learning resources. *Lecture Notes in Education Psychology and Public Media*, *7*(1), 634–642. doi:10.54254/2753-7048/7/2022980

Zhao, Y. (2020). A personalized English teaching design based on multimedia computer technology. *International Journal of Emerging Technologies in Learning*, *15*(8), 210–222. doi:10.3991/ijet.v15i08.13695

ADDITIONAL READING

Hsiao, I.-C. V., Hung, S.-T. A., & Huang, H.-T. D. (2023). The flipped classroom approach in an English for specific purposes (ESP) course: A quasi-experimental study on learners' self-efficacy, study process, and learning performances. *Journal of Research on Technology in Education*, *55*(3), 507–526. doi:10.1080/15391523.2021.1976329

Lai, Y., Saab, N., & Admiraal, W. (2022). University students' use of mobile technology in self-directed language learning: Using the integrative model of behavior prediction. *Computers & Education*, *179*, 1–13. doi:10.1016/j.compedu.2021.104413

Moorhouse, B. L., Kohnke, L., & Wan, Y. (2023). A systematic review of technology reviews in language teaching and learning journals. *RELC Journal*, *54*(2), 426–444. doi:10.1177/00336882221150810

Rintaningrum, R. (2023). Technology integration in English language teaching and learning: Benefits and challenges. *Cogent Education*, *10*(1), 1–21. doi:10.1080/2331186X.2022.2164690

Stockwell, G., & Reinders, H. (2019). Technology, motivation and autonomy, and teacher psychology in language learning: Exploring the myths and possibilities. *Annual Review of Applied Linguistics*, *39*, 40–51. doi:10.1017/S0267190519000084

KEY TERMS AND DEFINITIONS

Blended Learning: An instructional approach that combines face-to-face classroom instruction with online learning activities and resources.

Computer-Assisted Language Learning (CALL): The use of computers, digital technologies, and multimedia resources to support and facilitate language learning processes.

Digital Tools: Various technological resources and applications used in language learning, such as online platforms, mobile apps, virtual/augmented reality, gamification, and intelligent tutoring systems.

Flipped Classroom: A pedagogical model where students engage with instructional content online before class, and class time is dedicated to interactive activities, discussions, and collaborative work.

Learning Analytics: The measurement, collection, analysis, and reporting of data about learners and their contexts, with the purpose of understanding and optimizing learning and the environments in which it occurs.

Technological Pedagogical Content Knowledge (TPACK): A framework that describes the knowledge teachers need to effectively integrate technology into their teaching practices, comprising an understanding of content, pedagogy, and technology.

Chapter 8

The Impact of Visual Corrective Feedback on Pronunciation Accuracy in L2 Sound Production:
Empirical Evidence

Rizgar Qasim Mahmood
 https://orcid.org/0000-0002-5987-8884
The University of Wollongong, Australia

ABSTRACT

This chapter investigates the influence of visual corrective feedback (henceforth VCF) techniques on enhancing pronunciation accuracy among ESL learners (N = 40) from various countries and L1 backgrounds. Utilizing a mixed-methods approach, the research examines the efficacy of various VCF modalities, such as interactive software: Praat and YouGlish, in improving learners' pronunciation skills. Quantitative analysis involves pre- and post-assessment of pronunciation accuracy using standardized metrics. At the same time, qualitative data is gathered through learner interviews to gauge perceptions and experiences with VCF methods. The findings suggest a significant correlation between the use of VCF and enhanced vowel production accuracy. Additionally, the qualitative insights reveal positive learner attitudes towards VCF tools, highlighting their motivational and corrective influences on pronunciation improvement. This study offers several theoretical and pedagogical implications.

DOI: 10.4018/979-8-3693-3294-8.ch008

The Impact of Visual Corrective Feedback on Pronunciation Accuracy

1. INTRODUCTION

In the realm of second language acquisition (SLA), the importance of corrective feedback (CF) for rectifying learners' linguistic errors has been widely acknowledged as a crucial factor in the successful learning of a second language (L2), especially in L2 accurate pronunciation. L2 pronunciation accuracy remains a critical dimension of language acquisition, influencing effective communication and overall proficiency (Nguyen & Hung, 2021). Over the last 30 years, research has highlighted the significance of CF in language learning (Ellis et al., 2008; Liakina & Liakin, 2023; Lyster & Ranta, 1997; Mahmood, 2023). In this sense, CF can be seen as one of the methods of providing more input to L2 learners, previous scholars emphasized the role of input in L2 improvement. One type of input is through auditory or visual aids (Alahmadi, 2019; Ellis, 2015; VanPatten et al., 2004). The auditory and visual elements of language input play crucial roles in the development of accurate pronunciation skills (Derwing & Munro, 2005). In the past four decades, significant technological progress has given rise to various speech analysis tools. Among these, is the visual corrective feedback (VCF), also known as electronic visual feedback. The typical current VCF setup involves (a) a nonnative speaker recording the stimuli; (b) a visual representation of speech features, typically focusing on intonation contours; (c) a visual display comparing the nonnative speaker's production with that of a native speaker, often accompanied by corresponding auditory feedback; and (d) the nonnative participant re-recording in an attempt to replicate native-speaker productions (Olson, 2014; Olson, 2022; Olson & Offerman, 2021).

In recent years, there has been a notable focus on providing CF in L2 pronunciation teaching and instruction, responding to the heightened interest in L2 pronunciation (Lyster et al., 2013; Mahmood, 2023; Saito & Lyster, 2012). Various methods of CF provision, including explicit and implicit approaches, have been employed. With the advancement of technology, particularly the integration of computer-based programs, L2 pronunciation teaching has taken a significant leap forward. The use of learning technology, especially automatic speech recognition (ASR), presents a multitude of new possibilities for language pronunciation training (Chen, 2011; Hao-Jan Chen et al., 2024; Hsieh et al., 2023). The increasing speed of computers and the integration of multimedia enable the creation of more interactive and personalized learning environments, promising to enhance the traditional classroom model of language learning (Bashori et al., 2022).

Moreover, studies have explored the potential application of computer tools in developing a computer-assisted language learning system (CALL) (Wang & Young, 2012) and have assessed the effectiveness of CF within the system for learners across different age groups (Chau & Bui, 2023; Chen, 2022; Nazir et al., 2023; O'Brien et al., 2018). These investigations consistently indicated that learners, both adults and young learners, exhibited improved English pronunciation with detailed CF. However, limited research has delved into a specific type of pronunciation feedback – visual feedback – comprehensively.

While the existing literature has delved into the broader spectrum of CF, a notable gap exists concerning the specific exploration of VCF using computer programs. Previous studies have often explored the effects of visual CF without a comprehensive examination of the potential advantages brought by integrating advanced technological tools. This study aims to bridge this gap by scrutinizing how VCF, enhanced through the computer program: Praat, can contribute to L2 pronunciation accuracy. Furthermore, the integration of YouGlish as a tool for providing authentic pronunciation examples represents a novel approach in L2 pronunciation research. YouGlish, a web-based platform that sources authentic video examples from native speakers worldwide, offers learners exposure to diverse accents and contexts. Despite the potential benefits, limited research has systematically investigated its role in improving pronunciation accuracy within the framework of VCF. Previous studies have predominantly focused on homogeneous groups of ESL/EFL learners sharing similar cultural and language backgrounds (Offerman & Olson, 2023; Olson, 2022; Rehman & Flint, 2021). This homogeneity overlooks the diverse linguistic and cultural backgrounds that learners bring to the language learning environment. To address this gap, the present study emphasizes the necessity of examining the effects of VCF on learners' sound production from various cultural and language backgrounds. By doing so, this study aims to unravel potential variations in the effectiveness of VCF across a diverse learner population.

In this study, two vowels: /ɪ/ and /iː/ are under examination. These two close-front consonants are characterized by a high degree of constriction in the vocal tract and are produced with the tongue positioned close to the front of the mouth (Hillenbrand et al., 1995; Roach, 2009). These sounds are widely represented in languages worldwide and play a crucial role in speech perception and production. Their linguistic significance lies in their frequent occurrence in many languages' phonological systems, where they often serve as phonemic contrasts, distinguishing between different words or grammatical forms and have a high functional load. For instance, in English, the close front vowels /ɪ/ and /iː/ differentiate words like "bit" and "beat", respectively (Bohn & Flege, 1992; Rang & Moran, 2014; Suzukida & Saito, 2021). Moreover, the acoustic properties of close front consonants make them particularly interesting for study. They are characterized by high-frequency energy and relatively stable formant patterns, contributing to their perceptual salience in speech (Georgiou, 2022; Ladefoged & Johnson, 2014; Pillai & Delavari, 2012).

Therefore, this study has twofold significance: It contributes empirical evidence to the broader field of L2 pronunciation and offers practical insights for educators and curriculum developers. Understanding the efficacy of VCF, particularly within the context of modern technological tools, can inform pedagogical practices and enhance language learning experiences. Additionally, exploring the impact of VCF on learners from diverse backgrounds adds a crucial layer of understanding to facilitate more inclusive and effective language instruction. Therefore, this study addresses the following research questions.

1. To what extent does visual corrective feedback improve ESL learners' production of /ɪ/ and /iː/?
2. How do ESL learners perceive visual corrective feedback in teaching the sounds /ɪ/ and /iː/?

2. LITERATURE REVIEW

2.1. Theoretical Framework

Second Language Acquisition (SLA) is a complex phenomenon influenced by various theoretical perspectives. This study is grounded in the Interaction Hypothesis (IH) (Long, 1996), Sociocultural Theory (Vygotsky, 1978), and the Noticing Hypothesis proposed by Schmidt (1990). Together, these theories offer a comprehensive framework for understanding the role of CF, particularly in the visual domain, in the development of accurate pronunciation in second language learners.

The interaction hypothesis and the interaction approach as expounded by Michael Long and others (Carroll, 1999; Gass & Mackey, 2020; Long, 1996; Long, 1981), assert that language acquisition is intrinsically tied to meaningful interaction and feedback. In the context of second language pronunciation, this theory underscores the importance of CF in guiding learners towards linguistic accuracy. The concept of negotiation for meaning suggests that learners, through interactions, receive immediate feedback on linguistic errors, facilitating the refinement of their pronunciation skills. Moreover, the theory emphasizes the role of modified input, where feedback serves as a tool to expose learners to corrected forms, aiding in the internalization of accurate pronunciation.

Sociocultural Theory, rooted in the works of Lev Vygotsky (Vygotsky, 1978), posits that language learning is intricately linked to social interactions, cultural contexts, and collaborative learning experiences. Additionally, Schmidt's Noticing Hypothesis (1990) suggests that conscious awareness of L2 forms or differences between L1 and L2 forms is crucial for L2 development. In the realm of second language pronunciation, these theories collectively propose that VCF aligns with sociocultural and noticing perspectives. VCF operates within the Zone of Proximal Development (ZPD), providing a scaffold for learners just beyond their current proficiency level. It mediates cultural aspects of language learning by exposing learners to diverse accents and contexts, contributing to a richer sociolinguistic understanding (Lantolf, 2000, 2006; Lantolf, 2024; Lantolf & Pavlenko, 1995; Rassaei, 2014). The integration of technology, including computer-based programs and platforms like Praat and YouGlish, enhances social interaction in language learning, aligning with the sociocultural emphasis on the role of collaborative and interactive experiences in language development (Glăveanu et al., 2019; Ramani et al., 2019).

In this study, the integration of VCF situated within the intersection of Interaction hypothesis, Sociocultural, and Noticing theories, positions VCF as a pivotal element in the enhancement of second language pronunciation. Through tools like Praat and YouGlish, learners receive visual cues that complement traditional auditory feedback. The visual dimension serves to make linguistic forms more salient, aligning with the principles of interactionism. Simultaneously, it provides a culturally and socially rich learning experience, supporting sociocultural and noticing theories by exposing learners to diverse language use in authentic contexts. In addition to that, through the lens of the theoretical framework, the critical role of VCF in contributing to the nuanced understanding and improvement of second language pronunciation is emphasized. By adopting a comprehensive theoretical framework, this study aims to unravel the complex dynamics at play in the language acquisition process, offering insights that have implications for both theory and pedagogical practices in second language education.

2.2 The Importance of L2 Pronunciation Teaching

Mastering pronunciation is not only a fundamental aspect of effective communication but also holds the potential for fostering positive interactions and contributing values to various facets of life reliant on language and interpersonal effectiveness (Levis, 2018, 2022; O'Brien et al., 2018). Pronunciation, a much more significant and pervasive feature of communication than generally recognized, serves as the crucial starting point for all spoken language. Thoughts must be articulated in sound to be heard and transformed into a communicable message, making pronunciation indispensable for meaningful communication. Its significance extends beyond mere speech; pronunciation is essential for effective communication, ensuring that the conveyed message is not only audible but also comprehensible (Derwing & Munro, 2015; Derwing et al., 1998; Isaacs, 2009; Rochma, 2023).

Conversely, inadequate pronunciation, encompassing both individual phonemes and prosodic elements, can impede the understanding of the intended message and the interpretation of the underlying meaning. In more severe cases, it may lead to significant miscommunication, misunderstandings, and negative attitudes, and become a factor in discriminatory linguistic profiling, perpetuating various forms of social disadvantage (Levis, 2018, 2022).

The accuracy of pronunciation involves articulating phonemes in a manner that aligns with the recognized norms of a specific linguistic community. Achieving high accuracy necessitates the ability to both perceive and produce phonemes and their variations according to the established standards (Bohn & Flege, 2021; Flege, 1987; Jenkins, 2000; O'Brien, 2004). This process may involve redefining production targets to move away from inaccuracies, particularly those rooted in a different speech community or language, especially in the case of language learners and their native language (L1) (Flege, 1987).

Attaining pronunciation accuracy is facilitated by focusing on auditory features and sound articulation in both isolated and contextualized settings. However, dedicating attention to pronunciation can divert time and focus from other aspects of communication that typically demand speakers' attention. As a result, speakers often strive to automate pronunciation by following well-known routines for articulating phonemes and realizing broader phonological patterns of coarticulation and prosody (Flege et al., 1997; Flege et al., 1999; Piske et al., 2001).

In recent decades, the global prominence of English as an international language has reignited interest in pronunciation within L2 classrooms. It is now recognized as an integral component of effective communication. Contrastingly, historical approaches, such as listen-and-repeat exercises and situational language teaching, placed significant emphasis on the accurate pronunciation of individual sounds. These methods involved articulatory explanations, imitation, and memorization of language patterns through drills and dialogues, with a strong focus on correction (Larsen-Freeman & Anderson, 2013; Morley, 1991).

The role of pronunciation in communication surpasses general recognition, emerging as a pivotal and pervasive aspect. Serving as the fundamental gateway to spoken language, pronunciation plays a critical role as thoughts must be expressed in sound to be heard and transformed into a communicable message. Its significance extends beyond mere speech; pronunciation is essential for effective communication, ensuring that the conveyed message is not only audible but also comprehensible. The clarity of a person's pronunciation is vital, allowing listeners to discern words from the flow of speech and assemble them into meaningful, coherent patterns. Additionally, pronunciation projects information about the speaker and the communication context, leaving a distinct impression and establishing a shared foundation between the speaker and the listener, crucial for fostering effective communication (Levis & Pickering, 2004; Levis, 2022; Mahmood, 2023; O'Brien, 2004; O'Brien et al., 2018).

2.3 Technology and L2 Pronunciation Teaching

Technology is poised to play a pivotal role in the revitalization of pronunciation, as it has the potential to enhance and complement traditional teaching methods (Fouz-González, 2015; O'Brien et al., 2018). This is achieved by offering more personalised feedback and training opportunities (Hincks, 2015). Moreover, technology can alleviate the burden on teachers by facilitating autonomous learning and reducing the necessity for constant feedback (McCrocklin, 2016). The significance of technology has been particularly pronounced in recent years, especially during the global closure of schools due to the COVID-19 pandemic, where educators were compelled to transition to online instruction (Chau & Bui, 2023; Pastor, 2020).

In the area of pronunciation instruction, there has been a relatively limited focus on methodologies, with an emerging trend supporting the utilization of technology, particularly visualization. Speech analysis technology, offering visual depictions of speech features such as intonation, intensity, and formant transitions, is being explored for its potential in pronunciation instruction. The pedagogical implementation of visual representation varies, encompassing models of native speaker (NS) pronunciation, audio-visual modelling of NS productions, and simultaneous displays of L2 participant-produced speech alongside NS models (Offerman & Olson, 2016).

Initial studies predominantly delved into the effectiveness of VCF concerning suprasegmental features, especially intonation contours. While these studies have provided valuable insights (Anderson-Hsieh, 1992, 1994), there has been a more limited exploration of the consonantal level. Notably, Olson (2014) investigated the impact of VCF and model comparison, using spectrograms and waveforms, on the production of voiced stops by English-speaking learners of Spanish.

It is crucial to acknowledge that accurate pronunciation encompasses not only consonants but also vowels. Existing research, while promising, has primarily addressed consonantal aspects. For instance, Olson's work focused on voiced stops, leaving a gap in our understanding of the effects of VCF on learners' vowel accuracy. Therefore, further studies are warranted to comprehensively investigate the impact of VCF on improving learners' proficiency in vowel pronunciation.

Recently, Cengiz (2023) conducted a review of research on computer-assisted pronunciation teaching in L2 classes spanning the years 2010 to 2021. The analysis encompassed 26 studies, revealing that educators predominantly employed technologies in L2 instruction, particularly at the university level. Furthermore, the outcomes indicated that teachers played a crucial role in enhancing the efficacy of computer-assisted pronunciation teaching by providing support, motivation, and guidance to learners utilizing Computer-Assisted Pronunciation Training (CAPT) or technological tools. Similarly, Olson and Offerman (2021) investigated the effects of

VCF on L2 learners' pronunciation on consonant production, and the results revealed a noteworthy and enduring influence of VCF on L2 pronunciation. To be more specific, when L2 learners were given visual representations of both their utterances and those of NSs in the target language, facilitating a comparison process, there was a considerable decrease in Voice Onset Time (VOT). Furthermore, in a study conducted by Hardison (2004), both auditory-only and audiovisual experiments were utilized to support the idea that real-time visualizations can enhance L2 pronunciation. The findings from the research demonstrated that learners showed improvement not only in the production of segmental aspects but also in the accuracy of suprasegmental features. Notably, learners exhibited increased awareness of various aspects of their pronunciation, assigning attentional hierarchical levels.

Similarly, in a study conducted by Saito (2007), positive outcomes were observed concerning accuracy when Japanese learners of English, whose L1 was Japanese, utilized the speech software Praat to acquire the vowel /æ/. This was achieved by examining the differences between F1, with a particular focus on F2. Similarly, Motohashi-Siago and Hardison (2009), collaborated on research with L2 Japanese speakers of English, aiming to enhance accuracy in vowel length and geminates. The results from their studies support the advantages of employing speech software and suggest that utilizing visual cues from speech is more effective than providing auditory-only input.

In the same vein, a meta-analysis conducted by Hao-Jan Chen et al. (2024), the study examined the overall effectiveness of ASR in enhancing the pronunciation performance of ESL/EFL students. Analysing data from 15 studies spanning 2008 to 2021. The results of moderator analyses indicated that ASR with explicit CF was highly effective, while ASR with indirect feedback (e.g., ASR dictation) showed moderate effectiveness. Additionally, ASR demonstrated a substantial impact on segmental pronunciation but a smaller effect on suprasegmental pronunciation. The study also revealed that a medium to long treatment duration with ASR led to higher learning outcomes, and practising pronunciation with peers in an ASR condition had a large effect, whereas the effect was smaller when practising alone. Overall, ASR was found to be largely effective for adult and intermediate English learners, recommending its use for assisting L2 student pronunciation development.

Based on the reviewed studies, it can be interpreted that technology and computer-assisted programs have positive effects on L2 pronunciation development (Bashori et al., 2022; Dai & Wu, 2023; Evers & Chen, 2022; Hsieh et al., 2023; Kruk & Pawlak, 2023; Luo, 2016), but the effects have been more effective when oral or VCF was provided.

2.4. Visual Corrective Feedback and Pronunciation Improvement

In the field of SLA, it is widely acknowledged that providing CF on linguistic errors plays a crucial role in both the process and outcome of effective L2 learning. The theoretical advantages of CF stem from its capacity to stimulate learners' awareness, attention, and comprehension of linguistic structures, particularly when employing their L2 for conveying meaning (Ellis, 2016; Esterhazy, 2019; Lee & Lyster, 2017; Long, 2007; Lyster & Saito, 2010; Mackey, 2012; Saito, 2021). Additionally, scholars (e.g. Ha et al., 2021; Nassaji & Swain, 2000) argue that CF offers valuable opportunities for learners to engage in authentic communicative interactions, thereby contributing to the enhancement of their long-term proficiency in terms of accuracy, fluency, and automaticity (Lyster et al., 2013).

In the context of pronunciation instruction and teaching, the predominant form of CF is oral corrective feedback (OCF). This type of feedback is expressed verbally and can be given either during or after oral production. Immediate correction of errors during conversation is a common practice in providing oral feedback, with the primary goal of enhancing the accuracy of learners' spoken utterances (Kartchava & Nassaji, 2021; Lyster & Ranta, 1997). One type of CF which has been less researched compared to other types of CK is VCF.

"Visual corrective feedback consists of providing learners with visual representations of their speech, or some aspect of their speech, often accompanied by a visual representation of native speaker productions" (Olson, 2022, p. 1). VCF, specifically employing technology-mediated visual aids such as waveforms, spectrograms, and pitch contours (pitch tracings), has garnered support for many years (Anderson-Hsieh, 1994; Cucchiarini et al., 2008; Olson & Offerman, 2021). It is noteworthy that the tools for generating these visuals were initially designed as clinical instrumentation used by speech-language pathologists. Interestingly, these forms of visual display continue to be widely utilized in more contemporary CAPT systems (Offerman & Olson, 2016; Olson & Offerman, 2021). Therefore, VCF encompasses any form of instruction or training where second language learners receive feedback on their pronunciation through the utilization of a visual display (Offerman & Olson, 2023).

The incorporation of VCF in pronunciation training relies on two underlying assumptions. Firstly, it assumes that learners possess the capability to interpret visuals, enabling them to discern the similarities and differences between their speech and that of a native speaker. Secondly, it presupposes that once these differences are successfully identified, learners can effectively address the errors and enhance their pronunciation (Kartchava & Nassaji, 2021). Furthermore, VCF holds the potential for effectiveness by improving the ability of L2 learners to discern distinctions between their speech and that of a native speaker. This heightened awareness may contribute to a deeper understanding of acoustic differences already perceived successfully or introduce a new modality for recognizing differences that were previously overlooked. Drawing from the Noticing Hypothesis (Schmidt, 1990), which posits that awareness of L2 forms, especially differences between the L1 and L2, is a prerequisite for certain types of acquisition, there is a further suggestion that this noticing process is crucial for acquiring L2 pronunciation (Derwing & Munro, 2005).

Several previous studies have investigated the benefits of VCF on L2 pronunciation in general, and sound production specifically, and positive outcomes have been observed in various aspects of language learning using VCF. Noteworthy examples include the generation of novel utterances (Hardison, 2004), and the instruction of discourse-level intonation, as evidenced by studies conducted by Chun (2002) and Levis and Pickering (2004). Improvement in the production of intonation contours has been demonstrated across diverse language pairings, various learner profiles, and different styles of intonation contours, as explored by (Spaai & Hermes, 1993). While early research primarily concentrated on suprasegmental features, VCF has proven effective in significantly forcing various segmental features, including consonants and vowels (Offerman & Olson, 2023). For instance, Motohashi-Siago and Hardison (2009) reported notable improvement in the perceptual identification accuracy of singleton—geminate distinctions in L2 Japanese (L1 English) following training with waveforms and spectrograms compared to an audio-only control group (where learners solely received waveforms as feedback). Similarly, studies (Offerman & Olson, 2016; Olson, 2014; Olson, 2022; Olson & Offerman, 2021) demonstrated a substantial enhancement in the production of voice onset time for voiceless stop consonants among L2 learners of Spanish.

Concerning the impact of VCF on vowel production, the findings have displayed a certain degree of variability. Some studies have reported substantial enhancements in vowel production, particularly in terms of location within the vowel space, as illustrated by research conducted by Rehman and Flint (2021) and Saito (2007). However, contrasting results have been observed in other studies, with some indicating mixed outcomes or no discernible effect on vowel production, as exemplified by the works of Carey (2004). In the same vein, Chen et al. (2020) investigated ASR and immediate feedback. The results showed that learners improved significantly in producing /æ/-/ɛ/, but they continued having struggles with /i/-/ɪ/. Similarly, Olson (2022) investigates the potential enhancement of relative durational contrasts, such as stressed versus unstressed vowels, using VCF. However, the participants did not exhibit performance comparable to native Spanish speakers, as their vowel duration ratios fell below the anticipated Spanish norms. Moreover, the findings revealed that, in the pretest phase, learners tended to produce shorter stressed vowels and longer unstressed vowels, a deviation not observed in either English or Spanish. However, the studies reviewed above did not provide insights into how learners perceived the administered VCF. Therefore, it can be inferred that previous studies have not provided empirical evidence for or against the effectiveness of CF, particularly in the context of enhancing L2 vowel improvement.

Studying learner perceptions of CF is essential as it offers valuable insights into how learners perceive such feedback. Integrating this knowledge with findings from research on the effectiveness of CF can guide educators and enhance teaching practices for better outcomes. The focus on understanding learner preferences aligns with the overarching objective of maximizing the influence of CF in language learning (Basturkmen et al., 2004). While prior studies have examined the impact of VCF on learners' pronunciation and sound production, with a particular emphasis on consonants and, to a limited extent, vowels, there is a paucity of research that delves into and reports learners' perceptions of VCF (Bryfonski, 2023; Offerman & Olson, 2016).

Based on the reviewed literature, it is evident that more studies are needed to investigate the effects of VCF on L2 pronunciation, specifically regarding vowels. Previous findings have reported mixed results or no effects of VCF. Additionally, previous studies have primarily focused on monolingual learners. Therefore, the present study makes a substantial contribution to the field by addressing a notable gap. Firstly, it investigates the impact of VCF on L2 vowel production among learners hailing from diverse backgrounds and native speakers representing various countries. Secondly, it explores the learners' perceptions of the provided VCF, thereby enhancing our understanding of the nuanced aspects of VCF effectiveness across different linguistic and cultural contexts. To fulfil this goal, the current study employs two tools to provide VCF Praat (Boersma & Weenink, 2022) and YouGlish. Currently, Praat stands out as the most widely utilized software for delivering VCF. However, it is worth noting that some authors have observed that Praat is not explicitly tailored to cater to L2 learners as its primary audience (Olson, 2014).

3. METHODOLOGY

3.1 ESL Participants

This study involved forty ESL learners with diverse linguistic backgrounds, hailing from various countries. Participant selection was determined through the college's placement test, classifying them as pre-intermediate proficiency level. The participants, aged between 18 and 36 with a mean age of 23, were recruited from Latin American countries including Brazil, Colombia, and Ecuador, as well as predominantly Japan, Thailand, and Vietnam in the Asian region. It is essential to note that ethical approval was obtained for this study, and informed consent was secured from all participating students, ensuring compliance with ethical standards and the protection of participants' rights and privacy.

3.2 Native American Speaker Participants

Ten native speakers of American English from California, specifically Los Angeles, were selected for this study. Their ages ranged from 25 to 40. Each participant was presented with 15 minimal pairs for each vowel, namely /ɪ/, and /iː/. They were instructed to read the words as standard as possible, aiming to adhere to a North American accent.

3.3 Context and Course

Participants in this study were enrolled in a comprehensive one-month English pronunciation course, which took place five days a week at a language college in Sydney. Each daily session lasted for four hours. The course content encompassed both segmental elements, focusing on vowels and consonants, and suprasegmental features, including connected speech, intonation, and stress. The curriculum was thoughtfully designed to integrate speaking, listening, and extensive pronunciation practice.

It is noteworthy that, for the sake of maintaining consistency in this investigation, only two specific vowels were selected as the target features for detailed scrutiny within the course. This deliberate choice allows for a more focused and in-depth analysis of the chosen linguistic elements. Additionally, it aligns with the research objectives and enhances the precision of the study's findings.

3.4 Intervention

The study focused on a pair of vowels /ɪ/, and /iː/ present in words like "leave" and "live," "ship" and "sheep." The teacher, also the researcher, provided explicit VCF using Praat, comparing learners' sound production with native American English speakers as the baseline in the current study. Following the provision of VCF, participants practised extensively using ample examples sourced from YouGlish, incorporating exposure to the three included accents. The last 15 minutes of each class were dedicated to individual VCF, with additional explanations and feedback provided upon request.

3.5 Procedures

The participants followed a three-step process in receiving VCF. Initially, daily, they were provided with a list of five words, recorded them at home, and subsequently sent the recordings back to the teacher. In the classroom setting, following the presentation of accurate vowel production through authentic examples from native speakers and additional instances from YouGlish, the learners' productions were displayed on the screen and analysed using Praat (refer to Figure 1), then, the participants also analysed their productions visually (see Figure 2, and 3). Toward the end of the class, the teacher engaged in one-on-one sessions with each student, offering more explicit VCF and explanations utilizing Praat. For each recorded sample, the duration, as well as the first and second formant, were explained to guide the production of accurate vowels.

3.6 Data Collection

Data collection included pre-test and post-test assessments. On the first and last days of the course, participants read lists of words and sentences containing the target vowels, recorded by the teacher. Minimal pairs were carefully chosen to meet the study's objectives. Samples (30 words and 30 sentences) were annotated using Praat, measuring duration, and the first and second formant (F1 and F2) for each vowel. Post-test, a semi-structured interview was conducted with 20 learners to explore perceptions of visual pronunciation feedback. Data were analysed using a mixed-

Figure 1. A sample of VCF on vowel duration using Praat

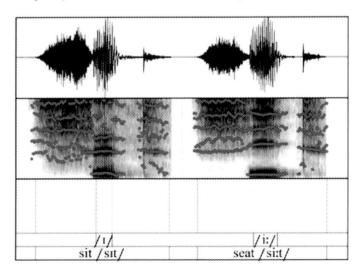

Figure 2. Sample spectrogram of the token "seat" and "sit" produced by a native English speaker

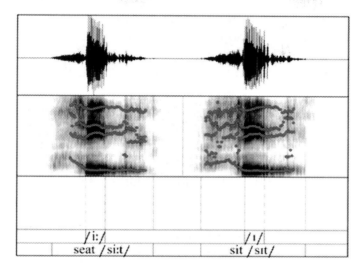

Figure 3. Sample spectrogram of the token "seat" and "sit" produced by an ESL participant

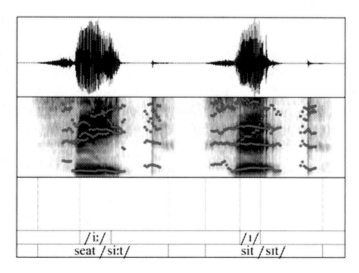

method approach, incorporating quantitative and qualitative analyses, particularly through thematic analysis. On the other hand, the native American speakers were tasked with reading the designated words and recording their pronunciation (*refer to Appendix A*). Subsequently, they sent back the recordings to the researcher.

3.7 Data Analysis

The data for the current study were collected quantitatively through task production, including reading words in isolation and reading target words in selected sentences containing the target vowels (/ɪ/ and /iː/), along with semi-structured interviews. Quantitative data collection was complemented by qualitative insights obtained through interviews.

The collected quantitative data were processed using Praat, a software commonly utilized for acoustic analysis in linguistics. The collected data were segmented and annotated within Praat, enabling the measurement and calculation of acoustic parameters such as vowel duration and F1 and F2 for each vowel instance in both tasks. This same procedure was replicated for the American English speakers, ensuring consistency in data collection and analysis across different participant groups.

The annotated data from the native American English speakers served as the baseline for measuring vowel production among ESL learners in the study. Once the relevant acoustic parameters (duration, F1, and F2) were measured, the data were prepared for statistical analysis.

Statistical analyses were conducted using SPSS version 26, a widely used software package for statistical analysis in various fields. This allowed for the exploration of patterns and relationships within the data, providing insights into the phonetic characteristics of vowel production among ESL learners in comparison to native speakers. Throughout the analysis process, efforts were made to ensure accuracy and consistency in data handling and interpretation. Any inconsistencies or errors identified during the analysis were addressed to maintain the integrity of the findings. This meticulous approach to data analysis enabled a comprehensive investigation into the phonetic features of vowel production among ESL learners, shedding light on potential areas for language acquisition and pronunciation improvement.

4. RESULTS

4.1 Effects of VCF on ESL Learners' Production /ɪ/ and /iː/

Following the coding and annotation of the data using Praat and information gathered from interviews, statistical and thematic analysis was employed. The outcomes of these analyses are presented in the subsequent sections.

To answer the first research question, a paired-sample t-test was conducted with raw vowel duration (ms), F1, and F2 as the dependent variables in both the pre-test and post-test. For the first vowel (i.e., /iː/) as a long vowel, the paired sample test in Table 1 shows the effects of VCF on the first vowel duration between the pre-test and the post-test. The mean difference in duration between the conditions was -3.900 seconds (SD = 1.586, SE = 0.355), with a 95% confidence interval ranging from -4.642 to -3.158 seconds. The t-test revealed a significant difference between the conditions, $t(19) = -10.996, p < .001$.

As shown in Table 2, a paired-sample t-test was conducted to examine the differences in F1 values between two conditions related to the /iː/ vowel. The mean difference ($M = 44.700; SD$ 1.418) was found to be statistically significant ($t(19) = 140.983, p < .001$). This suggests a substantial and reliable distinction in the F1 values between the two conditions, supporting the hypothesis that there is a significant difference in the production of the /iː/ vowel before and after the intervention. Overall, these findings suggest that the VCF intervention had a positive impact on the learners' vowel production, leading to more accurate and distinct articulation of the targeted vowel.

In terms of the effects of VCF on the target vowel's F2, as illustrated in Table 3, the results show that the mean difference ($M = 144.500; SD = 6.160$) was found to be statistically significant ($t(19) = 104.904, p < .001$). The standard deviation of the differences was 6.160, with a standard error of the mean at 1.377. The 95% confidence interval for the difference ranged from 141.617 to 147.383. This indicates a substantial and statistically significant difference in the F2 values within this target vowel. The positive mean difference suggests that the second measurement (F2) is consistently higher than the first measurement, providing evidence for a systematic shift in F2 values within the paired samples.

Table 1. Paired sample test: Duration of /iː/ in the pre-test and post-test

		Paired Differences					t	df	Sig. (2-Tailed)
		Mean	Std. Deviation	Std. Error Mean	95% Confidence Interval of the Difference				
					Lower	Upper			
/iː/	Duration - Duration	-3.900	1.586	.355	-4.642	-3.158	-10.996	19	.000

Table 2. Paired samples test: F1 of /iː/ from the pre-test and post-test

		Paired Differences					t	df	Sig. (2-Tailed)
		Mean	Std. Deviation	Std. Error Mean	95% Confidence Interval of the Difference				
					Lower	Upper			
/iː/	F1 - F1	44.700	1.418	.317	44.036	45.364	140.983	19	.000

Table 3. Paired samples test: F2 of /iː/ from the pre-test and post-test

		Paired Differences					t	df	Sig. (2-Tailed)
		Mean	Std. Deviation	Std. Error Mean	95% Confidence Interval of the Difference				
					Lower	Upper			
/iː/	F2 - F2	144.500	6.160	1.377	141.617	147.383	104.904	19	.000

Regarding the second target vowels i.e., /ɪ/ as a short vowel, the results from the paired samples correlations (Table 4) and the subsequent paired samples t-tests (Table 5) provide insights into the impact of the intervention on the measured variables.

As presented in Table 4, the mean difference ($M = 31.050$; $SD = .826$) was found to be statistically significant ($t(19) = 168.197$, $p < .001$), with the 95% confidence interval for the difference ranging from 30.664 to 31.436, this indicates that there is a substantial and highly statistically significant difference in the duration values within the second pair of the target vowel, /ɪ/. The positive mean difference suggests that the second measurement (Duration) is consistently higher than the first measurement, providing strong evidence for a systematic increase in duration values within the paired samples.

Concerning the F1 of the second target vowel (i.e., /ɪ/) as shown in Table 5, the results revealed that there was a statistically significant mean difference of ($M = -99.900$; $SD = 502$) ($t(19) = -198.964$, $p < .001$) in the F1 values for the second vowel /ɪ/. The 95% confidence interval for the difference ranged from -100.951 to -98.849. The negative mean difference suggests a systematic decrease in F1 values for the second vowel target, indicating a notable shift in acoustic characteristics. These systematic changes show the systematic approaches to providing VCF.

Similarly, regarding the F2 of the same vowel as presented in the same table (Table 5), the results indicate that there is a highly statistically significant mean difference of ($M = 552.650$; $SD = 650$) ($t(19) = 850.231$, $p < .001$) in the F2 values for the second vowel /ɪ/. The standard deviation of the differences, with a standard error

Table 4. Paired samples test duration of /ɪ/ from the pre-test and post-test

		Paired Differences					t	df	Sig. (2-Tailed)
		Mean	Std. Deviation	Std. Error Mean	95% Confidence Interval of the Difference				
					Lower	Upper			
/ɪ/	Duration - Duration	31.050	.826	.185	30.664	31.436	168.197	19	.000

of the mean (SEM) at 0.650. The 95% confidence interval for the difference ranged from 551.290 to 554.010. The positive mean difference implies a systematic increase in F2 values for the second vowel target, indicating a substantial shift in acoustic characteristics. This result indicates that VCF not only affects vowel durations but also acoustic characteristics of the target vowels in terms of place of articulations.

The statistical analysis of both target vowels demonstrates the remarkable effectiveness of integrating VCF through Praat with YouGlish in enhancing ESL learners' pronunciation and refining sound production accuracy. These findings underscore the potency of leveraging innovative tools like VCF using Praat and YouGlish to facilitate significant progress in ESL learners' pronunciation skills.

4.2 ESL Learners' Perceptions of VCF in Teaching the Sounds /ɪ/ and /iː/

To answer the second research question, an in-depth interview was conducted with 15 participants from which the results unveil a profound understanding of how VCF tools, notably Praat and YouGlish, impact the pronunciation journey of ESL learners.

Consistently, participants acknowledged the pivotal role of VCF in refining their sound production. Participant 1 articulated, *"The visual feedback was incredibly helpful! I could see where I lacked duration in words. The tools pinpointed my errors, making them easier to fix. My pronunciation improved significantly."* This sentiment echoed among participants, underscoring how visual aids served as a corrective mirror, enhancing speech clarity.

A prevalent theme emerged regarding the impact of VCF on stress placement within words. Participant 2 noted, *"At first, I didn't realize how my duration affected words. Seeing the vowel duration and formants helped me identify areas to work on. The improvement in my speech is noticeable now."* Participants attested that visual cues facilitated a nuanced understanding of vowel differences, leading to more accurate pronunciation.

Table 5. Paired samples test: F1 and F2 of /ɪ/ from the pre-test and post-test

		Paired Differences					t	df	Sig. (2-Tailed)
		Mean	Std. Deviation	Std. Error Mean	95% Confidence Interval of the Difference				
					Lower	Upper			
/ɪ/	F1 - F1	-99.900	2.245	.502	-100.951	-98.849	-198.964	19	.000
/ɪ/	F2 - F2	552.650	2.907	.650	551.290	554.010	850.231	19	.000

The reported increase in confidence was a noteworthy outcome of incorporating VCF. Participant 3 emphasized, *"Visual feedback showed my sound production issues. The vowel quality highlighted where I stumbled. It's amazing how it improved my pronunciation and confidence in speaking."* Learners expressed assurance in their pronunciation after integrating visual aids, positively impacting overall confidence levels.

Moreover, participants highlighted the practicality of integrating VCF into their language learning routine. Participant 4 reflected, *"The visual aid was an eye-opener. It showed where my vowels fell short. Now, I'm more conscious and confident. It's like I found missing pieces to improve my speech."* The user-friendly nature of visual feedback tools received praise, emphasizing their efficacy as self-correcting instruments easily integrated into individual practice sessions.

Participant 6 brought a unique perspective, stating, *"Visual feedback helped me identify errors, especially when reading in my native language, Spanish. I used to read words as they are written, but visual feedback helped me notice the difference."*

Another participant, Participant 7, expressed enthusiasm for YouGlish, saying, *"I loved using YouGlish as it gave me real samples of words from native speakers. It's interactive and helped me practice more."*

Despite the positive impact, participants mentioned challenges. Some found tools like Praat confusing and complicated. Participant 8 emphasized the need for well-trained teachers, stating, *"Using tools like Praat and YouGlish is useful, but sometimes it's time-consuming. Having a well-trained teacher in the class is necessary for accurate feedback."*

In essence, these narratives, seamlessly woven together, depict the holistic impact of VCF tools on ESL learners' pronunciation, encompassing vowel quality and duration, confidence, and the practicality of their language learning journey. The challenges voiced by participants underscore the importance of supportive teaching alongside technological tools.

5. DISCUSSION

The current study investigated the effects of visual corrective feedback (VCF) on L2 learners' sound production and their perceptions of VCF provision using technological and computer-assisted tools such as Praat and YouGlish in Australia as an ESL context. Feedback in general has been a controversial topic in L2 acquisition, and researchers have investigated this issue extensively, but in terms of pronunciation instruction and teaching, especially with the advancement of technology and the availability of several computer programs such as Praat, feedback provision has taken a new direction in the learning process. In that sense, VCF has drawn more attention recently than before, especially after the COVID-19 pandemic. Although previous studies examined the effectiveness of VCF on L2 sound productions, especially the consonants, previous findings reported mixed, sometimes, no effects of VCF on learners' vowel production development (Carey, 2004; Olson, 2022; Rehman & Flint, 2021). Therefore, this investigation delved into the issue, exploring the impact of VCF on vowel production among ESL learners.

In contrast to Olson's (2022) findings, where participants did not show performance comparable to native Spanish speakers, with vowel duration ratios falling below the expected Spanish norms, the current study demonstrates (i.e., RQ1) that ESL learners improved their accuracy in producing target vowels /ɪ/ and /iː/ compared to native American productions, especially following the provision of VCF. An inferred factor for the effectiveness of VCF in this study might be the fact that VCF was provided in a very structured methodology such as learners' home sample recordings followed by general in-class VCF, followed by ample examples using YouGlish, and finally strengthened with individual face-to-face VCF. This method of VCF provision confirms the effectiveness of the used theoretical framework such as the interaction hypothesis (Long, 1996; 1981; 2007), sociocultural theory (Vygotsky, 1978), and the noticing hypothesis proposed by Schmidt (1990). These theories emphasize active interaction between learners, teachers, and the used tools, and these tools have been considered as social factors which help learners improve their pronunciation beyond the Zone of Proximal Development (ZPD). Applying this method of feedback provision (i.e., through using Praat to provide visual feedback) enables learners to actively notice and process linguistic features. Furthermore, VCF effectiveness in this study could be due to the individual VCF as it enables learners to notice the difference between their vowel production and native speakers. This encouraged them to practice more by utilising the available tools. Additionally, offering explicit visual feedback through tools like Praat can be viewed as a mediating tool, as referenced in sociocultural theory. This approach involves leveraging learners' L1 and linguistic backgrounds to enhance the effectiveness of the provided feedback. Moreover, the outcomes of this study diverge from those of Chen et al. (2020), as the learners in this investigation demonstrated significant improvement in the production of /ɪ/ and /iː/ following the administration of VCF. This suggests that the utilization of VCF could potentially be more effective than relying solely on SRA and immediate feedback. Furthermore, this study reports learners' perceptions of VCF (i.e., RQ2) as none of the reviewed previous studies investigated this aspect. In contrast, learners' perceptions towards any learning tools are essential to guarantee a successful learning process (Basturkmen et al., 2004; Borg, 2003; Nunan, 1989). Although the findings revealed that ESL learners had positive perceptions of VCF and the used tools in the pronunciation course, they also reported some challenges such as using these tools could be time-consuming, learners need to learn how to use them properly, and a trained teacher must deliver the pronunciation lesson if technology and computer-assisted tools are used in the classroom. Yet overall, the learners' positive perceptions are promising to confirm the effectiveness of VCF, and to maintain this aspect of VCF, more support and training courses are needed prior to teaching pronunciation. Furthermore, the participants indicated that their confidence level and the ability to notice their errors have improved significantly after the provision of VCF. These findings are well-aligned with previous studies reports on the impact of technology usage on learners' pronunciation and confidence (Levis & Pickering, 2004; O'Brien et al., 2018).

6. CONCLUSION

This study illuminates two crucial findings regarding the effectiveness of visual feedback in an ESL context. Firstly, VCF can be a potent tool for improving ESL learners' vowel production, but its efficacy is contingent on a systematic and well-structured delivery process. The study's results underscore the significance of a phased implementation, involving home sample recordings, in-class feedback, YouGlish examples, and individual face-to-face sessions. Additionally, the pivotal role of a well-trained teacher, proficient in both pronunciation pedagogy and technology usage, is highlighted. This dual expertise ensures the seamless integration of VCF into the learning process, maximizing its impact on vowel production.

Secondly, learners exhibit positive perceptions of VCF, despite acknowledging challenges such as time consumption, the need for proper training, and a preference for a trained teacher in technology-assisted pronunciation lessons. The overall positive learner outlook underscores VCF's potential value, emphasizing the need for ongoing support and training initiatives to address challenges effectively. Educators should be responsive to learner concerns, guiding efficient tool usage and time management. These insights offer a promising avenue for the integration of VCF into ESL pronunciation courses, recognizing its positive impact on learners' attitudes.

This study offers several theoretical and pedagogical implications. The theoretical foundations of this study draw from Interaction Theory, Sociocultural Theory, and the Noticing Hypothesis. The findings align with these theories, emphasizing active interaction, social factors, and learners' awareness as crucial components in pronunciation instruction. Pedagogically, the study provides a model for educators, demonstrating the importance of a systematic approach and the need for teachers with dual expertise in pronunciation pedagogy and technology integration.

However, it is essential to acknowledge the limitations of this study. The focus on only two vowels and a limited participant pool of 40 necessitates caution in generalizing the findings. Future research endeavours could expand the scope by investigating VCF across a broader range of segmental and suprasegmental features, incorporating control groups for comparative analysis. Exploring VCF in diverse ESL contexts, considering factors such as language proficiency levels and cultural backgrounds, would contribute to a more comprehensive understanding of its impact. Moreover, ongoing exploration of learners' perceptions and the development of tailored support and training initiatives are crucial for sustaining the positive impact of VCF in pronunciation instruction.

In essence, these theoretical and pedagogical implications, along with a recognition of limitations and future research directions, provide educators and researchers with valuable insights for navigating the integration of VCF into ESL pronunciation instruction. This comprehensive approach ensures a nuanced understanding of VCF's potential benefits and challenges, paving the way for its effective implementation in language learning contexts.

REFERENCES

Alahmadi, N. S. (2019). The role of input in second language acquisition: An overview of four theories. *Bulletin of Advanced English Studies*, *3*(2), 70–78. doi:10.31559/baes2019.3.2.1

Anderson-Hsieh, J. (1992). Using electronic visual feedback to teach suprasegmentals. *System*, *20*(1), 51–62. doi:10.1016/0346-251X(92)90007-P

Anderson-Hsieh, J. (1994). Interpreting visual feedback on suprasegmentals in computer-assisted pronunciation instruction. *CALICO Journal*, *11*(4), 5–22. doi:10.1558/cj.v11i4.5-22

Bashori, M., Van Hout, R., Strik, H., & Cucchiarini, C. (2022). 'Look, I can speak correctly': Learning vocabulary and pronunciation through websites equipped with automatic speech recognition technology. *Computer Assisted Language Learning*, 1–29. doi:10.1080/09588221.2022.2080230

Basturkmen, H., Loewen, S., & Ellis, R. (2004). Teachers' Stated Beliefs about Incidental Focus on Form and their Classroom Practices. *Applied Linguistics*, *25*(2), 243–272. doi:10.1093/applin/25.2.243

Boersma, P., & Weenink, D. (2022). *Praat: doing phonetics by computer*. https://www.fon.hum.uva.nl/praat/

Bohn, O.-S., & Flege, J. E. (1992). The production of new and similar vowels by adult German learners of English. *Studies in Second Language Acquisition*, *14*(2), 131–158. doi:10.1017/S0272263100010792

Bohn, O.-S., & Flege, J. E. (2021). The revised speech learning model (SLM-r). In R. Wayland (Ed.), *Second language speech learning: Theoretical and empirical progress* (pp. 3–83). Cambridge University Press. doi:10.1017/9781108886901.002

Borg, S. (2003). Teacher cognition in language teaching: A review of research on what language teachers think, know, believe, and do. *Language Teaching*, *36*(2), 81–109. doi:10.1017/S0261444803001903

Bryfonski, L. (2023). Is seeing believing? The role of ultrasound tongue imaging and oral corrective feedback in L2 pronunciation development. *Journal of Second Language Pronunciation*, *9*(1), 103–129. doi:10.1075/jslp.22051.bry

Carey, M. (2004). CALL visual feedback for pronunciation of vowels: Kay Sona-Match. *CALICO Journal*, *21*(3), 571–601. doi:10.1558/cj.v21i3.571-601

Carroll, S. E. (1999). Putting 'input' in its proper place. *Second Language Research*, *15*(4), 337–388. doi:10.1191/026765899674928444

Cengiz, B. C. (2023). Computer-assisted pronunciation teaching: An analysis of empirical research. *Participatory Educational Research*, *10*(3), 72–88. doi:10.17275/per.23.45.10.3

Chau, M. K., & Bui, H. P. (2023). Technology-assisted teaching during the COVID-19 pandemic: L2 teachers' strategies and encountered challenges. In D. K. Sharma, S.-L. Peng, R. Sharma, & G. Jeon (Eds.), *Micro-electronics and telecommunication engineering. Lecture notes in networks and systems* (pp. 243–250). Springer Nature Singapore. doi:10.1007/978-981-19-9512-5_22

Chen, H. H.-J. (2011). Developing and evaluating an oral skills training website supported by automatic speech recognition technology. *ReCALL*, *23*(1), 59–78. doi:10.1017/S0958344010000285

Chen, M. (2022). Computer-aided feedback on the pronunciation of Mandarin Chinese tones: Using Praat to promote multimedia foreign language learning. *Computer Assisted Language Learning*, 1–26. doi:10.1080/09588221.2022.2037652

Chen, W.-H., Inceoglu, S., & Lim, H. (2020). Using ASR to improve Taiwanese EFL learners' pronunciation: Learning outcomes and learners' perceptions. *Proceedings of the 11th Pronunciation in Second Language Learning and Teaching conference*.

Chun, D. M. (2002). *Discourse intonation in L2: From theory and research to practice*. John Benjamins Publishing. doi:10.1075/lllt.1

Cucchiarini, C., Neri, A., & Strik, H. (2008). The effectiveness of computer-based speech corrective feedback for improving segmental quality in L2 Dutch. *ReCALL*, *20*(2), 225–243. doi:10.1017/S0958344008000724

Dai, Y., & Wu, Z. (2023). Mobile-assisted pronunciation learning with feedback from peers and/or automatic speech recognition: A mixed-methods study. *Computer Assisted Language Learning*, *36*(5-6), 861–884. doi:10.1080/09588221.2021.1952272

Derwing, T. M., & Munro, M. J. (2005). Second language accent and pronunciation teaching: A research-based approach. *TESOL Quarterly*, *39*(3), 379–397. doi:10.2307/3588486

Derwing, T. M., & Munro, M. J. (2015). *Pronunciation fundamentals: Evidence-based perspectives for L2 teaching and research*. John Benjamins Publishing Company. doi:10.1075/lllt.42

Derwing, T. M., Munro, M. J., & Wiebe, G. (1998). Evidence in favor of a broad framework for pronunciation instruction. *Language Learning*, *48*(3), 393–410. doi:10.1111/0023-8333.00047

Ellis, R. (2015). *Understanding second language acquisition* (2nd ed.). Oxford university press.

Ellis, R. (2016). Focus on form: A critical review. *Language Teaching Research*, *20*(3), 405–428. doi:10.1177/1362168816628627

Ellis, R., Sheen, Y., Murakami, M., & Takashima, H. (2008). The effects of focused and unfocused written corrective feedback in an English as a foreign language context. *System*, *36*(3), 353–371. doi:10.1016/j.system.2008.02.001

Esterhazy, R. (2019). Re-conceptualizing feedback through a sociocultural lens. In M. Henderson, R. Ajjawi, D. Boud, & E. Molloy (Eds.), The impact of feedback in higher education: Improving assessment outcomes for learners (pp. 67-82). Palgrave Macmillan Cham. doi:10.1007/978-3-030-25112-3_5

Evers, K., & Chen, S. (2022). Effects of an automatic speech recognition system with peer feedback on pronunciation instruction for adults. *Computer Assisted Language Learning*, *35*(8), 1869–1889. doi:10.1080/09588221.2020.1839504

Flege, J. E. (1987). The production of "new" and "similar" phones in a foreign language: Evidence for the effect of equivalence classification. *Journal of Phonetics*, *15*(1), 47–65. doi:10.1016/S0095-4470(19)30537-6

Flege, J. E., Bohn, O.-S., & Jang, S. (1997). Effects of experience on non-native speakers' production and perception of English vowels. *Journal of Phonetics, 25*(4), 437–470. doi:10.1006/jpho.1997.0052

Flege, J. E., MacKay, I. R. A., & Meador, D. (1999). Native Italian speakers' perception and production of English vowels. *The Journal of the Acoustical Society of America, 106*(5), 2973–2987. doi:10.1121/1.428116

Fouz-González, J. (2015). Trends and directions in computer-assisted pronunciation training. In J. A. Mompean & J. Fouz-González (Eds.), *Investigating English pronunciation: Trends and directions* (pp. 314–342). doi:10.1057/9781137509437_14

Gass, S. M., & Mackey, A. (2020). Input, interaction, and output in L2 acquisition. In B. VanPatten, G. D. Keating, & S. Wulff (Eds.), *Theories in second language acquisition: An introduction* (pp. 192–222). Routledge. doi:10.4324/9780429503986-9

Georgiou, G. P. (2022). The acquisition of /ɪ/–/iː/ is challenging: Perceptual and production evidence from Cypriot Greek speakers of English. *Behavioral Sciences (Basel, Switzerland), 12*(12), 469. doi:10.3390/bs12120469

Glăveanu, V. P., Ness, I. J., Wasson, B., & Lubart, T. (2019). Sociocultural perspectives on creativity, learning, and technology. In C. A. Mullen (Ed.), *Creativity under duress in education? Resistive theories, practices, and actions* (pp. 63–82). Springer International Publishing. doi:10.1007/978-3-319-90272-2_4

Hao-Jan Chen, H., Kuo-Wei Lai, K., & Thi-Nhu Ngo, T. (2024). The effectiveness of automatic speech recognition in ESL/EFL pronunciation: A meta-analysis. *ReCALL, 36*(1), 4–21. doi:10.1017/S0958344023000113

Hardison, D. M. (2004). Generalization of computer assisted prosody training: Quantitative and qualitative findings. *Language Learning & Technology, 8*(1), 34–52. http://llt.msu.edu/vol8num1/hardison/

Hillenbrand, J., Getty, L. A., Clark, M. J., & Wheeler, K. (1995). Acoustic characteristics of American English vowels. *The Journal of the Acoustical Society of America, 97*(5), 3099–3111. doi:10.1121/1.411872

Hincks, R. (2015). Technology and learning pronunciation. In M. Reed & J. M. Levis (Eds.), *The handbook of English pronunciation* (pp. 505–519). John Wiley & Sons. doi:10.1002/9781118346952.ch28

Hsieh, W.-M., Yeh, H.-C., & Chen, N.-S. (2023). Impact of a robot and tangible object (R&T) integrated learning system on elementary EFL learners' English pronunciation and willingness to communicate. *Computer Assisted Language Learning*, 1–26. doi:10.1080/09588221.2023.2228357

Isaacs, T. (2009). Integrating form and meaning in L2 pronunciation instruction. *TESL Canada Journal*, *27*(1), 1–12. doi:10.18806/tesl.v27i1.1034

Jenkins, J. (2000). *The phonology of English as an international language: New models, new norms, new goals.* Oxford University Press.

Kartchava, E., & Nassaji, H. (2021). Corrective feedback in second language teaching and learning. In E. Kartchava & H. Nassaji (Eds.), *The Cambridge handbook of corrective feedback in second language learning and teaching* (pp. 1–20). Cambridge University Press. doi:10.1017/9781108589789.001

Kruk, M., & Pawlak, M. (2023). Using internet resources in the development of English pronunciation: The case of the past tense -ed ending. *Computer Assisted Language Learning*, *36*(1-2), 205–237. doi:10.1080/09588221.2021.1907416

Ladefoged, P., & Johnson, K. (2014). *A course in phonetics.* Cengage Learning.

Lantolf, J. P. (2000). *Sociocultural theory and second language learning.* Oxford University Press.

Lantolf, J. P. (2006). Sociocultural theory and L2: State of the art. *Studies in Second Language Acquisition*, *28*(1), 67–109. doi:10.1017/S0272263106060037

Lantolf, J. P. (2024). On the value of explicit instruction: The view from sociocultural theory. *Language Teaching Research Quarterly*, *39*, 281–304. doi:10.32038/ltrq.2024.39.18

Lantolf, J. P., & Pavlenko, A. (1995). Sociocultural theory and second language acquisition. *Annual Review of Applied Linguistics*, *15*, 108–124. doi:10.1017/S0267190500002646

Larsen-Freeman, D., & Anderson, M. (2013). *Techniques and principles in language teaching* (3rd ed.). Oxford University Press.

Lee, A. H., & Lyster, R. O. Y. (2017). Can corrective feedback on second language speech perception errors affect production accuracy? *Applied Psycholinguistics*, *38*(2), 371–393. doi:10.1017/S0142716416000254

Levis, J., & Pickering, L. (2004). Teaching intonation in discourse using speech visualization technology. *System*, *32*(4), 505–524. doi:10.1016/j.system.2004.09.009

Levis, J. M. (2018). *Intelligibility, oral communication, and the teaching of pronunciation*. Cambridge University Press. doi:10.1017/9781108241564

Levis, J. M. (2022). Teaching pronunciation truths and lies. In C. Bardel, C. Hedman, K. Rejman, & E. Zetterholm (Eds.), *Exploring language education: Global and local perspectives* (pp. 39–72). Stockholm University Press. doi:10.16993/bbz.c

Liakina, N., & Liakin, D. (2023). Speech technologies and pronunciation training: What is the potential for efficient corrective feedback? In U. K. Alves & J. I. A. d. Albuquerque (Eds.), Second language pronunciation: Different approaches to teaching and training (pp. 287-312). Walter de Gruyter.

Long, M. (1996). The role of the linguistic environment in second language acquisition. In W. C. Ritchie & T. K. Bhatia (Eds.), *Handbook of second language acquisition* (pp. 413–468). Academic Press.

Long, M. H. (1981). Input, interaction, and second-language acquisition. *Annals of the New York Academy of Sciences*, *379*(1), 259–278. doi:10.1111/j.1749-6632.1981.tb42014.x

Long, M. H. (2007). *Problems in SLA*. Lawrence Erlbaum.

Luo, B. (2016). Evaluating a computer-assisted pronunciation training (CAPT) technique for efficient classroom instruction. *Computer Assisted Language Learning*, *29*(3), 451–476. doi:10.1080/09588221.2014.963123

Lyster, R., & Ranta, L. (1997). Corrective feedback and learner uptake: Negotiation of form in communicative classrooms. *Studies in Second Language Acquisition*, *19*(1), 37–66. doi:10.1017/S0272263197001034

Lyster, R., & Saito, K. (2010). Oral feedback in classroom SLA: A meta-analysis. *Studies in Second Language Acquisition*, *32*(2), 265–302. doi:10.1017/S0272263109990520

Lyster, R., Saito, K., & Sato, M. (2013). Oral corrective feedback in second language classrooms. *Language Teaching*, *46*(1), 1–40. doi:10.1017/S0261444812000365

Mackey, A. (2012). *Input, interaction, and corrective feedback in L2 learning*. Oxford University Press.

Mahmood, R. Q. (2023). Enhancing EFL speaking and pronunciation skills: Using explicit formal instruction in a Kurdish university. *Issues in Educational Research*, *33*(4), 1421–1440. http://www.iier.org.au/iier33/mahmood-abs.html

McCrocklin, S. M. (2016). Pronunciation learner autonomy: The potential of automatic speech recognition. *System, 57,* 25–42. doi:10.1016/j.system.2015.12.013

Morley, J. (1991). The pronunciation component in teaching English to speakers of other languages. *TESOL Quarterly, 25*(3), 481–520. doi:10.2307/3586981

Motohashi-Siago, M., & Hardison, D. M. (2009). Acquisition of L2 Japanese geminates: Training with waveform displays. *Language Learning & Technology, 13*(2), 29–47. http://llt.msu.edu/vol13num2/motohashisaigohardison.pdf

Nazir, F., Majeed, M. N., Ghazanfar, M. A., & Maqsood, M. (2023). A computer-aided speech analytics approach for pronunciation feedback using deep feature clustering. *Multimedia Systems, 29*(3), 1699–1715. doi:10.1007/s00530-021-00822-5

Nunan, D. (1989). *Designing tasks for the communicative classroom.* Cambridge University Press.

O'Brien, M. G. (2004). Pronunciation matters. *Die Unterrichtspraxis/Teaching German, 37*(1), 1-9. https://doi.org/https://doi.org/10.1111/j.1756-1221.2004.tb00068.x

O'Brien, M. G., Derwing, T. M., Cucchiarini, C., Hardison, D. M., Mixdorff, H., Thomson, R. I., Strik, H., Levis, J. M., Munro, M. J., Foote, J. A., & Levis, G. M. (2018). Directions for the future of technology in pronunciation research and teaching. *Journal of Second Language Pronunciation, 4*(2), 182–207. doi:10.1075/jslp.17001.obr

Offerman, H. M., & Olson, D. J. (2016). Visual feedback and second language segmental production: The generalizability of pronunciation gains. *System, 59,* 45–60. doi:10.1016/j.system.2016.03.003

Offerman, H. M., & Olson, D. J. (2023). Speech visualization for pronunciation instruction: Exploring instructor support in L2 learner attitudes toward visual feedback. In S. McCrocklin (Ed.), *Technological resources for second language pronunciation learning and teaching: Research-based approaches* (pp. 239–260). Rowman & Littlefield.

Olson, C. (2014). The conflicting themes of nonviolence and violence in ancient Indian asceticism as evident in the practice of fasting. *International Journal of Dharma Studies, 2*(1), 1. doi:10.1186/2196-8802-2-1

Olson, D. J. (2022). Visual feedback and relative vowel duration in L2 pronunciation: the curious case of stressed and unstressed vowels. *Proceedings of the 12th Pronunciation in Second Language Learning and Teaching Conference.* 10.31274/psllt.13353

Olson, D. J., & Offerman, H. M. (2021). Maximizing the effect of visual feedback for pronunciation instruction: A comparative analysis of three approaches. *Journal of Second Language Pronunciation, 7*(1), 89–115. doi:10.1075/jslp.20005.ols

Pastor, C. K. L. (2020). Sentiment analysis on synchronous online delivery of instruction due to extreme community quarantine in the Philippines caused by COVID-19 pandemic. *Asian Journal of Multidisciplinary Studies (Pangasinan), 3*(1), 1–6.

Pillai, S., & Delavari, H. (2012). The production of English monophthong vowels by Iranian EFL learners. *Poznán Studies in Contemporary Linguistics, 48*(3), 473–493. doi:10.1515/psicl-2012-0022

Piske, T., MacKay, I. R. A., & Flege, J. E. (2001). Factors affecting degree of foreign accent in an L2: A review. *Journal of Phonetics, 29*(2), 191–215. doi:10.1006/jpho.2001.0134

Ramani, S., Könings, K. D., Ginsburg, S., & van der Vleuten, C. P. M. (2019). Meaningful feedback through a sociocultural lens. *Medical Teacher, 41*(12), 1342–1352. doi:10.1080/0142159X.2019.1656804

Rang, O., & Moran, M. (2014). Functional loads of pronunciation features in nonnative speakers' oral assessment. *TESOL Quarterly, 48*(1), 176–187. doi:10.1002/tesq.152

Rassaei, E. (2014). Scaffolded feedback, recasts, and L2 development: A sociocultural perspective. *Modern Language Journal, 98*(1), 417–431. doi:10.1111/j.1540-4781.2014.12060.x

Rehman, I., & Flint, E. (2021). *Real-time visual acoustic feedback for nonnative vowel production.* Presentation presented at 12th Annual Pronunciation in Second Language Learning and Teaching Conference, Brock University, Canada.

Roach, P. (2009). *English phonetics and phonology: A practical course.* Cambridge University Press.

Rochma, A. F. (2023). Corrective oral feedback on students' errors in speaking courses. *Journal of English Language Teaching and Learning, 4*(2), 125–135. doi:10.18860/jetle.v4i2.20442

Saito, K. (2007). The influence of explicit phonetic instruction on pronunciation in EFL settings: The case of English vowels and Japanese learners of English. *The Linguistics Journal, 3*(3), 16–40.

Saito, K. (2021). Effects of corrective feedback on second language pronunciation development. In E. Kartchava & H. Nassaji (Eds.), *The Cambridge handbook of corrective feedback in second language learning and teaching* (pp. 407–428). Cambridge University Press. doi:10.1017/9781108589789.020

Saito, K., & Lyster, R. (2012). Effects of form-focused instruction and corrective feedback on L2 pronunciation development of /ɹ/ by Japanese learners of English. *Language Learning, 62*(2), 595–633. doi:10.1111/j.1467-9922.2011.00639.x

Schmidt, R. W. (1990). The role of consciousness in second language learning. *Applied Linguistics, 11*(2), 129–158. doi:10.1093/applin/11.2.129

Spaai, G. W. G., & Hermes, D. J. (1993). A visual display for the teaching of intonation. *CALICO Journal, 10*(3), 19–30. doi:10.1558/cj.v10i3.19-30

Suzukida, Y., & Saito, K. (2021). Which segmental features matter for successful L2 comprehensibility? Revisiting and generalizing the pedagogical value of the functional load principle. *Language Teaching Research, 25*(3), 431–450. doi:10.1177/1362168819858246

VanPatten, B., Williams, J., Rott, S., & Overstreet, M. (2004). *Form-meaning connections in second language acquisition.* Routledge. doi:10.4324/9781410610607

Vygotsky, L. S. (1978). *Mind in society development of higher psychological processes.* Harvard University Press. https://www.jstor.org/stable/j.ctvjf9vz4

Wang, Y. H., & Young, S. S.-C. (2012). Exploring young and adult learners' perceptions of corrective feedback in ASR-based CALL system. *British Journal of Educational Technology, 43*(3), E77–E80. doi:10.1111/j.1467-8535.2011.01275.x

ADDITIONAL READING

Brown, A. (2014). *Pronunciation and phonetics: A practical guide for English language teachers.* Routledge. doi:10.4324/9781315858098

Kang, O., Thomson, R., & Murphy, J. (2018). The Routledge handbook of contemporary English pronunciation. Routledge.

Murphy, J. (Ed.). (2017). *Teaching the pronunciation of English: focus on whole courses*. University of Michigan Press. doi:10.3998/mpub.8307407

Sardegna, V. G., & Jarosz, A. (2023). *English pronunciation teaching: Theory, practice and research findings* (1st ed.). Multilingual Matters.

Szpyra-Kozłowska, J. (2014). *Pronunciation in EFL instruction: A research-based approach*. Multilingual Matters. doi:10.21832/9781783092628

KEY TERMS AND DEFINITIONS

Automated Speech Recognition (ASR): Automated Speech Recognition is a technology that converts spoken language into written text using computer algorithms and machine learning. ASR systems are commonly used in applications like voice recognition software, virtual assistants, and language learning platforms to transcribe spoken words accurately.

Computer-Assisted Pronunciation Training (CAPT): Computer-Assisted Pronunciation Training refers to the use of technology, particularly computer programs or applications, to assist individuals in improving their pronunciation skills in a targeted language. CAPT often includes features like ASR for real-time feedback on pronunciation.

Educational Technology: Educational technology, often abbreviated as EdTech, encompasses the use of technology tools, resources, and digital platforms to enhance and support teaching and learning processes.

L2 Sound Production: It refers to the articulation of speech sounds in a second language acquired after the first language. It involves the reproduction of phonemes, intonation patterns, and other aspects of pronunciation specific to the target language.

Oral Corrective Feedback: Oral corrective feedback is a form of feedback provided in language learning contexts, specifically in response to spoken language. It involves correcting errors or providing guidance on pronunciation.

Pronunciation Instruction: Pronunciation instruction involves teaching and guiding individuals on how to articulate sounds, stress patterns, and intonation in a particular language. It is a component of language education aimed at improving learners' spoken language skills and ensuring effective communication.

Visual Feedback: Visual feedback refers to information or cues provided through visual means, such as images, waveforms, spectrograms, or any other visual representation. It can be used to enhance learning such as accurate production of sounds in pronunciation teaching.

The Impact of Visual Corrective Feedback on Pronunciation Accuracy

APPENDIX

A sample of the pre-test and the post-test comparing one participant with the baseline (the American speakers' measurements)

P.	\multicolumn{4}{c	}{Pre-test}					\multicolumn{4}{c	}{Baseline- American Speaker}
	V	D(ms)	F1	F2	V	D (ms)	F1	F2	Ave.	V	D (ms)	F1	F2
P1	/iː/	100	410	2710	iː	105	365	2575		/iː/	102	366	2577
	/ɪ/	85	432	2643	ɪ	56	530	2090		/ɪ/	61	531	2084

Note: P= Participant, V= vowel, D= duration, F= formant, and ave.= average

Chapter 9
The Role of Research in Applied Linguistics

Jacqueline Żammit
 https://orcid.org/0000-0002-3961-5286
University of Malta, Malta

ABSTRACT

This chapter shows the importance of research in applied linguistics. The chapter defines applied linguistics and explains the crucial function of research in this field. This defines teaching methods, laws, and interpretations for acquiring a language through definition and description. It consists of a section that discusses research methodologies in the area and language acquisition including quantitative as well as qualitative methods. Moreover, the chapter explains how different approaches are used to assess language teaching and learning environments including education and other factors that influence human knowledge. Finally, the chapter underscores the role played by research in applied linguistics urging for more investigations to improve understanding of language in daily life contexts.

INTRODUCTION

Applied linguistics represents an amalgamation of concepts and theories from diverse fields like anthropology, linguistics, sociology and psychology to address real-life problems. Applied linguistics focuses on the gap between theoretical linguistic insights and language application in various contexts especially concerning language policies, language testing and assessment, and the translation of languages (Cook, 2003). As Davis (2016) notes, applied linguistics encompasses several major areas which include methods of teaching languages, evaluation of languages, corpus linguistics,

DOI: 10.4018/979-8-3693-3294-8.ch009

and discourse analysis. Linguists seek to know how people acquire language in their communities. Additionally, they want to comprehend how language relates to the culture of a society (Norton, 2013).

Generally, applied linguistics is concerned with everyday issues or matters that are practical in nature. Scholars who belong to this discipline aim to improve teaching practices and address various challenges faced while learning languages (Spolsky, 2012). For example, first, scholars investigate various methods employed by teachers to instruct specific language aspects. They do this by studying the effects of multilingualism laws on English teaching. Second, they create ways to assess the effectiveness of these methods (Bachman & Palmer, 2010).

Research conducted within the framework of applied linguistics has contributed significantly to determining effective strategies for second language acquisition. Researchers have claimed that legislative decisions about language learning should be based on empirical evidence and studies that use dynamic research instruments. (Ellis, 2018). While applied linguistics contributes positively to the understanding and teaching of languages, it also comes with its share of controversies, such as debates over teaching methodologies, the role of native languages in education, and the implementation of language policies. These controversies often stem from differing perspectives on language acquisition and the best ways to promote multilingualism. Despite these challenges, the field continues to evolve and adapt, striving to improve language learning and teaching worldwide. Some emerging controversies regarding applied linguistics concern the validity of particular methodologies employed when doing research, the transferability of findings, and the ethics of applied linguistics (Shohamy & Or, 2013). The field has also ongoing debates on the role of technological change within language learning, on how far language is used by different people with its universality, as well on the relationship between identity and language. Accordingly, this field has evolved and continues to adapt in response to societal shifts and emerging trends. Scholars in this sophisticated subject try to address problems relating to languages and further deepen their conceptualization of language using theoretical frameworks and practical tools.

Applied linguistics research is important as it provides ways of understanding and addressing language obstacles that occur in real situations (Becker, 2023). Applied linguistics also has connections with various fields such as psychology, language teaching, and education which help to solve the problem of language barriers (Kramsch, 2017). Furthermore, applied linguistics needs significant research because it leads to policy-making, and comprehension of how language functions and is acquired. Furthermore, it is through studies in applied linguistics that great instructional strategies are found and that customized approaches can be made for different learners' needs (Ellis, 2021). Empirical and theoretical evaluation include discussions like the difference between task-based instruction and traditional grammar-centered mechanisms. Moreover, while assessing moods, planning mechanisms, and bilingual learning effects on academic success, research helps determine effective policies for languages (Garcia et al., 2016).

This kind of study may also lead to language assessment geared towards novel methods like holistic exams so as not to discriminate against any stakeholder or party unfairly during the process. In addition, many field techniques have shown considerable variables including motivation, age, and cognitive abilities among others when viewed from the perspective of a second or foreign language student (Ellis & Wulf, 2019). These insights form the basis for developing well-informed linguistic strategies and enhancing multilingualism. Another topic dealt with by researchers in this field regards community interests, such as loss of languages, and development issues calling for society-oriented projects aimed at preserving cultural heritage (McCarty et al., 2006). Such work tries to address issues affecting equity in communication approaches and fairness in linguistics. The field of linguistics ensures that language is a three-dimensional phenomenon that builds harmony among communities because it upholds life.

The Meaning of Applied Linguistics

Applied linguistics refers to the use of linguistic theories, methods, and insights derived from the study of language in actual activities involving its use (Cook, 2003). These include policy formulation, planning and enforcement as well as areas where language is impaired. An essential objective of this field is to use language models and empirical evidence to address language-related problems.

In higher education institutions applied linguistics research appears mainly in peer-reviewed journals, conference proceedings, or book chapters (Hall, 2016). Examples include *Applied Linguistics*, *Language Learning*, *TESOL Quarterly*, *Language Teaching Research*, and *Annual Review of Applied Linguistics*. These publications publish rigorous academic studies based on empirical research and theoretical discussions across all areas within applied linguistics.

Language education is a major area that has seen studies on effective approaches to teaching languages or second language learning strategies as well as technology-based influences on this process (Richards & Rodgers, 2014). Language policy and planning also play a significant role in addressing issues such as investigating countries' policies on multilingualism and examining how ideologies about languages influence decision-making regarding those languages. Additionally, they explore what occurs when policies are implemented through education systems (Spolsky, 2012).

Translation and interpreting studies discuss translation processes or quality assessment techniques for translated works. For Baker (2018), translation and interpreting studies encompass the examination of translation processes and quality

The Role of Research in Applied Linguistics

assessment techniques for translated works. Baker also investigates the roles of translators and interpreters in intercultural communication. Another branch of this field is testing, where researchers, like Bachman & Palmer (2010), investigate factors affecting performance (e.g., validity and reliability issues) that characterize most conventional second language tests, such as English. This can also involve developing proficiency exams alongside their validation or understanding differences between test takers' results to set standards. It can also involve developing proficiency exams alongside their validation or understanding differences between test takers' results to set standards (Bachman & Palmer, 2010).

Research has focused on aphasia, dyslexia, and other specific impairments and speech disorders, along with interventions for individuals affected by them (Bishop et al., 2017). Thus, the work of these researchers is in line with current academic sources in applied linguistics to contribute to ongoing scholarly discourse within the domain while maintaining academic rigor and credibility. They employ different theoretical frameworks and research methods to address diverse language problems encountered in various settings. The overall objective is an accurate understanding of language and its improved policies and practices.

The Importance of Research in Applied Linguistics

Research is a critical tool for understanding language and its application in practical terms. Through rigorous empirical studies, theoretical inquiries, and interdisciplinary collaborations, research in applied linguistics contributes to various aspects of language education, policy, assessment, and societal challenges. Let us delve into the importance of research in these areas.

Applied linguistic research helps identify effective teaching strategies by possessing efficient techniques and approaches that are specifically modified to address the individual needs or requirements of the students. Richards and Rodgers (2014) undertook a study to look at different approaches used in teaching languages. This research has made some significant contributions to improving the way teachers teach languages. Similarly, innovation's importance in learning a new language will be considered (Hubbard 2009). According to Hyland and Hyland (2019), research in applied linguistics shows how central task-based instruction is as well as what role teacher input plays while acquiring new vocabulary.

Applied linguistics research aims at moving ahead with and adopting policies on languages which guide our educational systems, federal services, and social cohesion among other things. Spolsky (2012) elucidated how important legislation about languages can influence people's mindsets or behaviour. Further, bilingual education frameworks are better understood through studies conducted by researchers such as Garcia et al. (2016 May (2012) also pointed out that studying applied linguistics helps at least the dialogue on language justice and diversity.

In addition to promoting fairness and validity of communicative competence tests, research carried out within applied linguistics helps develop good evaluation practices thereby ensuring that they are valid. The work done by Bachman and Palmer (2010) explored practical features of testing hypotheses about language use situations that were experimentally manipulated. Their findings highlight the importance of evaluative practices that are consistent with the goals of learning. Another study by Lantolf and Poehner (2011) explored dynamic assessment techniques, identifying new ways to assess second language abilities and helping learners develop their own.

Language Disorders

To understand the nature of such language difficulties as dyslexia and aphasia, one can undertake research in applied linguistics. According to Bisho et al. (2017), applied linguistics research provides evidence-based processes for diagnosing and treating such conditions.

According to Bisho et al. (2017), dyslexia is characterized by a reading disorder that affects a person's ability to read and comprehend written language. The condition involves problems with word recognition accuracy or fluency, poor spelling, and decoding skills. It mainly occurs due to a phonological deficit in language which often lacks expectations from other cognitive abilities or effective teaching within the classroom (Bisho et al., 2017).

Conversely, aphasia is a deficiency in one's ability to communicate effectively either orally or in writing, according to Bisho et al. (2017). Sometimes it happens suddenly right after a stroke or head injury while sometimes it develops slowly like when a tumor in the brain is growing or due to progressive neurological disease following certain patterns of symptom expression. This implies that aphasia impairs reading as well as writing alongside the expression and comprehension of oral communication.

Language disorders like those mentioned above are best understood through applied linguistics research because they seek to find out what causes them. Applied linguists who also specialize in language disorders can provide evidence that aids in the treatment of such disorders. In study cases involving diagnosed dyslexia, applied linguistics provides insights concerning the underlying causes of various learning disabilities, which often result in reading difficulties. Furthermore, these insights can guide the development of effective teaching strategies and intervention approaches. These methods are particularly beneficial during the early stages of school when intervention can have the most impact. In addition, applied linguists can inform cases wherein damage to specific brain regions leads to speech impairment, as they can aid in devising strategies aimed at improving communication in aphasic patients. Furthermore, this field also illuminates how language is impacted by damage to particular regions of the brain.

Language processing and communication pose unique problems for both dyslexia and aphasia. However, linguistic research can further illuminate these disorders, resulting in better strategies for diagnosing and treating them. This is what makes applied linguistics a prominent field for expanding knowledge about language disorders and enhancing the quality of life for those affected.

Societal Challenges

Moreover, applied linguistics research addresses issues such as linguistic disparities and language endangerment or revitalization. McCarty et al. (2006) carried out a study on indigenous peoples' grassroots efforts at language revival. This showed that some principles were based on society's perspectives. Norton (2013), for instance, explored how languages enable people to establish identities and achieve social justice. Such studies demonstrated the complex interplay between community, culture, and language.

Furthermore, the complex field of applied linguistics necessitates further research to address real-life linguistic obstacles in such contexts as education, testing, and law; this may produce positive transformations within those contexts. By focusing on a myriad of theoretical models and methods involved in this academic inquiry, researchers improve the knowledge base while enabling changes envisaged within linguistically oriented policies of different countries or states, including educational system updates among others.

A study conducted by Windle and Possas (2022) served as another typical case in which applied linguistics research solved real-world societal problems. It investigated the problem of translanguaging and inequality in education in the Global South, with a focus on Brazil. It identified translanguaging as a growing practice that supports multilingualism and identities, as well as a strategy that promotes minoritized migrant students' rights, thereby contributing to closing the social and racial gap. The focus is on the localized use of English so that teachers create conditions for developing critical language awareness.

Fang and Dovchin (2022) discussed the transformation in applied linguistics, which gradually contributes to reducing the power disparities among English speakers in the Global South. According to Sepúlveda et al. (2021), educational disparities lead to production disparities within the Global South. Educational delivery is impacted by cross-cultural factors which result in present-day topical issues like inequities. In line with these findings, Fang and Dovchin (2022) contended that it is important to critically approach educational linguistics in the southern hemisphere today while dealing with contemporary global issues such as disparity and discrimination between those who speak English there today.

Significance of Research in Addressing Language-Related Issues in Real Life

Interpreting and dealing with everyday language problems are key functions of research. It is an important approach in applied linguistics; a dynamic field that brings to light the complexities of various language settings and solves practical language problems. This is done through the use of several theoretical models and empirical studies that look into best teaching practices (Richards & Rodgers, 2014). Applied linguistic research helps teachers tailor their methods to suit every student's needs, thus ensuring better instruction and learning outcomes.

Research from applied linguistics also influences language policies. Intellectuals can provide relevant information to policymakers about language attitudes, planning methodologies, and the effects of legislation on diverse community contexts (Spolsky, 2012). Such a process would aid in formulating fairer language policies for enhancing diversity in language acquisition.

Moreover, applied linguistics research improves our understanding of how we learn and use languages. Understanding variables like age, language-related feedback, or personal motivation will help scholars develop theoretical frameworks on language enhancement (Ellis & Wulff, 2019). This field's studies reinforce the interpretation of second-language acquisition and inform the nature of effective interventions towards efficient educators. In addition, this research foregrounds current societal issues associated with language, including endangerment, preservation, revitalization, and so on. Researchers within this discipline can create culturally responsive interventions that involve partnerships with communities and interdisciplinary approaches to foster linguistic inclusivity. Therefore, researching issues related to applied linguistics is a potent tool for interpreting and handling real-life language problems.

Contributions by Applied Linguistics Research on Effective Language Teaching Methods

Applied linguistics has made significant contributions towards enhancing efficient teaching skills. Significant advancements in applied linguistics have greatly improved teaching efficiency. These advancements provide valuable information on the most effective teaching strategies available. Researchers in the field have consequently contributed through evidence-based frameworks alongside theoretical models, thereby prompting the establishment of quality educational outcomes and enabling effective language instruction (Richards & Rodgers, 2014). Therefore, applied linguistics has been instrumental in developing appropriate mechanisms for imparting knowledge in a foreign language including task-based language teaching, technology-enhanced language learning, feedback and error correction, content and language integrated learning, and individual differences in second/foreign language acquisition.

Task-based language teaching (TBLT) has received much attention in applied linguistics research for its efficacy in language classrooms. TBLT utilizes real-life tasks as the central unit of instruction, which has been shown to facilitate the quick acquisition of languages (Ellis, 2021). The method focuses on meaningful communication tasks both inside and outside the classroom, thus aiding students' language development (Ellis & Wulff, 2019). For instance, an investigation by Ellis and Wulff (2019) noted that TBLT helps students move around due to real-life conversations with other people outside school. To improve the outcomes of language learning activities, task-based approaches should be integrated into teaching methods.

Research on technology-enhanced language learning examines the incorporation of digital tools and resources into language classrooms. Technology is transforming linguistic pedagogy according to Hubbard (2009) who stressed on interactive media channels such as digital spaces and computer-assisted learning initiatives. This technology ensures that learners are involved in all kinds of learning environments thus making it a more inclusive environment (Hubbard, 2009). For example, Hubbard (2009) showed how digital tools provide interactive learning experiences catering for diverse learner needs. Research argues for leveraging technology to enhance language instruction and ensure equal access to language study materials.

The effectiveness of feedback mechanisms and error correction strategies in language education is being investigated by several scholars across various publications. Investigations have been conducted on different types of feedback given during student's English proficiency improvement processes. Hyland and Hyland (2019) claimed that constructive feedback from teachers can help students' English proficiency increase rapidly. Their research addressed feedback as a medium for helping language learners by providing them with a means of analyzing their production, thereby showing them how best they can improve what they say or write. Thus, good practices concerning feedback are important when it comes to learning languages.

Content and language integrated learning (CLIL) is another approach that combines the teaching of language with the instruction of other disciplines. Garcia et al. (2016) used translanguaging as a classroom strategy within the CLIL framework, drawing on bilingual resources to teach content knowledge across disciplinary boundaries. Their research explains how CLIL promotes authentic use of language and relevant development of linguistic skills necessary for second language acquisition. The integration of language learning into content instruction promotes interdisciplinary education, improving learners' language proficiency through contextually rich environments.

Furthermore, applied linguistics scholarship recognizes personal variations in language education. Consequently, such studies help adapt teaching methodologies to meet the needs of individual learners fairly. Richard and Rodgers (2014) examined such issues as cognitive style variables, attitudes toward languages, and learner motivation among others. These studies are important sources for developing an effective approach to teaching languages because they illuminate pedagogy through understanding innovative approaches, exploring various student needs, and knowing how to handle them effectively. Scholars can always strive towards promoting effective instruction in school while perfecting the outcomes through the utilization of evidence-based practices and theoretical insights.

Additionally, in the realm of applied linguistics, personal variations in language education are acknowledged. Consequently, studies like those conducted by Richard and Rodgers (2014), are considered important sources. These studies, which explore cognitive characteristics, attitudes towards languages, and learner motivation, among other subjects, contribute to the customization of instructional approaches to effectively meet the needs of individual learners. These significant sources shed light on teaching through their comprehension of innovative methodologies, examination of diverse student requirements, and adeptness in effectively addressing them. They offer a substantial contribution to the advancement of a proficient methodology for language instruction. Therefore, it is imperative for researchers to consistently endeavor to improve instruction in educational institutions by utilizing evidence-based techniques and theoretical insights to optimize the results.

The Impact of Research in Applied Linguistics on Language Policies

In formulating language policies, applied linguistics research based on empirical evidence about language uses, attitudes, and practices in different societal contexts is regarded as fundamental. These contributions go all along toward enlightening areas such as language planning and management, language rights, and equity, among others.

In discussing language policies, applied linguistics investigates attitudes held by societies, as well as ideologies on languages, dialects, and linguistic diversity. Researchers employ many methods to study such issues, which allow them to make claims like those made by Spolsky (2012). The elucidation of these attitudes helps policymakers to understand the complexities of different populations and more effectively develop appropriate policies that take into account not only linguistic diversity but also the special needs of particular language groups.

Applied linguistics plays a significant role in the discourse on language planning and management, thereby facilitating the analysis of their dynamics within societal contexts. For example, scholars are known for analyzing how various endangered languages can be preserved (McCarty et al., 2006). When it comes to evaluating the impact of multilingual education systems on learning outcomes as well as cultural diversity preservation, Garcia et al. (2016) explained that studies on the medium of instruction also play an important role. Based on the results of rigorous examination and assessment, researchers provide recommendations for making effective laws concerning issues of languages spoken by certain nations.

Consequently, this paper argues that applied linguistics plays an extremely vital role in framing language policies based on a comprehensive comprehension of language dynamics within sociocultural contexts. The area supports informed decision-making through interdisciplinary approaches thereby promoting just policies while advancing linguistic rights within multicultural environments.

Language Rights and Equity

Research conducted in this field serves as a basis for developing legislation, aiming to protect freedom while enhancing justice in society. Insight into regulations provides researchers with an opportunity to scrutinize them for any potential negative implications on how people use languages (May, 2012). Such a critical examination results in the formulation of policies targeting the provision of equal access to basic services such as education, government services, and employment regardless of one's mother tongue. Researchers advocate for the protection of language diversity, the rights of linguistic minorities in all sectors, free speech, and equal treatment for all. Their efforts help in the enactment of laws that not only safeguard this diversity but also promote human rights among speakers of minority languages. In pursuit of equity and inclusivity, applied linguistics research contributes towards making a legislative framework that ensures social cohesion is achieved through acknowledging cultural differences.

Dynamic applied linguistics research is necessary to evaluate the effectiveness of existing language policies and their impact on language usage patterns and societal attitudes. Researchers use different methodologies, such as qualitative and quantitative analyses, to comprehensively evaluate policy implementation outcomes in changing situations (Hornberger, 2006). This provides policymakers with evidence-based inputs, theoretical knowledge, and practical recommendations towards the development, adoption, and assessment of legislation on languages through rigorous evaluation methods. These strategies help decision-makers when planning policies based on empirical studies and community involvement that are used to address emerging trends concerning languages. Through cooperation with other people and the community at large, applied linguistics research facilitates the making of efficient laws that will promote language diversity while maintaining linguistic rights in multilingual environments.

The contribution of Research in Applied Linguistics to Understanding Language Acquisition and Use

The study of applied linguistics helps in understanding the acquisition and use of language. It does this by examining cognitive, social, and contextual variables that affect language-learning processes. The following sections present a review of how applied linguistic research enables the interpretation of language acquisition and utilization.

Factors Determining Language Acquisition

The process of language acquisition is a composite process influenced by various factors. Among these is age, which has been identified as one of the main areas that affect how well an individual can learn a new language. This results in young learners acquiring languages more easily and often to near-native proficiency levels. This phenomenon is commonly associated with the critical period hypothesis, which postulates that there exists an optimal time for acquiring language skills that ends around adolescence.

Furthermore, language learning involves feedback, which acts as a looking glass through which learners observe their own mistakes and adjust themselves accordingly. Feedback comes in different forms, including explicit feedback, such as direct error correction, and implicit feedback, like recasting a learner's erroneous statement into the correct sentence pattern. Furthermore, motivation plays a central role in language acquisition. It helps individuals to engage with the target language, persevere when they face challenges, and develop proficiency over time. The level of motivation for a learner greatly determines how fast or slowly they will acquire the second language.

Moreover, some individual differences, such as cognitive abilities, learning styles, and personality, also explain why people differ in terms of their rate do development of second languages. Some may be gifted in learning languages while others may thrive well within structured environments. Studies on second-language learning carried out by Ellis and Wulff (2019) and Ellis (2021) cite several important factors that can enhance foreign language competence among students, including memory, attention, instruction, and meaningful engagement with target languages, such as in the task-based language teaching model. Therefore, there are many aspects affecting success in acquiring another language: cognition, motivation, individual

The Role of Research in Applied Linguistics

characteristics, and many others should be taken into consideration when developing effective methods for teaching any kind of linguistic matter.

Language Learning Contexts

The contexts in which language acquisition takes place are quite varied and multi-faceted, with the environments involved playing a significant role in determining the process and outcomes of learning foreign languages. For instance, applied linguistics research has explored various classroom instructions, immersion programs, and global studies, each offering unique conditions and strategies for improving language proficiency.

On one hand, classroom instruction provides a structured environment for students to systematically acquire language skills. This means that they are given lessons by teachers who also help them to practice using the new language among themselves. However, the effectiveness of teaching through classrooms may depend on how a teacher uses his or her methods to teach, as well as the amount of motivation in a learner and the availability of resources.

On the other hand, immersion programs create more naturalistic situations for acquiring languages. In these programs, learners find themselves in an environment where the target language is used as a principal medium of communication. Such constant exposure to the language through various life situations can improve the comprehension and production abilities of learners. Nevertheless, the success of immersion programs often depends on learners' readiness to engage in extensive use of the language.

Kohler (2015) investigated an additional context, known globally as global studies, where students acquire languages within their cultural frameworks. This implies that such activities can facilitate the understanding of idiomatic expressions and cultural references linked to the use of specific words, thereby simplifying or even necessitating effective communication.

Comparing proficiency levels across these different educational settings will indeed help scholars identify optimum environments/methods for language acquisition. However, one should bear in mind that a perfect environment might not be the same for all individuals because each has unique characteristics that may influence learning style and purpose. Garcia et al., (2016) conducted research that stresses bilingualism's importance to fluency. Bilingualism enhances some cognitive skills like attentional control or problem solving, which can result in facilitating learning among the speakers as well as overall language acquisition. Furthermore, bilingual people have a deeper comprehension of the subtleties within languages, such as code-switching and translation, that contribute to the quality of their language usage.

Understanding these different contexts and how they influence language acquisition is important for anyone who wants to teach or learn new languages more efficiently. It can also explain how certain factors like being bilingual can lead to fluency in speaking.

Sociocultural Influences on Language Use Through an Applied Linguistics Perspective

Applied linguistics research, as viewed from the perspective of social uses of language, provides a profound understanding of how languages operate within society. Such investigations delve into sociolinguistic variables, giving us insights into how different places and cultures have diverse language applications.

Language is more than just a tool for communication, but also deeply interwoven with cultural practices, identity, and community involvement. These are not haphazard speech patterns that people or communities adopt; they are shaped by their social and cultural environments. These can function as signs to show the speaker's attachment to a particular community or sociocultural group.

May (2012) illustrates this aspect of language in use. His study centered on words spoken through speech acts to construct race, ethnicity, and political identities. It highlights the performativity of language, which implies that our words go beyond meaning—they do things, like constructing our social selves. Moreover, Hornberger's (2006) work widens our view on language's social uses. It gives invaluable information about the models that policymakers use to portray how sociopolitical factors affect the use of language. This research thus reveals how sociopolitical contexts influence the way people speak leading to an emphasis on how policy shapes practice and vice versa.

How applied linguistics research examines the social uses of language indicates that it has deep-seated relations with human beings' ways of life. This knowledge can lead to more inclusive and effective policies as far as using languages is concerned.

Research Methods in Applied Linguistics and Language Education

The methodologies used in applied linguistics research incorporate several strategies which investigate language-related ideas, guide teaching practices, and enhance our knowledge of applied linguistics.

Quantitative Research

Quantitative research is concerned with the collection and examination of numerical data to evaluate relationships and trends in terms of linguistic context. These approaches are crucial for increasing our knowledge of applied linguistics and language learning by providing systematic and empirical findings on various language learning issues.

Experimental studies are usually employed in linguistics to assess the effectiveness of different approaches to teaching languages, as well as techniques, interventions, and education aids. Experimental studies often involve independent variables such as methods of instruction being used to assess their effects on dependent variables like proficiency levels. For example, Norris and Ortega (2006) experimented to examine whether explicit instruction improved some aspects of second-language learners' grammatical competence.

Surveys mainly collect information on such things as attitudes towards a language or behaviour from large numbers of people. They perform a significant function by allowing researchers to quantify responses and identify developments within a given field of language use. A case in point is a study by Derakhshan and Taguchi (2021), which used surveys to find out what students think about the use of error correction at school during their acquisition process.

Correlational studies help establish links between two or more variables without manipulating some variables. This approach is often employed in determining whether vocabulary knowledge has an impact on reading comprehension or academic achievement. Proctor et al. (2006) used a correlation test to check the connection between bilinguals' level of English proficiency and academic success.

Quantitative content analysis covers systemic categorization and counting data to find patterns. It evaluates how languages are used across varied contexts including written genres, classroom talk, and networked communications. The quantitative content analysis of Pfeil and Zaphris (2010) included digital interaction themes.

Quantitative research studies in large-scale testing measure language proficiency and evaluate language programs at a macro level. The assessments often employ standardized tests that collect numerical information about learners' linguistic abilities and achievements. Common among them is the Test of English as a Foreign Language (TOEFL). This assessment is commonly employed in examining the English proficiency of non-native speakers. By utilizing systemic data collection and analysis mechanisms, quantitative methods constitute an important source of insights into teaching, learning, and using languages.

Qualitative Research

The importance of these approaches lies in their ability to provide a better understanding of how languages are used, learned, and taught through the emphasis on the contextualized experiences of individuals and communities. They involve lengthy reviews, analyses, and evaluations of qualitative data that is obtained from interviews or textual sources.

Ethnographic studies demand extensive fieldwork and participant observation to interpret language use within specific sociocultural contexts. These investigations offer rich descriptions of language practices, beliefs, and identities in multiple settings. Spolsky and Hult (2010) conducted an ethnographic study on multilingual educational settings for the examination of language policy and planning, providing thorough insights into language pedagogies as well as practices.

The method of discourse analysis analyzes social interaction where language was performed, emphasizing on how linguistic elements are negotiated with meaning in communicative spaces. Like conversational assessment, discourse analysis strategy reveals patterns of language use and power relations among various speech communities. Norton (2013) examined language and identity using discursive analysis in multilingual class sites which accentuated the significance of linguistic ideas upon the construction of learners' second-language acquisition.

Study cases require extensive examination of individual cases to investigate particular aspects connected with a given language topic. Case studies usually give detailed accounts of learning languages as well as initiatives adopted. McDonough and Mackey (2013) employed case studies that investigated the efficacy of correct input on English proficiency thus explaining error correction-based activities by educators' attitudes.

Narrative inquiry is a research methodology used in social sciences and humanities, which centers on the use of stories as data. Researchers collect these stories and then interpret them to understand the lived experiences and social contexts of the individuals involved. It's a way to understand and represent experiences through "story told" and "story analyzed." This method is often used in studies where the context and personal experience are important, such as education, social work, and psychology. It allows for a rich, detailed, and complex representation of human experiences and realities. Garcia et al. (2020) used narrative inquiry to establish the role that identity negotiation and investment played in L2 success.

Mixed Method Research

This method combines qualitative and quantitative research methods to provide a comprehensive understanding of language-related issues. The technique is effective in tackling the strengths and limitations of integrated approaches due to several data collection and analysis methods being used.

Mixed methods studies in applied linguistics involve collecting both numerical information as well as observational notes (qualitative). Combining these sources of information helps researchers triangulate findings, validate results, and gain better insights into complex language phenomena (Żammit, 2022). An example is Paltridge and Phakiti's (2015) study, which employed the mixed approach to investigate English language learners' language acquisition strategies. This study brought together survey data with qualitative interviews to give an accurate picture on how learners plan their learning activities.

This sequential explanatory design employs qualitative data collection techniques and analysis to either compare with quantitative series or interpret them The purpose of this method is for scholars to comprehend numerical outcomes better by revealing mechanisms or processes beneath them. For example, Mackey and Gass (2015) used a sequential explanatory design to examine the effects of mission complexity on second language development. It began by looking at numbers from language scalability tests and then carried out interviews to discover what first-year students do and think.

In contrast, convergent design involves the simultaneous collection of quantitative and qualitative data analyzed separately before comparison/integration during the interpretation stage. Through this approach, authors can shed light on various aspects of the research problem while studying complementary facets of linguistic phenomena. For instance, Morse (1994) utilized a convergent mechanism in researching teacher cognition related to teaching languages, using survey responses regarding teachers' beliefs alongside classroom practice-based qualitative data collection tactics. Thereafter, the study combined these findings for an inclusive understanding of teacher development within language education.

Embedded design represents a form of mixed methods research in which either a qualitative or quantitative approach takes center stage and the other serves as a supplement to provide more context. For example, Mackey and Bryfonski (2018) employed an embedded approach in evaluating corrective feedback effectiveness in language input. It interpreted quantitative findings from language proficiency efforts as well as incorporated qualitative interviews that aimed at capturing the participants' perceptions and experiences.

By employing these approaches, scholars working in applied linguistics can address research questions in a more comprehensive and nuanced way to enhance the validity and reliability of their findings. Through such sources of recent studies, among others like those stated above, researchers contribute towards increasing knowledge and applications within this field of study that apply to real-life situations.

Action Research

Action research is a process in which researchers and teachers work collaboratively to solve language-related issues in the real world. Its main aim is to foster practice, inform decision-making, and lead to positive transformation within educational contexts.

The point of action research is to bring together scholars, language teachers, and other stakeholders who have the mission of finding solutions to linguistic problems. Through these interactions, there are active engagements that happen through inter-ratings and conversations among all studies involved in integrative inquiry. For instance, Kemmis and McTaggart (2014) examined an example of collaborative action research as democratic decision-making and collaborative problem-solving activities in educational settings.

Action research often uses a cyclical approach involving planning, acting, observing, and reflecting; called the "Plan-Do-Study-Act" (PDSA) cycle. This iterative method helps practitioners to adopt interventions, collect information about their effectiveness, and make adjustments based on the feedback obtained. In her study case on action-research phases in language learning, Burns (2010) underscored the importance of systematic planning, data gathering, and interpretation as bases for informing practice.

Applied linguistics-oriented action research prioritizes addressing practical issues that would improve teaching-learning or conversational outcomes in real-world scenarios. By working with practitioners on developing interventions and implementing changes they may be able to assess their impact on language practices as well as outcomes from these practices. Costello's (2011) report used action research for language teacher development, confirming its great potential for motivating teachers' onward career growth and enhancing students' learning experiences.

Action research can empower teachers of languages and enable them to engage in reflective practice through critical appraisal of notions they hold dear concerning education. Ongoing reflection alongside investigation allows practitioners a deeper understanding of their teaching environments and more credible ways of dealing with linguistic matters. McNiff and Whitehead (2011) illustrated the role of interpretation in action research which can greatly contribute to professional growth when applied well. In applied linguistics, researchers and practitioners can use action research as a tool for meaningful study, partnership, and innovation to address language-related problems and improve educational outcomes under different conditions.

Corpus Linguistics

Corpus linguistics entails the systematic examination of comprehensive collections of natural language data, called corpora, to identify changes in patterns of linguistic use. This research methodology advances knowledge in elements of language such as lexis and semantics as well as its use across contexts.

The basis for corpus linguistics research consists of combining and annotating linguistic corpora which represent certain speech systems or groups. Corpora include written texts and spoken interactions and they are annotated with grammatical features, syntactic constituents, and semantic information, among other items. To illustrate this point, Egbert et al. (2022) covered the compilation and annotation process for the Corpus of Contemporary American English (COCA), a large-scale corpus used extensively by researchers employing the corpus linguistics approach.

Corpus linguistics enables scholars to undertake quantitative studies on language trends and frequencies that cut across different registers and genres. They employ statistical techniques together with computational tools to identify recurrent linguistic features, collocational patterns, or lexical connections based on the analysis of corpora. Gries' (2017) study examined the importance of investigating collocation assessment in corpus linguistics research to explore lexical co-occurrence cycles and semantic associations in large data sets.

Corpus linguistics research investigates language differences as well as alterations by examining various language phenomena within different social, cultural, and historical settings. Researchers analyze various types from different periods to trace developments in languages, identify new trends, or look into sociolinguistic variables that impact language use. Tagliamonte's (2015) study also looked into dimensions of dialect change using urban vernaculars through corpus-based approaches thereby revealing how English varieties continue being urbanized.

Language education is another area where corpus linguistics has practical applications, as it is used to inform course design, material development. and language pedagogy. Teachers refer to genuine communication samples to identify relevant trends, collocations and various speech situations useful for creating teaching materials and programs. For example, Anthony (2004) examined a case of incorporating corpus linguistics materials into language education where learners' abilities to interpret the texts were enhanced.

In the field of applied linguistics and language teaching, researchers utilize a broad spectrum of research techniques such as quantitative, qualitative, mixed methods strategy, action research, and corpus linguistics. These diverse methodologies allow them to address complex issues relating to language learning. The insights gained from this research can then be used to establish effective practices for language teaching. Furthermore, in response to the changing societal contexts, these research findings can guide the formulation of adaptive, evidence-based language policies. Therefore, the use of varied research techniques not only contributes to the advancement of knowledge in the field but also improves language education practices.

Advanced Applied Linguistics Research

Applied linguistics research is important for our understanding of language and its many applications in real-life situations. Scholars in applied linguistics have used rigorous, systematic research to investigate various aspects of language, ranging from language acquisition and language teaching to linguistic policy and communication disorders.

The development of language teaching and learning is the heartbeat of applied linguistics. This directly individuals' language proficiency and their communicative abilities. Scholars can aim to uncover effective teaching strategies, understand learner needs, and improve language education practices by applying empirical research and theoretical inquiry. Here I will discuss some ways in which studying this field enhances knowledge about language as well as how it relates to everyday life.

Research aimed at developing various pedagogical strategies for language teaching is carried out under applied linguistics. Teachers can determine whether diverse methods such as task-based language teaching (TBLT), communicative language teaching (CLT) or content-based instruction (CBI) are useful in improving learners' proficiency levels in languages with examples. A typical example is Sato and Loewen's (2019) study, in which they conducted a meta-analysis on instructed second language acquisition to determine the effectiveness of different instructional approaches and pedagogical techniques used.

Concerning instructional design development and curriculum progression, applied linguistics research looks into learner characteristics, motivations, and interests, among other features. Factors such as motivation, learner autonomy, and learning styles are investigated by researchers who want to adapt to various pupils' needs when teaching English. For instance, Dörnyei and Ushioda (2009) discussed inspiration among other matters related to L2 learning and claimed that there is a need to promote the intrinsic motivational ability and self-regulation of learners.

Exploring Language Learning Environments

Studies in applied linguistics focus on the effect of different learning environments, contexts, and innovations on language acquisition. The research looks at how face-to-face communication compares to digital learning spaces or blended learning models in developing a second language and fostering communicative competence. For instance, Stockwell (2021) scrutinized how using mobile-assisted language learning (MALL) could enable an exchange between students that is active as well as interactive in L2 classrooms.

Promoting Multilingualism and Intercultural Competence

Applied linguistics research supports multilingualism and intercultural competence in teaching languages. They look into strategies for integrating language instruction with culture, promoting cross-cultural awareness among learners, and enhancing positive attitudes towards linguistic diversity. For example, Byram and Wagner (2018), described how intercultural communicative competence is developed through foreign language education thereby highlighting the role of cultural objectives within the curriculum.

Research in teaching English as a second/foreign language helps us enrich our understanding of different aspects of society such as education, communication, and cultural exchanges employing empirical studies, theoretical frameworks, and pedagogical innovations.

This aspect forms part of applied linguistics research which shapes directly the way we use language, teach it, or accommodate it within societies. Researchers who specialize in applied linguistics may contribute to framing policies that consider issues related to multilingualism or civic rights on languages using both empirical studies as well as theoretical frameworks.

Applied linguistics research examines language ideologies and beliefs to help develop language policies. This way, it supports language planning processes that can be crucial in maintaining a good kind of justice. For example, Block (2018) explored how language ideologies influence the policy about what languages should be taught and how they should be taught in schools.

Applied linguistic studies investigate the implications of language planning initiatives for language use and learning. Consequently, they consider laws of languages being used in education such as bilingual learning frameworks and efforts towards revitalization of endangered languages. Hornberger and Johnson (2007) studied challenges encountered by countries' governments that have multilingualism as their official policy on language matters, thus pointing out the importance of involvement by community members.

In applied linguistics, research findings are used to support advocacy for linguistic rights and social justice in diverse sociopolitical contexts. Some areas where scholars focus their attention include language acts, legal statutes governing the use of languages, and movements fighting for linguistic rights. May (2015) took the initiative to look at political models concerning policy on this subject matter.

These studies play a role in ensuring developmen of policies guiding multilingual education that recognize multiple languages while encouraging all people's right to speak them. To achieve equal access to education for learners who speak different native tongues, researchers investigate the effectiveness or otherwise of various types of multilingual teaching models, methods employed when teaching second languages, and assessment strategies applied during evaluation exercises undertaken upon completion or within stages thereof. Creese and Blackledge (2015) focused on investigating the legal aspects associated with multi-linguistic instruction across various educational contexts, to indicate how language planning fosters inclusivity in learning arenas.

Such research has resulted in the making of decisions that were informed by language policy and planning, as well as the shaping of education policies. It has been possible due to empirical research, critical analysis, and advocacy work.

The improvement of communication technologies has revolutionized our daily lives by changing how we speak, learn, and relate to others. In addition, applied linguistics research aims at incorporating digital texts into language teaching, utilizing mobile phones for translation purposes and fostering intercultural exchanges. By harnessing these techniques, scholars can examine their efficiency levels, usability rate, and what they mean to instructors and learners when it comes to studying languages through experimentation or the use of theoretical models.

Exploring How Research in Applied Linguistics Enhances Comprehension of Language and its Practical Applications in Daily Life

Applied linguistics research examines the incorporation of digital assets and online resources into language learning spaces. Scholars study the use of computer-assisted language learning (CALL) programs, language learning apps, or online courses to increase learners' motivation, engagement, and proficiency levels in languages. For example, Hubbard (2009) examined how interactive multimedia resources such as blogs contribute to creating an autonomous learner.

Applied linguistics studies deal with virtual learning environments (VLEs) and immersive innovations in language education. They look at virtual reality (VR), augmented reality (AR), and digital gaming platforms as instruments that can be used for teaching foreign languages and promoting intercultural competence. For instance, Li et al. (2021) looked into the role of VR in L2 classrooms, focusing on its effects on student's ability to acquire a target language, comprehend cultural artifacts, and follow rules of conversation.

The place of social media sites and virtual communities in learning a second language is a subject of interest in applied linguistics research; therefore, scholars focus their attention on online communication patterns among L2 learners and teachers and how learners acquire L2 skills by interacting with peers and instructors via social networking sites such as Facebook or Twitter. According to Lamy and Zourou (2013), "the rise of social media has presented new opportunities for both collaborative writing activities" (p. 21).

Digital translation strategies as well as computer-mediated communication gadgets are other areas where applied linguistics researchers concentrate their investigations to enhance cross-language communications. Machine translation systems have been extensively researched by scientists who sought to understand their accuracy, usability within different contexts, cultural appropriateness, and so on; this topic is discussed further by O'Hagan and Ashworth (2002). Technology has also become the go-to for many who are not skilled in translation, whether medical or technical. Advanced communication technologies research involves empirical investigation, theoretical models, and pedagogical innovations in language learning, communicative practices, and cultural exchange in digital environments.

Addressing Societal Challenges

Addressing societal challenges through applied linguistics research entails dealing with such issues as linguistic diversity, language endangerment, language maintenance and language revitalization. In this area of expertise researchers also investigate how various initiatives are being made to preserve languages within given contexts (e.g. bilingual education) or what impact it will have on how people use a certain language in everyday life. A lot of research has been conducted to determine if some languages could be supported by law while others can survive naturally as a part of culture.

However, the lack of resources for mother tongue instruction in schools is a significant challenge to maintaining multilingualism in Africa (Simala & Ruteyaneka, 2014). This issue is not just about the scarcity of textbooks or learning materials in local languages. It extends to the shortage of trained teachers who are proficient in these languages and can effectively deliver the curriculum. Moreover, the situation is further complicated by the diverse linguistic landscape of the continent. Africa is home to over 2000 languages, making it one of the most linguistically diverse regions in the world. This diversity, while being a rich cultural asset, poses practical difficulties in implementing mother tongue instruction across all languages. Furthermore, there is often a societal preference for global languages like English or French, perceived as languages of opportunity. This perception can sometimes overshadow the benefits of mother tongue instruction, such as better understanding and retention of knowledge, and the promotion of cultural identity and diversity. Therefore, addressing this issue requires a multi-faceted approach. It involves not only increasing investment in educational resources but also training teachers, raising societal awareness about the benefits of mother tongue instruction, and advocating for supportive language policies. Through such comprehensive efforts, it may be possible to overcome the challenges and truly foster multilingualism in Africa.

Language endangerment and preservation is a common topic of applied linguistics research, particularly among indigenous and minority language communities. Issues that researchers have sought knowledge on include language documentation, revitalization methods, and community-based indigenous language programs to preserve linguistic heritage. A case in point was McCarty et al.'s (2006) study, which examined collaborative approaches to language revival; it pointed out the significance of community involvement and empowerment as a means of saving endangered languages.

Several studies in applied linguistics are geared towards linguistic rights campaigns and justice in varied sociopolitical contexts. In this regard, scholars focus on language policies, language planning projects, and movements fighting for linguistic freedom to address these injustices while promoting language diversity. One good example is the article of May (2017), which treated access to a given language as a human right, therefore advocating for the recognition and preservation of different languages as one major aspect constituting social justice.

The research in applied linguistics has enabled collaboration with communities towards culturally sensitive language interventions that help empower through learning oral communication skills. Researchers work hand-in-hand with speakers, instructors, or government policymakers when forming an environment for realising their mother tongue dreams or rather making materials including grassroots efforts that encourage multilingualism. For instance, Hinton and Hale (2001) showed how local-based revitalization programs can save endangered native languages, highlighting the significance of cultural renewal and intergenerational transmission.

Intercultural communication is a type of research in applied linguistics that promotes dialogue between individuals from divergent cultures by stressing cooperation across both linguistic and cultural boundaries. Language contact theories, attitudes toward English use worldwide, and communication techniques that facilitate intercultural dialogue are some of the areas of focus for researchers. For instance, in Kramsch's (1998) view, a language learner who has reached such an intercultural level recognizes the importance of practice empathy, reflexivity and critical knowledge while navigating through cultural issues. The understanding of how language can promote social inclusion, linguistic justice, and cultural diversity through applied linguistic research dealing with societal challenges is enhanced through empirical studies, theoretical foundations, and community involvement.

CONCLUSION

This chapter has shown the important role of research in applied linguistics. It also pointed out how applied linguistics research is a major component for addressing real-world language-related issues through critically analyzing the concept of applied linguistics and discussing research at length. In addition, this chapter argued that research is an essential part of applied linguistics because it shapes our linguistic landscapes by enhancing methods of teaching languages, giving information for language policies, and deepening our understanding of acquisition and use.

Moreover, variously explained in the chapter, diverse educational methodologies used by researchers have been indicated elsewhere. Thus, this section stressed on the significance of carrying out rigorous as well as systematic studies on language phenomena by providing a comprehensive overview of qualitative and quantitative approaches.

The need for research in applied linguistics cannot be overemphasized. Continuously probing and thoroughly investigating it day by day, we can find out how language works. Applied linguistics must continue to embrace research to guide innovation, inform practice, and foster an appreciation for the multi-faceted nature of language.

REFERENCES

Bachman, L. F., & Palmer, A. S. (2010). *Language assessment in practice: Developing language assessments and justifying their use in the real world.* Oxford University Press.

Baker, M. (2018). *In other words: A coursebook on translation* (3rd ed.). Routledge. doi:10.4324/9781315619187

Becker, A. (2023). Applied linguistics communities of practice: Improving the research-practice relationship. *Applied Linguistics, 2023*, 1–20. doi:10.1093/applin/amad010

Bishop, D. V., Snowling, M. J., Thompson, P. A., & Greenhalgh, T. (2017). Catalise: A multinational and multidisciplinary Delphi consensus study. Identifying language impairments in children. *PLoS One, 12*(6), e0179498. Advance online publication. doi:10.1371/journal.pone.0158753 PMID:27392128

Block, D. (2018). Language, education and neoliberalism: Critical studies in sociolinguistics. *ELT Journal, 72*(4), 452–454. doi:10.1093/elt/ccy035

Burns, A. (2010). *Doing action research in English language teaching: A guide for practitioners*. Routledge.

Byram, M., & Wagner, M. (2018). Making a difference: Language teaching for intercultural and international dialogue. *Foreign Language Annals*, *51*(1), 140–151. doi:10.1111/flan.12319

Cook, G. (2003). *Applied linguistics*. Oxford University Press.

Costello, P. J. M. (2011). *Effective Action Research: Developing Reflective Thinking and Practice Continuum Research Methods*. Bloomsbury Publishing.

Creese, A., & Blackledge, A. (2015). Translanguaging and identity in educational settings. *Annual Review of Applied Linguistics*, *35*, 20–35. doi:10.1017/S0267190514000233

Derakhshan, A., & Taguchi, N. (2021). The Routledge handbook of second language acquisition and pragmatics. *Applied Linguistics*, *42*(5), 1029–1032. doi:10.1093/applin/amz031

Dörnyei, Z., & Ushioda, E. (Eds.). (2009). *Motivation, language identity and the L2 self*. Multilingual Matters. doi:10.21832/9781847691293

Egbert, J., Biber, D., & Gray, B. (2022). *Designing and evaluating language corpora: A practical framework for corpus representativeness*. Cambridge University Press. doi:10.1017/9781316584880

Ellis, N. C., & Wulff, S. (2019). Cognitive approaches to second language acquisition. In J. W. Schwieter & A. Benati (Eds.), *The Cambridge handbook of language learning* (pp. 41–61). Cambridge University Press. doi:10.1017/9781108333603.003

Ellis, R. (2021). Task-based language teaching. In H. Mohebbi & C. Coombe (Eds.), *Research questions in language education and applied linguistics* (pp. 133–136). Springer., doi:10.1007/978-3-030-79143-8_25

Faez, F., Martini, J., & Pavia, N. (2022). Research methods in applied linguistics and language education: Current considerations, recent innovations, and future directions. *ELT Journal*, *76*(2), 276–296. doi:10.1093/elt/ccab091

Fang, F., & Dovchin, S. (2022). Reflection and reform of applied linguistics from the Global South: Power and inequality in English users from the Global South. *Applied Linguistics Review*, *2022*(0). Advance online publication. doi:10.1515/applirev-2022-0072

García, O., Flores, N., & Spotti, M. (Eds.). (2020). *The Oxford handbook of language and society*. Oxford University Press.

García, O., Johnson, S. I., & Seltzer, K. (2016). *The translanguaging classroom: Leveraging student bilingualism for learning*. Brookes Publishing.

Gries, S. T. (2017). *Quantitative corpus linguistics with R: A practical introduction* (2nd ed.). Routledge.

Hall, G. (Ed.). (2016). *The Routledge handbook of English language teaching*. Routledge. doi:10.4324/9781315676203

Hinton, L., & Hale, K. (2001). *The green book of language revitalization in practice*. Academic Press. doi:10.1163/9789004261723

Hornberger, N. H. (2006). Frameworks and models in language policy and planning. In T. Ricento (Ed.), *An introduction to language policy: Theory and method* (pp. 24–41). Blackwell Publishing.

Hornberger, N. H., & Johnson, D. C. (2007). Slicing the onion ethnographically: Layers and spaces in multilingual language education policy and practice. *TESOL Quarterly, 41*(3), 509–532. doi:10.1002/j.1545-7249.2007.tb00083.x

Hubbard, P. (Ed.). (2009). *Computer-assisted language learning: Critical concepts in linguistics*. Routledge.

Hyland, K., & Hyland, F. (2019). *Feedback in second language writing: Contexts and issues*. Cambridge University Press., doi:10.1017/9781108635547

Kemmis, S., & McTaggart, R. (2014). *The action research planner: Doing critical participatory action research*. Springer. doi:10.1007/978-981-4560-67-2

Kramsch, C. (1998). *Language and culture*. Oxford University Press.

Kramsch, C. (2017). Applied linguistic theory and second/foreign language education. In N. Van Deusen-Scholl & S. May (Eds.), *Second and foreign language education. Encyclopedia of language and education* (pp. 3–14). Springer., doi:10.1007/978-3-319-02246-8_1

Lamy, M.-N., & Zourou, K. (Eds.). (2013). *Social networking for language education*. Palgrave Macmillan. doi:10.1057/9781137023384

Lantolf, J. P., & Poehner, M. E. (2011). Dynamic assessment in the classroom: Vygotskian praxis for second language development. *Language Teaching Research, 15*(1), 11–33. doi:10.1177/1362168810383328

Li, M., Pan, Z., Sun, Y., & Yao, Z. (2021). Virtual reality in foreign language learning: A review of the literature. In *IEEE 7th International Conference on Virtual Reality (ICVR)* (pp. 302–307). IEEE. 10.1109/ICVR51878.2021.9483842

Mackey, A., & Gass, S. M. (2015). *Second language research: Methodology and design* (2nd ed.). Routledge. doi:10.4324/9781315750606

Mackey, A. J., & Bryfonski, L. (2018). Mixed methodology. In A. Phakiti, P. De Costa, L. Plonsky, & S. Starfield (Eds.), *The Palgrave handbook of applied linguistics research methodology* (pp. 103–121). Palgrave., doi:10.1057/978-1-137-59900-1_5

May, S. (2012). *Language and minority rights: Ethnicity, nationalism and the politics of language*. Routledge.

May, S. (2015). Language policy and political theory. In F. M. Hult & D. C. Johnson (Eds.), *Research methods in language policy and planning: A practical guide* (pp. 45–55). Wiley. doi:10.1002/9781118340349.ch5

McCarty, T. L., Romero-Little, M. E., & Zepeda, O. (2006). Native American youth discourses on language shift and retention: Ideological cross-currents and their implications for language planning. *International Journal of Bilingual Education and Bilingualism*, 9(5), 659–677. doi:10.2167/beb386.0

McDonough, K., & Mackey, A. (Eds.). (2013). *Second language interaction in diverse educational contexts*. John Benjamins Publishing Company., doi:10.1075/lllt.34

McNiff, J., & Whitehead, J. (2011). *All you need to know about action research* (2nd ed.). Sage.

Morse, J. M. (1994). *Critical issues in qualitative research methods*. Sage Publications.

Norris, J. M., & Ortega, L. (Eds.). (2006). *Synthesizing research on language learning and teaching*. John Benjamins Publishing Company., doi:10.1075/lllt.13

Norton, B. (2013). *Identity and language learning: Extending the conversation*. Multilingual Matters., doi:10.21832/9781783090563

O'Hagan, M., & Ashworth, D. (Eds.). (2002). *Translation-mediated communication in a digital world: Facing the challenges of globalization and localization*. Multilingual Matters., doi:10.21832/9781853595820

Paltridge, B., & Phakiti, A. (Eds.). (2015). *Research methods in applied linguistics: A practical resource*. Bloomsbury Publishing.

Pfeil, U., & Zaphiris, P. (2010). Applying qualitative content analysis to study online support communities. *Universal Access in the Information Society*, *9*(1), 1–16. doi:10.1007/s10209-009-0154-3

Phakiti, A., De Costa, P., Plonsky, L., & Starfield, S. (Eds.). (2018). *The Palgrave handbook of applied linguistics research methodology.* Palgrave Macmillan. doi:10.1057/978-1-137-59900-1

Piller, I. (2017). *Intercultural communication: A critical introduction.* Edinburgh University Press. doi:10.1515/9781474412926

Proctor, C. P., August, D., Carlo, M., & Snow, C. E. (2006). The intriguing role of Spanish language vocabulary knowledge in predicting English reading comprehension. *Journal of Educational Psychology*, *98*(1), 159–169. doi:10.1037/0022-0663.98.1.159

Richards, J. C., & Rodgers, T. S. (2014). *Approaches and methods in language teaching.* Cambridge University Press. doi:10.1017/9781009024532

Sato, M., & Loewen, S. (2019). *Evidence-based second language pedagogy: A collection of instructed second language acquisition studies.* Routledge. doi:10.4324/9781351190558

Sepúlveda, D., Horvitz, M. M., Joiko, S., & Ortiz Ruiz, F. (2021). Education and the production of inequalities across the Global South and North. *Journal of Sociology (Melbourne, Vic.)*, *58*(3), 144078332110600. doi:10.1177/14407833211060059

Spolsky, B. (Ed.). (2012). *The Cambridge handbook of language policy.* Cambridge University Press., doi:10.1017/CBO9780511979026

Spolsky, B., & Hult, F. M. (Eds.). (2010). *The handbook of educational linguistics.* Wiley-Blackwell.

Stockwell, G. (2021). *Mobile assisted language learning: Concepts, contexts, and challenges.* Cambridge University Press., doi:10.1017/9781108652087

Tagliamonte, S. A. (2015). *Making waves: The story of variationist sociolinguistics.* Wiley-Blackwell. doi:10.1002/9781118455494

Windle, J., & Possas, L. A. (2022). Translanguaging and educational inequality in the Global South: Stance-taking amongst Brazilian teachers of English. *Applied Linguistics*, *44*(2), 312–327. Advance online publication. doi:10.1093/applin/amac067

ADDITIONAL READING

Carter, R., McCarthy, M., Mark, G., & O-Keefe, A. (2016). *English grammar today: An A-Z of spoken and written grammar*. Cambridge University Press

Crystal, D. (2019). *The Cambridge Encyclopedia of the English language* (3rd ed.). Cambridge University Press.

Davies, A. (2016). *An introduction to applied linguistics: From practice to theory*. Edinburgh University Press.

Ellis, R. (2008). *The study of second language acquisition* (2nd ed.). Oxford University Press.

Gass, S. M., & Mackey, A. (2015). *The Routledge handbook of second language acquisition*. Routledge.

Hornby, A. S. (2014). *Oxford advanced learner's dictionary*. Oxford University Press.

May, S. (2014). *The multilingual turn: Implications for SLA, TESOL, and bilingual education*. Routledge., doi:10.4324/9780203113493

Ortega, L. (2009). *Understanding second language acquisition*. Routledge.

Ricento, T., Peled, Y., & Ives, P. (Eds.). (2015). *Language policy and political theory: Building bridges, assessing breaths*. Springer. doi:10.1007/978-3-319-15084-0

Richards, J. C., & Schmidt, R. (2013). *Longman dictionary of language teaching and applied linguistics*. Routledge. doi:10.4324/9781315833835

Swan, M., & Walter Ur, P. (2012). *A course in language teaching: Practice and theory*. Cambridge University Press.

Yule, G. (2016). *The study of language* (6th ed.). Cambridge University Press.

Żammit, J. (2022). Mixed methods to study the interlanguage of adult learners of Maltese as a second language. *Asian Journal of Social Science and Management Technology, 4*(3), 79–93.

KEY TERMS AND DEFINITIONS

Action Research: Experiments designed for solving specific problems or challenges of the current practice by hands-on professionals. The goal of action research is to develop practical answers to the needs of the given situation and provide feedback and evaluation to enhance professional practice.

Applied Linguistics: This is an interdisciplinary Androscoggin, which includes linguistic theories, methods, and findings that offer solutions to practical language problems. These include subjects such as foreign language education, translation services, language policy in areas like testing of languages and speech abnormalities.

Corpus Linguistics: Corpus linguistics refers to a kind of language research that uses large collections of authentic samples (Butler 2010). Computational techniques are employed in corpus linguistics in order to analyze lengths of words, sentence lengths, types of words used in sentences and phrases (Sinclair 2004).

Language Acquisition: Thematic process whereby people learn one or more languages leading them into understanding symbols such as grammar rules, vocabulary among other communicative skills.

Language Policies: These are official rules that govern the use or non-use on differentiations among others regarding a particular issue. They pertain human rights connected with communication variation between individuals educational systems.

Language Teaching Methods: These attempts include using contextualized language teaching (CLT), task-based language teaching (TBLT), content-based instruction (CBI) approaches for the realization second-language learning strategies.

Mixed Methods Research: Mixed-methods designs bridge qualitative and quantitative research in terms of scope when trying to understand phenomena fully. These designs aim at enriching both sides through a comprehensive analysis of complex phenomena.

Qualitative Research: Research methods aimed at studying subjective perspectives from individual interviewee's point-of-view interpreted through participant observation conducted during fieldwork activities done as part of ethnographic research; these interpretations also encompassed all data collection methods for this study.

Quantitative Research: In general, this involves quantifying large quantities of numbers to generalize patterns, trends and relationships. Quantitative research is usually based on the application of various statistical techniques to confirm or disapprove certain hypotheses and derive conclusions from it.

Research Methods: This refers to a systematical approach when conducting research which enables the researcher to perform procedures and techniques that will allow him/her to study language-related phenomena as well as answer research questions in applied linguistics. They can be either quantitative or qualitative methods.

Chapter 10
Vietnamese EFL Teachers' and Students' Perceptions of Using Translanguaging in Language-Integrated Literature Courses:
A Qualitative Study

Tuyet-Nhung Thi Nguyen
Tra Vinh University, Vietnam

Phuong-Nam Thi Nguyen
Tra Vinh University, Vietnam

Ngoc-Tai Huynh
Tra Vinh University, Vietnam

ABSTRACT

This chapter reports a case study on Vietnamese EFL student and teacher perceptions of the benefits and difficulties of using translanguaging in literature courses. Using semi-structured interviews and thematic analysis, this study engaged seven students and five teachers to address the research questions. The results revealed that the students perceived benefits in using Vietnamese in teaching English literature courses, including improving understanding and analyses of literary works, cultural connections, and group interactions. Similarly, the teachers recognized benefits such as increasing comprehension, student engagement, cultural awareness, and confidence. However, students encountered difficulties related to the use of colloquial language, translation complexities, and cultural disparities. Likely, teachers observed diminishing student engagement, hindrances to students' English language proficiency, and comprehension difficulties. These results thereby contribute to the existing understanding of translanguaging in the classroom.

DOI: 10.4018/979-8-3693-3294-8.ch010

1. INTRODUCTION

The significance of literature in language education extends beyond language acquisition, impacting students' cultural awareness, critical thinking, and personal growth. Integrating literature courses in English as a Foreign Language (EFL) settings enhances language structures, vocabulary, and reading skills while providing authentic materials for student engagement (Khan & Alasmari, 2018). However, teaching literature in EFL contexts presents challenges related to student preferences, language proficiency barriers, and instructional strategies (Hussein, 2016). The intricate nature of literature necessitates tailored interventions to support students' language development and literary analysis. Because literary works evoke empathy and emotions and improve theory of mind, such works serve as significant cultural and artistic expressions (Kidd & Castano, 2013).

In parallel, exploring the use of translanguaging in EFL classrooms offers promising benefits for enhancing the engagement, understanding, and language skills of students. Translanguaging deepens comprehension, facilitates learning explanations, and improves writing performance (Berlianti & Pradita, 2021; Liando et al., 2023; Sun & Zhang, 2022). In addition, translanguaging contributes to students' identity development, fostering confidence, metalinguistic awareness, and inclusive learning environments (Garcia & Kleifgen, 2019; Makalela, 2015; Moses et al., 2021; Wang, 2022). Moreover, the use of translanguaging has been linked to the development of students' identity and confidence, leading to an in-depth understanding of content and enhancing language-learning experiences (Makalela, 2015; Wang, 2022). It also fosters critical metalinguistic awareness, confidence in performing literacies, and the creation of inclusive learning environments (Garcia & Kleifgen, 2019; Moses et al., 2021). These aspects collectively emphasize the positive influence of translanguaging on students' language proficiency, social–emotional development, and identity construction.

The aforementioned research on the benefits and challenges of literature courses and translanguaging in EFL classrooms suggests that by incorporating translanguaging practices in EFL contexts, educators may enhance students' language proficiency, social–emotional development, and critical engagement with literary texts. To this end, however, exploring the perceptions of teachers and students, particularly the use of a native language in literature courses for English majors, is essential.

To date, nonetheless, limited research has made such an attempt. To address this gap, the present study explores the perceptions of Vietnamese EFL lecturers and English majors regarding the benefits and challenges of using translanguaging in literature courses in the Vietnamese EFL context. Examining the perspectives of educators and learners on the integration of translanguaging practices, this study aims to elucidate the effective utilization of native language resources in enhancing language acquisition and literary analysis in EFL settings. The insights gained from this investigation have the potential to inform pedagogical strategies, curriculum development, and teacher training programs in the Vietnamese EFL context, ultimately enhancing the quality of literature education for English majors. Based on the aforementioned objectives, this study aims to address the following research questions.

1. How do Vietnamese EFL teachers perceive the benefits and challenges using translanguaging in literature courses?
2. How do English majors perceive the benefits and challenges of using translanguaging in literature courses?

2. LITERATURE REVIEW

2.1. Definitions of Translanguaging

According to Cenoz and Gorter (2021, p. 3), the term "translanguaging" originates from bilingual education in Welsh and was first used in Welsh as "trawsieithu." In terms of processes and functions, Wright and Baker (2017, p. 280) defined translanguaging as "the process of making meaning, shaping experiences, understandings and knowledge through the use of two languages" (as cited in Cenoz & Gorte, 2021, p. 5). In this sense, translanguaging highlights the essential roles of multimodal semiotic resources, including gestures, objects, visual signals, touch, tone, sounds, and words (García & Wei, 2014). From this approach, the emphasis shifts from switching between two fixed languages as modes to the communicative inventiveness of the individual agent.

Cenoz and Gorter (2021) noted that various linguistics resources are always available for multilingual speakers to use. However, depending on the social context, translanguaging practices can be prominent. For instance, when school regulations do not prohibit students from using various languages in class, students can use their resources in more creative ways (Cenoz & Gorter, 2021). In bilingual contexts, the purposeful use of translanguaging enhances the bilingual identities of students and aids in the development of their academic language and topic expertise (Abourehab & Azaz, 2020; Creese & Blackledge, 2015; Cummins, 2019). In teaching EFL, translanguaging refers to the practice of utilizing multiple languages or language varieties in communication and learning. Translanguaging is considered a pedagogical method that allows for the use of students' first language as a resource to facilitate language learning (Liu & Fang, 2022). It also challenges the traditional monolingual framework and encourages the adoption of a new mindset that embraces students' entire linguistic potential (Nagy, 2018). Moreover, translanguaging is related to teaching EFL because it allows for the use of students' entire linguistic repertoire, including their first language, in the classroom (Liando et al., 2023; Nagy, 2018).

In summary, translanguaging is a concept that has gained recognition in bilingual and EFL teaching contexts. In this study, translanguaging refers to the spontaneous switching between two distinct languages to enhance the communicative creativity of the individual. Specifically, the present research employs the term translanguaging to describe instances where Vietnamese teachers and students utilize their first language (L1), Vietnamese, within literature courses for English majors.

2.2. Challenges of Teaching Literature Courses to EFL Students in an English Studies Program

Along with benefits, teaching literature in EFL contexts also presents various challenges that impact instructors and students. The primary issues faced in delivering literature courses in EFL settings revolve around student preferences, language proficiency barriers, and instructional approaches.

One of the key challenges lies in incorporating students' literature preferences and attitudes into teaching practices to enhance literary and language competence. Studies have affirmed that aligning teaching strategies with students' interests can significantly improve learning outcomes (Yilmaz, 2011). However, accommodating diverse preferences while maintaining academic standards poses a notable challenge for instructors. Language proficiency is another major obstacle for EFL students studying literature. Low language levels hinder students' comprehension and engagement with literary texts, impacting their overall performance in literature courses (Hussein, 2016). Addressing these proficiency barriers requires tailored interventions to support language development alongside literary analysis.

Motivating EFL students to actively participate in literature courses remains a persistent issue. Negative attitudes toward English literature, cultural misperceptions, and intrinsic demotivating factors may contribute to student disengagement (Lam, 2017). Creating a supportive and engaging learning environment that fosters interest in literature is crucial but challenging in EFL contexts. In addition, adapting teaching methodologies to suit the needs of EFL learners presents a considerable challenge for instructors. Balancing linguistic competence development with literary content, selecting appropriate teaching approaches, and integrating reflective writing skills pose complexities in the delivery of literature courses (Febriani et al., 2022). Ensuring that teaching methods effectively enhance students' critical thinking abilities and language proficiency requires continuous pedagogical refinement (Miri & Hung, 2021).

Although there are recommendations for integrating literature into EFL classrooms, implementing these suggestions effectively remains a challenge. Ensuring the seamless integration of literary materials to meet language teaching objectives, addressing student needs, and aligning course content with students' aptitudes require a nuanced approach (Vo, 2024). Overcoming the challenges of incorporating translanguaging in EFL contexts necessitates strategic planning and instructional innovation.

In conclusion, the multifaceted challenges in teaching literature courses in EFL contexts demand proactive measures to address student preferences, language proficiency issues, motivational barriers, and instructional complexities. By recognizing and navigating these challenges, instructors can enhance the learning experiences and literary engagement of EFL students.

2.3. Advantages of Translanguaging in EFL Contexts

Several studies have explored the potential benefits of using translanguaging in enhancing EFL students' engagement and understanding. Berlianti and Pradita (2021) observed that translanguaging in the classroom deepens students' understanding of sociopolitical engagement, critical thinking, and metalinguistic awareness. Furthermore, Moses et al. (2021) contended that translanguaging promotes the use of students' language skills to create meaning. The aforementioned researchers also highlighted the importance of fostering educational settings that encourage the growth of bilingual identities. By incorporating opportunities for students to utilize their language skills in writing letters, teachers can create an inclusive learning environment that encourages bilingualism and supports student growth. Such opportunities also allows teachers to draw on their own linguistic resources and teaching strategies, fostering a sense of authenticity and confidence in their pedagogical approach. These studies underscore the significance of translanguaging in shaping students' linguistic and cultural identities as well as their confidence in using multiple languages.

Various studies have also demonstrated the potential benefits of translanguaging in enhancing student engagement, comprehension, and language skills in diverse EFL contexts. Alasmari et al. (2022) reported that EFL students utilize their entire linguistic repertoire to facilitate communication and improve comprehension. The findings indicated that teachers generally have a favorable opinion of translanguaging, recognizing its effectiveness in aiding students' comprehension of intricate concepts and facilitating communication inside and outside the classroom. Furthermore, Panezai et al. (2022) also showed that the use of multiple languages in classrooms facilitates meaningful communication. Chaika (2023) further supported the benefits of using translanguaging in EFL contexts by reporting that translanguaging strategies effectively promote language learning by encouraging meaningful communication, providing comprehension support, and creating a supportive language environment. Students showed greater motivation and engagement as they could use their native languages to understand and communicate complex ideas, connecting their first languages with the language used in class.

Similarly, Liando et al. (2023) confirmed that translanguaging enhances students' understanding by providing a more convenient way to explain learning materials. This aligns with the positive perceptions of translanguaging found by Muis (2023), who observed that lecturers expressed positive perceptions of translanguaging in the EFL classroom in terms of it making their English teaching effective and helping the students understand the teaching and learning material well. Furthermore, Greenier (2023) showed that in primary EFL classrooms in China, translanguaging between English and Chinese is commonly used for meaning making (through preparation and expansion), collaboration, and empowerment, which have the potential to facilitate different procedures of formative assessment by furthering understanding and expression, stimulating critical thinking and exploration, maintaining interest and engagement, and promoting autonomy and peer learning.

The use of translanguaging has been linked to the development of students' identity and confidence. Makalela (2015) found that translanguaging techniques afforded affective and social advantages to participants, leading to an in-depth understanding of the content. From the participants' metacognitive reflections, the class was unconventional and effective in helping them show who they were, enhancing what they brought with them from outside the classroom, and gaining a deeper understanding of the target language and its cultural content. In other words, translanguaging reinforced their sense of self and promoted a feeling of inclusion inside the classroom. Similarly, Wang (2022) observed that students made full use of translanguaging practices, enhancing their confidence in language-learning experiences.

These findings collectively suggest that translanguaging positively influences students' language proficiency and social–emotional development. The implications of these studies are notable for EFL pedagogy. Such results suggest that translanguaging can be a valuable tool for enhancing students' language skills, engagement, and understanding in EFL classrooms. However, the contrasting findings regarding the impact of translanguaging on English language development highlight the need for further research to understand the nuanced effects of translanguaging in different EFL contexts.

2.4. Translanguaging Challenges in EFL Contexts

Although there are potential benefits to employing translanguaging in EFL teaching, there are several challenges that must be addressed. One of the challenges is that teachers encounter difficulties in effectively utilizing translanguaging pedagogy in classroom settings owing to the need for a comprehensive understanding of the linguistic competencies of both the students and the teachers themselves (Walter, 2022). This highlights the importance of addressing linguistic competence as a fundamental challenge in the implementation of translanguaging in teaching and learning English in Vietnam.

Jiang et al. (2022) argued that the attitudes and perceptions of stakeholders, including teachers and students, play a crucial role in the successful implementation of translanguaging. The existing research has shown that students express a need for translanguaging as a strategy for learning and teaching in EFL and English as the Medium of Instruction classrooms. In addition, the attitudes of university English as a Second Language instructors toward translanguaging in the classroom have been identified as a significant factor that influences its incorporation into English language teaching pedagogy (Burton & Rajendram, 2019).

In the context of Vietnam, cultural and linguistic diversity necessitates a nuanced approach such as translanguaging that considers the full linguistic repertoire of students and the sociocultural context in which teaching and learning occur for the creation of an effective translanguaging environment. Therefore, addressing the attitudes and perceptions of stakeholders is essential for overcoming challenges in implementing translanguaging in the Vietnamese context. Moreover, the successful implementation of translanguaging requires strategic and intentional pedagogical use, as opposed to spontaneous use, to realize its benefits fully (Goodman & Tastanbek, 2020). This requirement underscores the need for explicit training and support for teachers to effectively incorporate translanguaging pedagogies into their teaching practice. In addition to linguistic competence and stakeholder attitudes, specific cultural and contextual factors must be considered in the implementation of translanguaging (Cenoz & Gorter, 2011).

The present research explores the perceptions of Vietnamese EFL lecturers and English majors concerning the use of translanguaging in literature courses. This attempt is significant because it is linked to the benefits and challenges of teaching literature courses to EFL students in English studies programs.

3. METHODOLOGY

3.1. Research Design

This study employs a qualitative approach to thoroughly examine the perspectives and experiences of Vietnamese EFL instructors and English majors regarding the use of translanguaging in literature classrooms. Qualitative methodologies enable a comprehensive exploration of participants' viewpoints, facilitating the capture of detailed and intricate narratives that may be overlooked by quantitative approaches (Mirhosseini, 2020).

3.2. Participants

The study includes five EFL lecturers from Vietnam who are now teaching literary classes and seven English majors who are currently enrolled in these classes at a university in Vietnam (Table 1). In the English studies program at this university, students must take three compulsory literature courses with a total of eight credits in three different semesters. To ensure that a wide variety of opinions are represented, a purposeful sampling approach is followed. This selection process includes teacher participants who have varied levels of English teaching experience and teaching experience in different literature courses. Meanwhile, the student participants are in their third or final year and have all experienced at least two literary courses. The inclusion of lecturers and students in the study allows for the collection of numerous perspectives, which, in turn, enriches the analysis and provides a comprehensive grasp of the topic under investigation.

3.3. Data Collection Method

The chosen approach for data collection of this study involves the utilization of 12 semi-structured interviews with Vietnamese lecturers and students. In semi-structured interviews, questions and prompts are employed flexibly, although the interviewer prepares a question list and topics prior to conducting the interview. The interviewer can even offer more opportunities for respondents to develop their opinions towards the researcher's interested topics (Denscombe, 2007).

Rabionet (2011) asserts that semi-structured interview is different from unstructured interview in that semi-structured interviewing techniques allow interviewers to direct the conversation towards the topics of interest. This type of interviewing approach is especially appropriate when researchers are interested in exploring participants' perceptions and attitudes regarding a certain topic (Glesne, 2011). This is particularly relevant to the research aim of the present study, as the primary aim this study is to explore viewpoints of Vietnamese EFL lecturers' and students' viewpoints on the advantages and disadvantages of using native language (i.e., Vietnamese language) in language-integrated literature courses.

Specifically, each interview comprises two main sections to investigate the perceptions of lecturers and students in terms of benefits and difficulties of using translanguaging in their literature classes. The first step in preparation involves establishing the study's goals and identifying important themes connected to

Table 1. Participant background

	Gender	Years of Teaching English	Years of Teaching Literature	Literature Courses
Teacher 1	Female	29	10	British literatureAmerican literatureWorld literature
Teacher 2	Female	20	6	British literatureAmerican literatureWorld literature
Teacher 3	Female	10	5	American literatureWorld literature
Teacher 4	Female	10	3	British literatureAmerican literature
Teacher 5	Male	3	1	American literature
	Gender	Age	Years of Learning English	Literature Courses
Student 1	Female	22	14	British literatureAmerican literatureWorld literature
Student 2	Female	23	14	British literatureAmerican literatureWorld literature
Student 3	Female	21	13	British literatureAmerican literature
Student 4	Female	22	14	British literatureAmerican literatureWorld literature
Student 5	Male	21	13	British literatureAmerican literature
Student 6	Male	22	14	British literatureAmerican literatureWorld literature
Student 7	Male	21	13	British literatureAmerican literature

translanguaging in language-integrated literature courses, then developing open-ended questions that enable a thorough examination of participants' perspectives and personal experiences. During the interviews, researchers carefully listen to participants' responses, asking for more details and explanations when necessary. Interviewers strike a balance between adhering to a structured framework and embracing spontaneous conversation to uncover unforeseen insights. After the interviews, researchers carefully examined the gathered data, identifying common themes and detailed perspectives to report on the findings with the hope of contributing to a deeper understanding of language learning and teaching dynamics in this context.

3.4. Data Analysis Procedure

Thematic analysis (TA) was employed to analyze the collected data of the present study. Thematic analysis is a method for identifying, analyzing, and interpreting patterns of meaning within qualitative data (Clarke, 2017; Herzog et al., 2019). It is a flexible and accessible approach that can be applied across various theoretical frameworks and research paradigms (Clarke, 2017). Given the research aims of this study, thematic analysis is a vital method for analyzing the information collected from the interviews with Vietnamese lecturers and students. This process involves organizing data into themes that make sense and interpreting these themes based on the study's objectives. By carefully examining the qualitative data, the researchers identified patterns, variations, and subtle details in how the teachers and students viewed the use of Vietnamese in literature classes. In addition, allowing the participants to validate the interpretations through member checking adds credibility to the research findings by ensuring the accuracy of the data. Table 2 summarizes the main themes regarding the perceived benefits and challenges of using Vietnamese in literature courses for English majors.

Table 2. Main themes and sub-themes regarding the perceived benefits and challenges of using Vietnamese in literature courses for English majors

Themes	Students' Viewpoints	Teachers' Viewpoints
Benefits of using Vietnamese in literature courses	Enhanced understanding and analysis of literary worksCultural connection and confidence buildingImproved group interactions and communication	Enhanced understanding and comprehensionSupporting student engagement and participationFacilitating cultural understandingEncouraging confidence and idea development
Challenges of using Vietnamese literature courses	Use of colloquial language and slang during discussionsComplexities of translating from Vietnamese to EnglishCultural disparities in analyzing literary works	Decrease in student engagement and concentrationImpeding English language proficiency and comprehension

4. RESULTS

An analysis showed that the students perceived the use of Vietnamese as enhancing their understanding and analysis of literary works while fostering cultural connection and confidence building. Furthermore, it improved group interactions and communication. The teachers also highlighted the benefits of using Vietnamese in terms of enhancing student understanding and comprehension, supporting student engagement and participation, facilitating cultural understanding, and encouraging confidence and idea development. However, the challenges identified by the students included the use of colloquial language and slang, complexities in translation, and cultural disparities in literary analysis. In addition, the teachers raised concerns regarding potential negative effects on engagement, risks of overdependence on L1 for English language development, and the importance of regulating language use for English proficiency.

4.1. Teachers' Perceptions of the Benefits and Challenges of Using L1 (Vietnamese)

4.1.1. Teachers' Perceptions of the Benefits of Using L1 (Vietnamese)

Through an analysis of the responses from the teacher participants, four key themes regarding the benefits of using Vietnamese in literature courses have been identified: enhancing understanding and comprehension, supporting student engagement and participation, facilitating cultural understanding, and encouraging confidence and idea development. These themes are discussed in detail below.

Of the five teacher participants, three (Teachers 2, 3, and 4) stress the importance of using Vietnamese to support students' comprehension in literature courses for English majors. These teachers advocate initiating discussions in Vietnamese before transitioning to English analysis to ensure that students understand the task at hand and can delve into complex literary analyses effectively. For instance, Teacher 2 recommends discussions in Vietnamese as a precursor to English analysis. The teacher justifies this suggestion with a specific case:

An example of how I integrate Vietnamese into the learning process is during the analysis phase in literature. I often prompt students to analyze based on themes or characters, requiring them to express their thoughts in English. However, before they delve into their analysis, I encourage them to first discuss in Vietnamese to ensure they understand the task at hand. (Teacher 2)

This consideration indicates the importance of establishing a linguistic bridge for students to comprehend the nuances of literary analysis effectively. Teacher 3 echoes this sentiment by highlighting the pivotal role of Vietnamese in setting the groundwork for comprehension. Teacher 3 asserts,

I find that utilizing Vietnamese in specific ways can be highly effective, especially when clarity is essential. When students face challenges in understanding complex literary concepts, I incorporate Vietnamese strategically to provide a clearer explanation, facilitating a deeper comprehension of the material. (Teacher 3)

The aforementioned statement demonstrates the significance of using Vietnamese to provide a clear and structured foundation for students to navigate complex literary concepts with ease. Teacher 4 further reinforces the pedagogical value of incorporating Vietnamese to establish a firm understanding of the subject matter, saying,

Personally, I incorporate Vietnamese in literature courses to ensure that students have a thorough understanding of the subject matter. By using Vietnamese, I aim to simplify concepts and offer explanations that resonate more deeply with the students, enhancing their grasp of the literary content. (Teacher 4)

This explanation emphasizes the role of Vietnamese in simplifying concepts and fostering a deeper connection between students and the literary content. Overall, the perspectives of Teachers 2, 3, and 4 show the consensus on the importance of using Vietnamese to provide a solid foundation for students' comprehension in English literature courses. Their shared experiences in using Vietnamese in literature courses for English majors suggest that by initiating discussions in Vietnamese before transitioning to English analysis, EFL teachers can pave the way for a comprehensive understanding of complex literary themes and characters, creating a conducive learning environment wherein language serves as a catalyst for enhanced student comprehension and engagement with the material.

The incorporation of the Vietnamese language in classroom discussions within English literature courses serves as a catalyst for enhancing student engagement and fostering a dynamic learning environment. Teachers 2, 3, 4, and 5 highlight the positive aspects of using Vietnamese to empower students, promote active participation, and create a supportive and inclusive setting that is conducive to collaborative learning. Teacher 2 mentions the positive impact of Vietnamese on student participation and expression during discussions. This teacher recalls,

When students engage in discussions using Vietnamese, there is a noticeable increase in their participation and expression. The use of Vietnamese encourages students to

articulate their thoughts more freely, leading to dynamic and engaging interactions within the classroom setting. (Teacher 2)

The use of Vietnamese allows students to articulate their thoughts more freely, leading to dynamic and engaging interactions within the classroom setting. This approach boosts student confidence and fosters a vibrant exchange of ideas, enriching the learning experience for all. Similarly, Teacher 3 focuses on creating an empowering environment wherein students feel encouraged to share their perspectives and actively engage with the material using Vietnamese. By incorporating their native language to facilitate discussions, Teachers 3 and 5 cultivate a dynamic learning atmosphere that values diverse viewpoints and promotes active participation. This approach fosters a sense of ownership and inclusivity, nurturing a collaborative learning environment. These teachers observe,

By incorporating Vietnamese to facilitate discussions, I aim to create an environment where students feel empowered to contribute their perspectives and engage meaningfully with the material. This approach fosters a dynamic learning atmosphere that encourages diverse viewpoints and active participation. (Teacher 3)

Integrating Vietnamese into classroom discussions creates a relaxed and focused learning environment. Students are able to concentrate on the material at hand and engage effectively with the content, leading to a more immersive and productive learning experience. (Teacher 5)

The above experiences suggest that by allowing students to use Vietnamese in discussions, regardless of their language proficiency, teachers can create a setting where all learners feel encouraged and valued. This inclusive environment enhances collaboration, promotes mutual respect, and enriches the overall learning experience for students of varying linguistic backgrounds, as asserted by Teacher 4:

The inclusive approach of allowing students to use their native language promotes a supportive learning environment where all students, regardless of their language abilities, feel encouraged to participate in discussions. This inclusive environment enhances collaboration and enhances the overall learning experience. (Teacher 4)

The integration of the Vietnamese language into English studies programs emerges as a helpful tool for fostering cultural understanding, inclusivity, and idea development among students. Teachers 1 and 4 both emphasize the transformative impact of incorporating Vietnamese in enriching students' learning experiences, promoting deeper engagement with cultural themes, and empowering students to explore diverse perspectives within the literary domain.

Teacher 1 acknowledges the value of Vietnamese integration in promoting cultural understanding and inclusivity within English studies programs. By incorporating Vietnamese, students are exposed to diverse cultural perspectives, enhancing their language skills and academic performance. This approach fosters idea generation and development and nurtures student growth within a collaborative and inclusive learning environment, creating a space for the exchange of cultural perspectives and fostering a deeper appreciation for diversity. Teacher 1 said,

I personally think that using Vietnamese in English studies programs, especially for difficult subjects like literature, serves as a valuable tool in fostering cultural understanding and promoting inclusivity. I observe that my students have the opportunity to engage with diverse cultural perspectives, enhancing their language skills and academic performance. (Teacher 1)

Teacher 4 echoes this sentiment by highlighting the strategic use of Vietnamese to encourage students to delve deeper into literary themes and cultural contexts. Through the incorporation of Vietnamese, students gain insights into diverse cultural perspectives, enriching their learning experience and fostering a deeper understanding of cultural nuances. This approach enhances their educational journey and cultivates a more profound appreciation of diverse cultural contexts within the literary realm.

For me, the use of Vietnamese in literature courses encourages my students to explore and delve deeper into literary themes and cultural contexts. By incorporating Vietnamese, my students are able to enrich their learning experience by gaining insights into diverse cultural perspectives. (Teacher 4)

These teachers emphasize the role of Vietnamese in promoting cultural understanding, inclusivity, and academic growth among students. By integrating Vietnamese into English studies programs, educators can facilitate increased engagement with cultural themes and perspectives, enriching students' learning experiences and nurturing a more profound appreciation of diverse cultural contexts within the literary domain.

Of the five teachers, three (Teachers 2, 3, and 4) observe the role of Vietnamese in encouraging confidence, idea development, and academic growth among students. By allowing students to organize their thoughts in Vietnamese before translating them into English, the teachers in the present investigation believe that they can facilitate confidence building and idea articulation.

Allowing students to organize their thoughts in Vietnamese before translating them into English fosters confidence and idea development. This enables students to articulate their ideas more effectively and ensures a smoother transition between languages, enhancing their overall comprehension and expression in the study of literature. (Teacher 2)

This enhancement indicates that through the intentional use of the Vietnamese language, teachers can foster confidence, idea development, and student engagement in the study of literature courses. In other words, by encouraging students to organize their thoughts, providing necessary support, preventing isolation due to language barriers, and enhancing cultural understanding, teachers create a supportive and dynamic learning environment that promotes idea exploration, academic growth, and enriched learning experiences for students. Teachers 3 and 4 elaborate on this point:

The incorporation of Vietnamese enables me to check my students' understanding and provide the necessary support during my lessons. Specifically, I can identify areas where students may require additional assistance, fostering a supportive learning environment conducive to idea development when learning literature courses. (Teacher 3)

From my experience, the appropriate use of Vietnamese in literature courses for English majors can help prevent my students from feeling isolated or disengaged due to language barriers. (Teacher 4)

In summary, the insights of Teachers 3 and 4, along with the perspectives of Teacher 2, underscore the multifaceted benefits of integrating Vietnamese into English studies programs. This integration promotes cultural understanding, inclusivity, confidence building, and idea development. Thus, the use of Vietnamese enriches students' learning experiences, nurtures engagement with diverse cultural perspectives, and fosters a supportive and enriching environment that is conducive to academic growth and idea exploration in the literature courses for English majors.

4.1.2. Teachers' Perceptions of the Challenges of Using L1 (Vietnamese)

Of the five teachers involved, Teachers 3, 4, and 5 express concerns regarding the negative effects of the overdependence on students' native language (L1) with respect to their engagement and focus, highlighting the difficulties of incorporating Vietnamese into English literature classes for English majors. Furthermore, Teachers 3 and 4 raise concerns about students becoming too reliant on their native language for their English language development. In particular, Teacher 1, an experienced lecturer with 30 years of teaching, explicitly states her preference for using English over Vietnamese when teaching literature courses to English majors, despite acknowledging the value of students' native language (Vietnamese).

Teachers 3, 4, and 5 provide discerning observations regarding the topic of student overdependence and concentration, elaborating on the disadvantages of incorporating Vietnamese (L1) into English literature courses designed for English majors. These teachers mention the risks of relying excessively on Vietnamese (L1) for students studying English literature as part of their major. Teacher 3 observes, "If students use too much Vietnamese in the classroom, when I organize activities that require the use of English exclusively, students seem to lack motivation to participate because they are not confident in using English immediately."

Similarly, Teacher 4 shares concerns about students becoming overly dependent on their native language, saying, "I fear that students might depend too much on Vietnamese, which could hinder their understanding of English." This indicates Teacher 4's recognition of the risks involved with the excessive use of Vietnamese in impeding students' English skills and overall comprehension.

Moreover, Teacher 3 expresses concerns regarding distracting students and reducing their concentration by using Vietnamese, stating, "I worry that speaking in Vietnamese could distract students and decrease their focus." This shows Teacher 3's awareness of how language barriers can affect student learning and engagement.

Similarly, Teacher 5, a young lecturer, ponders the effects of prolonged Vietnamese discussions, stating, "If I keep explaining in Vietnamese for too long, it tends to make students lose focus." Teacher 5 thus observes the challenge of balancing language use to maintain students' attention and prevent distractions that could hinder their learning process.

Given these perspectives, Teachers 3, 4, and 5 clearly recognize the crucial importance of using Vietnamese appropriately in literature classrooms for effective language teaching. Their concerns highlight the balance required to ensure that incorporating students' native language (i.e., Vietnamese) does not detract from students' attention, motivation, and academic progress.

Teachers 3 and 4, who have a decade of teaching English experience, discuss the importance of language skills and understanding. Both teachers hold the belief that if Vietnamese is excessively used in the classroom, it negatively impacts students' English language proficiency development and comprehension abilities. These teachers explain,

There is a need to consider when and why Vietnamese is necessary. Without this consideration, students may become dependent on Vietnamese and form habits

that deter them from participating in English opportunities, thereby limiting their English language development and proficiency. (Teacher 3)

I observe that some students tend to use Vietnamese to translate literary works. While this may help them understand the text, it limits their opportunities to read in English. Therefore, when translation tools are not available, the reading comprehension abilities of these students are affected. (Teacher 4)

Teachers 3 and 4 emphasize the importance of regulating language use to improve students' English proficiency and understanding. Their perspectives reveal the challenges that educators face in managing language complexities to help students succeed in English while acknowledging the role of Vietnamese in aiding comprehension.

Conversely, Teacher 1 focuses on enhancing English language proficiency by encouraging students to engage in English conversations, demonstrating a commitment to strengthening language skills in an English-focused curriculum for English-major students.

Teacher 1 highlights her desire for students to excel in English by fully promoting English conversations, stating, "Therefore, I aspire for the students to achieve their goal of mastering English by encouraging them to converse in English as much as they can." This underscores Teacher 1's dedication to creating an English-speaking environment that motivates students to enhance their language abilities through active communication. Teacher 1's perspective emphasizes the importance of providing opportunities for students to engage in meaningful language interactions in English rather than in Vietnamese, promoting their development and proficiency in English within an immersive learning environment.

In summary, the discussions among the teachers elucidate the complexities and considerations involved in language integration and proficiency, particularly in the context of English literature courses for English majors. The concerns raised regarding the balance between using Vietnamese (L1) and promoting English language development underscore the challenges faced by educators in fostering effective language-learning environments. By emphasizing the importance of regulating language use, incentivizing English dialogues, and prioritizing English interactions, these teachers demonstrate a shared commitment to enhancing students' English skills while acknowledging the role of the Vietnamese language in the learning process. Their insights serve to emphasize the ongoing efforts and dedication of educators in navigating language barriers to ensure students' success and mastery of English in educational settings.

4.2. Students' Perceptions of the Benefits and Challenges of Using Vietnamese in Literature Courses

4.2.1. Students' Perceptions of the Benefits of Using Vietnamese in Literature Courses

In analyzing the responses shared by the students regarding the use of Vietnamese in literature courses for English majors, several recurring themes have emerged, illustrating the diverse benefits and impacts of incorporating multiple languages in academic pursuits. Specifically, through a comprehensive analysis of the data provided by the students, it becomes evident that the themes of enhanced understanding and analysis of literary works, cultural connection and confidence building, and improved group interaction and communication collectively indicate the multifaceted advantages of utilizing Vietnamese alongside English in literature studies.

Of the seven student participants, all specifically mention the benefits of using Vietnamese (L1) in understanding and analyzing literary works. Each student shares unique insights, reflections, testimonials, and experiences to highlight the importance of employing Vietnamese in conjunction with English to amplify their comprehension of dense themes, literary tools, plotlines, and characters embedded within the literature courses of the English studies program.

For instance, Students 1 and 2 stress the valuable role of Vietnamese in enriching their understanding of literary devices and narrative intricacies. Student 1 explains the following:

Employing both English and Vietnamese in the learning process aids in an effortless understanding of the storyline and an analysis of the literary devices contained in the text. An excellent example is confronting a new piece of work laden with unfamiliar words possessing multiple meanings. Merging English–Vietnamese and Vietnamese–English helps me grasp the plot more seamlessly. (Student 1)

This statement underscores the critical role of Vietnamese in equipping students with an enriched understanding of complex literary components. Student 2 echoes the previous statement with a similar sentiment:

A considerable amount of complex knowledge in literature, such as themes and topics, was made clear to me when my teacher explained it in Vietnamese. (Student 2)

Similarly, Students 3, 5, and 7 acknowledge the crucial role of Vietnamese in decoding complex plotlines, unfamiliar literary terms, and concepts. These students disclose the following:

Indeed, literature is replete with terms and concepts that are incredibly challenging to grasp without a strong English foundation. (Student 3)

Applying Vietnamese proves advantageous when studying literature courses, specifically when studying classic works of literature. (Student 5)

Specifically, the use of the translanguaging approach enables the students to delve deeper into texts, analyze complex literary concepts, and engage critically with the material. Student 7 notes,

Using multiple languages in the literature classes helps me understand the text more clearly and analyze and understand the story effectively. (Student 7)

This sentiment underscores how the integration of Vietnamese alongside English promotes a comprehensive analysis of characters, themes, and literary devices, leading to a profound understanding of literary texts among students. The positive feedback from these students demonstrates that integrating Vietnamese with English in literature courses can enhance student engagement with texts, hone their analytical skills, and enrich their understanding of the cultural and linguistic dimensions in literature. Their insights indicate the importance of language diversity in nurturing a more nuanced and comprehensive understanding of literary works.

The remaining two students (Students 4 and 6) highlight the benefits of integrating Vietnamese with English in enhancing communication skills and fostering critical thinking. Student 4 draws attention to how Vietnamese deepens their text understanding, stating, "Utilizing multiple languages in literature class enables me to understand the texts more profoundly." This sentiment highlights the role of language diversity in bolstering comprehension and promoting a robust analysis of literary works. Similarly, Student 6 accentuates the positive influence of using Vietnamese in classroom communication, noting, "The use of Vietnamese in literature class invigorates the lesson, making it less monotonous." Taken together, these insights underscore how the integration of Vietnamese with English in literature courses not only elevates communication skills but also stimulates critical thinking, forming a dynamic and collaborative learning environment that enhances students' overall academic experiences in English studies programs.

Four of the seven students (Students 1, 2, 5, and 7) discuss the theme of cultural interface and confidence augmentation. These students acknowledge the significance of utilizing Vietnamese alongside English in literature courses for English majors. Specifically, the use of Vietnamese in English literature classes does more than augment students' comprehension; it cultivates a potent cultural linkage, as articulated by Student 3:

Indeed, literature is replete with terminology and notions that can be exceedingly challenging to grasp for learners who lack a solid foundation in English. Consequently, a blend of languages becomes crucial in literature classes to facilitate my grasp of the contexts, including historical and social contexts, as well as to better understand the significance of the works and the moral lessons intertwined with reality. (Student 3)

Furthermore, Student 5 reflects,

The tandem use of my native tongue and English in studying literature aided me in manifesting my cultural identity. For example, when the theme of a work discusses the role of women in American society, I often compare it with the role of women in Vietnamese culture to observe similarities and differences, thereby helping me to have a more comprehensive perspective and more confidence in expressing my opinions. (Student 5)

This perspective underscores the importance of integrating Vietnamese to reflect cultural identity, thereby allowing students to forge deeper connections with literary works from various viewpoints. This cultural linkage accentuates the learning experience and bolsters students' confidence in articulating their ideas effectively. Student 7 affirms the role of Vietnamese in confidence reinforcement: "The incorporation of diverse languages in literature classes simplifies my understanding of the lessons and allows me to confidently show my views because I understand the lessons well." This remark highlights how linguistic diversity influences comprehension and student confidence in their engagement with academic content as well as their successful expression of ideas.

In the cohort of seven students, two participants (Students 4 and 6) explicitly address the topic of advanced group interactions and communication. Through a combination of their insights and experiences, these students emphasize the manner in which the concurrent utilization of Vietnamese and English languages fosters improved communication, promotes efficacious teamwork, and enriches group dialogues, particularly within the context of literature courses that form an integral part of English studies programs. In scenarios involving group projects, by integrating Vietnamese, the level of effective communication and collaboration among students has increased noticeably.

Student 4 draws attention to this point by stating, "Because literature is literary, it is full of vague ideas and very complicated terms. Some students may find it easy to understand these, but for others it might be like going into unknown territory. Because of this, mixing languages is the best way for everyone to share their thoughts and ideas. Just to give you an example, whenever we practice for group presentations, we always talk in Vietnamese so that everyone can understand. Also, using Vietnamese gives us the power to be more creative, which is hard to do with just English."

Likewise, Student 6 underscores the collaborative advantages of the use of Vietnamese and English in discussions, remarking, "When collaborating in groups, the use of both Vietnamese and English empowers members to become more assertive in voicing their opinions, utilizing a richer vocabulary, and avoiding potential monotony within the group." This observation accentuates how the purposeful introduction of Vietnamese encourages a more engaging and dynamic group setting, stimulating active participation and a multitude of viewpoints in literature-related dialogues.

In conclusion, the incorporation of Vietnamese in literature courses for English majors offers a myriad of benefits that enrich the learning experience and foster further engagement with literary works. From enhancing comprehension and cultural connections to promoting confidence and effective communication, the use of multiple languages plays a pivotal role in nurturing students' analytical and interpretive skills in the literary domain. By embracing the diversity of languages, students can develop a holistic understanding of literary texts, interact in collaborative learning environments, and cultivate a deeper appreciation for the cultural nuances embedded within literary works.

4.2.2. Students' Perceptions of the Benefits of Using Vietnamese in Literature Courses

In the interviews with the student participants, several key themes emerged regarding the challenges of using L1 (Vietnamese) in literature courses for English majors. One prominent challenge was the use of colloquial language and slang during their discussions with classmates in literature courses. Student 1, for instance, aptly articulates this challenge, stating,

Using colloquial language in discussions can be confusing for others. It's like we're speaking different languages within the same language. (Student 1)

This sentiment is echoed by Student 2, who emphasizes the importance of striking a balance between linguistic expression and clarity to facilitate effective communication in group discussions. This student states the following:

When slang is used, it can create a barrier to understanding. We need to find a balance between being expressive and being clear when using Vietnamese in literature courses for English majors. (Student 2)

Moreover, the students discuss their concerns regarding the complexities of translating from Vietnamese to English during academic discourse. For instance, Student 3 highlights the time-consuming nature of translation, emphasizing the need to convey the essence of discussions accurately across languages. This student recalls,

I usually analyze the details or characters of literary works in Vietnamese first, so it could take more time to transfer them into English. (Student 3)

Students 4 and 7 further elaborate on the challenges of maintaining meaning during translation, noting the meticulous attention required to ensure that all points are effectively communicated in both languages. One student asserts,

Sometimes the meaning gets lost in translation. We have to be careful when switching between Vietnamese and English to ensure our points are understood. (Student 4)

Holding a similar viewpoint, the other states,

I cannot deny that sometimes translation can lead to cultural barriers, or the differences in writing styles between languages can make it difficult for me to fully appreciate the meaning of the sentences. (Student 7)

These insights elucidate the meticulous nature of linguistic transitions and the need for proficient translation skills to facilitate comprehension when using L1 in EFL classrooms. In addition to linguistic challenges, the students mention challenges relating to the cultural disparities inherent in analyzing literary works written in English (Students 5 and 6). Student 5 stresses the significance of understanding cultural contexts in literature, noting the challenges posed by differences between Vietnam and other nations in interpreting thematic elements:

Understanding the cultural context is crucial in literature. The differences between Vietnam and other countries can make it challenging to interpret certain themes. (Student 5)

Student 6 further underscores the pivotal role of cultural nuances in literary analysis, emphasizing the imperative of expanding cultural awareness to appreciate the depth of the works under study. This student claims,

Cultural nuances play a significant role in literary analysis. We need to expand our cultural awareness to appreciate the depth of the works we study. (Student 6)

These reflections indicate the importance of cultural literacy and cross-cultural understanding in navigating the complexities of literary analysis within a multicultural context.

Overall, these insights elucidate the intricate dynamics of incorporating Vietnamese into literature courses for English majors, highlighting the cognitive, emotional, and pedagogical considerations involved in navigating linguistic diversity to enhance learning and comprehension in the study of literature. The students' varied experiences offer valuable perspectives regarding the challenges and benefits of using multiple languages in the educational context, underscoring the importance of a thoughtful integration of linguistic resources to enrich the literary learning experience.

5. DISCUSSION

This chapter explores the perspectives of teachers and students on using Vietnamese in literature courses for English majors. The data analysis of the responses from the teacher and student participants in the present study finds a shared recognition of the benefits and challenges associated with incorporating Vietnamese into the academic setting, particularly in literature courses. Both the teachers and students agree on key points regarding the use of Vietnamese in literature courses. Moreover, the participants emphasize how the incorporation of Vietnamese enhances understanding and engagement with literary works. Herein, the Vietnamese EFL students indicate that using Vietnamese alongside English aids in unraveling complex themes and characters, fostering a deeper comprehension of the materials. Similarly, the Vietnamese EFL teachers emphasize the pedagogical benefits of using Vietnamese to support students' analytical skills and further their engagement with literary concepts. These results align with previous studies on translanguaging (Alasmari et al., 2022; Berlianti & Pradita, 2021).

Second, the findings herein support the point that translanguaging can address the persistent issue of motivating EFL students to actively participate in learning activities. Specifically, researchers have found that translanguaging promotes language learning and student engagement (Chaika, 2023), and using Vietnamese in literature courses may help in balancing linguistic competence development and literary content. Third, translanguaging practices promote collaboration, empowerment, and meaningful communication (Greenier, 2023), and the present study finds that incorporating Vietnamese enriches students' understanding and expression.

The findings herein can address several challenges encountered in teaching literature, especially in EFL contexts. For instance, addressing language proficiency barriers through tailored interventions and linguistic support is crucial, as highlighted in the studies conducted by Hussein (2016). In addition, challenges related to student motivation, engagement, and adapting teaching methodologies are recognized in the findings of the present study, which is consistent with previous research on translanguaging (Chaika, 2023; Febriani et al., 2022).

Regarding the literature on translanguaging, researchers in the field of language teaching, including multilingual environments and EFL settings, have been investigating this concept extensively (Berlianti & Pradita, 2021; Garcia & Kleifgen, 2019; Liando et al., 2023; Makalela, 2015; Moses et al., 2021; Sun & Zhang, 2022; Wang, 2022). Currently, diverse academic perspectives exist regarding the value of translanguaging practices in foreign language classrooms. Some studies have identified the benefits of translanguaging in language classrooms, whereas many others have observed the disadvantages of using a native language in foreign language classes (Cenoz & Gorter, 2011; Goodman & Tastanbek, 2020; Jiang et al., 2022; Walter, 2022). These debates have led to a lack of consensus, causing foreign language teachers to hesitate in experimenting with incorporating native languages into their classrooms. One of the main aims of the current research is to clarify the value of using a native language in foreign language classrooms and to address the concerns of teachers and scholars with respect to the role of translanguaging by exploring the perspectives of the two main stakeholders in English language teaching and learning environments: students and English specialist teachers. Specifically, this study aims to clarify the value of translanguaging in literature classes within an English studies program in Vietnam. The findings of the study evince diverse points that align and contrast with previous research on the advantages and disadvantages of using translanguaging in EFL contexts.

6. CONCLUSION

In conclusion, the insights gleaned from the present chapter, which explores the use of Vietnamese in literature courses for English majors, present valuable strategies for addressing the challenges encountered in teaching literature within EFL contexts. By acknowledging and accommodating student preferences, overcoming language proficiency barriers, fostering motivation and engagement, adapting teaching methodologies, and integrating literary materials, educators can enhance the learning experience and foster a deeper connection with literature among EFL students. This endeavor will allow for the multifaceted obstacles present in delivering literature courses within EFL settings to be overcome.

The alignment and complementarity of the findings herein with previous research on translanguaging in EFL contexts indicate the significance of implementing innovative strategies to enhance language learning and comprehension while considering cultural and contextual factors. The interplay between students' and teachers' viewpoints on incorporating Vietnamese into literature courses illuminates the diverse benefits and challenges associated with integrating different languages in academia. By navigating these complexities and leveraging the strengths of linguistic diversity, students and teachers can both contribute to a dynamic and enriched learning environment that encourages an in-depth engagement with literary works and fosters cultural understanding within English studies programs.

It should be noted that one limitation of this study is its exclusive focus on the perspectives of students and teachers within a specific academic setting, which potentially limits the generalizability of the findings. Therefore, future research should consider broadening the participant pool to encompass diverse populations and educational contexts. Incorporating mixed-method approaches and longitudinal studies could provide a more comprehensive understanding of the effects of using Vietnamese in literature courses. In addition, exploring different pedagogical strategies and assessing student outcomes in terms of language proficiency, cultural understanding, and academic performance would offer valuable insights for educators and curriculum developers, enabling further advancements in language education and cultural integration.

REFERENCES

Abourehab, Y., & Azaz, M. (2023). Pedagogical translanguaging in community/heritage Arabic language learning. *Journal of Multilingual and Multicultural Development*, *44*(5), 398–411. doi:10.1080/01434632.2020.1826496

Alasmari, M., Qasem, F., Ahmed, R., & Alrayes, M. (2022). Bilingual teachers' translanguaging practices and ideologies in online classrooms in Saudi Arabia. *Heliyon*, *8*(9), e10537. doi:10.1016/j.heliyon.2022.e10537

Berlianti, D., & Pradita, I. (2021). Translanguaging in an EFL classroom discourse: To what extent it is helpful for the students? *Communication in Humanity and Social Science*, *1*(1), 42–46. doi:10.21924/chss.1.1.2021.14

Burton, J., & Rajendram, S. (2019). Translanguaging-as-resource: University ESL instructors' language orientations and attitudes toward translanguaging. *TESL Canada Journal*, *36*(1), 21–47. doi:10.18806/tesl.v36i1.1301

Cenoz, J., & Gorter, D. (2011). Focus on multilingualism: A study of trilingual writing. *Modern Language Journal*, *95*(3), 356–369. doi:10.1111/j.1540-4781.2011.01206.x

Cenoz, J., & Gorter, D. (2021). *Pedagogical translanguaging*. Cambridge University Press.

Chaika, O. (2023). *Translanguaging in multilingual classrooms: A case study analysis*. Philological Review. doi:10.31499/2415-8828.1.2023.281366

Clarke, V., & Braun, V. (2017). Thematic analysis. *The Journal of Positive Psychology*, *12*(3), 297–298. doi:10.1080/17439760.2016.1262613

Creese, A., & Blackledge, A. (2015). Translanguaging and identity in educational settings. *Annual Review of Applied Linguistics*, *35*, 20–35. doi:10.1017/S0267190514000233

Cummins, J. (2019). The emergence of translanguaging pedagogy: A dialogue between theory and practice. *Journal of Multilingual Education Research*, *9*(13), 19–36.

Denscombe, M. (2007). *The good research guide: For small-scale social research projects* (3rd ed.). Open University Press.

Febriani, R. B., Rukmini, D., Mujiyanto, J., & Yuliasri, I. (2022). Lecturers' perception on the implementation of approaches to teaching literature in EFL classrooms. *Studies in English Language and Education*, *9*(1), 349–364. doi:10.24815/siele.v9i1.21035

García, O., & Wei, L. (2014). *Translanguaging: Language, bilingualism and education*. Palgrave Macmillan. doi:10.1057/9781137385765

Glesne, C. (2011). *Becoming qualitative researchers: An introduction* (4th ed.). Pearson.

Goodman, B., & Tastanbek, S. (2020). Making the shift from a codeswitching to a translanguaging lens in English language teacher education. *TESOL Quarterly*, *55*(1), 29–53. doi:10.1002/tesq.571

Greenier, V., Liu, X., & Xiao, Y. (2023). Creative translanguaging in formative assessment: Chinese teachers' perceptions and practices in the primary EFL classroom. *Applied Linguistics Review*, *0*(0). Advance online publication. doi:10.1515/applirev-2023-0085

Herzog, C., Handke, C., & Hitters, E. (2019). *Analyzing talk and text II: Thematic analysis*. Springer.

Hussein E. T. Al-Emami A. H. (2016). Challenges to teaching English literature at the University of Hail: instructors' perspective. *Arab World English Journal (AWEJ)*, *7*(4). https://doi.org/ doi:10.31219/osf.io/wnech

Jiang, Z., Zhang, L., & Mohamed, N. (2022). Researching translanguaging as a feasible pedagogical practice: Evidence from Chinese English-as-a-foreign-language students' perceptions. *RELC Journal*, *53*(2), 371–390. doi:10.1177/00336882221113653

Kidd, D., & Castano, E. (2013). Reading literary fiction improves theory of mind. *Science*, *342*(6156), 377–380. doi:10.1126/science.1239918

Lam, M. (2017). The motivational dimension of language teaching. *Language Teaching*, *50*(3), 301–346. doi:10.1017/S0261444817000088

Liando, N., Dallyono, R., Tatipang, D., & Lengkoan, F. (2023). Among English, Indonesian and local language: Translanguaging practices in an Indonesian EFL classroom. *Indonesian Journal of Applied Linguistics*, *13*(1), 204–216. doi:10.17509/ijal.v13i1.58270

Liu, Y., & Fang, F. (2022). Translanguaging theory and practice: How stakeholders perceive translanguaging as a practical theory of language. *RELC Journal*, *53*(2), 391–399. doi:10.1177/0033688220939222

Makalela, L. (2015). Moving out of linguistic boxes: The effects of translanguaging strategies for multilingual classrooms. *Language and Education*, *29*(3), 200–217. doi:10.1080/09500782.2014.994524

Mirhosseini, S. A. (2020). *Doing qualitative research in language education*. Springer Nature. doi:10.1007/978-3-030-56492-6

Miri, A. M., & Hung, B. P. (2021). Contextualizing second language writing in literature courses: Locality of pedagogy for innovative practices. In *Futuristic and linguistic perspectives on teaching writing to second language students* (pp. 287–306). IGI Global. doi:10.4018/978-1-7998-6508-7.ch017

Moses, L., Hajdun, M., & Aguirre, A. (2021). Translanguaging together: Building bilingual identities con nuevos amigos. *The Reading Teacher*, *75*(3), 291–304. doi:10.1002/trtr.2060

Muis, S., Salija, K., Nur, S., & Sakkir, G. (2023). Translanguaging in EFL classroom at a private university in south Sulawesi. Eduline. *Journal of Education and Learning Innovation*, *3*(3), 396–406. doi:10.35877/454RI.eduline1904

Nagy, T. (2018). On translanguaging and its role in foreign language teaching. *Acta Universitatis Sapientiae. Philologica*, *10*(2), 41–53. doi:10.2478/ausp-2018-0012

Panezai, A., Channa, L. A., & Bibi, B. (2022). Translanguaging in higher education: Exploring interactional spaces for meaning-making in the multilingual universities of Pakistan. *International Journal of Bilingual Education and Bilingualism*, *26*(4), 514–527. doi:10.1080/13670050.2022.2124842

Rabionet, S. E. (2011). How I learned to design and conduct semi-structured interviews: An ongoing and continuous journey. *The Qualitative Report*, *16*(2), 563.

Sun, P., & Zhang, L. (2022). Effects of translanguaging in online peer feedback on Chinese university English-as-a-foreign-language students' writing performance. *RELC Journal, 53*(2), 325–341. doi:10.1177/00336882221089051

Vo, L. H. (2024). Teaching English literature in the Vietnamese EFL context: Towards a language and literature integrated model. In H. P. Bui, T. C. Bang, & C. H. Nguyen (Eds.), *Exploring contemporary English language education practices*. IGI Global.

Walter, Y. (2022). Translanguaging pedagogy in cameroon EFL/ESL secondary classrooms. *International Journal of English Language Teaching, 10*(7), 31–49. doi:10.37745/ijelt.13/vol10n73149

Wang, P. (2022). Relooking at the roles of translanguaging in English as a Foreign Language classes for multilingual learners: Practices and implications. *Frontiers in Psychology, 13*, 850649. Advance online publication. doi:10.3389/fpsyg.2022.850649

Wright, W. E., & Baker, C. (2017). Key concepts in bilingual education. *Bilingual and Multilingual Education*, 65-79. doi:10.1007/978-3-319-02258-1_2

Yilmaz, K. (2011). The cognitive perspective on learning: Its theoretical underpinnings and implications for classroom practices. *The Clearing House: A Journal of Educational Strategies, Issues and Ideas, 84*(5), 204–212. doi:10.1080/00098655.2011.568989

ADDITIONAL READING

Huang, X., & Chalmers, H. (2023). Implementation and effects of pedagogical translanguaging in EFL classrooms: A systematic review. *Languages (Basel, Switzerland), 8*(3), 1–20. doi:10.3390/languages8030194

Kao, Y. T. (2023). Exploring translanguaging in Taiwanese CLIL classes: An analysis of teachers' perceptions and practices. *Language, Culture and Curriculum, 36*(1), 100–121. doi:10.1080/07908318.2022.2033762

Karabassova, L., & San Isidro, X. (2023). Towards translanguaging in CLIL: A study on teachers' perceptions and practices in Kazakhstan. *International Journal of Multilingualism, 20*(2), 556–575. doi:10.1080/14790718.2020.1828426

Sobkowiak, P. (2022). Translanguaging practices in the EFL classroom-the Polish context. *Linguistics and Education, 69*, 101020. Advance online publication. doi:10.1016/j.linged.2022.101020

Yuvayapan, F. (2019). Translanguaging in EFL classrooms: Teachers' perceptions and practices. *Journal of Language and Linguistic Studies*, *15*(2), 678–694. doi:10.17263/jlls.586811

KEY TERMS AND DEFINITIONS

Colloquial Language: Informal, everyday language that is used in casual or relaxed settings.

Cultural Understanding: The ability to comprehend, appreciate, and respect the beliefs, values, customs, traditions, and behaviors of people from different cultural backgrounds.

EFL: English as a Foreign Language.

Engagement: The level of active participation, involvement and interest in a given task.

Inclusive Learning Environment: An educational environment that welcomes and supports individuals from diverse backgrounds, abilities, and identities in the process of acquiring a new language.

L1: The native language, Vietnamese.

Translanguaging: Vietnamese teachers and students utilize their first language (L1), Vietnamese, within English literature courses for English majors.

Compilation of References

A, A. M. (2019). The use of technology in English language teaching. *Frontiers in Education Technology, 2*(3), 168-180. doi:10.22158/fet.v2n3p168

Abarghoui, M. A., & Taki, S. (2018). Measuring the effectiveness of using "Memrise" on high school students' perceptions of learning EFL. *Theory and Practice in Language Studies, 8*(12), 1758–1765. doi:10.17507/tpls.0812.25

Abatabaee Farani, S., & Pishghadam, R. (2021). Examining emotion in sense-based teaching: A cognitive task of sentence comprehension. *Language Related Research, 12*(4), 73–104. doi:10.29252/LRR.12.4.3

Abourehab, Y., & Azaz, M. (2023). Pedagogical translanguaging in community/heritage Arabic language learning. *Journal of Multilingual and Multicultural Development, 44*(5), 398–411. doi:10.1080/01434632.2020.1826496

Adamakis, M., & Dania, A. (2021). Validity of emotional intelligence scale in pre-service physical education teachers. *Journal of Physical Education and Sport, 21*(1), 54–59. doi:10.7752/jpes.2021.01007

Adipat, S., Chotikapanich, R., Laksana, K., Busayanon, K., Piatanom, P., Ausawasowan, A., & Elbasouni, I. (2023). Technological pedagogical content knowledge for professional teacher development. *Academic Journal of Interdisciplinary Studies, 12*(1), 173–182. doi:10.36941/ajis-2023-0015

Afifa, S., Yelfiza, Y., & Merina, Y. (2022). Cyberbullying found in commentary on English educational Youtube channel for high school students. *Edumaspul: Jurnal Pendidikan, 6*(1), 717–722. doi:10.33487/edumaspul.v6i1.2039

Ainy, S. (2006). *Use of literature in developing learner's speaking skills in Bangladeshi EFL contexts* [Doctoral dissertation]. University of Nottingham.

Akintunde, A. F., & Angulu, Y. D. (2020). Technology in language learning: An effective innovation but not without Its challenges. *Sapientia Foundation Journal of Education Sciences and Gender Studies, 2*(4), 25–35.

Akinwamide, T. K. (2012). The influence of process approach on English as second language students' performances in essay writing. *English Language Teaching*, *5*(3), 16–29.

Alahmadi, N. S. (2019). The role of input in second language acquisition: An overview of four theories. *Bulletin of Advanced English Studies*, *3*(2), 70–78. doi:10.31559/baes2019.3.2.1

Alani, F. S., & Hawas, A. T. (2021). Factors Affecting Students Academic Performance: A Case Study of Sohar University. *Psychology and Education*, *58*(5), 4624–4635.

Alanoca, M. (2019). Emotional Intelligence Program to improve The Teaching-Learning Process of The English Language in Teaching and Translation of Language. *Educación Superior*, *6*(2), 14–23.

Alasmari, M., Qasem, F., Ahmed, R., & Alrayes, M. (2022). Bilingual teachers' translanguaging practices and ideologies in online classrooms in Saudi Arabia. *Heliyon*, *8*(9), e10537. doi:10.1016/j.heliyon.2022.e10537

Alavi, S. M., Nemati, M., & Dorri Kafrani, J. (2020). Error gravity analysis of IELTS students' academic writing task 2. *International Journal of Language Studies*, *14*(1).

Albatti, H. (2023). Blended learning in English language teaching and learning: A focused study on a reading and vocabulary building course. *World Journal of English Language*, *13*(5), 121–130. doi:10.5430/wjel.v13n5p121

Alharbi, B. (2021). Mobile learning age: Implications for future language learning skills. *Psychology (Savannah, Ga.)*, *58*(2), 862–867. doi:10.17762/pae.v58i2.1960

Alier, M., Guerrero, M. J. C., Amo, D., Severance, C., & Fonseca, D. (2021). Privacy and e-learning: A pending task. *Sustainability (Basel)*, *13*(9206), 1–17. doi:10.3390/su13169206

Alisha, F., Safitri, N., Santoso, I., & Siliwangi, I. (2019). Students' difficulties in writing EFL. *Professional Journal of English Education*, *2*(1), 20–25. doi:10.22460/project.v2i1.p20-25

Al-Jarf, R. (2022). Learning vocabulary in the app store by EFL college students. *International Journal of Social Science And Human Research*, *5*(1), 216–225. doi:10.47191/ijsshr/v5-i1-30

Alodwan, T. A. A., & Ibnian, S. S. K. (2014). The effect of using the process approach to writing on developing university students' essay writing skills in EFL. *Review of Arts and Humanities*, *3*(2), 139–155.

Anderson-Hsieh, J. (1992). Using electronic visual feedback to teach suprasegmentals. *System*, *20*(1), 51–62. doi:10.1016/0346-251X(92)90007-P

Anderson-Hsieh, J. (1994). Interpreting visual feedback on suprasegmentals in computer-assisted pronunciation instruction. *CALICO Journal*, *11*(4), 5–22. doi:10.1558/cj.v11i4.5-22

Angelucci, T. C., & María Isabel Pozzo, M. I. (2020). Errors and mistakes in foreign language learning: Drawing boundaries from the discourse of Argentine teachers. In E. Vanderheiden & C. Mayer (Eds.), *Mistakes, errors and failures across cultures: Navigating potentials* (pp. 383–398). Springer. doi:10.1007/978-3-030-35574-6_20

Compilation of References

Aomr, J., Seng, G., & Kapol, N. (2020). Relationship between willingness to communicate in English and classroom environment among Libyan EFL learners. *Universal Journal of Educational Research*, *8*(2), 605–610. doi:10.13189/ujer.2020.080232

Arias, J., Soto-Carballo, J. G., & Pino-Juste, M. R. (2022). Emotional intelligence and academic motivation in primary school students. *Psicologia: Reflexão e Crítica*, *35*(1), 14–23. doi:10.1186/s41155-022-00216-0

Ariyanti, A., & Fitriana, R. (2017, October). EFL students' difficulties and needs in essay writing. In *International Conference on Teacher Training and Education 2017 (ICTTE 2017)* (pp. 32-42). Atlantis Press. 10.2991/ictte-17.2017.4

Arnó-Macià, E., & Mancho-Barés, G. (2015). The role of content and language in content and language integrated learning (CLIL) at university: Challenges and implications for ESP. *English for Specific Purposes*, *37*, 63–73. doi:10.1016/j.esp.2014.06.007

Auliyah, R., & Arrasyid, F. I. (2019). Revealing process-based and writers' choice of academic essay writing in undergraduate EFL learners. *ELT Echo: The Journal of English Language Teaching in Foreign Language Context*, *4*(1), 49–61. doi:10.24235/eltecho.v4i1.4478

Aydin, F. (2017). Willingness to communicate among intermediate-level adult Turkish EFL learners: Underlying factors. *Journal of Qualitative Research in Education*, *5*(3), 109–137. doi:10.14689/issn.2148-2624.1.5c3s5m

Azizah, S. N., Supriyono, Y., & Andriani, A. (2022). Projecting communicative language teaching (CLT) implementation in teaching spoken language at secondary school. *Journal of English Teaching Applied Linguistics and Literatures*, *5*(2), 179–197. doi:10.20527/jetall.v5i2.12873

Bachman, L. F., & Palmer, A. S. (2010). *Language assessment in practice: Developing language assessments and justifying their use in the real world*. Oxford University Press.

Bagheri, M. S., & Riasati, M. J. (2016). EFL graduate students' IELTS writing problems and students' and teachers' beliefs and suggestions regarding writing skill improvement. *Journal of Language Teaching and Research*, *7*(1), 198. doi:10.17507/jltr.0701.23

Bahrani, T. (2011). Technology as an assessment tool in language learning. *International Journal of English Linguistics*, *1*(2), 295–298. doi:10.5539/ijel.v1n2p295

Baker, B. A. (2012). Individual differences in rater decision-making style: An exploratory mixed-methods study. *Language Assessment Quarterly*, *9*(3), 225–248. doi:10.1080/15434303.2011.637262

Baker, M. (2018). *In other words: A coursebook on translation* (3rd ed.). Routledge. doi:10.4324/9781315619187

Bang, T. C. (2024). English in higher education: navigating Vietnam's academic landscape. In H. P. Bui, T. C. Bang, & C. H. Nguyen (Eds.), *Teacher and student perspectives on bilingual and multilingual education* (pp. 34–50). IGI Global. doi:10.4018/979-8-3693-5365-3.ch003

Bashori, M., Van Hout, R., Strik, H., & Cucchiarini, C. (2022). 'Look, I can speak correctly': Learning vocabulary and pronunciation through websites equipped with automatic speech recognition technology. *Computer Assisted Language Learning*, 1–29. doi:10.1080/09588221.2022.2080230

Başöz, T., & Erten, I. (2018). Investigating tertiary level EFL learners' willingness to communicate in English. *English Language Teaching*, *11*(3), 78–87. doi:10.5539/elt.v11n3p78

Basturkmen, H., Loewen, S., & Ellis, R. (2004). Teachers' Stated Beliefs about Incidental Focus on Form and their Classroom Practices. *Applied Linguistics*, *25*(2), 243–272. doi:10.1093/applin/25.2.243

Bata, S., & Castro, C. (2021). English as a foreign language students' emotional intelligence management when taking speaking exams. *Profile: Issues in Teachers' Professional Development*, *23*(2), 245–261. https://doi.org/.v23n2.8837 doi:10.15446/profile

Bataineh, A. (2014). The effect of teaching literature on EFL students' pragmatic competence. *Journal of Education and Practice*, *5*(3), 137–156.

Batista-Toledo, S., & Gavilan, D. (2022). Implementation of blended learning during COVID-19. *Encyclopedia*, *2*(4), 1763–1772. doi:10.3390/encyclopedia2040121

Baum, S., & McPherson, M. (2019). The Human Factor: The Promise & Limits of Online Education. *Daedalus*, *148*(4), 235–254. doi:10.1162/daed_a_01769

Becker, A. (2023). Applied linguistics communities of practice: Improving the research-practice relationship. *Applied Linguistics*, *2023*, 1–20. doi:10.1093/applin/amad010

Begimbetova, G., Abdigapbarova, U., Abdulkarimova, G., Pristupa, E., Issabayeva, D., & Kurmangaliyeva, N. (2022). *Use of ICT in CLIL-classes for the future teachers training*. 2022 the 4th International Conference on Modern Educational Technology (ICMET), New York.

Belkhir, A., & Benyelles, R. (2017). Identifying EFL learners essay writing difficulties and sources: a move towards solution the case of second year EFL learners at Tlemcen University. *International Journal of Learning, Teaching and Educational Research*, *16*(6), 80-88. https://www.ijlter.net/index.php/ijlter/article/view/811/816

Benyo, A. (2020). CALL in English language teaching. *International Journal of Advanced Science and Technology*, *29*(3), 1390–1395. http://sersc.org/journals/index.php/IJAST/article/view/6098

Berlianti, D., & Pradita, I. (2021). Translanguaging in an EFL classroom discourse: To what extent it is helpful for the students? *Communication in Humanity and Social Science*, *1*(1), 42–46. doi:10.21924/chss.1.1.2021.14

Bishop, D. V., Snowling, M. J., Thompson, P. A., & Greenhalgh, T. (2017). Catalise: A multinational and multidisciplinary Delphi consensus study. Identifying language impairments in children. *PLoS One*, *12*(6), e0179498. Advance online publication. doi:10.1371/journal.pone.0158753 PMID:27392128

Compilation of References

Block, D. (2018). Language, education and neoliberalism: Critical studies in sociolinguistics. *ELT Journal*, *72*(4), 452–454. doi:10.1093/elt/ccy035

Boardman, A. C., & Frydenberg, J. (2008). *Writing to communicate 2* (3rd ed.). Pearson Education.

Boersma, P., & Weenink, D. (2022). *Praat: doing phonetics by computer*. https://www.fon.hum.uva.nl/praat/

Bohn, O.-S., & Flege, J. E. (1992). The production of new and similar vowels by adult German learners of English. *Studies in Second Language Acquisition*, *14*(2), 131–158. doi:10.1017/S0272263100010792

Bohn, O.-S., & Flege, J. E. (2021). The revised speech learning model (SLM-r). In R. Wayland (Ed.), *Second language speech learning: Theoretical and empirical progress* (pp. 3–83). Cambridge University Press. doi:10.1017/9781108886901.002

Borg, S. (2003). Teacher cognition in language teaching: A review of research on what language teachers think, know, believe, and do. *Language Teaching*, *36*(2), 81–109. doi:10.1017/S0261444803001903

Botes, E., Dewaele, J. M., & Greiff, S. (2020). The Foreign Language Classroom Anxiety Scale and Academic Achievement: An Overview of the Prevailing Literature and a Meta-Analysis. *Journal for the Psychology of Language Learning*, *2*(1), 26–56. doi:10.52598/jpll/2/1/3

Brown, A. (2018). Mastering verb tenses in English essay writing. *Journal of Language Learning*, *15*(2), 45–58. doi:10.1111/joll.12345

Brudermann, C. A. (2015). Computer-mediated online language learning programmes vs. tailor-made teaching practices at university level: A foul relationship or a perfect match? *Open Learning*, *30*(3), 267–281. doi:10.1080/02680513.2015.1100069

Brumfit, C. J., & Carter, R. A. (Eds.). (1986). Literature and language teaching. Oxford University Press.

Bryfonski, L. (2023). Is seeing believing? The role of ultrasound tongue imaging and oral corrective feedback in L2 pronunciation development. *Journal of Second Language Pronunciation*, *9*(1), 103–129. doi:10.1075/jslp.22051.bry

Budiartha, C. I. W. E., & Vanessa, A. (2021). Process approach and collaborative learning analysis on students' academic writing. *ELTR Journal*, *5*(1), 19–37. doi:10.37147/eltr.v5i1.89

Budiarti, Y. (2022). Language Learning Strategies, Gender, and Motivation in Foreign Language Context. *Journal of English as A Foreign. Language Teaching Research*, *2*(1), 19–33. doi:10.31098/jefltr.vil.780

Bui, H. P., Nguyen, L. T., & Nguyen, T. V. (2023). An investigation into EFL pre-service teachers' academic writing strategies. *Heliyon*, *9*(3), E13743. doi:10.1016/j.heliyon.2023.e13743

Bui, H. P. (2022). Vietnamese EFL students' use and misconceptions of cohesive devices in writing. *SAGE Open*, *12*(3). Advance online publication. doi:10.1177/21582440221126993

Bui, H. P. (2023). L2 teachers' strategies and students' engagement in virtual classrooms: A multidimensional perspective. In *Lecture Notes in Networks and System* (Vol. 617, pp. 205–213). Springer. doi:10.1007/978-981-19-9512-5_18

Bui, H. P. (2023). Vietnamese university EFL teachers' and students' beliefs and teachers' practices regarding classroom assessment. *Language Testing in Asia*, *13*(1), 10. doi:10.1186/s40468-023-00220-w

Bui, H. P., Hoang, V. Q., & Nguyen, N. H. (2022). Encouraging Vietnamese students' willingness to communicate inside English L2 classrooms. *Language Related Research*, *13*(5), 1–23. doi:10.52547/LRR.13.5.17

Bui, H. P., & Nguyen, T. T. T. (2022). Classroom assessment and learning motivation: Insights from secondary school EFL classrooms. *International Review of Applied Linguistics in Language Teaching*, *0*(0). Advance online publication. doi:10.1515/iral-2022-0020

Bui, T. H. (2022). English teachers' integration of digital technologies in the classroom. *International Journal of Educational Research Open*, *3*, 1–15. doi:10.1016/j.ijedro.2022.100204

Bujang, S., Heromi, N. A., & Hadil, H. (2023). Issues and gaps in emotional intelligence studies. *Science International (Lahore)*, *35*(1), 39–44.

Bulqiyah, S., Mahbub, M., & Nugraheni, D. A. (2021). Investigating Writing Difficulties in Essay Writing: Tertiary Students' Perspectives. *English Language Teaching Educational Journal*, *4*(1), 61–73. doi:10.12928/eltej.v4i1.2371

Burns, A. (2010). *Doing action research in English language teaching: A guide for practitioners.* Routledge.

Burton, J., & Rajendram, S. (2019). Translanguaging-as-resource: University ESL instructors' language orientations and attitudes toward translanguaging. *TESL Canada Journal*, *36*(1), 21–47. doi:10.18806/tesl.v36i1.1301

Byram, M., & Wagner, M. (2018). Making a difference: Language teaching for intercultural and international dialogue. *Foreign Language Annals*, *51*(1), 140–151. doi:10.1111/flan.12319

Canals, L., Granena, G., Yilmaz, Y., & Malicka, A. (2021). The relative effectiveness of immediate and delayed corrective feedback in video-based computer-mediated communication. *Language Teaching Research*. Advance online publication. doi:10.1177/13621688211052793

Carey, M. (2004). CALL visual feedback for pronunciation of vowels: Kay Sona-Match. *CALICO Journal*, *21*(3), 571–601. doi:10.1558/cj.v21i3.571-601

Carroll, S. E. (1999). Putting 'input' in its proper place. *Second Language Research*, *15*(4), 337–388. doi:10.1191/026765899674928444

Compilation of References

Carter, R. A., & Long, M. N. (1991). *Teaching Literature*. Longman.

Cassell, M. (2023). Language technology applications: Current developments and future implications. *Journal of Linguistics and Communication Studies*, 2(2), 83–89. doi:10.56397/JLCS.2023.06.11

Celce-Murcia, M., Larsen-Freeman, D., & Williams, H. A. (1983). *The grammar book: An ESL/EFL teacher's course*. Rowley.

Cengiz, B. C. (2023). Computer-assisted pronunciation teaching: An analysis of empirical research. *Participatory Educational Research*, 10(3), 72–88. doi:10.17275/per.23.45.10.3

Cenoz, J., & Gorter, D. (2011). Focus on multilingualism: A study of trilingual writing. *Modern Language Journal*, 95(3), 356–369. doi:10.1111/j.1540-4781.2011.01206.x

Cenoz, J., & Gorter, D. (2021). *Pedagogical translanguaging*. Cambridge University Press.

Ceylan, N. O. (2019). Student perceptions of difficulties in second language writing. *Journal of Language and Linguistic Studies*, 15(1), 151–157. doi:10.17263/jlls.547683

Chaika, O. (2023). *Translanguaging in multilingual classrooms: A case study analysis*. Philological Review. doi:10.31499/2415-8828.1.2023.281366

Chapelle, C. A. (2001). *Computer applications in second language acquisition: foundations for teaching, testing and research*. Cambridge University Press. doi:10.1017/CBO9781139524681

Chau, M. K., & Bui, H. P. (2023). Technology-assisted teaching during the COVID-19 pandemic: L2 teachers' strategies and encountered challenges. In *Lecture Notes in Networks and Systems* (Vol. 617, pp. 243–250). Springer.

Chau, M. K., & Bui, H. P. (2023). Technology-assisted teaching during the COVID-19 pandemic: L2 teachers' strategies and encountered challenges. In D. K. Sharma, S.-L. Peng, R. Sharma, & G. Jeon (Eds.), *Micro-electronics and telecommunication engineering. Lecture notes in networks and systems* (pp. 243–250). Springer Nature Singapore. doi:10.1007/978-981-19-9512-5_22

Chen, H. H.-J. (2011). Developing and evaluating an oral skills training website supported by automatic speech recognition technology. *ReCALL*, 23(1), 59–78. doi:10.1017/S0958344010000285

Chen, M. (2022). Computer-aided feedback on the pronunciation of Mandarin Chinese tones: Using Praat to promote multimedia foreign language learning. *Computer Assisted Language Learning*, 1–26. doi:10.1080/09588221.2022.2037652

Chen, W.-H., Inceoglu, S., & Lim, H. (2020). Using ASR to improve Taiwanese EFL learners' pronunciation: Learning outcomes and learners' perceptions. *Proceedings of the 11th Pronunciation in Second Language Learning and Teaching conference*.

Chen, X., Dewaele, J., & Zhang, T. (2022). Sustainable development of EFL/ESL learners' willingness to communicate: The effects of teachers and teaching styles. *Sustainability (Basel)*, 14(1), 1–21. doi:10.3390/su14010396

Chien, S.-C. (2012). Students' use of writing strategies and their English writing achievements in Taiwan. *Asia Pacific Journal of Education*, *32*(1), 93–112. doi:10.1080/02188791.2012.655240

Choi, S.-Y., & Li, S. (2012). Corrective feedback and learner uptake in a child ESOL classroom. *RELC Journal*, *43*(3), 331–351. doi:10.1177/0033688212463274

Chomsky, N. (1965). *Aspects of the theory of syntax*. MIT Press.

Chuang, H.-H., Yang, Y.-F., & Liu, H.-C. (2010, December). *What digital divide factors matter in the motivation to use technology to learn English? A case of low SES young learners in Taiwan*. 2009 Joint Conferences on Pervasive Computing (JCPC), Tamsui, Taiwan.

Chun, D. M. (2002). *Discourse intonation in L2: From theory and research to practice*. John Benjamins Publishing. doi:10.1075/lllt.1

Clarke, V., & Braun, V. (2017). Thematic analysis. *The Journal of Positive Psychology*, *12*(3), 297–298. doi:10.1080/17439760.2016.1262613

Coffin, C., Curry, M., Goodman, S., Hewings, A., Lillis, T., & Swann, J. (2003). *Teaching academic writing: A toolkit for higher education London*. Routledge.

Cohen, A. D., & Wang, I. K. H. (2018). Fluctuation in the functions of language learner strategies. *System*, *74*, 169–182. doi:10.1016/j.system.2018.03.011

Collie, J., & Slater, S. (1987). *Literature in the language classroom: a resource book of ideas and activities*. Cambridge University Press.

Cook, G. (2003). *Applied linguistics*. Oxford University Press.

Corder, S. P. (1975). Error analysis, interlanguage and second language acquisition. *Language Teaching*, *8*(04), 201–218. doi:10.1017/S0261444800002822

Cosgun, G., & Atay, D. (2021). Fostering critical thinking, creativity, and language skills in the EFL classroom through problem-based learning. *International Journal of Curriculum and Instruction*, *13*(3), 2360–2385. https://ijci.globets.org/index.php/IJCI/article/view/583

Costello, P. J. M. (2011). *Effective Action Research: Developing Reflective Thinking and Practice Continuum Research Methods*. Bloomsbury Publishing.

Crasnich, S., & Lumbell, L. (2005). Improving argumentative writing by fostering argumentative speech. Effective learning and teaching of writing: A Handbook of Writing in Education, 181–196.

Creese, A., & Blackledge, A. (2015). Translanguaging and identity in educational settings. *Annual Review of Applied Linguistics*, *35*, 20–35. doi:10.1017/S0267190514000233

Creswell, J. W. (2012). *Educational research: Planning, conducting, and evaluating quantitative and qualitative research* (4th ed.). Pearson.

Creswell, J. W., & Creswell, J. D. (2017). *Research design: Qualitative, Quantitative, and Mmixed methods approaches*. Sage Publications.

Compilation of References

Creswell, J. W., & Creswell, J. D. (2018). *Research Design: Qualitative, Quantitative, and Mixed Methods Approaches*. Sage Publications.

Cucchiarini, C., Neri, A., & Strik, H. (2008). The effectiveness of computer-based speech corrective feedback for improving segmental quality in L2 Dutch. *ReCALL*, *20*(2), 225–243. doi:10.1017/S0958344008000724

Cullen, P. (2017). *The key to IELTS success*. Cambridge University Press.

Cumming, A., Kantor, R., & Powers, D. E. (2002). Decision making while rating ESL/EFL writing tasks: A descriptive framework. *Modern Language Journal*, *86*(1), 67–96. doi:10.1111/1540-4781.00137

Cummins, J. (2019). The emergence of translanguaging pedagogy: A dialogue between theory and practice. *Journal of Multilingual Education Research*, *9*(13), 19–36.

Dai, Y., & Wu, Z. (2023). Mobile-assisted pronunciation learning with feedback from peers and/or automatic speech recognition: A mixed-methods study. *Computer Assisted Language Learning*, *36*(5-6), 861–884. doi:10.1080/09588221.2021.1952272

Dash, B. B. (2022). Digital tools for teaching and learning English language in 21st century. *International Journal of English and Studies*, *4*(2), 8–13. doi:10.47311/IJOES.2022.4202

Davis, A. (2003). Teachers' and students' beliefs regarding aspects of language learning. *Evaluation and Research in Education*, *17*(4), 207–222. doi:10.1080/09500790308668303

De Smet, A., Mettewie, L., Galand, B., Hiligsmann, P., & Van Mensel, L. (2018). Classroom Anxiety and Enjoyment in CLIL and non-CLIL: Does the Target Language Matter? *Studies in Second Language Learning and Teaching*, *8*(1), 47–71. doi:10.14746/ssllt.2018.8.1.3

Demirel, E. (2011). Take it step by step: Following a process approach to academic writing to overcome student anxiety. *Journal of Academic Writing*, *1*(1), 222–227. doi:10.18552/joaw.v1i1.28

Denscombe, M. (2007). *The good research guide: For small-scale social research projects* (3rd ed.). Open University Press.

Derakhshan, A., Eslami, Z. R., & Ghandhari, N. (2021). Investigating the interplay of emotional intelligence and inter-language pragmatic competence in Iranian lower-intermediate EFL learners. *Journal of Issues in Language Teaching*, *10*(1), 37–66. doi:10.22054/ilt.2020.54334.527

Derakhshan, A., & Taguchi, N. (2021). The Routledge handbook of second language acquisition and pragmatics. *Applied Linguistics*, *42*(5), 1029–1032. doi:10.1093/applin/amz031

Derwing, T. M., & Munro, M. J. (2005). Second language accent and pronunciation teaching: A research-based approach. *TESOL Quarterly*, *39*(3), 379–397. doi:10.2307/3588486

Derwing, T. M., & Munro, M. J. (2015). *Pronunciation fundamentals: Evidence-based perspectives for L2 teaching and research*. John Benjamins Publishing Company. doi:10.1075/lllt.42

Derwing, T. M., Munro, M. J., & Wiebe, G. (1998). Evidence in favor of a broad framework for pronunciation instruction. *Language Learning*, *48*(3), 393–410. doi:10.1111/0023-8333.00047

Dewaele, J. M. (2019). The effect of classroom emotions, attitudes toward English, and teacher behavior on willingness to communicate among English Foreign Language Learners. *Journal of Language and Social Psychology*, *38*(4), 523–535. doi:10.1177/0261927X19864996

Dewaele, J. M., & Dewaele, L. (2018). Learner-internal and learner-external predictors of willingness to communicate in the FL classroom. *Journal of the European Second Language Association*, *2*(1), 24–37. doi:10.22599/jesla.37

Dewaele, J. M., & Dewaele, L. (2020). Are Foreign Language Learners' Enjoyment and Anxiety Specific to the Teacher? An Investigation Into the Dynamics of Learners' Classroom Emotions. *Studies in Second Language Learning and Teaching*, *10*(1), 45–65. doi:10.14746/ssllt.2020.10.1.3

Dewaele, J. M., Magdalena, A. F., & Saito, K. (2019). The Effect of Perception of Teacher Characteristics on Spanish EFL Learners' Anxiety and Enjoyment. *Modern Language Journal*, *103*(2), 412–427. doi:10.1111/modl.12555

Dewaele, J. M., & Pavelescu, L. (2021). The relationship between incommensurable emotions and willingness to communicate in English as a foreign language: A multiple case study. *Innovation in Language Learning and Teaching*, *15*(1), 66–80. doi:10.1080/17501229.2019.1675667

Divaharan, S., & Atputhasamy, L. (2002). An attempt to enhance the quality of cooperative learning through peer assessment. *Journal of Educational Enquiry*, *3*(2), 72–83.

Divsar, H., & Tahriri, A. (2009). Investigating the effectiveness of an integrated approach to teaching literature in a EFK context. *Journal of Pan-Pacific Association of Applied Linguistics*, *13*(2), 105–116.

Do, N. C. (2002). Vietnamese EFL students' critical thinking in an English literature course. *Journal of Ethnic and Cultural Studies*, *9*(1), 77–94.

Dooly, M., Thrasher, T., & Sadler, R. (2023). "Whoa! incredible!:" language learning experiences in virtual reality. *RELC Journal*, *54*(2), 321–339. doi:10.1177/00336882231167610

Dörnyei, Z., & Ushioda, E. (Eds.). (2009). *Motivation, language identity and the L2 self*. Multilingual Matters. doi:10.21832/9781847691293

Duff, A., & Maley, A. (1990). *Literature*. Oxford University Press.

Duong, T. M., Tran, N. Y., Ha, A. T., & Phung, Y. (2020). The impact of emotional intelligence on performance: A closer look at individual and environmental factors. *Journal of Asian Finance Economics and Business*, *7*(1), 183–193. doi:10.13106/jafeb.2020.vol7.no1.183

Ebadi, S., & Ebadijalal, M. (2022). The effect of Google Expeditions virtual reality on EFL learners' willingness to communicate and oral proficiency. *Computer Assisted Language Learning*, *35*(8), 1975–2000. doi:10.1080/09588221.2020.1854311

Compilation of References

Egbert, J., Biber, D., & Gray, B. (2022). *Designing and evaluating language corpora: A practical framework for corpus representativeness.* Cambridge University Press. doi:10.1017/9781316584880

Elachachi, H. H. (2015). Exploring cultural barriers in EFL Arab learners' writing. *Procedia: Social and Behavioral Sciences*, *199*, 129–136. doi:10.1016/j.sbspro.2015.07.496

Ellis, N. C., & Wulff, S. (2019). Cognitive approaches to second language acquisition. In J. W. Schwieter & A. Benati (Eds.), *The Cambridge handbook of language learning* (pp. 41–61). Cambridge University Press. doi:10.1017/9781108333603.003

Ellis, R. (2015). *The study of second language acquisition* (2nd ed.). Oxford University Press.

Ellis, R. (2015). *Understanding second language acquisition* (2nd ed.). Oxford university press.

Ellis, R. (2016). Focus on form: A critical review. *Language Teaching Research*, *20*(3), 405–428. doi:10.1177/1362168816628627

Ellis, R. (2017). Oral corrective feedback in L2 classroom: What we know so far. In H. Nassaji & E. Kartchava (Eds.), *Corrective feedback in second language teaching and learning: Research, theory, applications, implications* (pp. 3–18). Taylor & Francis. doi:10.4324/9781315621432-2

Ellis, R. (2021). Explicit and implicit oral corrective feedback. In H. Nassaji & E. Kartchava (Eds.), *The Cambridge handbook of corrective feedback in second language learning and teaching* (pp. 341–364). Cambridge University Press. doi:10.1017/9781108589789.017

Ellis, R. (2021). Task-based language teaching. In H. Mohebbi & C. Coombe (Eds.), *Research questions in language education and applied linguistics* (pp. 133–136). Springer., doi:10.1007/978-3-030-79143-8_25

Ellis, R., & Barkhuizen, G. (2005). *Analysing learner language.* Oxford University Press.

Ellis, R., Sheen, Y., Murakami, M., & Takashima, H. (2008). The effects of focused and unfocused written corrective feedback in an English as a foreign language context. *System*, *36*(3), 353–371. doi:10.1016/j.system.2008.02.001

Esterhazy, R. (2019). Re-conceptualizing feedback through a sociocultural lens. In M. Henderson, R. Ajjawi, D. Boud, & E. Molloy (Eds.), The impact of feedback in higher education: Improving assessment outcomes for learners (pp. 67-82). Palgrave Macmillan Cham. doi:10.1007/978-3-030-25112-3_5

Evans, S., & Green, C. (2007). Why EAP is necessary: A survey of Hong Kong tertiary students. *Journal of English for Academic Purposes*, *6*(1), 3–17. doi:10.1016/j.jeap.2006.11.005

Evers, K., & Chen, S. (2022). Effects of an automatic speech recognition system with peer feedback on pronunciation instruction for adults. *Computer Assisted Language Learning*, *35*(8), 1869–1889. doi:10.1080/09588221.2020.1839504

Faez, F., Martini, J., & Pavia, N. (2022). Research methods in applied linguistics and language education: Current considerations, recent innovations, and future directions. *ELT Journal*, *76*(2), 276–296. doi:10.1093/elt/ccab091

Fakhrurazzy. (2011). *Teaching English as a Foreign Language for Teachers in Indonesia*. State University of Malang Press.

Fang, F., & Dovchin, S. (2022). Reflection and reform of applied linguistics from the Global South: Power and inequality in English users from the Global South. *Applied Linguistics Review*, *2022*(0). Advance online publication. doi:10.1515/applirev-2022-0072

Fan, X., Liu, K., Wang, X., & Yu, J. (2023). Exploring mobile apps in English learning. *Journal of Education. Humanities and Social Sciences*, *8*, 2367–2374. doi:10.54097/ehss.v8i.4996

Fareed, M., Ashraf, A., & Bilal, M. (2016). ESL learners' writing skills: Problems, factors and suggestions. *Journal of Education and Social Sciences*, *4*(2), 81–92. doi:10.20547/jess0421604201

Febriani, R. B., Rukmini, D., Mujiyanto, J., & Yuliasri, I. (2022). Lecturers' perception on the implementation of approaches to teaching literature in EFL classrooms. *Studies in English Language and Education*, *9*(1), 349–364. doi:10.24815/siele.v9i1.21035

Fernández Barrionuevo, E., Villoria Prieto, J., González Fernández, F. T., & Baena Extremera, A. (2020). Willingness to communicate in a foreign language in the four skills. Sex and age differences. *Espiral. Cuadernos del Profesorado*, *13*(27), 192–203. doi:10.25115/ecp.v13i27.3359

Fernández, S. G. (2018). Rendimiento Académico en Educación Superior: Desafíos para el Docente y Compromiso del Estudiante [Academic Performance in Higher Education: Challenges for the Teacher and Student Commitment]. *Revista Científica de la UCSA*, *5*(3), 55–63. doi:10.18004/ucsa/2409-8752/2018.005(03)055-063

Firoozjahantigh, M., Fakhri Alamdari, E., & Marzban, A. (2021). Investigating the effect of process-based instruction of writing on the IELTS writing task two performance of Iranian EFL learners: Focusing on hedging & boosting. *Cogent Education*, *8*(1), 1881202. doi:10.1080/2331186X.2021.1881202

Flege, J. E. (1987). The production of "new" and "similar" phones in a foreign language: Evidence for the effect of equivalence classification. *Journal of Phonetics*, *15*(1), 47–65. doi:10.1016/S0095-4470(19)30537-6

Flege, J. E., Bohn, O.-S., & Jang, S. (1997). Effects of experience on non-native speakers' production and perception of English vowels. *Journal of Phonetics*, *25*(4), 437–470. doi:10.1006/jpho.1997.0052

Flege, J. E., MacKay, I. R. A., & Meador, D. (1999). Native Italian speakers' perception and production of English vowels. *The Journal of the Acoustical Society of America*, *106*(5), 2973–2987. doi:10.1121/1.428116

Flower, L., & Hayes, J. R. (1981). A cognitive process theory of writing. *College Composition and Communication*, *32*(4), 365–387. doi:10.2307/356600

Compilation of References

Fojtík, R. (2018). Problems of distance education. *ICTE Journal*, *7*(1), 14–23. doi:10.2478/ijicte-2018-0002

Fouz-González, J. (2015). Trends and directions in computer-assisted pronunciation training. In J. A. Mompean & J. Fouz-González (Eds.), *Investigating English pronunciation: Trends and directions* (pp. 314–342). doi:10.1057/9781137509437_14

Fryer, L. K., Nakao, K., & Thompson, A. (2019). Chatbot learning partners: Connecting learning experiences, interest and competence. *Computers in Human Behavior*, *93*, 279–289. doi:10.1016/j.chb.2018.12.023

Fu, M., & Li, S. (2020). The effect of immediate and delayed correcitve feedback on L2 development. *Studies in Second Language Acquisition*, 1–33. doi:10.1017/S0272263120000388

Galbraith, D. (2009). Cognitive Models of Writing. *German as a Foreign Language Journal*, *2*(3), 7–22. http://www.gfl-journal.de/2-2009/galbraith.pdf

Gárate, M., & Melero, A. (2005). Teaching how to write argumentative texts at primary school. In G. Rijlaarsdam, H. van den Bergh, & M. Couzijn (Eds.), *Effective learning and teaching of writing. Studies in writing* (Vol. 14). Springer. doi:10.1007/978-1-4020-2739-0_22

Garcia, M., & Nguyen, T. (2021). Understanding and using conjunctions in English essay writing. *TESOL Quarterly*, *18*(1), 32–47. doi:10.1111/tesq.12345

García, O., Flores, N., & Spotti, M. (Eds.). (2020). *The Oxford handbook of language and society*. Oxford University Press.

García, O., Johnson, S. I., & Seltzer, K. (2016). *The translanguaging classroom: Leveraging student bilingualism for learning*. Brookes Publishing.

García, O., & Wei, L. (2014). *Translanguaging: Language, bilingualism and education*. Palgrave Macmillan. doi:10.1057/9781137385765

Gass, S. M., & Mackey, A. (2020). Input, interaction, and output in L2 acquisition. In B. VanPatten, G. D. Keating, & S. Wulff (Eds.), *Theories in second language acquisition: An introduction* (pp. 192–222). Routledge. doi:10.4324/9780429503986-9

Georgiou, G. P. (2022). The acquisition of /ɪ/–/iː/ is challenging: Perceptual and production evidence from Cypriot Greek speakers of English. *Behavioral Sciences (Basel, Switzerland)*, *12*(12), 469. doi:10.3390/bs12120469

Ghadirzade Toosy, S., & Haniyeh Jajarmi, H. (2023). ESQ in L2 Willingness to Communicate and Communicative Ability. *Journal of Business. Tongxin Jishu*, 15–27. doi:10.56632/bct.2023.2202

Gielen, S., Peeters, E., Dochy, F., Onghena, P., & Struyven, K. (2010). Improving the effectiveness of peer feedback for learning. *Learning and Instruction*, *20*(4), 304–315. doi:10.1016/j.learninstruc.2009.08.007

Gilakjani, A. P. (2012). An analysis of factors affecting the ue of computer technology in English language teaching and learning. *International Journal of Information and Education Technology*, *2*(2), 135–142. doi:10.7763/IJIET.2012.V2.96

Ginusti, G. N. (2023). The implementation of digital technology in online project-based learning during pandemic: EFL students' perspectives. *J-SHMIC: Journal of English for Academic*, *10*(1), 13–25. doi:10.25299/jshmic.2023.vol10(1).10220

Glăveanu, V. P., Ness, I. J., Wasson, B., & Lubart, T. (2019). Sociocultural perspectives on creativity, learning, and technology. In C. A. Mullen (Ed.), *Creativity under duress in education? Resistive theories, practices, and actions* (pp. 63–82). Springer International Publishing. doi:10.1007/978-3-319-90272-2_4

Glesne, C. (2011). *Becoming qualitative researchers: An introduction* (4th ed.). Pearson.

Gold, H. (2019). "My Father Sits in the Dark" by Jerome Weidman. In J. R. Bryer (Ed.), *Why I Like This Story* (pp. 162–167). Boydell & Brewer. doi:10.1017/9781787445352.024

Gönen, S. İ. K. (2019). A qualitative study on a situated experience of technology integration: Reflections from pre-service teachers and students. *Computer Assisted Language Learning*, *32*(3), 163–189. doi:10.1080/09588221.2018.1552974

Goodman, B., & Tastanbek, S. (2020). Making the shift from a codeswitching to a translanguaging lens in English language teacher education. *TESOL Quarterly*, *55*(1), 29–53. doi:10.1002/tesq.571

Greenier, V., Liu, X., & Xiao, Y. (2023). Creative translanguaging in formative assessment: Chinese teachers' perceptions and practices in the primary EFL classroom. *Applied Linguistics Review*, *0*(0). Advance online publication. doi:10.1515/applirev-2023-0085

Gries, S. T. (2017). *Quantitative corpus linguistics with R: A practical introduction* (2nd ed.). Routledge.

Guía, E., Camacho, V. L., Orozco-Barbosa, L., Luján, V. M. B., Penichet, V. M. R., & Pérez, M. L. (2016). Introducing IoT and wearable technologies into task-based language learning for young children. *IEEE Transactions on Learning Technologies*, *9*(4), 366–378. doi:10.1109/TLT.2016.2557333

Guijarro Sanz, M. (2022). Fossilized mistakes in Spanish relative clauses learned by Chinese students. *International Review of Applied Linguistics in Language Teaching*, *60*(4), 1227–1251. doi:10.1515/iral-2021-0062

Guillén, G., Sawin, T., & Avineri, N. (2020). Zooming out of the crisis: Language and human collaboration. *Foreign Language Annals*, *53*(2), 320–328. doi:10.1111/flan.12459

Guillén, M., Monferrer, D., Rodríguez, A., & Moliner, M. (2021). Does emotional intelligence influence academic performance? The role of compassion and engagement in education for sustainable development. *Sustainability (Basel)*, *13*(4), 1–18. doi:10.3390/su13041721

Guslyakova, N. I., & Guslyakova, A. V. (2020). Emotional Intelligence as a Driving Force in the Study of Foreign Languages in Higher Education. *Proceedings IFTE*, 781-792. DOI: 10.3897/ap.2.e0781

Haider, M. Z., & Chowdhury, T. A. (2012). Promoting CLT within a computer assisted learning environment: A survey of the communicative English course of FLTC. *English Language Teaching*, 5(8), 91–102. doi:10.5539/elt.v5n8p91

Hajar, A. (2019). A Critical Review of Research on Language Learning Strategies Used by Arab Learners of English. *Studies in Self-Access Learning Journal*, 10(3), 239–257. doi:10.37237/100303

Halimi, F., Al Shammari, I., & Navarro, C. (2021). Emotional intelligence and academic achievement in higher education. *Journal of Applied Research in Higher Education*, 13(2), 485–503. doi:10.1108/JARHE-11-2019-0286

Hall, G. (Ed.). (2016). *The Routledge handbook of English language teaching*. Routledge. doi:10.4324/9781315676203

Hammad, E. A. (2016). Palestinian university students' problems with EFL essay writing in an instructional setting. *Teaching EFL writing in the 21st century Arab world: Realities and Challenges*, 99-124. doi:10.1057/978-1-137-46726-3_5

Hamoud, K., Hashim, A. S., & Awadh, W. A. (2018). Predicting student performance in higher education institutions. *International Journal of Interactive Multimedia and Artificial Intelligence*, 5(2), 26–31. doi:10.9781/ijimai.2018.02.004

Hampel, R., & Stickler, U. (2012). The use of videoconferencing to support multimodal interaction in an online language classroom. *ReCALL*, 24(2), 116–137. doi:10.1017/S095834401200002X

Hao-Jan Chen, H., Kuo-Wei Lai, K., & Thi-Nhu Ngo, T. (2024). The effectiveness of automatic speech recognition in ESL/EFL pronunciation: A meta-analysis. *ReCALL*, 36(1), 4–21. doi:10.1017/S0958344023000113

Hardison, D. M. (2004). Generalization of computer assisted prosody training: Quantitative and qualitative findings. *Language Learning & Technology*, 8(1), 34–52. http://llt.msu.edu/vol8num1/hardison/

Hartono, D., Basthomi, Y., Widiastuti, O., & Prastiyowati, S. (2022). The impacts of teacher's oral corrective feedback to students' psychological domain: A study on EFL speech production. *Cogent Education*, 9(1), 1–19. doi:10.1080/2331186X.2022.2152619

Hattie, J., & Timperley, H. (2007). The power of feedback. *Review of Educational Research*, 77(1), 81–112. doi:10.3102/003465430298487

Ha, X. V., & Murray, J. C. (2020). Corrective feedback: Beliefs and practices of Vietnamese primary EFL teachers. *Language Teaching Research*, 27(1), 137–167. doi:10.1177/1362168820931897

Ha, X. V., Nguyen, L. T., & Hung, B. P. (2021). Oral corrective feedback in English as a foreign language classrooms: A teaching and learning perspective. *Heliyon*, *7*(7), e07550. doi:10.1016/j.heliyon.2021.e07550

Hernández Sampiero, R., Fernández Collado, C., & Baptista Lucio, P. (2014). *Metodología de la investigación* [Research methodology]. McGraw-Hill.

Herzog, C., Handke, C., & Hitters, E. (2019). *Analyzing talk and text II: Thematic analysis*. Springer.

Hillenbrand, J., Getty, L. A., Clark, M. J., & Wheeler, K. (1995). Acoustic characteristics of American English vowels. *The Journal of the Acoustical Society of America*, *97*(5), 3099–3111. doi:10.1121/1.411872

Hincks, R. (2015). Technology and learning pronunciation. In M. Reed & J. M. Levis (Eds.), *The handbook of English pronunciation* (pp. 505–519). John Wiley & Sons. doi:10.1002/9781118346952.ch28

Hinton, L., & Hale, K. (2001). *The green book of language revitalization in practice*. Academic Press. doi:10.1163/9789004261723

Hişmanoğlu, M. (2005). Teaching English through literature. *Journal of Language and Linguistic Studies*, *1*(1), 53–66.

Hoang, V. Q., & Bui, H. P. (2023). Encouraging EFL students' willingness to communicate inside Vietnamese high school classrooms: Teachers' strategies and students' beliefs. *Applied Research on English Language*, *12*(2), 19–44. doi:10.22108/ARE.2022.134674.1968

Hornberger, N. H. (2006). Frameworks and models in language policy and planning. In T. Ricento (Ed.), *An introduction to language policy: Theory and method* (pp. 24–41). Blackwell Publishing.

Hornberger, N. H., & Johnson, D. C. (2007). Slicing the onion ethnographically: Layers and spaces in multilingual language education policy and practice. *TESOL Quarterly*, *41*(3), 509–532. doi:10.1002/j.1545-7249.2007.tb00083.x

Hsieh, W.-M., Yeh, H.-C., & Chen, N.-S. (2023). Impact of a robot and tangible object (R&T) integrated learning system on elementary EFL learners' English pronunciation and willingness to communicate. *Computer Assisted Language Learning*, 1–26. doi:10.1080/09588221.2023.2228357

Huang, J. (2022). Task-based language teaching and rigorous instruction in beginning English as a second language classrooms. *New Directions for Adult and Continuing Education*, *2022*(175), 59–70. doi:10.1002/ace.20468

Hubbard, P. (Ed.). (2009). *Computer-assisted language learning: Critical concepts in linguistics*. Routledge.

Hung, B. P., & Khoa, B. T. (2022). Communication strategies for interaction in social networks: a multilingual perspective. In I. Priyadarshini & R. Sharma (Eds.), *Artificial intelligence and cybersecurity* (pp. 2008–2020). CRC Press, Taylor & Francis.

Hung, B. P., Quang, N. N., Nguyen, L. T., & Viet, N. T. (2021). A cross-linguistic approach to analysing cohesive devices in expository writing by Asian EFL teachers. *3L: Language, Linguistics. Literature, 27*(2), 16–30. doi:10.17576/3L-2021-2702-02

Hung, B. P., & Van, L. T. (2018). Depicting and outlining as pre-writing strategies: Experimental results and learners' opinions. *International Journal of Instruction, 11*(2), 451–464. doi:10.12973/iji.2018.11231a

HusseinE. T.Al-EmamiA. H. (2016). Challenges to teaching English literature at the University of Hail: instructors' perspective. *Arab World English Journal (AWEJ), 7*(4). https://doi.org/doi:10.31219/osf.io/wnech

Hyland, K., & Hyland, F. (2019). *Feedback in second language writing: Contexts and issues.* Cambridge University Press., doi:10.1017/9781108635547

Inyang, J. B. (2017). The use of information and communication technologies (ICTS) in foreign language teaching in Nigeria: Prospects and challenges. *International Journal of Arts and Humanities, 6*(1), 124–134. doi:10.4314/ijah.v6i1.11

Iqbal, J., Asghar, M. Z., Ashraf, M. A., & Yi, X. (2022). The impacts of emotional intelligence on students' study habits in blended learning environments: The mediating role of cognitive engagement during COVID-19. *Behavioral Sciences (Basel, Switzerland), 12*(1), 14–33. doi:10.3390/bs12010014

Isaacs, T. (2009). Integrating form and meaning in L2 pronunciation instruction. *TESL Canada Journal, 27*(1), 1–12. doi:10.18806/tesl.v27i1.1034

Isariyawat, C., Yenphech, C., & Intanoo, K. (2020). The role of literature and literary texts in an EFL context: Cultural awareness and language skills. *Journal of Language and Linguistic Studies, 16*(3), 1320–1333. doi:10.17263/jlls.803748

Issah, M. (2018). Change Leadership: The Role of Emotional Intelligence. *SAGE Open, 8*(3), 1–6. doi:10.1177/2158244018800910

Jabali, O. (2018). Students' attitudes towards EFL university writing: A case study at An-Najah National University, Palestine. *Heliyon, 4*(11), e00896. Advance online publication. doi:10.1016/j.heliyon.2018.e00896

Jaime Romero, B., Castillejos López, W., & Reyes Toxqui, A. (2021). Intencionalidades y resistencias en el aprendizaje del inglés: Referentes para diseñar estrategias didácticas efectivas [Intentionalities and resistances in English language learning: references for designing effective teaching strategies]. *Revista de Investigación Educativa de la REDIECH, 12*, 1–19. doi:10.33010/ie_rie_rediech.v12i0.1013

Jebreil, N., Azizifar, A., & Gowhary, H. (2015). Investigating the effect of anxiety of male and female Iranian EFL learners on their writing performance. *Procedia: Social and Behavioral Sciences, 185*, 190–196. Advance online publication. doi:10.1016/j.sbspro.2015.03.360

Jenkins, J. (2000). *The phonology of English as an international language: New models, new norms, new goals.* Oxford University Press.

Jeong, K.-O. (2016). Integrating a web-based platform to promote creativity and authenticity in language classrooms. *International Journal of Knowledge and Learning, 11*(2), 127–136. doi:10.1504/IJKL.2016.079752

Jiang, Z., Zhang, L., & Mohamed, N. (2022). Researching translanguaging as a feasible pedagogical practice: Evidence from Chinese English-as-a-foreign-language students' perceptions. *RELC Journal, 53*(2), 371–390. doi:10.1177/00336882221113653

Jordan, R. R. (1997). *English for Academic Purposes: A Guide and Resource Book for Teachers.* Cambridge University Press. doi:10.1017/CBO9780511733062

Jouzdani, M., Biria, R., & Mohammadi, M. (2015). The effect of product-based and process-based teaching on writing efficiency of Iranian EFL learners. *International Journal of Research Studies in Language Learning, 1*(1), 1–6.

Kalsoom, T., Jabeen, S., Alshraah, S. M., Khasawneh, M. A. S., & Al-Awawdeh, N. (2024). Using technological-based models as digital tutors for enhancing reading and writing proficiency of foreign language undergraduates. *Kurdish Studies, 12*(1), 1716–1733. doi:10.58262/ks.v12i1.118

Kannan, M., & Meenakshi, S. (2023). A critical overview of the implementation of language-immersion through the use of mobile apps. *Theory and Practice in Language Studies, 13*(1), 186–191. doi:10.17507/tpls.1301.21

Kant, R. (2019). Emotional intelligence: A study on university students. *Journal of Education and Learning, 13*(4), 441–446. https://doi.org/.13592 doi:10.11591/edulearn.v13i4

Kartchava, E., & Nassaji, H. (2021). Corrective feedback in second language teaching and learning. In E. Kartchava & H. Nassaji (Eds.), *The Cambridge handbook of corrective feedback in second language learning and teaching* (pp. 1–20). Cambridge University Press. doi:10.1017/9781108589789.001

Kassem, M. A. M. (2018). Balancing technology with pedagogy in English language classroom: Teachers' perspective. *International Journal of English Language Teaching, 6*(9), 1–19.

Katsaris, T. (2019). The Willingness to Communicate (WTC): Origins, significance, and propositions for the L2/FL classroom. *Journal of Applied Languages and Linguistics, 3*(2), 31–42.

Kaur, D. J., Saraswat, N., & Alvi, I. (2023). Technology-enabled language leaning: Mediating role of collaborative learning. *Journal of Language and Education, 9*(1), 89–101. doi:10.17323/jle.2023.12359

Kemmis, S., & McTaggart, R. (1988). *The action research planner, 3rd.* Deakin University.

Kemmis, S., & McTaggart, R. (2014). *The action research planner: Doing critical participatory action research.* Springer. doi:10.1007/978-981-4560-67-2

Khabbazbashi, M. (2012). *On topic validity in speaking tests*. Cambridge University Press.

Khatib, M., & Alizadeh, I. (2012). Critical thinking skills through literary and non-literary texts in English classes. *International Journal of Linguistics, 4*(4), 563–580. doi:10.5296/ijl.v4i4.2928

Khoa, B. T., Hung, B. P., & Hejsalem-Brahmi, M. (2023). Qualitative research in social sciences: Data collection, data analysis and report writing. *International Journal of Public Sector Performance Management, 12*(1-2), 187–209. doi:10.1504/IJPSPM.2023.132247

Kidd, D., & Castano, E. (2013). Reading literary fiction improves theory of mind. *Science, 342*(6156), 377–380. doi:10.1126/science.1239918

Kim, S. H. (2015). Communicative language learning and curriculum development in the digital environment. *Asian Social Science, 11*(12), 337–352. doi:10.5539/ass.v11n12p337

Kozhevnikova, E. (2014). Exposing students to authentic materials as a way to increase students' language proficiency and cultural awareness. *Procedia: Social and Behavioral Sciences, 116*, 4462–4466. doi:10.1016/j.sbspro.2014.01.967

Kraklow, D., & Slimon, J. (2016). Using process-based writing instruction to change student attitudes about writing. *NCYU Inquiry in Applied Linguistics*, 78.

Kramsch, C. (1998). *Language and culture*. Oxford University Press.

Kramsch, C. (2017). Applied linguistic theory and second/foreign language education. In N. Van Deusen-Scholl & S. May (Eds.), *Second and foreign language education. Encyclopedia of language and education* (pp. 3–14). Springer., doi:10.1007/978-3-319-02246-8_1

Krashen, S. D. (1982). *Principles and practice in second language acquisition*. Pergamon.

Kruk, M., & Pawlak, M. (2023). Using internet resources in the development of English pronunciation: The case of the past tense -ed ending. *Computer Assisted Language Learning, 36*(1-2), 205–237. doi:10.1080/09588221.2021.1907416

Kukulska-Hulme, A. (2016). *Personalization of language learning through mobile technologies*. Cambridge University Press.

Kumar, M. N., & Prasad, B. B. N. (2022). Acquisition of English language through language laboratories- a paradigm shift in language learning. *International Journal of English Learning and Teaching Skills, 4*(4), 1–9. doi:10.15864/ijelts.4409

Kumar, T., Shet, J. P., & Parwez, M. A. (2022). Technology-integration experiences in ELT classrooms as an effective tool: A theoretical study. *Journal for Educators. Teachers and Trainers, 13*(1), 51–60. doi:10.47750/jett.2022.13.01.006

Kung, S.-C. (2005). Guiding EFL learners in the use of web resources. *GEMA: Online Journal of Language Studies, 5*(2), 50–62.

Kupchyk, L., & Litvinchuk, A. (2021). Constructing personal learning environments through ICT mediated foreign language instruction. *Journal of Physics: Conference Series*, *1840*(1), 1–15. doi:10.1088/1742-6596/1840/1/012045

Kushkiev, P. (2019). The role of positive emotions in second language acquisition: Some critical considerations. *Mextsol Journal*, *43*(4), 1–10.

Ladefoged, P., & Johnson, K. (2014). *A course in phonetics*. Cengage Learning.

Lai, C. (2019). Technology and learner autonomy: An argument in favor of the nexus of formal and informal language learning. *Annual Review of Applied Linguistics*, *39*, 52–58. doi:10.1017/S0267190519000035

Lam, M. (2017). The motivational dimension of language teaching. *Language Teaching*, *50*(3), 301–346. doi:10.1017/S0261444817000088

Lamy, M.-N., & Zourou, K. (Eds.). (2013). *Social networking for language education*. Palgrave Macmillan. doi:10.1057/9781137023384

Landrieu, Y., De Smedt, F., Van Keer, H., & De Wever, B. (2023). Argumentation in collaboration: The impact of explicit instruction and collaborative writing on secondary school students' argumentative writing. *Reading and Writing*. Advance online publication. doi:10.1007/s11145-023-10439-x

Lantolf, J. P. (2000). *Sociocultural theory and second language learning*. Oxford University Press.

Lantolf, J. P. (2006). Sociocultural theory and L2: State of the art. *Studies in Second Language Acquisition*, *28*(1), 67–109. doi:10.1017/S0272263106060037

Lantolf, J. P. (2024). On the value of explicit instruction: The view from sociocultural theory. *Language Teaching Research Quarterly*, *39*, 281–304. doi:10.32038/ltrq.2024.39.18

Lantolf, J. P., & Pavlenko, A. (1995). Sociocultural theory and second language acquisition. *Annual Review of Applied Linguistics*, *15*, 108–124. doi:10.1017/S0267190500002646

Lantolf, J. P., & Poehner, M. E. (2011). Dynamic assessment in the classroom: Vygotskian praxis for second language development. *Language Teaching Research*, *15*(1), 11–33. doi:10.1177/1362168810383328

Larsen-Freeman, D., & Anderson, M. (2013). *Techniques and principles in language teaching* (3rd ed.). Oxford University Press.

Larsen-Freeman, D., & Long, M. H. (2014). *An introduction to second language acquisition research*. Routledge. doi:10.4324/9781315835891

Lazar, G. (1993). *Literature and language teaching: a guide for teachers and trainers*. Cambridge University Press. doi:10.1017/CBO9780511733048

Lee, A. H., & Lyster, R. O. Y. (2017). Can corrective feedback on second language speech perception errors affect production accuracy? *Applied Psycholinguistics*, *38*(2), 371–393. doi:10.1017/S0142716416000254

Lee, J. S. (2022). The role of grit and classroom enjoyment in EFL learners' willingness to communicate. *Journal of Multilingual and Multicultural Development*, *43*(5), 452–468. doi:10.1080/01434632.2020.1746319

Lee, J. S., & Hsieh, J. C. (2019). Affective variables and willingness to communicate of EFL learners in in-class, out-of-class, and digital contexts. *System*, *82*(1), 63–73. doi:10.1016/j.system.2019.03.002

Lee, L. (2002). Enhancing learners' communication skills through synchronous electronic Iieraction and task-based instruction. *Foreign Language Annals*, *35*(1), 16–24. doi:10.1111/j.1944-9720.2002.tb01829.x

Lee, S. N., & Tajino, A. (2008). Understanding students' perceptions of difficulty with academic writing for teacher development: A case study of the university of Tokyo writing program. *Kyoto University*, *14*, 1–11.

Lestari, M., & Wahyudin, A. Y. (2020). Language Learning Strategies of Undergraduate EFL Students. *Journal of English Language Teaching and Learning*, *1*(1), 25–30. doi:10.33365/jeltl.v1i1.242

Le, T. T. D. (2023). Grammatical Error Analysis of EFL Learners' English Writing Samples: The Case of Vietnamese Pre-intermediate Students. *International Journal of TESOL & Education*, *3*(4), 1–14. doi:10.54855/ijte.23341

Levis, J. M. (2018). *Intelligibility, oral communication, and the teaching of pronunciation*. Cambridge University Press. doi:10.1017/9781108241564

Levis, J. M. (2022). Teaching pronunciation truths and lies. In C. Bardel, C. Hedman, K. Rejman, & E. Zetterholm (Eds.), *Exploring language education: Global and local perspectives* (pp. 39–72). Stockholm University Press. doi:10.16993/bbz.c

Levis, J., & Pickering, L. (2004). Teaching intonation in discourse using speech visualization technology. *System*, *32*(4), 505–524. doi:10.1016/j.system.2004.09.009

Li, M., Pan, Z., Sun, Y., & Yao, Z. (2021). Virtual reality in foreign language learning: A review of the literature. In *IEEE 7th International Conference on Virtual Reality (ICVR)* (pp. 302–307). IEEE. 10.1109/ICVR51878.2021.9483842

Liakina, N., & Liakin, D. (2023). Speech technologies and pronunciation training: What is the potential for efficient corrective feedback? In U. K. Alves & J. I. A. d. Albuquerque (Eds.), *Second language pronunciation: Different approaches to teaching and training* (pp. 287-312). Walter de Gruyter.

Liando, N., Dallyono, R., Tatipang, D., & Lengkoan, F. (2023). Among English, Indonesian and local language: Translanguaging practices in an Indonesian EFL classroom. *Indonesian Journal of Applied Linguistics*, *13*(1), 204–216. doi:10.17509/ijal.v13i1.58270

Li, C., Dewaele, J. M., & Jiang, G. (2019). The Complex Relationship between Classroom Emotions and EFL Achievement in China. *Applied Linguistics Review*, *11*(3), 1–26. doi:10.1515/applirev-2018-0043

Li, F. (2022). The impact of the flipped classroom teaching model on EFL learners' language learning: Positive changes in learning attitudes, perceptions and performance. *World Journal of English Language*, *12*(5), 136–147. doi:10.5430/wjel.v12n5p136

Li, G. (2023). On flipped classroom teaching of college English listening under the "Internet Plus" model. *Frontiers in Educational Research*, *6*(6), 101–104. doi:10.25236/FER.2023.060622

Lightbown, P. M., & Spada, N. (1999). *How languages are learned*. Oxford University Press.

Lin, L., Lam, W. I., & Tse, S. K. (2021). Motivational strategies, language learning strategies, and literal and inferential comprehension in second language Chinese reading: A structural equation modeling study. *Frontiers in Psychology*, *12*, 1–13. doi:10.3389/fpsyg.2021.707538

Li, S. (2010). The effectiveness of corrective feedback in SLA: A meta-analysis. *Language Learning*, *60*(2), 309–365. doi:10.1111/j.1467-9922.2010.00561.x

Li, S., Ellis, R., & Kim, J. (2018). The influence of pre-task grammar instruction on L2 learning: An experimental study. *Studies in English Education*, *23*(4), 831–857. doi:10.22275/SEE.23.4.03

Li, S., & Vuono, A. (2019). Twenty-five years of research on oral and written corrective feedback in System. *System*, *84*, 93–109. doi:10.1016/j.system.2019.05.006

Liu, M. (2022). The Relationship between Students' Study Time and Academic Performance and its Practical Significance. *BCP Education & Psychology*, *7*, 1–4. doi:10.54691/bcpep.v7i.2696

Liu, Y., & Fang, F. (2022). Translanguaging theory and practice: How stakeholders perceive translanguaging as a practical theory of language. *RELC Journal*, *53*(2), 391–399. doi:10.1177/0033688220939222

Liu, Y., & Garcia, M. (2018). Incorporating supporting evidence in English essay writing: Strategies for non-native speakers. *Journal of English for Academic Purposes*, *20*(2), 54–68. doi:10.1016/j.jeap.2018.01.001

Liu, Y.-J., Zhou, Y.-G., Li, Q.-L., & Ye, X.-D. (2022). Impact study of the learning effects and motivation of competitive modes in gamified learning. *Sustainability (Basel)*, *14*(11), 1–14. doi:10.3390/su14116626

Li, Z., & Bonk, C. J. (2023). Self-directed language learning with Duolingo in an out-of-class context. *Computer Assisted Language Learning*, 1–23. Advance online publication. doi:10.1080/09588221.2023.2206874

Compilation of References

Long, M. (1996). The role of the linguistic environment in second language acquisition. In W. C. Ritchie & T. K. Bhatia (Eds.), *Handbook of second language acquisition* (pp. 413–468). Academic Press.

Long, M. H. (1981). Input, interaction, and second-language acquisition. *Annals of the New York Academy of Sciences, 379*(1), 259–278. doi:10.1111/j.1749-6632.1981.tb42014.x

Long, M. H. (2007). *Problems in SLA*. Lawrence Erlbaum.

Lubis, N. H., & Fithriani, R. (2023). Investigating vocational high school teachers' challenges in integrating computer assisted instruction (CAI) into EFL classes. *Jurnal Paedagogy, 10*(3), 809–819. doi:10.33394/jp.v10i3.7731

Luo, B. (2016). Evaluating a computer-assisted pronunciation training (CAPT) technique for efficient classroom instruction. *Computer Assisted Language Learning, 29*(3), 451–476. doi:10.1080/09588221.2014.963123

Lyddon, P. A. (2019). A reflective approach to digital technology implementation in language teaching: Expanding pedagogical capacity by rethinking substitution, augmentation, modification, and redefinition. *TESL Canada Journal, 36*(3), 186–200. doi:10.18806/tesl.v36i3.1327

Lyster, R. (2004). Differential effects of prompts and recasts in form-focused instruction. *Studies in Second Language Acquisition, 26*(3), 399–432. doi:10.1017/S0272263104263021

Lyster, R., & Mori, H. (2006). Interactional feedback and instructional counterbalance. *Studies in Second Language Acquisition, 28*(2), 269–300. doi:10.1017/S0272263106060128

Lyster, R., & Ranta, L. (1997). Corrective feedback and learner uptake: Negotiation of form in communicative classrooms. *Studies in Second Language Acquisition, 19*(1), 37–66. doi:10.1017/S0272263197001034

Lyster, R., & Saito, K. (2010). Oral feedback in classroom SLA. *Studies in Second Language Acquisition, 32*(2), 265–302. doi:10.1017/S0272263109990520

Lyster, R., Saito, K., & Sato, M. (2013). Oral corrective feedback in second language classrooms. *Language Teaching, 46*(1), 1–40. doi:10.1017/S0261444812000365

MacCann, C., Jiang, Y., Brown, L. E. R., Double, K. S., Bucich, M., & Minbashian, A. (2020). Emotional intelligence predicts academic performance: A meta-analysis. *Psychological Bulletin, 146*(2), 150–186. doi:10.1037/bul0000219

MacIntyre, P. D. (2020). Expanding the Theoretical Base for the Dynamics of Willingness to Communicate. *Studies in Second Language Learning and Teaching, 10*(1), 111–131. doi:10.14746/ssllt.2020.10.1.6

MacIntyre, P. D., & Gregersen, T. (2021). The Idiodynamic Method: Willingness to Communicate and Anxiety Processes Interacting in Real Time. *International Review of Applied Linguistics in Language Teaching, 60*(1), 67–84. doi:10.1515/iral-2021-0024

MacIntyre, P. D., & Wang, L. (2021). Willingness to communicate in the L2 about meaningful photos: Application of the pyramid model of WTC. *Language Teaching Research*, 25(6), 878–898. doi:10.1177/13621688211004645

MacIntyre, P. D., Wang, L., & Khajavy, G. H. (2020). Thinking Fast and Slow About Willingness to Communicate: A Two-systems View. *Eurasian Journal of Applied Linguistics*, 6(3), 443–458. doi:10.32601/ejal.834681

Mackey, A. (2012). *Input, interaction, and corrective feedback in L2 learning*. Oxford University Press.

Mackey, A. J., & Bryfonski, L. (2018). Mixed methodology. In A. Phakiti, P. De Costa, L. Plonsky, & S. Starfield (Eds.), *The Palgrave handbook of applied linguistics research methodology* (pp. 103–121). Palgrave., doi:10.1057/978-1-137-59900-1_5

Mackey, A., & Gass, S. M. (2015). *Second language research: Methodology and design* (2nd ed.). Routledge. doi:10.4324/9781315750606

Mackey, A., Oliver, R., & Leeman, J. (2003). Interactional input and the incorporation of feedback: An exploration of NS–NNS and NNS–NNS adult and child dyads. *Language Learning*, 53(1), 35–66. doi:10.1111/1467-9922.00210

MacKey, A., & Philp, J. (1998). Conversational interaction and second language development: Recasts, responses, and red herrings? *Modern Language Journal*, 82(3), 338–356. doi:10.1111/j.1540-4781.1998.tb01211.x

Maharani, A. A. P. (2022). Exploring writing instruction-based process writing approach in tertiary level of EFL argumentative writing classroom. *Journal Santiaji Pendidikan*, 12(2), 158–167.

Mahmood, R. Q. (2023). Enhancing EFL speaking and pronunciation skills: Using explicit formal instruction in a Kurdish university. *Issues in Educational Research*, 33(4), 1421–1440. http://www.iier.org.au/iier33/mahmood-abs.html

Mahmud, A., Chanda Antor, S., & Al Zabir, A. (2020). Factor Affecting the Academic Performance of University Students. *Social Work Education*, 7(3), 373–382. doi:10.25128/2520-6230.20.3.11.

Makalela, L. (2015). Moving out of linguistic boxes: The effects of translanguaging strategies for multilingual classrooms. *Language and Education*, 29(3), 200–217. doi:10.1080/09500782.2014.994524

Mandasari, B., & Oktaviani, L. (2018). English Language Learning Strategies: An Exploratory Study of Management and Engineering Students. *Premise: Journal of English Education and Applied Linguistics*, 7(2), 61–78. doi:10.24127/pj.v7i2.1581

Marenzi, I., Kupetz, R., Nejdl, W., & Zerr, S. (2010). *Supporting active learning in CLIL through collaborative search*. International Conference on Web-Based Learning, Shanghai, China. 10.1007/978-3-642-17407-0_21

Compilation of References

Maroko, G. M. (2010) The authentic materials approach in the teaching of functional writing in the classroom. In *The new decade and (2nd) FL Teaching: The initial phase Rudolf Reinelt*. Research Laboratory EU Matsuyama. http://web.iec.ehime-u.ac.jp/reinelt/raineruto2/5%20Geoffrey%20M%20Maroko.pdf

Marue, M. G., & Pantas, M. B. (2019). Challenges in descriptive essay writing: A case of Indonesian EFL leaners. *International Journal of Innovation, Creativity and Change, 8*(12), 88-103. https://www.ijicc.net/images/vol8iss12/81205_Marue_2019_E1_R.pdf

Matsuda, P. K. (2003). Second language writing in the twentieth century: A situated historical perspective. *Exploring the Dynamics of Second Language Writing, 1*, 15–34. doi:10.1017/CBO9781139524810.004

May, S. (2012). *Language and minority rights: Ethnicity, nationalism and the politics of language*. Routledge.

May, S. (2015). Language policy and political theory. In F. M. Hult & D. C. Johnson (Eds.), *Research methods in language policy and planning: A practical guide* (pp. 45–55). Wiley. doi:10.1002/9781118340349.ch5

McCarty, T. L., Romero-Little, M. E., & Zepeda, O. (2006). Native American youth discourses on language shift and retention: Ideological cross-currents and their implications for language planning. *International Journal of Bilingual Education and Bilingualism, 9*(5), 659–677. doi:10.2167/beb386.0

McCrocklin, S. M. (2016). Pronunciation learner autonomy: The potential of automatic speech recognition. *System, 57*, 25–42. doi:10.1016/j.system.2015.12.013

McDonough, K., & Mackey, A. (Eds.). (2013). *Second language interaction in diverse educational contexts*. John Benjamins Publishing Company., doi:10.1075/lllt.34

McDougald, J. S., Gómez, D. P. D., Gutiérrez, L. S. Q., & Córdoba, F. G. S. (2023). Listening to CLIL practitioners: An overview of bilingual teachers' perceptions in Bogota. *Colombian Applied Linguistics Journal, 25*(1), 97–117. doi:10.14483/22487085.18992

McNiff, J., & Whitehead, J. (2011). *All you need to know about action research* (2nd ed.). Sage.

Méndez López, M. G. (2020). Emotions attributions of ELT pre-service teachers and their effects on teaching practice. *Profile: Issues in Teachers'. Professional Development (Philadelphia, Pa.), 22*(1), 15–28. doi:10.15446/profile.v22n1.78613

Méndez López, M. G. (2022). Emotions experienced by secondary school students in English classes in México. *Colombian Applied Linguistics Journal, 24*(2), 219–233. doi:10.14483/22487085.18401

Menggo, S., & Darong, H. C. (2022). Blended learning in ESL/EFL class. *LLT Journal: A Journal on Language and Language Teaching, 25*(1), 132-148. doi:10.24071/llt.v25i1.4159

Mirhosseini, S. A. (2020). *Doing qualitative research in language education*. Springer Nature. doi:10.1007/978-3-030-56492-6

Miri, A. M., & Hung, B. P. (2021). Contextualizing second language writing in literature courses: Locality of pedagogy for innovative practices. In *Futuristic and linguistic perspectives on teaching writing to second language students* (pp. 287–306). IGI Global. doi:10.4018/978-1-7998-6508-7.ch017

Mısır, H. (2018). Digital literacies and interactive multimedia-enhanced tools for language teaching and learning. *International Online Journal of Education & Teaching*, 5(3), 514–523.

Mohammad, T., & Khan, S. I. (2023). Flipped classroom: An effective methodology to improve writing skills of EFL students. *World Journal of English Language*, 13(5), 468–474. doi:10.5430/wjel.v13n5p468

Mohammed, A. M. K. A. (2023). Authenticity in the language classroom and its effect on ELF learners' language proficiency. *Brock Journal of Education*, 11(1), 78–87. doi:10.37745/bje.2023/vol11n17889

Moore, R., & Fodrey, B. (2021). *Distance Education and Technology Infrastructure: Strategies and Opportunities*. Springer.

Moqbel, M. S. S., & Al-Kadi, A. M. T. (2023). Foreign language learning assessment in the age of ChatGPT: A theoretical account. *Journal of English Studies in Arabia Felix*, 2(1), 71–84. doi:10.56540/jesaf.v2i1.62

Morley, J. (1991). The pronunciation component in teaching English to speakers of other languages. *TESOL Quarterly*, 25(3), 481–520. doi:10.2307/3586981

Morse, J. M. (1994). *Critical issues in qualitative research methods*. Sage Publications.

Moses, L., Hajdun, M., & Aguirre, A. (2021). Translanguaging together: Building bilingual identities con nuevos amigos. *The Reading Teacher*, 75(3), 291–304. doi:10.1002/trtr.2060

Motohashi-Siago, M., & Hardison, D. M. (2009). Acquisition of L2 Japanese geminates: Training with waveform displays. *Language Learning & Technology*, 13(2), 29–47. http://llt.msu.edu/vol13num2/motohashisaigohardison.pdf

Muis, S., Salija, K., Nur, S., & Sakkir, G. (2023). Translanguaging in EFL classroom at a private university in south Sulawesi. Eduline. *Journal of Education and Learning Innovation*, 3(3), 396–406. doi:10.35877/454RI.eduline1904

Myhill, D. (2009). Becoming a designer: Trajectories of linguistic development. In The Sage Handbook of Writing Development (pp. 402-13). Sage Publications.

Nagy, T. (2018). On translanguaging and its role in foreign language teaching. *Acta Universitatis Sapientiae. Philologica*, 10(2), 41–53. doi:10.2478/ausp-2018-0012

Nagy, T. (2021). Using technology for foreign language learning: The teacher's role. *Central European Journal of Educational Research*, *3*(2), 23–28. doi:10.37441/cejer/2021/3/2/9347

Nassaji, H. (2018). *Errors versus mistakes. Teaching grammar.* doi:10.1002/9781118784235. eelt0059

Nassaji, H. (2009). Effects of recasts and elicitations in dyadic interaction and the role of feedback explicitness. *Language Learning*, *59*(2), 411–452. doi:10.1111/j.1467-9922.2009.00511.x

Nassaji, H. (2015). *The interactional feedback dimension in instructed second language learning: Linking theory, research, and practice.* Bloomsbury.

Nassaji, H. (2016). Anniversary article interactional feedback in second language teaching and learning: A synthesis and analysis of current research. *Language Teaching Research*, *20*(4), 535–562. doi:10.1177/1362168816644940

Nassaji, H., & Kartchava, E. (Eds.). (2021). *The Cambridge handbook of corrective feedback in second language learning and teaching.* Cambridge University Press. doi:10.1017/9781108589789

Nassar, Y. H., Al-Motrif, A., Abuzahra, S., Aburezeq, I. M., Dweikat, F. F., Helali, M. M., ... Gimeno, A. R. (2023). The impacts of blended learning on English education in higher education. *World Journal of English Language*, *13*(6), 449–458. doi:10.5430/wjel.v13n6p449

Nation, I. S. P. (2001). *Learning vocabulary in another language.* Cambridge University Press. doi:10.1017/CBO9781139524759

Nazir, F., Majeed, M. N., Ghazanfar, M. A., & Maqsood, M. (2023). A computer-aided speech analytics approach for pronunciation feedback using deep feature clustering. *Multimedia Systems*, *29*(3), 1699–1715. doi:10.1007/s00530-021-00822-5

Nazli, K., & Yahya, U. (2023). The role of computer-assisted language learning (CALL) in language teachers' professional development. *Pakistan Languages and Humanities Review*, *7*(1), 1–11. doi:10.47205/plhr.2023(7-I)01

Negoescu, A. G., & Mitrulescu, C. M. (2023). Using technology to increase students' motivation for learning a foreign language. *International conference: Knowledge-based Organization*, *29*(2), 210-214. 10.2478/kbo-2023-0059

Nehe, B. M., Mualimah, E. N., Bastaman, W. W., Arini, I., & Purwantiningsih, S. (2023). Exploring English learners' experiences of using mobile language learning applications. *Jurnal Teknologi Pendidikan*, *25*(1), 76–90. doi:10.21009/jtp.v25i1.34883

Nenotek, S. A., Tlonaen, Z. A., & Manubulu, H. A. (2022). Exploring university students' difficulties in writing English academic essay. *Al-Ishlah: Jurnal Pendidikan*, *14*(1), 909–920. doi:10.35445/alishlah.v14i1.1352

Ngo, H. K., & Yunus, M. M. (2021). Flipped classroom in English language teaching and learning: A systematic literature review. *International Journal of Academic Research in Business & Social Sciences*, *11*(3), 185–196. doi:10.6007/IJARBSS/v11-i3/8622

Nguyen, L. Q., & Le, H. V. (2022). Improving L2 learners' IELTS task 2 writing: The role of model essays and noticing hypothesis. *Language Testing in Asia, 12*(1), 58. doi:10.1186/s40468-022-00206-0

Nguyen, L. T., Bui, H. P., & Ha, X. V. (2024). Scaffolding in genre-based L2 writing classes: Vietnamese EFL teachers' beliefs and practices. *IRAL. International Review of Applied Linguistics in Language Teaching, 62*(1), 1–19. doi:10.1515/iral-2023-0125

Nguyen, L. T., & Newton, J. (2021). Enhancing EFL teachers' pronunciation pedagogy through professional learning: A Vietnamese case study. *RELC Journal, 52*(1), 77–93. doi:10.1177/0033688220952476

Nguyen, N. H. T., Nguyen, N. T. M., & Nguyen, T. T. T. (2021). Difficulties in writing an essay of English-majored sophomores at Tay Do University, in Vietnam. *European Journal of English Language Teaching, 6*(5), 1–15. doi:10.46827/ejel.v6i5.3851

Nguyen, N. H. T., Pham, T. U., & Phan, T. M. U. (2020). Difficulties in writing essays of English majored sophomores at Tay Do University, Vietnam. *European Journal of English Language Teaching, 6*(2), 1–14. https://oapub.org/edu/index.php/ejel/article/view/3518

Nguyen, T. K. T. (2022). A study of Vietnamese teachers' perceptions and practice in teaching English literature in the context of English as a Lingua Franca. *HNUE Journal of Science, 67*(3), 3–13. doi:10.18173/2354-1075.2022-0039

Nguyen, T. T. N. (2023). Exploring Vietnamese EFL students' perceptions towards literature courses in English Studies program. *International Journal of Language Instruction, 2*(3), 80–96. doi:10.54855/ijli.23234

Nikula, T. (2015). Hands-on tasks in CLIL science classrooms as sites for subject-specific language use and learning. *System, 54*, 14–27. doi:10.1016/j.system.2015.04.003

Nordin, S. M. (2017). The best of two approaches: Process/genre-based approach to teaching writing. *English Teaching*, 11.

Norris, J. M., & Ortega, L. (Eds.). (2006). *Synthesizing research on language learning and teaching*. John Benjamins Publishing Company., doi:10.1075/lllt.13

Norton, B. (2013). *Identity and language learning: Extending the conversation*. Multilingual Matters., doi:10.21832/9781783090563

Nunan, D. (1989). *Designing tasks for the communicative classroom*. Cambridge University Press.

Nurmala, I., Irianto, S., Franchisca, S., Amsa, H., & Susanti, R. (2023). Technology-enhanced language learning: A meta-analysis study on English language teaching tools. *Journal of Education, 6*(1), 2188–2195. doi:10.31004/joe.v6i1.3221

O'Brien, M. G. (2004). Pronunciation matters. *Die Unterrichtspraxis/Teaching German, 37*(1), 1-9. https://doi.org/https://doi.org/10.1111/j.1756-1221.2004.tb00068.x

O'Brien, M. G., Derwing, T. M., Cucchiarini, C., Hardison, D. M., Mixdorff, H., Thomson, R. I., Strik, H., Levis, J. M., Munro, M. J., Foote, J. A., & Levis, G. M. (2018). Directions for the future of technology in pronunciation research and teaching. *Journal of Second Language Pronunciation, 4*(2), 182–207. doi:10.1075/jslp.17001.obr

O'Connor, P. J., Hill, A., Kaya, M., & Martin, B. (2019). The Measurement of Emotional Intelligence: A Critical Review of the Literature and Recommendations for Researchers and Practitioners. *Frontiers in Psychology, 10*, 1–19. doi:10.3389/fpsyg.2019.01116

O'Hagan, M., & Ashworth, D. (Eds.). (2002). *Translation-mediated communication in a digital world: Facing the challenges of globalization and localization.* Multilingual Matters., doi:10.21832/9781853595820

Oddone, C. (2011). Using videos from YouTube and websites in the CLIL classroom. *Studies about. Languages (Basel, Switzerland), 0*(18), 105–110. doi:10.5755/j01.sal.0.18.417

Offerman, H. M., & Olson, D. J. (2016). Visual feedback and second language segmental production: The generalizability of pronunciation gains. *System, 59*, 45–60. doi:10.1016/j.system.2016.03.003

Offerman, H. M., & Olson, D. J. (2023). Speech visualization for pronunciation instruction: Exploring instructor support in L2 learner attitudes toward visual feedback. In S. McCrocklin (Ed.), *Technological resources for second language pronunciation learning and teaching: Research-based approaches* (pp. 239–260). Rowman & Littlefield.

Okpe, A. A., & Onjewu, M. A. (2017). Difficulties of Learning Essay Writing: The Perspective of Some Adult EFL Learners in Nigeria. *International Journal of Curriculum and Instruction, 9*(2), 198–205. https://ijci.globets.org/index.php/IJCI/article/view/82

Oktan, D., & Kaymakamoğlu, S. E. (2017). Using literary texts in EFL classrooms: Cultural awareness and vocabulary enrichment. *International Journal of New Trends in Arts, Sports & Science Education, 6*(4).

Oliver, R. (2000). Age differences in negotiation and feedback in classroom and pairwork. *Language Learning, 50*(1), 119–151. doi:10.1111/0023-8333.00113

Oliver, R., & Adams, R. (2021). Oral corrective feedback. In H. Nassaji & E. Kartchava (Eds.), *The Cambridge handbook of corrective feedback in second language learning and teaching* (pp. 187–206). Cambridge University Press. doi:10.1017/9781108589789.010

Oliver, R., & Azkarai, A. (2017). Review of child second language acquisition: Examining theories and research. *Annual Review of Applied Linguistics, 37*, 62–76. doi:10.1017/S0267190517000058

Olson, C. (2014). The conflicting themes of nonviolence and violence in ancient Indian asceticism as evident in the practice of fasting. *International Journal of Dharma Studies, 2*(1), 1. doi:10.1186/2196-8802-2-1

Olson, D. J. (2022). Visual feedback and relative vowel duration in L2 pronunciation: the curious case of stressed and unstressed vowels. *Proceedings of the 12th Pronunciation in Second Language Learning and Teaching Conference.* 10.31274/psllt.13353

Olson, D. J., & Offerman, H. M. (2021). Maximizing the effect of visual feedback for pronunciation instruction: A comparative analysis of three approaches. *Journal of Second Language Pronunciation*, 7(1), 89–115. doi:10.1075/jslp.20005.ols

Özgür Küfi, E. (2023). Activation of Content-Schemata for Scaffolding L2 Writing: Voices from a Turkish Context. *Journal of Psycholinguistic Research*, 52(6), 2405–2427. doi:10.1007/s10936-023-10002-3

Paltridge, B., & Phakiti, A. (Eds.). (2015). *Research methods in applied linguistics: A practical resource*. Bloomsbury Publishing.

Panezai, A., Channa, L. A., & Bibi, B. (2022). Translanguaging in higher education: Exploring interactional spaces for meaning-making in the multilingual universities of Pakistan. *International Journal of Bilingual Education and Bilingualism*, 26(4), 514–527. doi:10.1080/13670050.2022.2124842

Partido, B. B., & Stafford, R. (2018). Association between emotional intelligence and academic performance among dental hygiene students. *Journal of Dental Education*, 82(9), 974–979. doi:10.21815/JDE.018.094

Pastor, C. K. L. (2020). Sentiment analysis on synchronous online delivery of instruction due to extreme community quarantine in the Philippines caused by COVID-19 pandemic. *Asian Journal of Multidisciplinary Studies (Pangasinan)*, 3(1), 1–6.

Pegrum, M. (2019). *Mobile lenses on learning languages and literacies on the move*. Springer., doi:10.1007/978-981-15-1240-7

Peixoto, I., & Muniz, M. (2022). Emotional Intelligence, Intelligence and Social Skills in Different Areas of Work and Leadership. *Psico-USF*, 27(2), 237–250. doi:10.1590/1413-82712022270203

Pellegrino, E., Santo, M. D., & Vitale, G. (2013). Integrating learning technologies and autonomy: a CLIL course in linguistics. *Procedia- Social and Behavioral Sciences*, 106(2023), 1514-1522. doi:10.1016/j.sbspro.2013.12.171

Peng, J. E. (2019). The roles of multimodal pedagogic effects and classroom environment in willingness to communicate in English. *System*, 82(1), 161–173. doi:10.1016/j.system.2019.04.006

Pereira, J. (2013). Video game meets literature: language learning with interactive fiction. *E-TEALS: AN E-JOURNAL of Teacher Education and Applied Language Studies*, 4, 19-45.

Petek, E., & Bedir, H. (2018). An adaptable teacher education framework for critical thinking in language teaching. *Thinking Skills and Creativity*, 28, 56–72. doi:10.1016/j.tsc.2018.02.008

Petersen, S. A., Procter-Legg, E., & Cacchione, A. (2013). Creativity and mobile language learning using LingoBee. *International Journal of Mobile and Blended Learning*, 5(3), 34–51. doi:10.4018/jmbl.2013070103

Compilation of References

Pfeil, U., & Zaphiris, P. (2010). Applying qualitative content analysis to study online support communities. *Universal Access in the Information Society*, *9*(1), 1–16. doi:10.1007/s10209-009-0154-3

Phakiti, A., De Costa, P., Plonsky, L., & Starfield, S. (Eds.). (2018). *The Palgrave handbook of applied linguistics research methodology*. Palgrave Macmillan. doi:10.1057/978-1-137-59900-1

Pham, T. N., & Duong, D. T. (2022). Using Kahoot! in vocabulary learning: Evidence from a Vietnamese higher education context. *VNU Journal of Foreign Studies*, *38*(3), 138–152. doi:10.25073/2525-2445/vnufs.4849

Phuong, W. T. N. (2021). Difficulties in studying writing of English-majored sophomores at a university in Vietnam. *European Journal of Education Studies*, *8*(10). Advance online publication. doi:10.46827/ejes.v8i10.3962

Pichugin, V., Panfilov, A., & Volkova, E. (2022). The effectiveness of online learning platforms in foreign language teaching. *World Journal on Educational Technology: Current Issues*, *14*(5), 1357–1372. doi:10.18844/wjet.v14i5.7861

Pillai, S., & Delavari, H. (2012). The production of English monophthong vowels by Iranian EFL learners. *Poznán Studies in Contemporary Linguistics*, *48*(3), 473–493. doi:10.1515/psicl-2012-0022

Piller, I. (2017). *Intercultural communication: A critical introduction*. Edinburgh University Press. doi:10.1515/9781474412926

Piske, T., MacKay, I. R. A., & Flege, J. E. (2001). Factors affecting degree of foreign accent in an L2: A review. *Journal of Phonetics*, *29*(2), 191–215. doi:10.1006/jpho.2001.0134

Pratiwi, K. D. (2016). Students Difficulties in Writing English. A Study at the Third Semester Students of English Education Program of UNIB in Academic Year 2011-2012). *Journal of Linguistics and Language Teaching*, *3*(1). Advance online publication. doi:10.29300/ling.v3i1.106

Pregowska, A., Masztalerz, K., Garlińska, M., & Osial, M. (2021). A worldwide journey through distance education. *Education Sciences*, *11*(3), 1–26. doi:10.3390/educsci11030118

Proctor, C. P., August, D., Carlo, M., & Snow, C. E. (2006). The intriguing role of Spanish language vocabulary knowledge in predicting English reading comprehension. *Journal of Educational Psychology*, *98*(1), 159–169. doi:10.1037/0022-0663.98.1.159

Purnama, Y. (2022). The use of information and communication technology as learning sources in English language learning. *International Journal of Multidisciplinary Research and Analysis*, *5*(9), 2302–2304. doi:10.47191/ijmra/v5-i9-02

Purwaningtyas, T., Nurkamto, J., & Kristina, D. (2023). EFL teacher intervention in mediating students' interaction in web-based collaborative writing environment using Google Docs. *Voice of English Language Education Society*, *7*(1), 135–144. doi:10.29408/veles.v7i1.7912

Rabionet, S. E. (2011). How I learned to design and conduct semi-structured interviews: An ongoing and continuous journey. *The Qualitative Report, 16*(2), 563.

Rahimi, M., & Karkami, F. H. (2015). The role of teachers' classroom discipline in their teaching effectiveness and students' language learning motivation and achievement: A path method. *Iranian Journal of Language Teaching Research, 3*(1), 57–82. https://eric.ed.gov/?id=EJ1127336

Rahman, M. W., Farid, K. S., & Tanny, N. Z. (2022). Determinants of Students' Academic Performance at the University Level. *International Journal of Agricultural Science, Research and Technology in Extension and Education Systems, 11*(4), 213–222. 20.1001.1.22517588.2021.11.3.1

Rahmat, N. H. (2020). Knowledge Transforming in Writing: An Analysis of Read-to-Write Process. *European Journal of English Language Teaching, 594*(4), 1–17. doi:10.46827/ejel.v5i4.3103

Ramani, S., Könings, K. D., Ginsburg, S., & van der Vleuten, C. P. M. (2019). Meaningful feedback through a sociocultural lens. *Medical Teacher, 41*(12), 1342–1352. doi:10.1080/0142159X.2019.1656804

Ramírez Espinosa, A., & Hernández Gaviria, F. (2022). Learning strategies in action. *Revista Boletín Redipe, 11*(4), 67–83. doi:10.36260/rbr.v11i04.1802

Rang, O., & Moran, M. (2014). Functional loads of pronunciation features in nonnative speakers' oral assessment. *TESOL Quarterly, 48*(1), 176–187. doi:10.1002/tesq.152

Ranta, L., & Lyster, R. (2007). A cognitive approach to improving immersion students' oral language abilities: The awareness-practice-feedback sequence. In R. DeKeyser (Ed.), *Practice in a second language: Perspectives from applied linguistics and cognitive psychology* (pp. 141–160). Cambridge University Press. doi:10.1017/CBO9780511667275.009

Rashtchi, M., Porkar, R., & Saeed, S. F. G. M. (2019). Product-based, process-based, and genre-based Instructions in expository writing: Focusing on EFL learners' performance and strategy use. *European Journal of Education Studies*.

Rassaei, E. (2013). Corrective feedback, learners' perceptions, and second language development. *System, 41*(1), 472–483. doi:10.1016/j.system.2013.05.002

Rassaei, E. (2014). Scaffolded feedback, recasts, and L2 development: A sociocultural perspective. *Modern Language Journal, 98*(1), 417–431. doi:10.1111/j.1540-4781.2014.12060.x

Rehman, I., & Flint, E. (2021). *Real-time visual acoustic feedback for nonnative vowel production*. Presentation presented at 12th Annual Pronunciation in Second Language Learning and Teaching Conference, Brock University, Canada.

Resnik, P., & Dewaele, J. M. (2020). Trait Emotional Intelligence, Positive and Negative Emotions in First and Foreign Language Classes: A Mixed-methods Approach. *System, 94*, 1–20. doi:10.1016/j.system.2020.102324

Richards, J. C., & Rodgers, T. S. (2014). *Approaches and methods in language teaching*. Cambridge University Press. doi:10.1017/9781009024532

Richards, J. C., & Schmidt, R. (2002). *Dictionary of language teaching and applied linguistics* (3rd ed.). Longman.

Roach, P. (2009). *English phonetics and phonology: A practical course.* Cambridge University Press.

Robles Bello, M. A., Sánchez Teruel, D., & Moreno, M. G. (2021). Psychometric properties of the Emotional Quotient Inventory: Youth Version-EQ-i:YV in Spanish adolescents with Down syndrome. *Journal of Applied Research in Intellectual Disabilities, 34*(1), 77–89. doi:10.1111/jar.12787

Rochma, A. F. (2023). Corrective oral feedback on students' errors in speaking courses. *Journal of English Language Teaching and Learning, 4*(2), 125–135. doi:10.18860/jetle.v4i2.20442

Rocque, S. R. (2022). Evaluating the effectiveness of mobile applications in enhancing learning and development. *International Journal of Innovative Technologies in Social Science, 3*(35), 1–8. doi:10.31435/rsglobal_ijitss/30092022/7847

Rogulska, O., Rudnitska, K., Mahdiuk, O., Drozdova, V., Lysak, H., & Korol, S. (2023). The today's linguistic paradigm: the problem of investigating emotional intelligence in the learning of a foreign language. *Revista Românească pentru Educaţie Multidimensională, 15*(4), 458-473. https://doi.org/ doi:10.18662/rrem/15.4/804

Romano, L., Tang, X., Hietajärvi, L., Salmela-Aro, K., & Fiorilli, C. (2020). Students' trait emotional intelligence and perceived teacher emotional support in preventing burnout: The moderating role of academic anxiety. *International Journal of Environmental Research and Public Health, 17*(13), 4771–4786. doi:10.3390/ijerph17134771

Roothooft, H., & Breeze, R. (2016). A comparison of EFL teachers' and students' attitudes to oral corrective feedback. *Language Awareness, 25*(4), 318–335. doi:10.1080/09658416.2016.1235580

Ru, M. (2022). Research on the new model of data-driven teaching decision-making for university minority language majors. *Frontiers in Psychology, 13*, 1–8. doi:10.3389/fpsyg.2022.901256

Rumble, G. (2019). *The planning and management of distance education.* Routledge. doi:10.4324/9780429288661

Sabti, A. A., Md Rashid, S., Nimehchisalem, V., & Darmi, R. (2019). The Impact of writing anxiety, writing achievement motivation, and writing self-efficacy on writing performance: A correlational study of Iraqi tertiary EFL Learners. *SAGE Open, 9*(4). doi:10.1177/2158244019894289

Sadeghi, M. (2019). A shift from classroom to distance learning: Advantages and limitations. International. *Journal of Research in English Education, 4*(1), 80–88. doi:10.29252/ijree.4.1.80

Šafranj, J., & Zivlak, J. (2019). Effects of big five personality traits and fear of negative evaluation on foreign language anxiety. *Croatian Journal of Education, 21*(1), 275–306. doi:10.15516/cje.v21i1.2942

Saito, K. (2007). The influence of explicit phonetic instruction on pronunciation in EFL settings: The case of English vowels and Japanese learners of English. *The Linguistics Journal, 3*(3), 16–40.

Saito, K. (2012). Effects of instruction on L2 pronunciation development: A synthesis of 15 quasi-experimental intervention studies. *TESOL Quarterly, 46*(4), 842–854. doi:10.1002/tesq.67

Saito, K. (2021). Effects of corrective feedback on second language pronunciation development. In E. Kartchava & H. Nassaji (Eds.), *The Cambridge handbook of corrective feedback in second language learning and teaching* (pp. 407–428). Cambridge University Press. doi:10.1017/9781108589789.020

Saito, K., & Lyster, R. (2012). Effects of form-focused instruction and corrective feedback on L2 pronunciation development of /ɹ/ by Japanese learners of English. *Language Learning, 62*(2), 595–633. doi:10.1111/j.1467-9922.2011.00639.x

Sánchez Álvarez, N., Berrios Martos, M. P., & Extremera, N. (2020). A meta-analysis of the relationship between emotional intelligence and academic performance: A multi-stream comparison. *Frontiers in Psychology, 11*, 1517. doi:10.3389/fpsyg.2020.01517

Sarhady, T. (2015). The effect of product/process-oriented approach to teaching and learning writing skill on university student performances. *International Journal of Language and Applied Linguistics, 1*(2), 7–12.

Sato, M. (2017). Oral peer corrective feedback: Multiple theoretical perspectives. In H. Nassaji & E. Kartchava (Eds.), *Corrective feedback in second language teaching and learning: Research, theory, applications, implications* (pp. 19–34). Routledge. doi:10.4324/9781315621432-3

Sato, M., & Loewen, S. (2019). *Evidence-based second language pedagogy: A collection of instructed second language acquisition studies*. Routledge. doi:10.4324/9781351190558

Savvidou, C. (2004). An Integrated Approach to Teaching Literature in the EFL Classroom. *The Internet TESL Journal, 10*(12). Available at http://iteslj.org/Techniques/Savvidou-Literature.html

Saykili, A. (2018). Distance education: Definitions, generations, key concepts, and future directions. *International Journal of Contemporary Educational Research, 5*(1), 2–17.

Schachter, J. (1991). Corrective feedback in historical perspective. *Second Language Research, 7*(2), 89–102. doi:10.1177/026765839100700202

Schmidt, R. W. (1990). The role of consciousness in second language learning. *Applied Linguistics, 11*(2), 129–158. doi:10.1093/applin/11.2.129

Selinker, L. (1972). Interlanguage. *International Review of Applied Linguistics in Language Teaching, 10*(1-4), 209–232. doi:10.1515/iral.1972.10.1-4.209

Seng, H. Z., Mustafa, N. C., Halim, H. A., Rahmat, N. H., & Amali, N. A. K. (2023). An Investigation of Direct and Indirect Learning Strategies in Learning Foreign Languages. *International Journal of Academic Research in Business & Social Sciences, 13*(3), 322–338. doi:10.6007/IJARBSS/v13-i3/16492

Compilation of References

Sepúlveda, D., Horvitz, M. M., Joiko, S., & Ortiz Ruiz, F. (2021). Education and the production of inequalities across the Global South and North. *Journal of Sociology (Melbourne, Vic.)*, 58(3), 144078332110600. doi:10.1177/14407833211060059

Setyowati, S., Sukmawan, S., & El-Sulukiyyah, A. A. (2021). The effect of literature as authentic materials for writing essays in a blended learning setting. *International Seminar on Language, Education, and Culture, KnE. Social Sciences*, 2021, 195–208.

Sewart, D., Keegan, D., & Holmberg, B. (2020). *Distance education: International perspectives*. Routledge.

Shadiev, R., & Liang, Q. (2024). A review of research on AR-supported language learning. *Innovation in Language Learning and Teaching*, 18(1), 78–100. doi:10.1080/17501229.2023.2229804

Sheen, Y. (2011). Comparing oral and written corrective feedback. In Corrective feedback, individual differences and second language learning (pp. 113-127). Springer. doi:10.1007/978-94-007-0548-7_6

Sheen, Y. (2004). Corrective feedback and learner uptake in communicative classrooms across instructional settings. *Language Teaching Research*, 8(3), 263–300. doi:10.1191/1362168804lr146oa

Sheen, Y. (2010). Introduction: The role of oral and written corrective feedback in SLA. *Studies in Second Language Acquisition*, 32(2), 169–179. doi:10.1017/S0272263109990489

Shinde, K., & Bhangale, R. (2017). A model based on IoT for improving programming language skills among students. *International Journal of Students'. Research Technology Management*, 5(2), 38–40. doi:10.18510/ijsrtm.2017.521

Shirvan, M. E., Khajavy, G. H., MacIntyre, P. D., & Taherian, T. (2019). A meta-analysis of L2 willingness to communicate and its three high-evidence correlates. *Journal of Psycholinguistic Research*, 48(6), 1241–1267. doi:10.1007/s10936-019-09656-9

Shrawan, A. (2019). *The language of literature and its meaning: A comparative study of Indian and western aesthetics*. Cambridge Scholars Publishing.

Silva, T. (1993). Toward an Understanding of the Distinct Nature of L2 Writing: The ESL Research and Its Implications. *TESOL Quarterly*, 27(4), 657. Advance online publication. doi:10.2307/3587400

Simonson, M., Zvacek, S. M., & Smaldino, S. (2019). *Teaching and Learning at a Distance: Foundations of Distance Education*. IAP.

Simpson, A., Maltese, A. V., Anderson, A., & Sung, E. (2020). Failures, errors, and mistakes: A systematic review of the literature. In E. Vanderheiden & C. H. Mayer (Eds.), *Mistakes, errors and failures across cultures*. Springer. doi:10.1007/978-3-030-35574-6_18

Sinha, K. K. (2022). Role of modern technology in teaching and learning the English language in Indian educational institutions. *Indonesian Journal of English Language Studies, 8*(2), 71–82. doi:10.24071/ijels.v8i2.4713

Soepriyanti, H., Waluyo, U., Syahrial, E., & Hoesni, R. K. (2022). Pre-service English teachers' lived experiences in implementing technology for teaching practice. *Technium Education and Humanities, 3*(1), 16–26. doi:10.47577/teh.v3i1.7810

Softa, V. L. (2022). Technology as a method of teaching and learning foreign languages. *Intercultural Communication, 1*(7), 81–90. doi:10.13166/ic/712022.4948

Spaai, G. W. G., & Hermes, D. J. (1993). A visual display for the teaching of intonation. *CALICO Journal, 10*(3), 19–30. doi:10.1558/cj.v10i3.19-30

Spolsky, B. (Ed.). (2012). *The Cambridge handbook of language policy*. Cambridge University Press., doi:10.1017/CBO9780511979026

Spolsky, B., & Hult, F. M. (Eds.). (2010). *The handbook of educational linguistics*. Wiley-Blackwell.

Stanlee, T. J., Swanto, S., Din, W. A., & Edward, E. I. (2022). English language educators' approaches to integrate technology in the 21st century education practices. *International Journal of Education Psychology and Counseling, 7*(48), 301–307. doi:10.35631/IJEPC.748022

Stockwell, G. (2021). *Mobile assisted language learning: Concepts, contexts, and challenges*. Cambridge University Press., doi:10.1017/9781108652087

Subandowo, D., & Sárdi, C. (2023). Academic essay writing in an English medium instruction environment: Indonesian graduate students' experiences at Hungarian universities. *Ampersand (Oxford, UK), 11*, 100158. doi:10.1016/j.amper.2023.100158

Sujana, I. M., Waluyo, U., Fitriana, E., & Sudiarta, I. W. (2023). The potentials and limitations of applying content and language integrated learning (CLIL) approach to English teaching for medical students. *World Journal of English Language, 13*(2), 331–335. doi:10.5430/wjel.v13n2p331

Suleman, Q., Hussain, I., Syed, M. A., Parveen, R., Lodhi, I. S., & Mahmood, Z. (2019). Association between emotional intelligence and academic success among undergraduates: A cross-sectional study in KUST. *PLoS One, 14*(7), 1–22. doi:10.1371/journal.pone.0219468

Sun, P., & Zhang, L. (2022). Effects of translanguaging in online peer feedback on Chinese university English-as-a-foreign-language students' writing performance. *RELC Journal, 53*(2), 325–341. doi:10.1177/00336882221089051

Suzukida, Y., & Saito, K. (2021). Which segmental features matter for successful L2 comprehensibility? Revisiting and generalizing the pedagogical value of the functional load principle. *Language Teaching Research, 25*(3), 431–450. doi:10.1177/1362168819858246

Swain, M. (1985). Communicative competence: Some roles of comprehensible input and comprehensible output in its development. In S. Gass & C. Madden (Eds.), *Input in second language acquisition* (pp. 235–253). Newbury House.

Syed, H. A., & Kuzborska, I. (2018). Dynamics of factors underlying willingness to communicate in a second language. *Language Learning Journal*, 1–49. doi:10.1080/09571736.2018.1435709

Tafazoli, D., María, E. G., & Abril, C. A. H. (2019). Intelligent language tutoring system: Integrating intelligent computer-assisted language learning into language education. *International Journal of Information and Communication Technology Education*, *15*(3), 60–74. doi:10.4018/IJICTE.2019070105

Tagliamonte, S. A. (2015). *Making waves: The story of variationist sociolinguistics*. Wiley-Blackwell. doi:10.1002/9781118455494

Tan, H. Y.-J., Kwok, J. W.-J., Neo, M., & Neo, T.-K. (2010, December 5-8). *Enhancing student learning using multimedia and web technologies: students' perceptions of an authentic learning experience in a Malaysian classroom*. ASCILITE- Australian Society for Computers in Learning in Tertiary Education Annual Conference, Sydney, Australia.

Tang, T., & Williams, J. (2000). Who have better learning styles - East Asian or Western students? *Proceedings of the fifth European Learning Styles Information Network Conference*.

Teh, W. (2021). Communicative language teaching (CLT) in the context of online learning: A literature review. *International Journal of TESOL & Education*, *1*(2), 65–71. doi:10.11250/ijte.01.02.004

Teng, F. (2023). Language learning strategies. In Z. Wen, R. Sparks, A. Biedroń., & F. Teng (Eds.), Cognitive individual differences in second language acquisition: Theories, assessment, and pedagogy (pp. 147-173). De Gruyter. doi:10.1515/9781614514749-008

Thanh, P. T. H., & Gillies, R. (2010). Designing a culturally appropriate format of formative peer assessment for Asian students: The case of Vietnamese students. *International Journal of Educational Reform*, *19*(2), 72–85. doi:10.1177/105678791001900201

Thao, L. T., Thuy, P. T., Thi, N. H., Yen, P. H., Thu, H. A., & Tra, N. H. (2023). Impacts of Emotional Intelligence on Second Language Acquisition: English Major Students' Perspectives. *SAGE Open*, *13*(4), 1–15. doi:10.1177/21582440231212065

Thurairasu, V. (2022). Gamification-based learning as the future of language learning: An overview. *European Journal of Humanities and Social Sciences*, *2*(6), 62–69. doi:10.24018/ejsocial.2022.2.6.353

Toba, R., Noor, W. N., & Sanu, L. O. (2019). The current issues of Indonesian EFL students' writing skills: Ability, problem, and reason in writing comparison and contrast essay. *Dinamika Ilmu*, *19*(1), 57–73. doi:10.21093/di.v19i1.1506

Tran, L. T. (2007). Learners' motivation and identity in the Vietnamese EFL writing classroom. *English Teaching*, *6*(1), 151–163. https://files.eric.ed.gov/fulltext/EJ832183.pdf

Traxler, J. (2018). Distance learning: Predictions and possibilities. *Education Sciences*, *8*(1), 1–13. doi:10.3390/educsci8010035

Trinh, Q. L., & Truc, N. T. (2014). Enhancing Vietnamese learners' ability in writing argumentative essays. *Journal of Asia TEFL*, *11*(2). http://journal.asiatefl.org/main/main.php?inx_journals=40&inx_contents=50&main=1&sub=2&submode=3&PageMode=JournalView&s_title=Enhancing_Vietnamese_Learners_Ability_in_Writing_Argumentative_Essays

Troussas, C., Chrysafiadi, K., & Virvou, M. (2019). An intelligent adaptive fuzzy-based inference system for computer-assisted language learning. *Expert Systems with Applications*, *127*, 85–96. doi:10.1016/j.eswa.2019.03.003

Truong, K. N. (2005). *Issues of Literature classrooms: An Investigation into the role of Literature in Language Classrooms at Hue College of Sciences* [BA thesis]. Hue University, Vietnam.

Truscott, J. (1999). The case for "The case against grammar correction in L2 writing classes": A response to Ferris. *Journal of Second Language Writing*, *8*(2), 111–122. doi:10.1016/S1060-3743(99)80124-6

Truscott, J. (2007). The effect of error correction on learners' ability to write accurately. *Journal of Second Language Writing*, *16*(4), 255–272. doi:10.1016/j.jslw.2007.06.003

Tseng, C. C. (2019). Senior high school teachers' beliefs about EFL writing instruction. *Taiwan Journal of TESOL*, *16*(1), 1–39.

UCLES. (1996). *The IELTS handbook*. UCLES publications.

Uysal, H. H. (2009). A critical review of the IELTS writing test. *ELT Journal*, *64*(3), 314–320. doi:10.1093/elt/ccp026

van der Westhuizen, J., Tshabalala, M., & Stanz, K. (2020). Mistakes, errors and failures: Their hidden potential in cultural contexts – The power of a professional culture. In E. Vanderheiden & C. H. Mayer (Eds.), *Mistakes, errors and failures across cultures*. Springer. doi:10.1007/978-3-030-35574-6_30

Vanderheiden, E., & Mayer, C. H. (2020). "There is a crack in everything. That's how the light gets in": An introduction to mistakes, errors and failure as resources. In E. Vanderheiden & C. H. Mayer (Eds.), *Mistakes, errors and failures across cultures*. Springer. doi:10.1007/978-3-030-35574-6_1

VanPatten, B., Williams, J., Rott, S., & Overstreet, M. (2004). *Form-meaning connections in second language acquisition*. Routledge. doi:10.4324/9781410610607

Varnosfadrani, A. D., & Basturkmen, H. (2009). The effectiveness of implicit and explicit error correction on learners' performance. *System*, *37*(1), 82–98. doi:10.1016/j.system.2008.04.004

Vesely-Maillefer, A. K., & Saklofske, D. H. (2020). *Emotional Intelligence and the Next Generation of Teachers*. Springer.

Compilation of References

Vo, L. H. (2024). Teaching English literature in the Vietnamese EFL context: Towards a language and literature integrated model. In H. P. Bui, T. C. Bang, & C. H. Nguyen (Eds.), *Exploring contemporary English language education practices*. IGI Global.

Volk, H., Kellner, K., & Wohlhart, D. (2015). Learning analytics for English language teaching. *Journal of Universal Computer Science, 21*(1), 156–174.

Vurdien, R. (2019). Videoconferencing: Developing students' communicative competence. *Journal of Foreign Language Education and Technology, 4*(2), 269–298.

Vygotsky, L. S. (1978). *Mind in society development of higher psychological processes*. Harvard University Press. https://www.jstor.org/stable/j.ctvjf9vz4

Walter, Y. (2022). Translanguaging pedagogy in cameroon EFL/ESL secondary classrooms. *International Journal of English Language Teaching, 10*(7), 31–49. doi:10.37745/ijelt.13/vol10n73149

Waluyo, B., & Bucol, J. L. (2021). The impact of gamified vocabulary learning using Quizlet on low-proficiency students. *Computer-Assisted Language Learning Electronic Journal, 22*(1), 158-179.

Wang, J. Q. (2019). Classroom intervention for integrating simulation games into language classrooms: An exploratory study with the SIMs 4. *CALL-EJ, 20*(2), 101–127.

Wang, P. (2022). Relooking at the roles of translanguaging in English as a Foreign Language classes for multilingual learners: Practices and implications. *Frontiers in Psychology, 13*, 850649. Advance online publication. doi:10.3389/fpsyg.2022.850649

Wang, Y. H., & Young, S. S.-C. (2012). Exploring young and adult learners' perceptions of corrective feedback in ASR-based CALL system. *British Journal of Educational Technology, 43*(3), E77–E80. doi:10.1111/j.1467-8535.2011.01275.x

Wang, Y., & Xie, Q. (2022). Diagnostic assessment of novice EFL learners' discourse competence in academic writing: A case study. *Language Testing in Asia, 12*(1), 1–24. doi:10.1186/s40468-022-00197-y

Warschauer, M., & Healey, D. (1998). Computers and language learning: An overview. *Language Teaching, 31*(2), 57–71. doi:10.1017/S0261444800012970

Weda, S., Atmowardoyo, H., Rahman, F., Said, M. M., & Sakti, A. E. F. (2021). Factors affecting learners' willingness to communicate in EFL classroom at higher institution in Indonesia. *International Journal of Instruction, 14*(2), 719–734. doi:10.29333/iji.2021.14240a

Weerasinghe, M., Biener, V., Grubert, J., Quigley, A. J., Toniolo, A., Pucihar, K. Č., & Kljun, M. (2022). Vocabulary: Learning vocabulary in AR supported by keyword visualisations. *IEEE Transactions on Visualization and Computer Graphics, 28*(11), 3748–3758. doi:10.1109/TVCG.2022.3203116

Weidman, J. (1935). *My father sits in the dark.* Available at https://msanaknudsen.weebly.com/uploads/9/3/6/8/9368722/my_father_sits_in_the_dark_by_jerome_weidma1.pdf

Weng, X., & Chiu, T. K. F. (2023). Instructional design and learning outcomes of intelligent computer assisted language learning: Systematic review in the field. *Computers and Education: Artificial Intelligence, 4*, 1–12. doi:10.1016/j.caeai.2022.100117

Westervelt, L. (1998). *Teaching writing using the process-oriented approach.* Academic Press.

White, F. D., & Billings, S. J. (2008). *The well-crafted argument.* Houghton Mifflin Company.

White, R., & Arndt, V. (1991). *Process writing.* Longman London.

Wibowo, H., & Raihani, S. (2019). The effectiveness of Hellotalk app on English writing skills. *Lingua Jurnal Pendidikan Bahasa, 15*(2). Advance online publication. doi:10.34005/lingua.v15i2.581

Widodo, H. P. (2008). Process-based academic essay writing instruction in an EFL context. *IKIP Negeri Malang: Jurnal Bahasa Dan Seni Tahun, 36*.

Windle, J., & Possas, L. A. (2022). Translanguaging and educational inequality in the Global South: Stance-taking amongst Brazilian teachers of English. *Applied Linguistics, 44*(2), 312–327. Advance online publication. doi:10.1093/applin/amac067

Wong, S. S. H., & Lim, S. W. H. (2018). Prevention–permission–promotion: A review of approaches to errors in learning. *Educational Psychologist, 54*(1), 1–19. doi:10.1080/00461520.2018.1501693

Wright, W. E., & Baker, C. (2017). Key concepts in bilingual education. *Bilingual and Multilingual Education*, 65-79. doi:10.1007/978-3-319-02258-1_2

Xu, L., & Zhang, L. J. (2019). L2 doctoral students' experiences in thesis writing in an English-medium university in New Zealand. *Journal of English for Academic Purposes, 41*, 100779. doi:10.1016/j.jeap.2019.100779

Yaguara, J. A., Salinas, N. P. V., & Caviche, J. C. O. (2021). Exploring the implementation of CLIL in an EFL virtual learning environment. *Latin American Journal of Content and Language Integrated Learning, 14*(2), 187–214. doi:10.5294/laclil.2021.14.2.1

Yaman, İ. (2015). Digital divide within the context of language and foreign language teaching. *Procedia: Social and Behavioral Sciences, 176*, 766–771. doi:10.1016/j.sbspro.2015.01.538

Yan, C. (2022). Research on Student Academic Performance Prediction Methods. *Highlights in Science. Engineering and Technology, 24*, 1–7.

Yan, Q., Zhang, L. J., & Cheng, X. (2021). Implementing classroom-based assessment for young EFL learners in the Chinese context: A case study. *The Asia-Pacific Education Researcher, 30*(6), 541–552. doi:10.1007/s40299-021-00602-9

Compilation of References

Yan, Z. (2021). English as a foreign language teachers' critical thinking ability and L2 students' classroom engagement. *Frontiers in Psychology*, *12*, 773138. Advance online publication. doi:10.3389/fpsyg.2021.773138

Yashima, T., MacIntyre, P. D., & Ikeda, M. (2018). Situated Willingness to Communicate in an L2: Interplay of Individual Characteristics and Context. *Language Teaching Research*, *22*(1), 115–137. doi:10.1177/1362168816657851

Yilmaz, K. (2011). The cognitive perspective on learning: Its theoretical underpinnings and implications for classroom practices. *The Clearing House: A Journal of Educational Strategies, Issues and Ideas*, *84*(5), 204–212. doi:10.1080/00098655.2011.568989

Yimwilai, S. (2015). An integrated approach to teaching literature in an EFL classroom. *English Language Teaching*, *8*(2), 14–21. doi:10.5539/elt.v8n2p14

Zarrinabadi, N., Lou, N. M., & Darvishnezhad, Z. (2021). To praise or not to praise? Examining the effects of ability vs. effort praise on speaking anxiety and willingness to communicate in EFL classrooms. *Innovation in Language Learning and Teaching*, *17*(1), 1–14. doi:10.1080/17501229.2021.1938079

Zhang, Y. (2023). Research on technology-mediated task-based teaching approach in oral English teaching based on the Chinese context. *Frontiers in Humanities and Social Sciences*, *3*(6), 12–16. doi:10.54691/fhss.v3i6.5137

Zhao, B. X. (2023). Educational inequality: The role of digital learning resources. *Lecture Notes in Education Psychology and Public Media*, *7*(1), 634–642. doi:10.54254/2753-7048/7/2022980

Zhao, Y. (2020). A personalized English teaching design based on multimedia computer technology. *International Journal of Emerging Technologies in Learning*, *15*(8), 210–222. doi:10.3991/ijet.v15i08.13695

Zhoc, K. C. H., Chung, T. S. H., & King, R. B. (2018). Emotional intelligence (EI) and self-directed learning: Examining their relation and contribution to better student learning outcomes in higher education. *British Educational Research Journal*, *44*(6), 982–1004. doi:10.1002/berj.3472

Zhou, L., Xi, Y., & Lochtman, K. (2023). The relationship between second language competence and willingness to communicate: The moderating effect of foreign language anxiety. *Journal of Multilingual and Multicultural Development*, *44*(2), 129–143. doi:10.1080/01434632.2020.1801697

Zhuo C., Zhang, P. (2020). Trait Emotional Intelligence and Second Language Performance: A Case Study of Chinese EFL Learners. *Journal of Multilingual and Multicultural Development*, 1–15. https://doi.org/.2020.1767633 doi:10.1080/01434632

Zhu, W. (2001). Performing argumentative writing in English: Difficulties, processes, and strategies. *TESL Canada Journal*, *19*(1), 34–50. doi:10.18806/tesl.v19i1.918

Zormanová, L. (2021). Learning strategies applied by university students in distance learning. *International Journal of Research in E-learning*, *7*(1), 1–20. doi:10.31261/IJREL.2021.7.1.04

About the Contributors

Truong Cong Bang is the Director of Studies and Lecturer in English at the Institute of Foreign Languages, University of Economics and Law (Vietnam National University) in Ho Chi Minh City, Vietnam. He holds a PhD from the University of Newcastle, Australia. His research interests focus on teaching and learning English at universities, and motivational theories, particularly the constructs of expectancy-value and self-efficacy.

Cuong Huy Nguyen serves as Dean of School of Languages, International University, Vietnam National University in Ho Chi Minh City. He earned a master's degree in TESOL from Canberra University in 2007 and a PhD in Curriculum and Instruction from Michigan State University in 2017. His primary research interests include self-directed and socioemotional language learning.

Hung Phu Bui holds a Ph.D in English Language Education. He is now a researcher lecturer at School of Foreign Languages, University of Economics Ho Chi Minh City, Vietnam. He has edited and authored many books on language teaching and linguistics and has been invited to make plenary and keynote talks at many international conferences. His research interests include applying cognitive linguistics in second language teaching, sociocultural theory, and L2 classroom assessment.

* * *

Thanh-Hai L. Cao (Ph.D in American Studies) is a senior lecturer in American Studies and International Studies at the University of Foreign Languages and International Studies (HUFLIS), Hue University, Vietnam. Her research interests revolve around issues relating to race, class and gender in American society, Asian American Studies, Cross-cultural communication and World Englishes. She is also a researcher in English and American literature.

About the Contributors

Isabel María Garcia Conesa has a degree in English Studies from the University of Alicante and a PhD from the National University of Distance Education (UNED). She is currently working as a full time lecturer at the Centro Universitario de la Defensa in San Javier (Spain). She has been awarded a scholarship by the Franklin Institute (University of Alcala de Henares, Spain) and the Radcliffe Institute for Advanced Study (Harvard University, USA), where she conducted a pre-doctoral research stay in the year 2012. Among her main lines of research, we can highlight the role of different women in literature and culture of the United States in contrast to Francophone writers with publication in Spanish journals like Revista Estudios Humanísticos (University of León), Tonos Digital (University of Murcia), Dossiers Feministes (University Jaime I), Prisma Social, Raudem (University of Almeria), Camino Real (University of Alcala de Henres), or Nomadas (University Complutense of Madrid). She also focuses on the study of the history of the teaching of English and gender studies with publications in journals such as Revista Feminismo (University of Alicante) or even Quaderns Digitals.

Chau Thi Hoang Hoa, PhD. is an EFL teacher of Tra Vinh university, Vietnam. Her research interests are teaching EFF in general education, teachers' education, and integrating cultures into teaching EFF. She is especially interested in studying a diversity of strategies to integrate culture into teaching EFL in upper secondary education in Vietnam to build learners' intercultural communicative competence.

Ngoc-Tai Huynh (PhD in Education) is a lecturer of School of Foreign Languages, Tra Vinh University. His research and teaching focus on Multimodal semiotics, Applied and Educational Linguistics, English, Bilingual and cultural education. He has presented at various international conferences, contributed to two book chapters published on IGI Global, Multilingual Matters, and Springer. He also published a number of journal articles on Social Semiotics, Australian Journal of Teacher Education, and Journal of Early Childhood Teacher Education.

Antonio D. Juan has a degree in English Studies from the University of Murcia and a PhD from the National University of Distance Education (UNED) with the positive accreditation by the ANECA body, being given the Extraordinary Doctorate Award. He is currently working as a professor at the University of Granada. He has been awarded a scholarship by University College (Cork, Ireland), the Franklin Institute (University of Alcala de Henares, Spain) and the Radcliffe Institute for Advanced Study (Harvard University, USA), where he conducted a pre-doctoral research visit in the year 2012. He is currently a member of the scientific committee of several national and international journals as well as a member of the editorial board of several international journals. He also belongs to the organizing and scientific committee of several conferences organized by the Athens Institute for Education and Research (Greece). Among his main lines of research we can emphasize the following aspects: cultural studies in the United States; gender issues associated with the role of women in the Anglo-American literature; or the teaching practice and process of English.

Rizgar Mahmood pursued his academic endeavours at California State University, Northridge in the USA, where he earned a master's degree in Linguistics/TESL. After graduating in 2019, he devoted himself to teaching as an assistant lecturer at Salahaddin University, Erbil in Iraqi Kurdistan until 2022. Currently, he is pursuing his PhD in Applied Linguistics/Second Language Acquisition, exploring the effectiveness of pronunciation instruction and corrective feedback on the development of L2 learners' pronunciation.

Phuong-Nam Thi Nguyen (PhD in the English Language and Literature) currently works at the School of Foreign Languages, Tra Vinh University – Vietnam. Her research is in the area of second language acquisition and foreign language literature. She is interested in intervention research in language teaching. Dr Phuong Nam has published a wide range of papers in Scopus Indexed journals such as Journal of Culture and Education, Asian EFL Journal and presented at various international conferences on TESOL and linguistics.

Tuyet-Nhung Thi Nguyen has joined the staff of School of Foreign Languages since 2009. She earned a BA in English Education in 2008 and MA degree in TESOL in 2015. She has published several peer-review journals and presented at various international conferences. Currently, Ms. Nhung is a PhD candidate in the field of English language teaching methodologies at Tra Vinh University.

Lien-Huong Vo (Ph.D. in Linguistics) is a senior lecturer of Linguistics and Translation Studies at the University of Foreign Languages and International Studies (HUFLIS), Hue University, Vietnam. Her research expertise pertains to Theoretical Linguistics, Educational Linguistics, and Translation Studies, focusing on pragmatics, discourse analysis and translation competence between English and Vietnamese. She is also an NSM (Natural Semantic Metalanguage) practitioner. She is also interested in creative ways of teaching language and literature.

Mai Vo is an English postgraduate with a profound passion for English language and education. Having pursued her Master's degree in theory and methodology of teaching English, she is dedicated to honing her teaching skills and pedagogical techniques related to IELTS with the intention in contributing her knowledge to shed a light on the difficulties that EFL learners often struggle with when learning IELTS, particularly writing skills. Additionally, she hopes to gain more practical experience to play a pivotal role in empowering and assisting EFL learners, especially those in rural areas, to succeed in their English language learning.

Thanh Vo obtained a bachelor's degree in English Linguistics and Literature, and a Master's degree in TESOL awarded by University of Social Sciences and Humanities, Vietnam National University, Ho Chi Minh City. Also at this university, he currently serves as a full-time lecturer at Faculty of English Linguistics and Literature. Up to now, he has had eight-year experience in EFL teaching at tertiary level. He is also a Ph.D student in TESOL. His research interests include second language acquisition, language assessment, technology-assisted language learning, and intercultural communication in language teaching.

Jacqueline Żammit is a lecturer and researcher specializing in applied linguistics. With over fifteen years of pedagogical experience, she has worked with schools and academic institutions teaching languages. Dr. Żammit is currently involved in lecturing at University, research and design consultancy for second language acquisition, is actively publishing articles, presenting at conferences, and writing books on the subject. Her research interests include second language acquisition, computer-assisted language learning, interculturalism, and adult education. Additionally, she serves as a reviewer for academic journals and holds the position of Associate Editor for a Springer journal. Dr. Żammit also dedicates time to teaching, coordinating pedagogy, supervising students' theses, and contributing to projects like the 'Ġabra' online dictionary and an Augmented Reality Project to create stories.

Index

(Inter)Cultural Awareness 116-117

A

Academic Performance 40-41, 45-48, 50-51, 56-59, 61-69, 76, 92, 95, 233, 244
Action Research 1-2, 8, 17, 20, 142, 206-207, 214-216, 218
Applied Linguistics 20, 36, 65, 92-93, 98, 109-110, 112-113, 115, 128, 147, 150-151, 156, 179, 183, 187, 190-203, 205-214, 216-219, 245-246
Applied Linguistics Research 190-202, 208-213, 216-217
Argumentative Essay 1, 3, 9, 15
Authentic Material 117-118, 130
Automated Speech Recognition (ASR) 188

B

Blended Learning 91, 129, 134-136, 146-147, 151-153, 156, 208

C

Class Participation 70, 77-79, 84-88, 96
Colloquial Language 220, 230, 240, 248
Computer-Assisted Language Learning (CALL) 133, 152, 156, 210
Computer-Assisted Pronunciation Training (CAPT) 164, 184, 188
Confidence 24, 29, 31, 71, 73, 79, 105, 173-176, 178, 220-221, 224-225, 230, 232-234, 237-240
Corpus Linguistics 190, 207, 215, 219

Corrective Feedback (CF) 98, 100, 115, 159
Critical Thinking Skills 127-128, 135
Cultural Awareness 116-117, 128-130, 141, 150, 220-221, 241
Cultural Understanding 143, 230, 232-234, 244, 248

D

Difficulty 20, 25, 28-31, 39, 138
Digital Tools 131-132, 135-136, 139-141, 143, 148, 157, 197
Distance Education 40-43, 62, 64-67, 69

E

Educational Technology 147, 153, 158, 187-188
EFL 1-8, 18-21, 23-28, 30-38, 63-64, 67, 89-92, 94-95, 109-110, 112-122, 127-130, 146, 148, 150-151, 153, 155, 160, 165, 180, 182-184, 186-188, 220-227, 231, 241-248
Emerging Technologies 131, 143-145, 156
Emotional Intelligence 40-41, 44-50, 54-56, 58-67, 69-71, 73-75, 78, 81, 88-96
Engagement 13-14, 30, 33, 38, 63-64, 91, 104, 136, 138, 141-143, 200, 210, 220-221, 223-225, 230-231, 233-235, 238-240, 242-244, 248
English 2, 5-6, 8, 18-24, 26-30, 33-39, 41, 46-50, 56-59, 61-66, 68, 70-71, 76, 82-84, 89-95, 98, 102, 110-111, 115-121, 127-129, 131-156, 160, 163, 165, 167, 169, 171-172, 179,

Index

181-183, 185-188, 191, 193, 195-197, 203-205, 207-209, 211-212, 214-215, 217-218, 220-223, 225-227, 229-233, 235-248

English Essay Writing 23, 26, 28, 34-36

English Literature 116-121, 127-128, 220, 223, 231, 234-236, 238, 245, 247-248

English Proficiency 197, 203-204, 230, 236

Essay 1, 3, 5-16, 18, 21-24, 26-31, 33-39

Explicit 31, 35, 69, 97, 102-104, 107, 110, 114, 159, 165, 169-170, 177, 183-184, 187, 200, 203, 226

F

Flipped Classroom 134, 136, 141, 150-152, 156-157

I

IELTS Writing Task 2 1-10, 15-16

Implicit 69, 97, 103, 110, 114, 159, 200

Inclusive Learning Environment 224, 233, 248

Integrated Teaching Model 130

Interaction 41, 51-53, 56-58, 60-61, 91, 107-108, 111-112, 117, 123, 134, 136, 138, 141, 144-145, 149, 153, 161-162, 177-178, 182, 184, 203-204, 216, 237

Intercultural Awareness 130

Intercultural Communicative Competence 130, 209

L

L1 25, 96, 100, 158, 161, 163, 165, 167, 177, 223, 230, 234-237, 240-241, 248

L2 Sound Production 158, 188

Language Acquisition 66, 68, 92, 94, 97-99, 104-105, 109-113, 133, 136-138, 140, 144, 147, 159, 161-162, 172, 179, 181-184, 187, 190-191, 196-197, 200-202, 205, 208, 214, 217-219, 221-222

Language Development 71, 98, 100-101, 104-105, 107, 111, 113, 116-117, 127, 136, 162, 197, 205, 215, 221, 223, 225, 230, 235-236

Language Pedagogy 132, 158, 207, 217

Language Policies 190-191, 196, 198-199, 208-209, 212-213, 219

Language Proficiency 47, 94, 99, 108, 117, 120-121, 134-135, 138, 141, 143, 145, 150-151, 179, 198, 201, 203, 205, 208, 220-221, 223-225, 232, 235-236, 242-244

Language Teaching Methods 196, 219

Learning Analytics 131, 143, 155, 157

Learning Strategies 38, 40-41, 43-44, 46-51, 56-69, 104, 192, 219

Literature Courses 118, 129-130, 220-224, 226-231, 233-240, 242-244, 246, 248

M

Mixed Methods Research 205, 219

O

Oral Corrective Feedback (OCF) 97, 101, 115, 166

P

Pedagogical Frameworks 131

Perceptions 8, 20-21, 34, 74, 113, 119, 128-129, 146, 150-151, 154, 158, 168, 170, 175-180, 187, 205, 220-221, 225-227, 230, 234, 237, 240, 245, 247-248

Personal Growth 120-122, 126-127, 221

Praat 158, 160, 162, 165, 168-170, 172, 175-177, 179-180

Process-Based Writing Instruction 1-10, 12-17, 20, 22

Prompts 12-13, 102-104, 108, 111, 115, 227

Pronunciation Instruction 164, 166, 176, 178-179, 181, 183, 185-186, 188

Q

Qualitative Research 34-35, 90, 190, 204, 216, 219, 246

Quantitative Research 203-204, 219

R

Recast 103-104, 115
Research Methods 193, 202, 204, 214, 216, 219

S

Secondary Education 49, 70, 78, 95-96
Sound Production 158, 160, 167-169, 175-176, 188
Students' Performance 10-11, 15, 17, 98-99

T

Task Response 2-6, 8-12, 15-16, 22
Task Response Criterion 2-6, 8-11, 15-16
Technological Pedagogical Content Knowledge (TPACK) 139, 157
Technology Integration 131-136, 139-145, 148, 156, 178
Tertiary Education 23, 30, 32, 154

Translanguaging 195, 197, 214-215, 217, 221-226, 228, 238, 242-248

U

University Students 6, 18, 25, 32, 35-36, 41, 47-49, 58-60, 65, 67, 69, 92, 95, 115, 119, 156

V

Vietnamese 1, 3, 18, 23-24, 26-32, 34-36, 38, 90-91, 95, 109-110, 112, 114, 116-117, 119, 127-129, 153, 220-223, 226-227, 229-244, 247-248
Visual Corrective Feedback 158-159, 161, 166, 176
Visual Feedback 159-160, 175-180, 185-186, 188

W

Willingness to Communicate 70-71, 88-96, 148, 183

Publishing Tomorrow's Research Today

Uncover Current Insights and Future Trends in Education with IGI Global's Cutting-Edge Recommended Books

Print Only, E-Book Only, or Print + E-Book.
Order direct through IGI Global's Online Bookstore at www.igi-global.com or through your preferred provider.

ISBN: 9781668493007
© 2023; 234 pp.
List Price: US$ 215

ISBN: 9798369300749
© 2024; 383 pp.
List Price: US$ 230

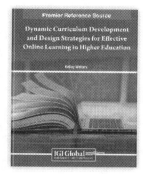

ISBN: 9781668486467
© 2023; 471 pp.
List Price: US$ 215

ISBN: 9781668465387
© 2024; 389 pp.
List Price: US$ 215

ISBN: 9781668475836
© 2024; 359 pp.
List Price: US$ 215

ISBN: 9781668444238
© 2023; 334 pp.
List Price: US$ 240

Do you want to stay current on the latest research trends, product announcements, news, and special offers? Join IGI Global's mailing list to receive customized recommendations, exclusive discounts, and more.
Sign up at: www.igi-global.com/newsletters.

Scan the QR Code here to view more related titles in Education.

www.igi-global.com   Sign up at www.igi-global.com/newsletters   facebook.com/igiglobal   twitter.com/igiglobal   linkedin.com/igiglobal

Ensure Quality Research is Introduced to the Academic Community

Become a Reviewer for IGI Global Authored Book Projects

 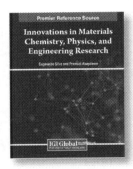 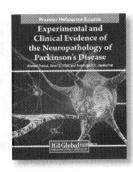 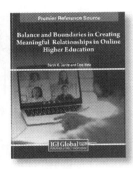

The overall success of an authored book project is dependent on quality and timely manuscript evaluations.

Applications and Inquiries may be sent to:
development@igi-global.com

Applicants must have a doctorate (or equivalent degree) as well as publishing, research, and reviewing experience. Authored Book Evaluators are appointed for one-year terms and are expected to complete at least three evaluations per term. Upon successful completion of this term, evaluators can be considered for an additional term.

If you have a colleague that may be interested in this opportunity, we encourage you to share this information with them.

www.igi-global.com

Publishing Tomorrow's Research Today
IGI Global's Open Access Journal Program
Including Nearly 200 Peer-Reviewed, Gold (Full) Open Access Journals across IGI Global's Three Academic Subject Areas: Business & Management; Scientific, Technical, and Medical (STM); and Education

Consider Submitting Your Manuscript to One of These Nearly 200 Open Access Journals for to Increase Their Discoverability & Citation Impact

Web of Science Impact Factor	Web of Science Impact Factor	Web of Science Impact Factor	Web of Science Impact Factor
6.5	4.7	3.2	2.6
JOURNAL OF Organizational and End User Computing	JOURNAL OF Global Information Management	INTERNATIONAL JOURNAL ON Semantic Web and Information Systems	JOURNAL OF Database Management

Choosing IGI Global's Open Access Journal Program Can Greatly Increase the Reach of Your Research

Higher Usage
Open access papers are 2-3 times more likely to be read than non-open access papers.

Higher Download Rates
Open access papers benefit from 89% higher download rates than non-open access papers.

Higher Citation Rates
Open access papers are 47% more likely to be cited than non-open access papers.

Submitting an article to a journal offers an invaluable opportunity for you to share your work with the broader academic community, fostering knowledge dissemination and constructive feedback.

Submit an Article and Browse the IGI Global Call for Papers Pages

We can work with you to find the journal most well-suited for your next research manuscript.
For open access publishing support, contact: journaleditor@igi-global.com

Publishing Tomorrow's Research Today
IGI Global
e-Book Collection

Including Essential Reference Books Within Three Fundamental Academic Areas

Business & Management
Scientific, Technical, & Medical (STM)
Education

- Acquisition options include Perpetual, Subscription, and Read & Publish
- No Additional Charge for Multi-User Licensing
- No Maintenance, Hosting, or Archiving Fees
- Continually Enhanced Accessibility Compliance Features (WCAG)

| Over 150,000+ Chapters | Contributions From 200,000+ Scholars Worldwide | More Than 1,000,000+ Citations | Majority of e-Books Indexed in Web of Science & Scopus | Consists of Tomorrow's Research Available Today! |

Recommended Titles from our e-Book Collection

Innovation Capabilities and Entrepreneurial Opportunities of Smart Working
ISBN: 9781799887973

Advanced Applications of Generative AI and Natural Language Processing Models
ISBN: 9798369305027

Using Influencer Marketing as a Digital Business Strategy
ISBN: 9798369305515

Human-Centered Approaches in Industry 5.0
ISBN: 9798369326473

Modeling and Monitoring Extreme Hydrometeorological Events
ISBN: 9781668487716

Data-Driven Intelligent Business Sustainability
ISBN: 9798369300497

Information Logistics for Organizational Empowerment and Effective Supply Chain Management
ISBN: 9798369301593

Data Envelopment Analysis (DEA) Methods for Maximizing Efficiency
ISBN: 9798369302552

Request More Information, or Recommend the IGI Global e-Book Collection to Your Institution's Librarian

For More Information or to Request a Free Trial, Contact IGI Global's e-Collections Team: eresources@igi-global.com | 1-866-342-6657 ext. 100 | 717-533-8845 ext. 100

Are You Ready to Publish Your Research?

IGI Global
Publishing Tomorrow's Research Today

IGI Global offers book authorship and editorship opportunities across three major subject areas, including Business, STM, and Education.

Benefits of Publishing with IGI Global:

- Free one-on-one editorial and promotional support.
- Expedited publishing timelines that can take your book from start to finish in less than one (1) year.
- Choose from a variety of formats, including Edited and Authored References, Handbooks of Research, Encyclopedias, and Research Insights.
- Utilize IGI Global's eEditorial Discovery® submission system in support of conducting the submission and double-blind peer review process.
- IGI Global maintains a strict adherence to ethical practices due in part to our full membership with the Committee on Publication Ethics (COPE).
- Indexing potential in prestigious indices such as Scopus®, Web of Science™, PsycINFO®, and ERIC – Education Resources Information Center.
- Ability to connect your ORCID iD to your IGI Global publications.
- Earn honorariums and royalties on your full book publications as well as complimentary content and exclusive discounts.

Join Your Colleagues from Prestigious Institutions, Including:

Australian National University
Massachusetts Institute of Technology
JOHNS HOPKINS UNIVERSITY
HARVARD UNIVERSITY
COLUMBIA UNIVERSITY IN THE CITY OF NEW YORK

Learn More at: www.igi-global.com/publish
or by Contacting the Acquisitions Department at: acquisition@igi-global.com